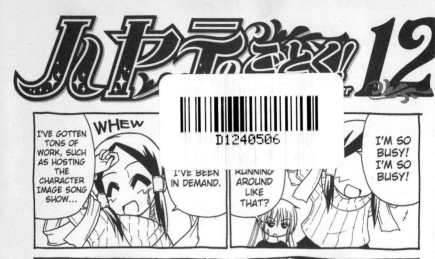

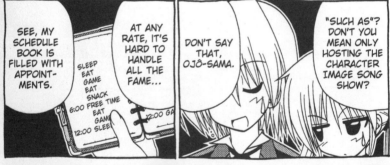

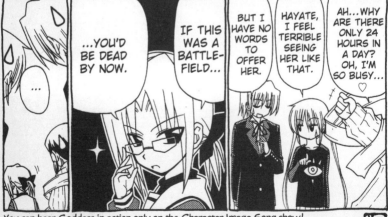

ハヤテのごとく! 12

I'M SO BUSY! I'M SO BUSY!
RUNNING AROUND LIKE THAT?
I'VE BEEN IN DEMAND.
WHEW
I'VE GOTTEN TONS OF WORK, SUCH AS HOSTING THE CHARACTER IMAGE SONG SHOW...
"SUCH AS"? DON'T YOU MEAN ONLY HOSTING THE CHARACTER IMAGE SONG SHOW?
DON'T SAY THAT, OJÔ-SAMA.
AT ANY RATE, IT'S HARD TO HANDLE ALL THE FAME...
SEE, MY SCHEDULE BOOK IS FILLED WITH APPOINT-MENTS.
SLEEP
EAT
GAME
EAT
SNACK
6:00 FREE TIME
EAT
GAME
12:00 SLEE
12:00 GA
AH...WHY ARE THERE ONLY 24 HOURS IN A DAY? OH, I'M SO BUSY...♡
HAYATE, I FEEL TERRIBLE SEEING HER LIKE THAT.
BUT I HAVE NO WORDS TO OFFER HER.
IF THIS WAS A BATTLE-FIELD...
...YOU'D BE DEAD BY NOW.
...
You can hear Goddess in action only on the Character Image Song show!

八田

HAYATE THE COMBAT BUTLER
VOL. 12
Shonen Sunday Edition

STORY AND ART BY
KENJIRO HATA

English Adaptation/Mark Giambruno
Translation/Yuki Yoshioka & Cindy H. Yamauchi
Touch-up Art & Lettering/Hudson Yards
Design/Yukiko Whitley
Editor/Shaenon K. Garrity

Editor in Chief, Books/Alvin Lu
Editor in Chief, Magazines/Marc Weidenbaum
VP, Publishing Licensing/Rika Inouye
VP, Sales & Product Marketing/Gonzalo Ferreyra
VP, Creative/Linda Espinosa
Publisher/Hyoe Narita

HAYATE NO GOTOKU! 12 by Kenjiro HATA © 2007 Kenjiro HATA
All rights reserved. Original Japanese edition published in 2007 by Shogakukan Inc., Tokyo.

The rights of the author(s) of the work(s) in this publication to be so identified have been asserted in accordance with the Copyright, Designs and Patents Act 1988. A CIP catalogue record for this book is available from the British Library.

Printed in Canada

Published by VIZ Media, LLC
P.O. Box 77010
San Francisco, CA 94107

10 9 8 7 6 5 4 3 2 1
First printing, August 2009

www.viz.com

WWW.SHONENSUNDAY.COM

Hayate
the Combat Butler

12

KENJIRO HATA

CONTENTS

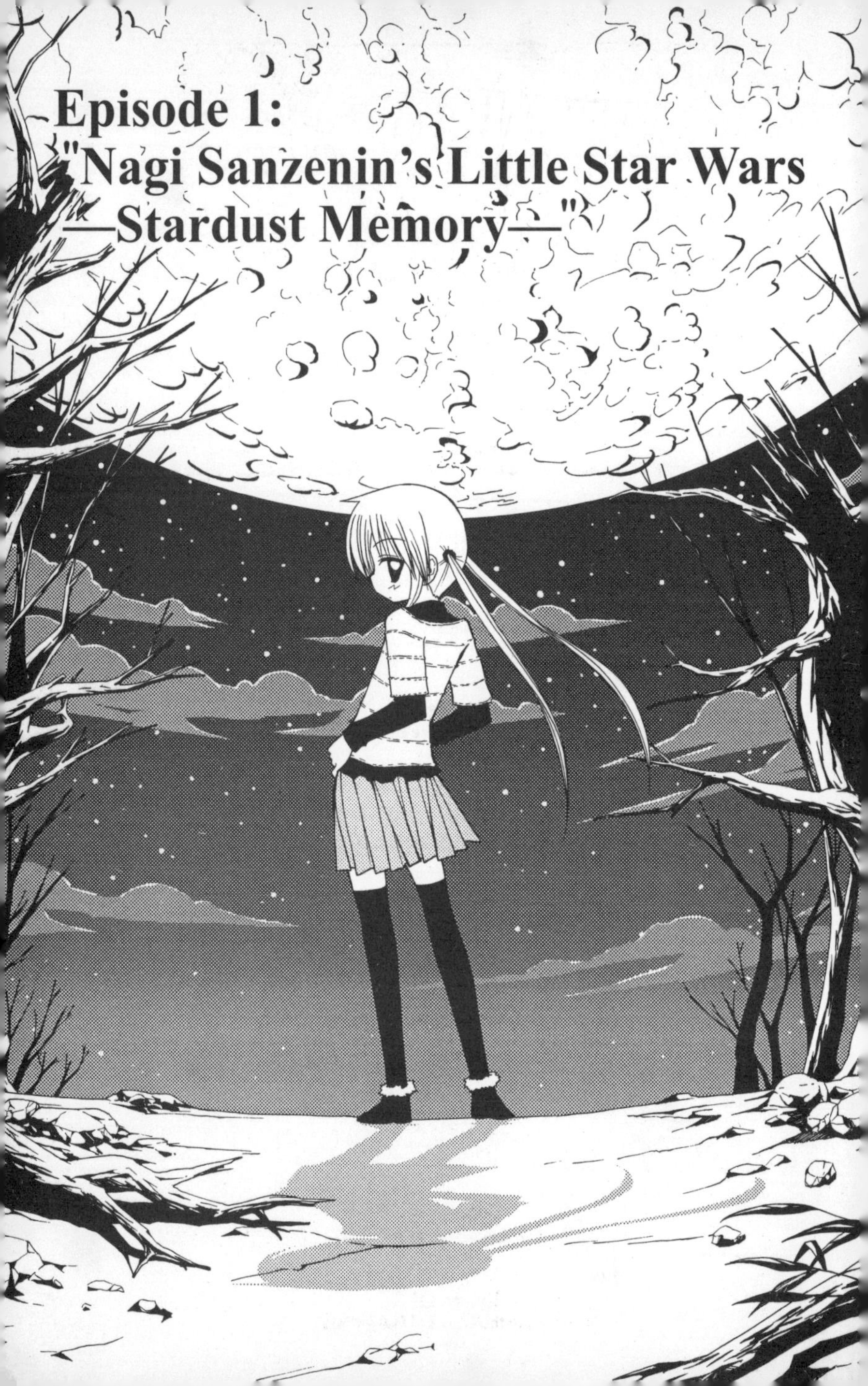
Episode 1:
"Nagi Sanzenin's Little Star Wars
—Stardust Memory—"

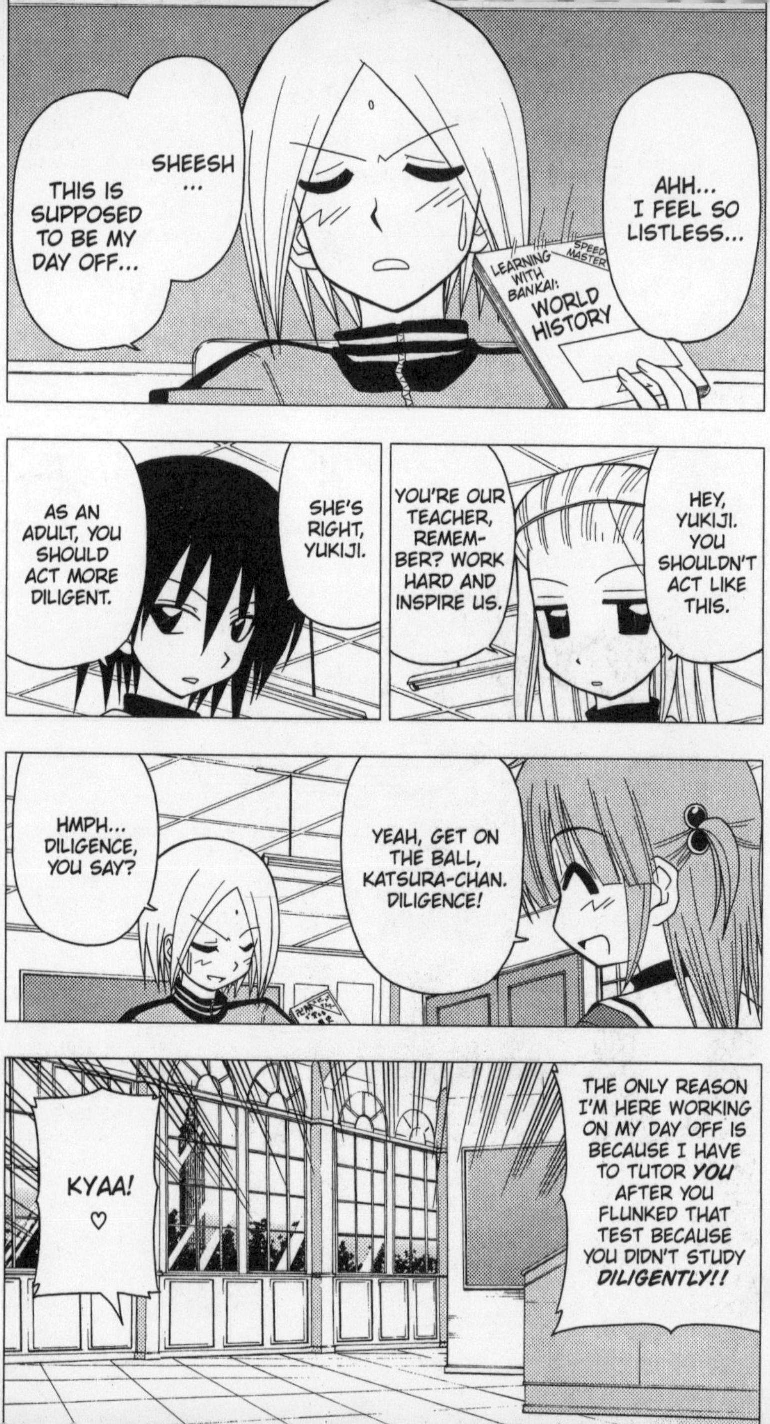
AHH... I FEEL SO LISTLESS...
SPEED MASTER
LEARNING WITH BANKAI: WORLD HISTORY
SHEESH ...
THIS IS SUPPOSED TO BE MY DAY OFF...
HEY, YUKIJI. YOU SHOULDN'T ACT LIKE THIS.
YOU'RE OUR TEACHER, REMEMBER? WORK HARD AND INSPIRE US.
SHE'S RIGHT, YUKIJI.
AS AN ADULT, YOU SHOULD ACT MORE DILIGENT.
YEAH, GET ON THE BALL, KATSURA-CHAN. DILIGENCE!
HMPH... DILIGENCE, YOU SAY?
THE ONLY REASON I'M HERE WORKING ON MY DAY OFF IS BECAUSE I HAVE TO TUTOR ***YOU*** AFTER YOU FLUNKED THAT TEST BECAUSE YOU DIDN'T STUDY ***DILIGENTLY!!***
KYAA! ♡

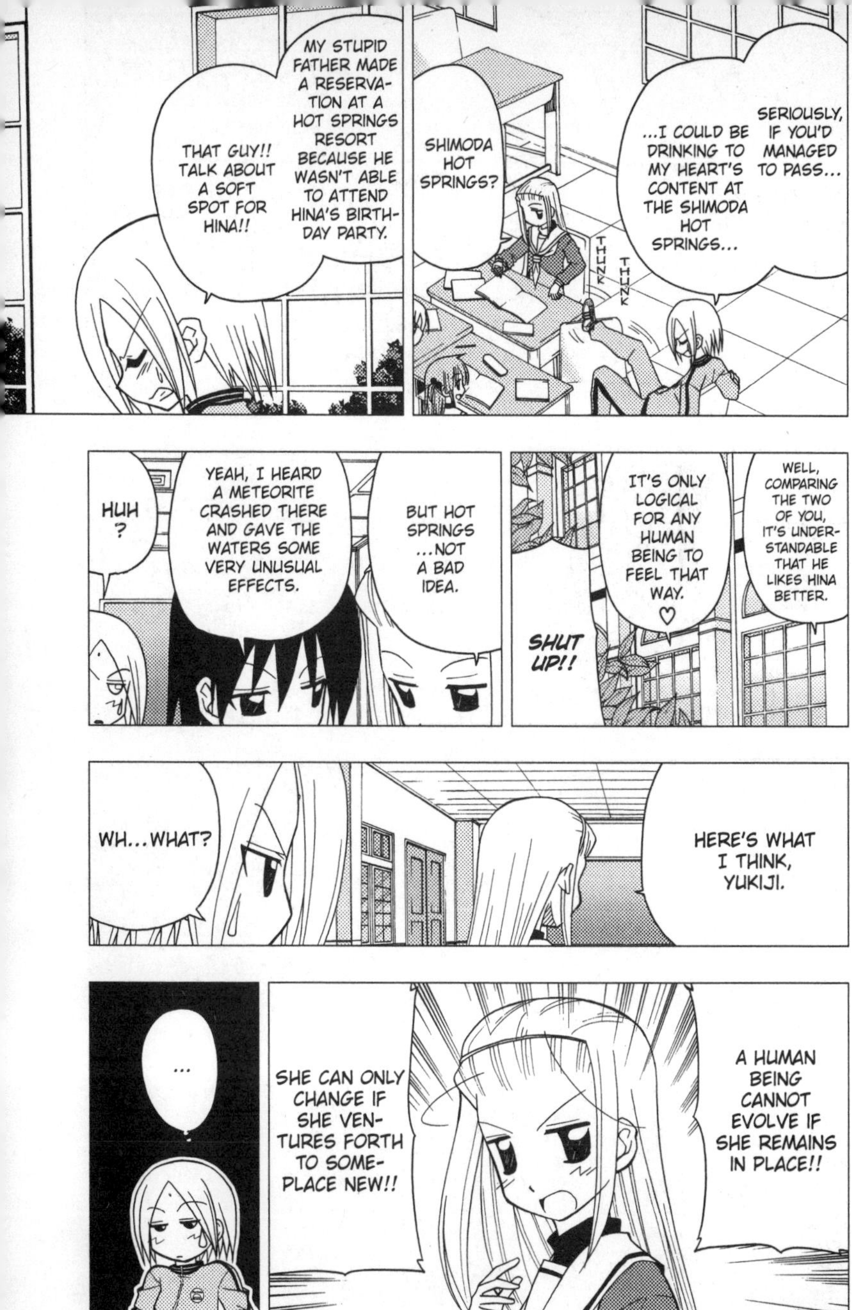
SERIOUSLY, IF YOU'D MANAGED TO PASS...
...I COULD BE DRINKING TO MY HEART'S CONTENT AT THE SHIMODA HOT SPRINGS...
THUNK
THUNK
SHIMODA HOT SPRINGS?
MY STUPID FATHER MADE A RESERVATION AT A HOT SPRINGS RESORT BECAUSE HE WASN'T ABLE TO ATTEND HINA'S BIRTHDAY PARTY.
THAT GUY!! TALK ABOUT A SOFT SPOT FOR HINA!!
WELL, COMPARING THE TWO OF YOU, IT'S UNDERSTANDABLE THAT HE LIKES HINA BETTER.
IT'S ONLY LOGICAL FOR ANY HUMAN BEING TO FEEL THAT WAY. ♡
SHUT UP!!
BUT HOT SPRINGS ...NOT A BAD IDEA.
YEAH, I HEARD A METEORITE CRASHED THERE AND GAVE THE WATERS SOME VERY UNUSUAL EFFECTS.
HUH?
HERE'S WHAT I THINK, YUKIJI.
WH...WHAT?
A HUMAN BEING CANNOT EVOLVE IF SHE REMAINS IN PLACE!!
SHE CAN ONLY CHANGE IF SHE VENTURES FORTH TO SOMEPLACE NEW!!
...

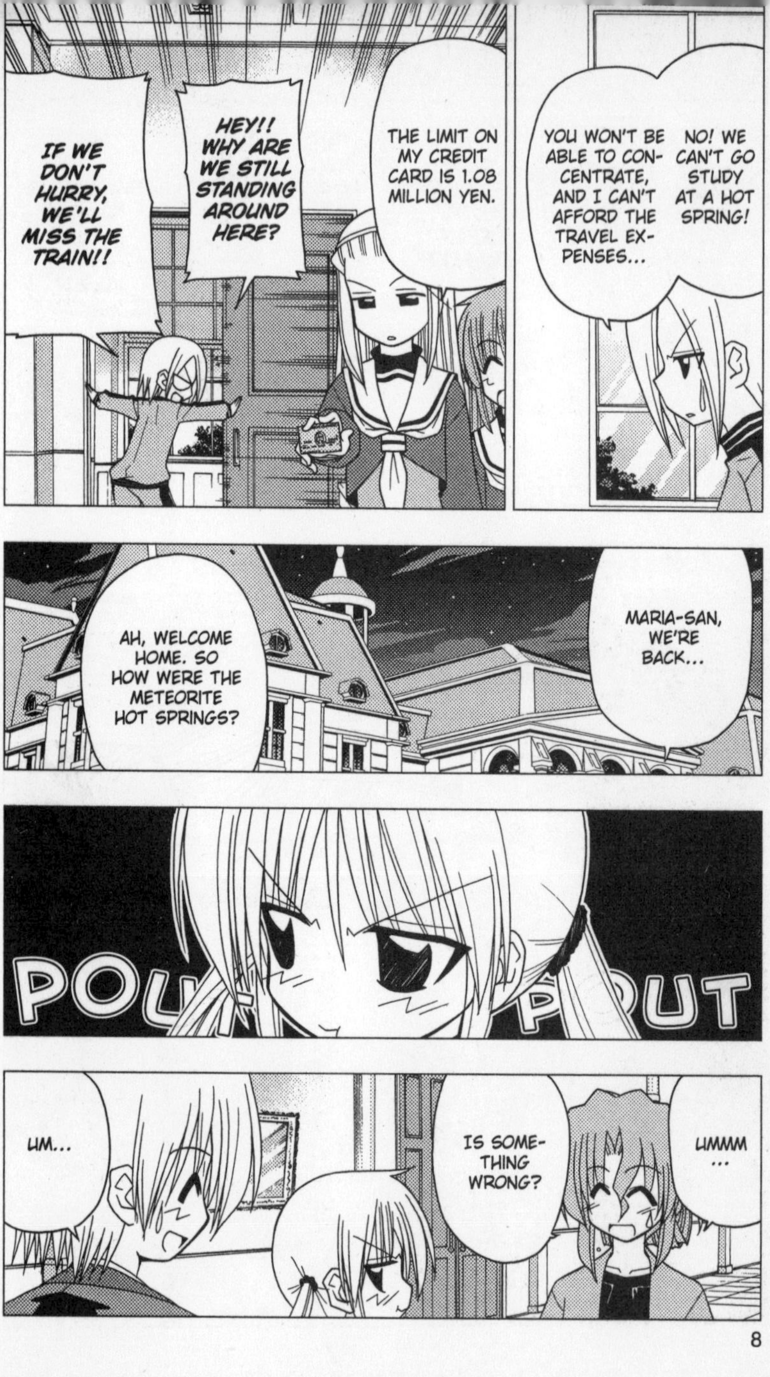
NO! WE CAN'T GO STUDY AT A HOT SPRING!
YOU WON'T BE ABLE TO CON-CENTRATE, AND I CAN'T AFFORD THE TRAVEL EX-PENSES...
THE LIMIT ON MY CREDIT CARD IS 1.08 MILLION YEN.
HEY!! WHY ARE WE STILL STANDING AROUND HERE?
IF WE DON'T HURRY, WE'LL MISS THE TRAIN!!
MARIA-SAN, WE'RE BACK...
AH, WELCOME HOME. SO HOW WERE THE METEORITE HOT SPRINGS?
POU
POUT
UMMM...
IS SOME-THING WRONG?
UM...

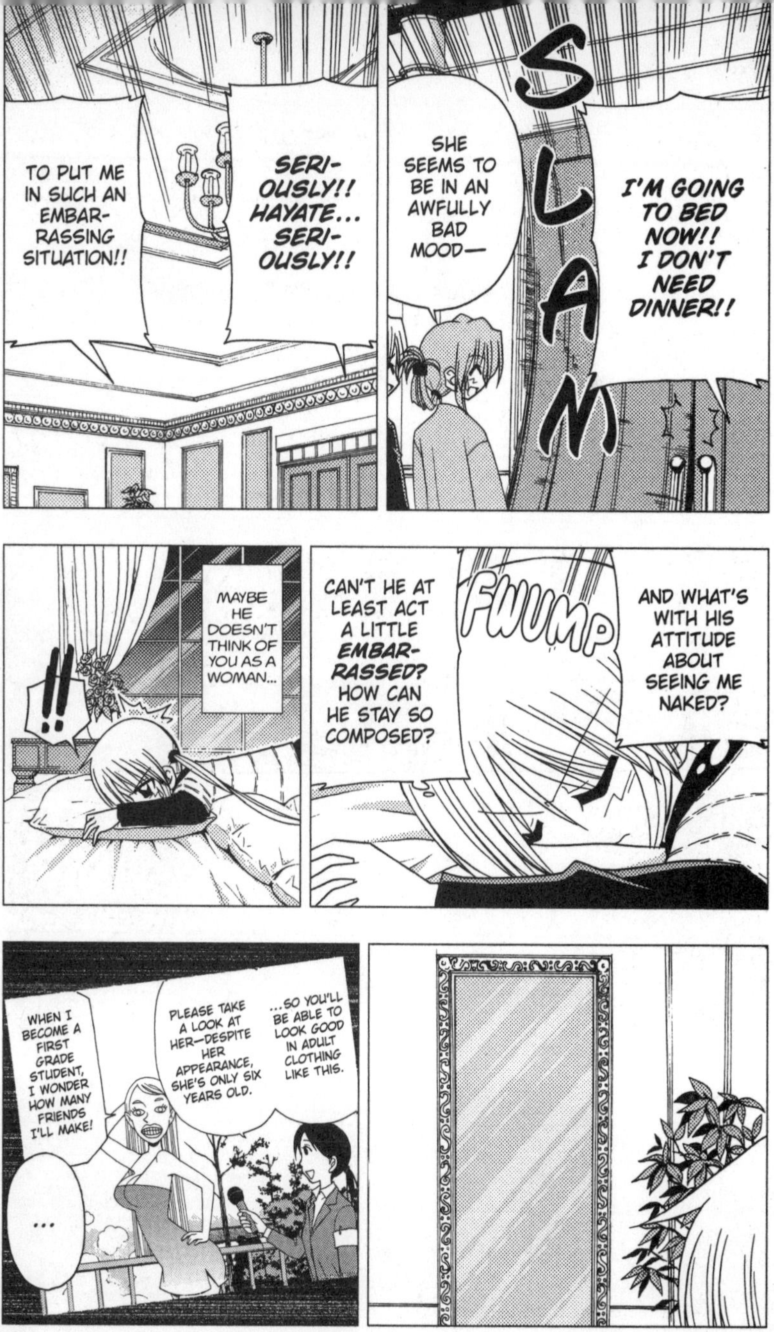
I'M GOING TO BED NOW!! I DON'T NEED DINNER!!
SLAM
SHE SEEMS TO BE IN AN AWFULLY BAD MOOD—
SERI-OUSLY!! HAYATE... SERI-OUSLY!!
TO PUT ME IN SUCH AN EMBAR-RASSING SITUATION!!
FWUMP
AND WHAT'S WITH HIS ATTITUDE ABOUT SEEING ME NAKED?
CAN'T HE AT LEAST ACT A LITTLE EMBAR-RASSED? HOW CAN HE STAY SO COMPOSED?
MAYBE HE DOESN'T THINK OF YOU AS A WOMAN...
!!
...SO YOU'LL BE ABLE TO LOOK GOOD IN ADULT CLOTHING LIKE THIS.
PLEASE TAKE A LOOK AT HER—DESPITE HER APPEARANCE, SHE'S ONLY SIX YEARS OLD.
WHEN I BECOME A FIRST GRADE STUDENT, I WONDER HOW MANY FRIENDS I'LL MAKE!
...

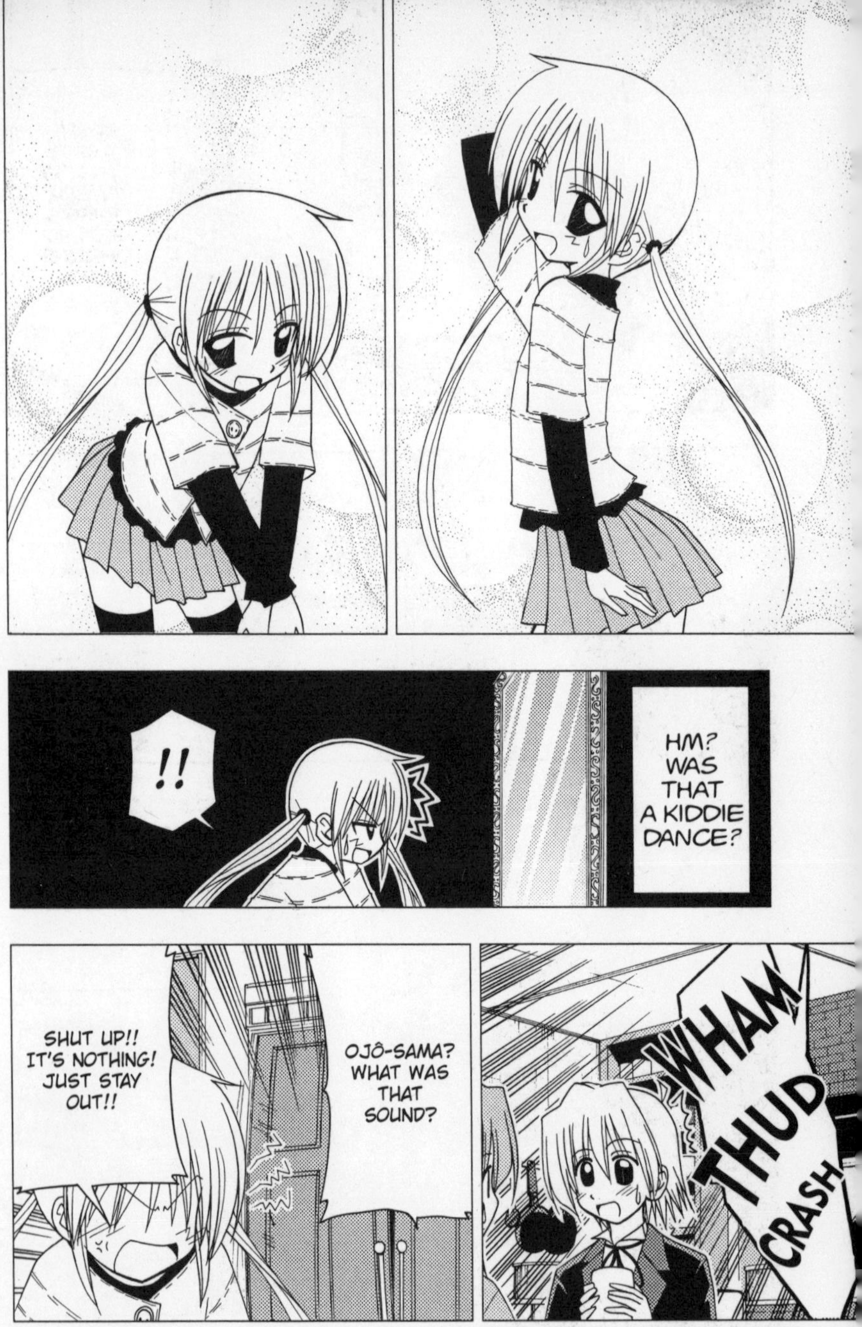
HM? WAS THAT A KIDDIE DANCE?
!!
WHAM
THUD
CRASH
OJÔ-SAMA? WHAT WAS THAT SOUND?
SHUT UP!! IT'S NOTHING! JUST STAY OUT!!

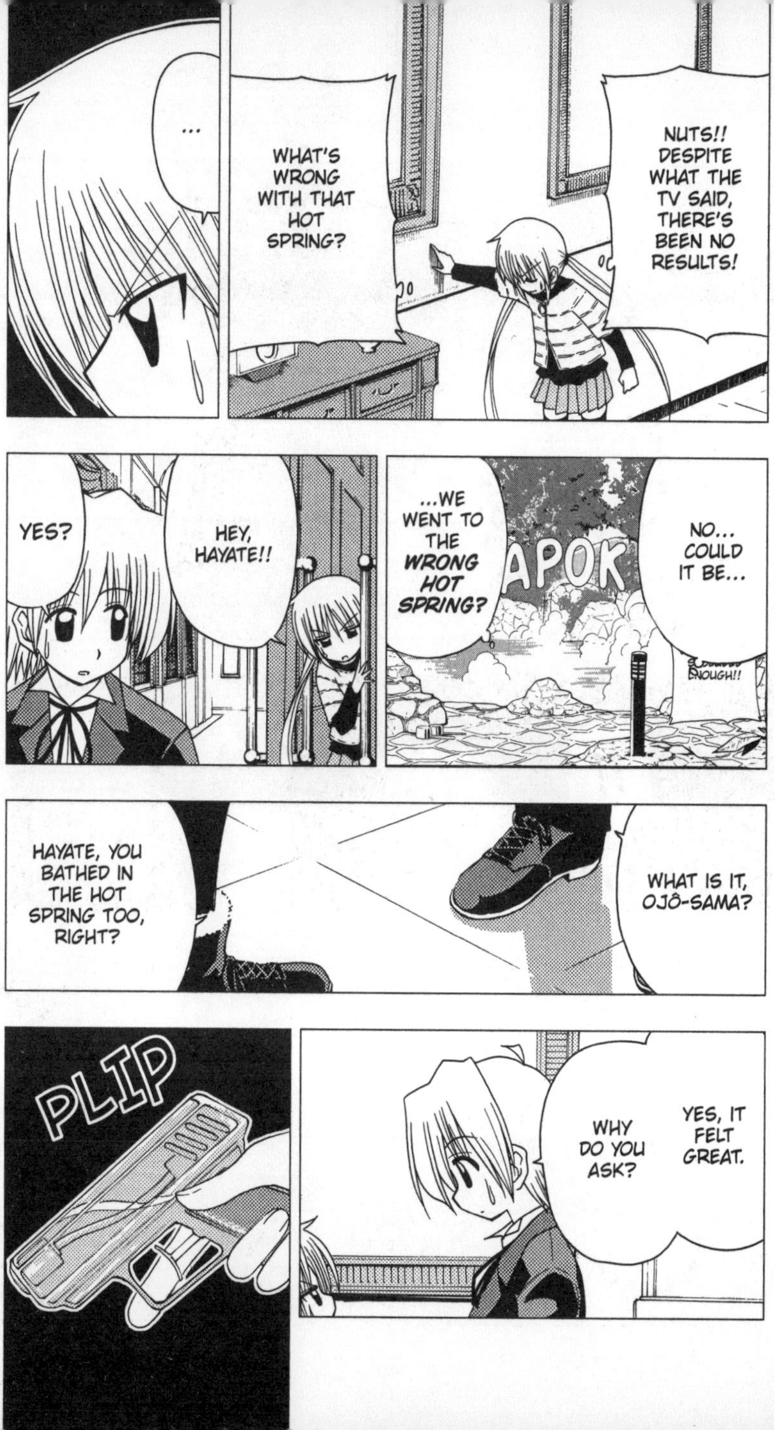
NUTS!! DESPITE WHAT THE TV SAID, THERE'S BEEN NO RESULTS!
WHAT'S WRONG WITH THAT HOT SPRING?
...
NO... COULD IT BE...
APOK
...WE WENT TO THE *WRONG HOT SPRING*?
HEY, HAYATE!!
YES?
WHAT IS IT, OJÔ-SAMA?
HAYATE, YOU BATHED IN THE HOT SPRING TOO, RIGHT?
YES, IT FELT GREAT.
WHY DO YOU ASK?
PLIP

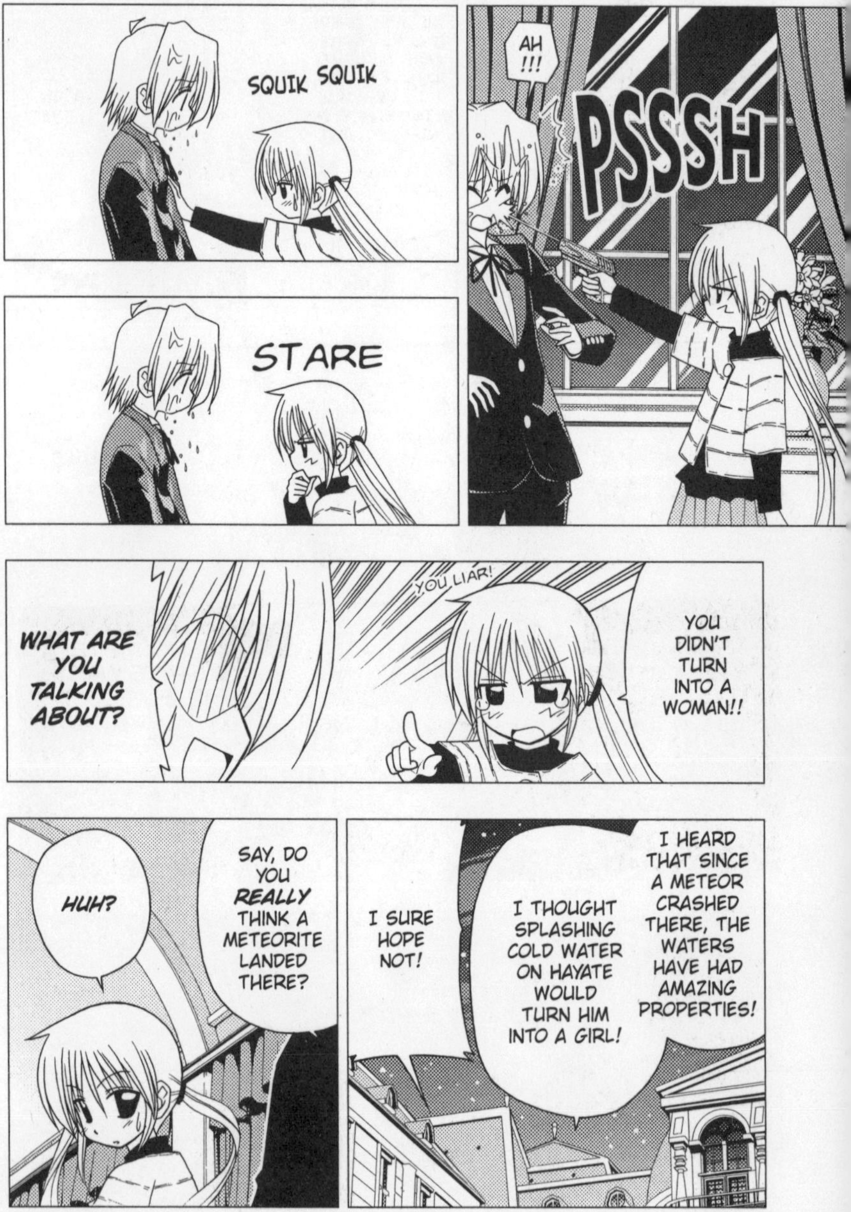
AH !!!
PSSSH
SQUIK SQUIK
STARE
YOU DIDN'T TURN INTO A WOMAN!!
YOU LIAR!
WHAT ARE YOU TALKING ABOUT?
I HEARD THAT SINCE A METEOR CRASHED THERE, THE WATERS HAVE HAD AMAZING PROPERTIES!
I THOUGHT SPLASHING COLD WATER ON HAYATE WOULD TURN HIM INTO A GIRL!
I SURE HOPE NOT!
SAY, DO YOU REALLY THINK A METEORITE LANDED THERE?
HUH?

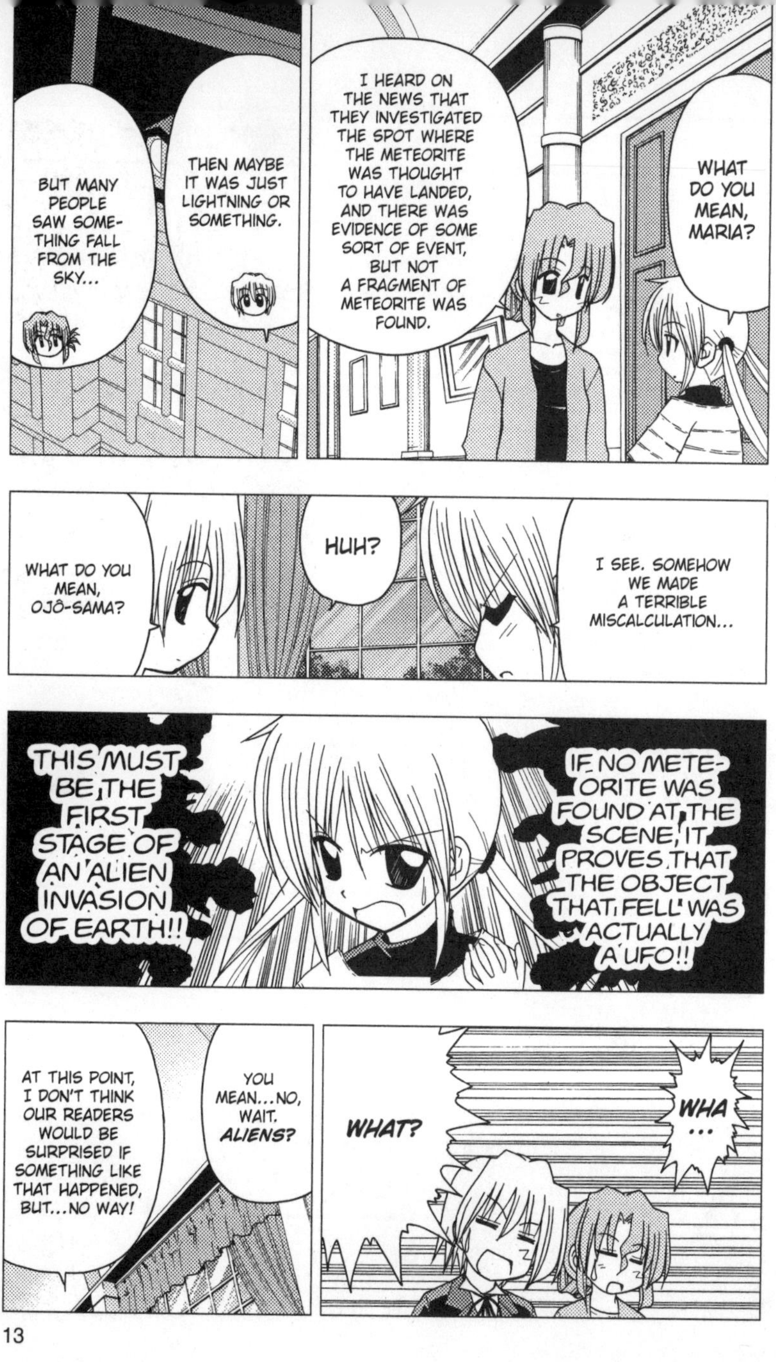
WHAT DO YOU MEAN, MARIA?
I HEARD ON THE NEWS THAT THEY INVESTIGATED THE SPOT WHERE THE METEORITE WAS THOUGHT TO HAVE LANDED, AND THERE WAS EVIDENCE OF SOME SORT OF EVENT, BUT NOT A FRAGMENT OF METEORITE WAS FOUND.
THEN MAYBE IT WAS JUST LIGHTNING OR SOMETHING.
BUT MANY PEOPLE SAW SOME-THING FALL FROM THE SKY...
I SEE. SOMEHOW WE MADE A TERRIBLE MISCALCULATION...
HUH?
WHAT DO YOU MEAN, OJÔ-SAMA?
IF NO METE-ORITE WAS FOUND AT THE SCENE, IT PROVES THAT THE OBJECT THAT FELL WAS ACTUALLY A UFO!!
THIS MUST BE THE FIRST STAGE OF AN ALIEN INVASION OF EARTH!!
WHA...
WHAT?
YOU MEAN...NO, WAIT. ALIENS?
AT THIS POINT, I DON'T THINK OUR READERS WOULD BE SURPRISED IF SOMETHING LIKE THAT HAPPENED, BUT...NO WAY!

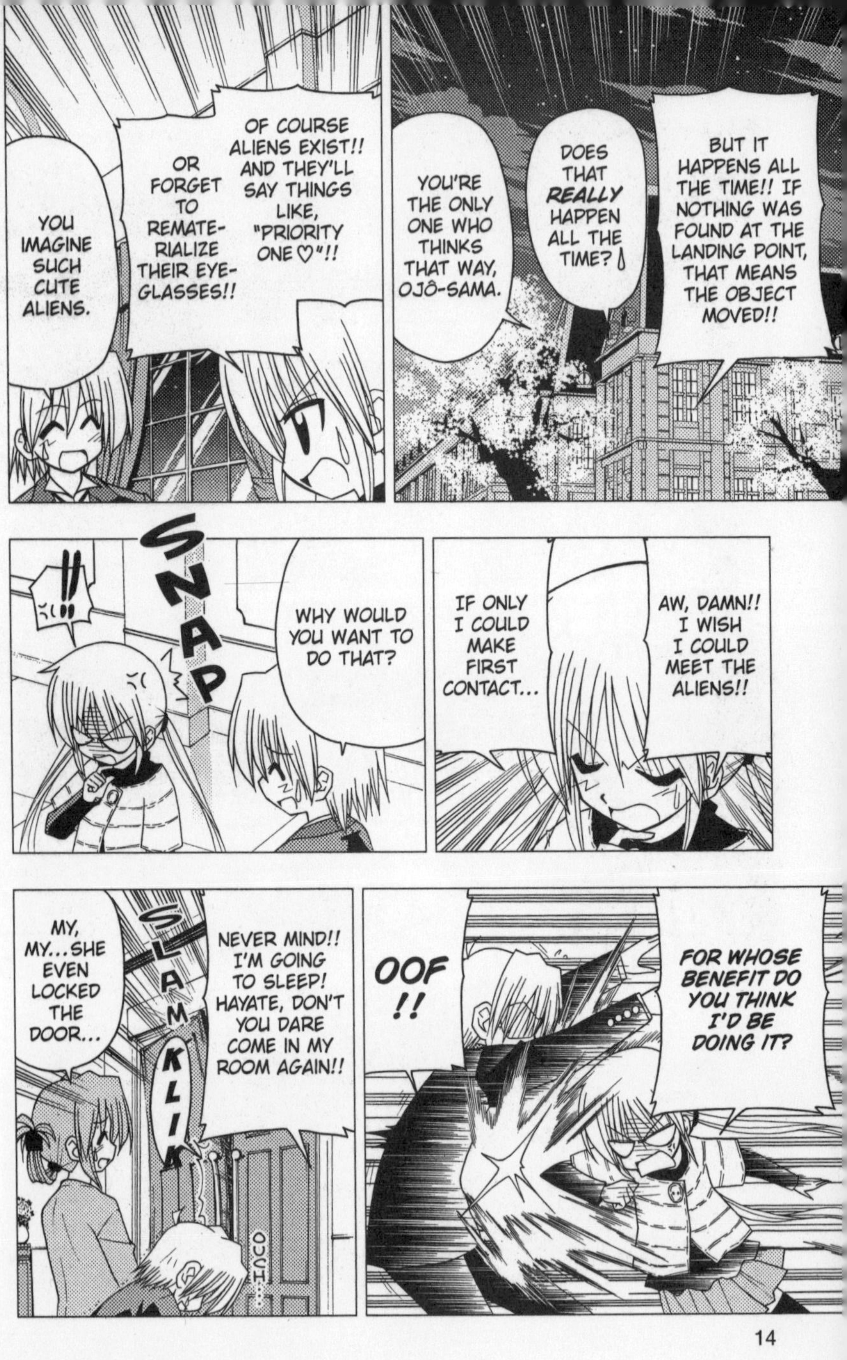
BUT IT HAPPENS ALL THE TIME!! IF NOTHING WAS FOUND AT THE LANDING POINT, THAT MEANS THE OBJECT MOVED!!
DOES THAT *REALLY* HAPPEN ALL THE TIME?
YOU'RE THE ONLY ONE WHO THINKS THAT WAY, OJÔ-SAMA.
OF COURSE ALIENS EXIST!! AND THEY'LL SAY THINGS LIKE, "PRIORITY ONE♡"!!
OR FORGET TO REMATERIALIZE THEIR EYEGLASSES!!
YOU IMAGINE SUCH CUTE ALIENS.
AW, DAMN!! I WISH I COULD MEET THE ALIENS!!
IF ONLY I COULD MAKE FIRST CONTACT...
WHY WOULD YOU WANT TO DO THAT?
SNAP
!!
FOR WHOSE BENEFIT DO YOU THINK I'D BE DOING IT?
OOF!!
NEVER MIND!! I'M GOING TO SLEEP! HAYATE, DON'T YOU DARE COME IN MY ROOM AGAIN!!
SLAM
KLIK
MY, MY...SHE EVEN LOCKED THE DOOR...
OUCH...

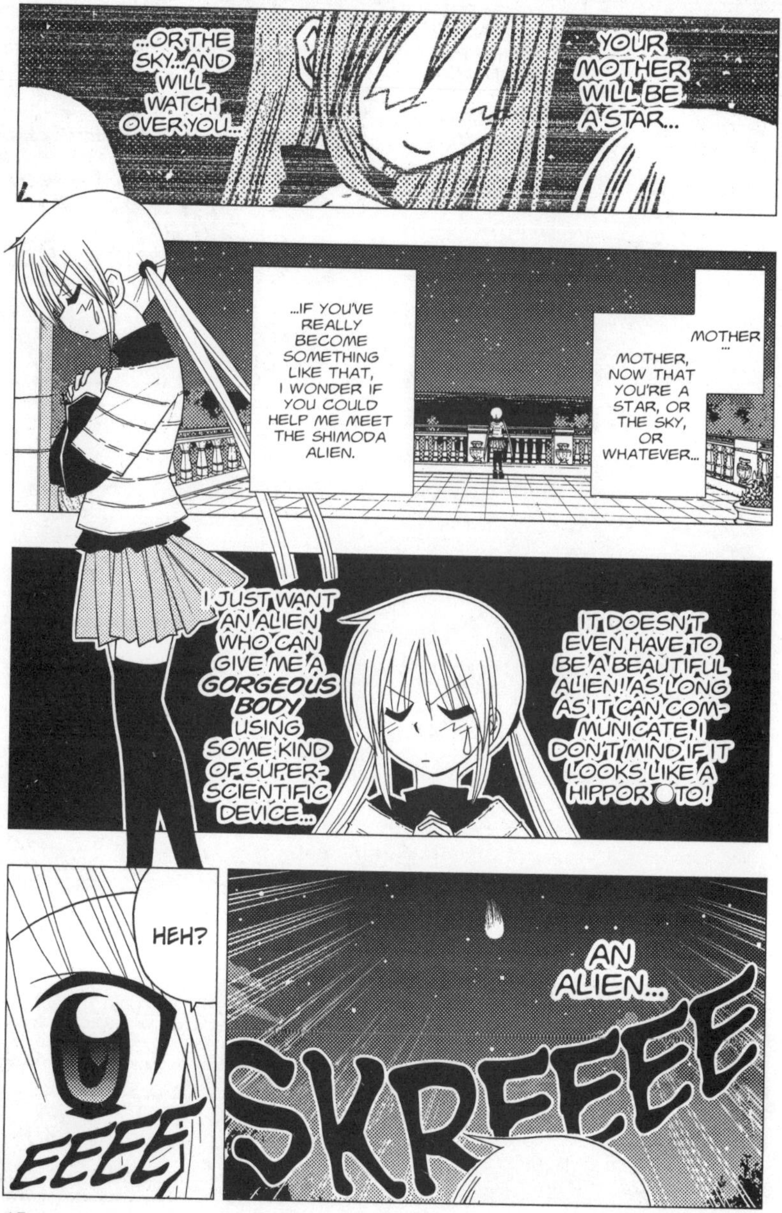
YOUR MOTHER WILL BE A STAR...
...OR THE SKY...AND WILL WATCH OVER YOU...
MOTHER...
MOTHER, NOW THAT YOU'RE A STAR, OR THE SKY, OR WHATEVER...
...IF YOU'VE REALLY BECOME SOMETHING LIKE THAT, I WONDER IF YOU COULD HELP ME MEET THE SHIMODA ALIEN.
IT DOESN'T EVEN HAVE TO BE A BEAUTIFUL ALIEN! AS LONG AS IT CAN COMMUNICATE, I DON'T MIND IF IT LOOKS LIKE A HIPPOR○TO!
I JUST WANT AN ALIEN WHO CAN GIVE ME A GORGEOUS BODY USING SOME KIND OF SUPER-SCIENTIFIC DEVICE...
AN ALIEN...
SKREEE
HEH?
EEEE

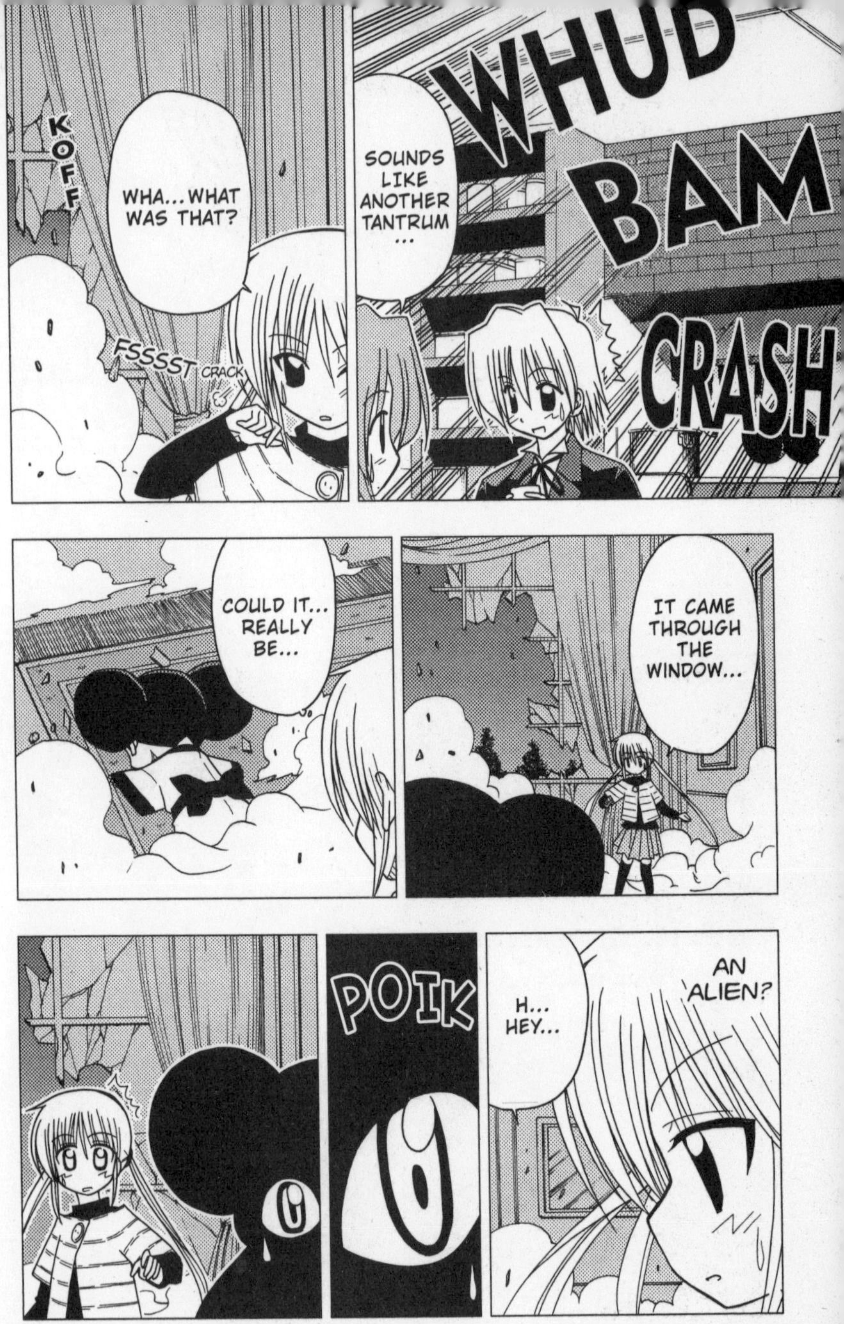
WHUD
BAM
CRASH
SOUNDS LIKE ANOTHER TANTRUM...
KOFF
WHA...WHAT WAS THAT?
FSSSST
CRACK
IT CAME THROUGH THE WINDOW...
COULD IT... REALLY BE...
AN ALIEN?
H... HEY...
POIK

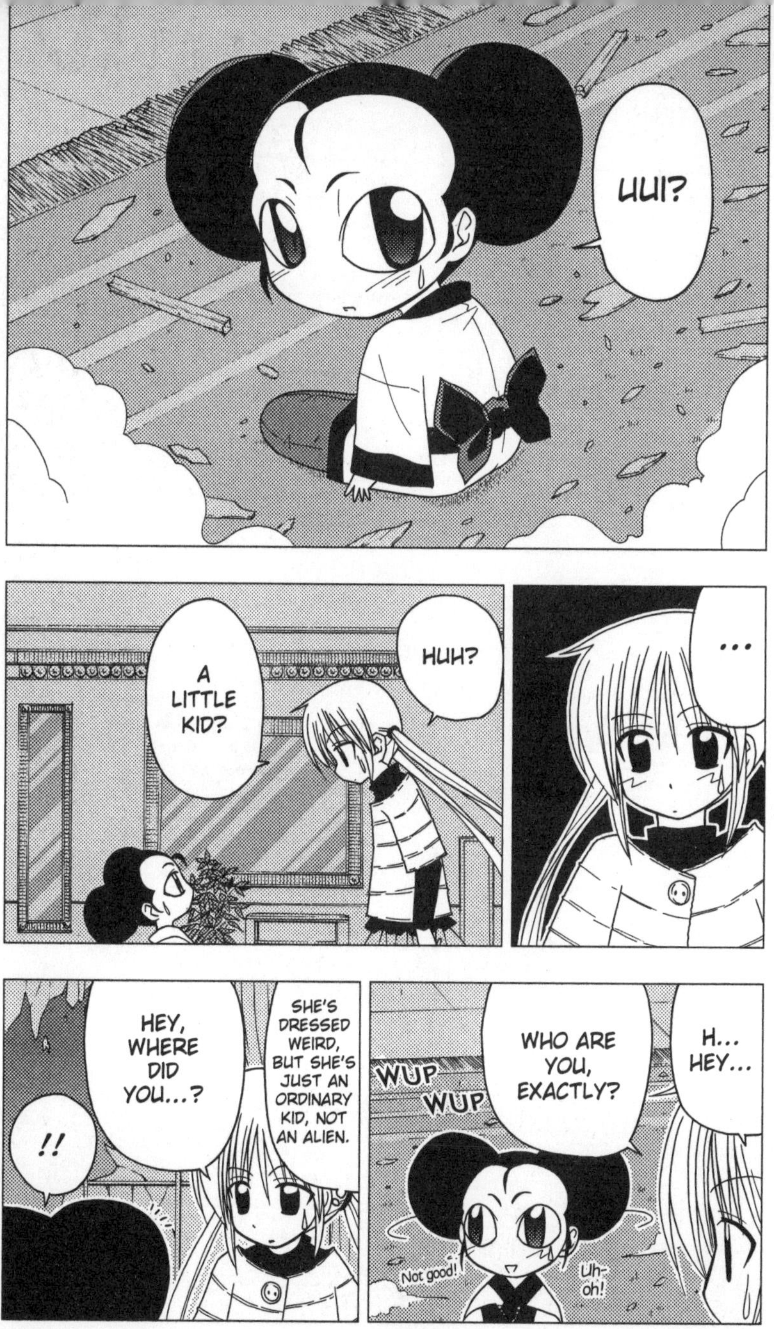
UUI?
...
HUH?
A LITTLE KID?
H... HEY...
WHO ARE YOU, EXACTLY?
WUP WUP
Uh-oh!
Not good!
SHE'S DRESSED WEIRD, BUT SHE'S JUST AN ORDINARY KID, NOT AN ALIEN.
HEY, WHERE DID YOU...?
!!

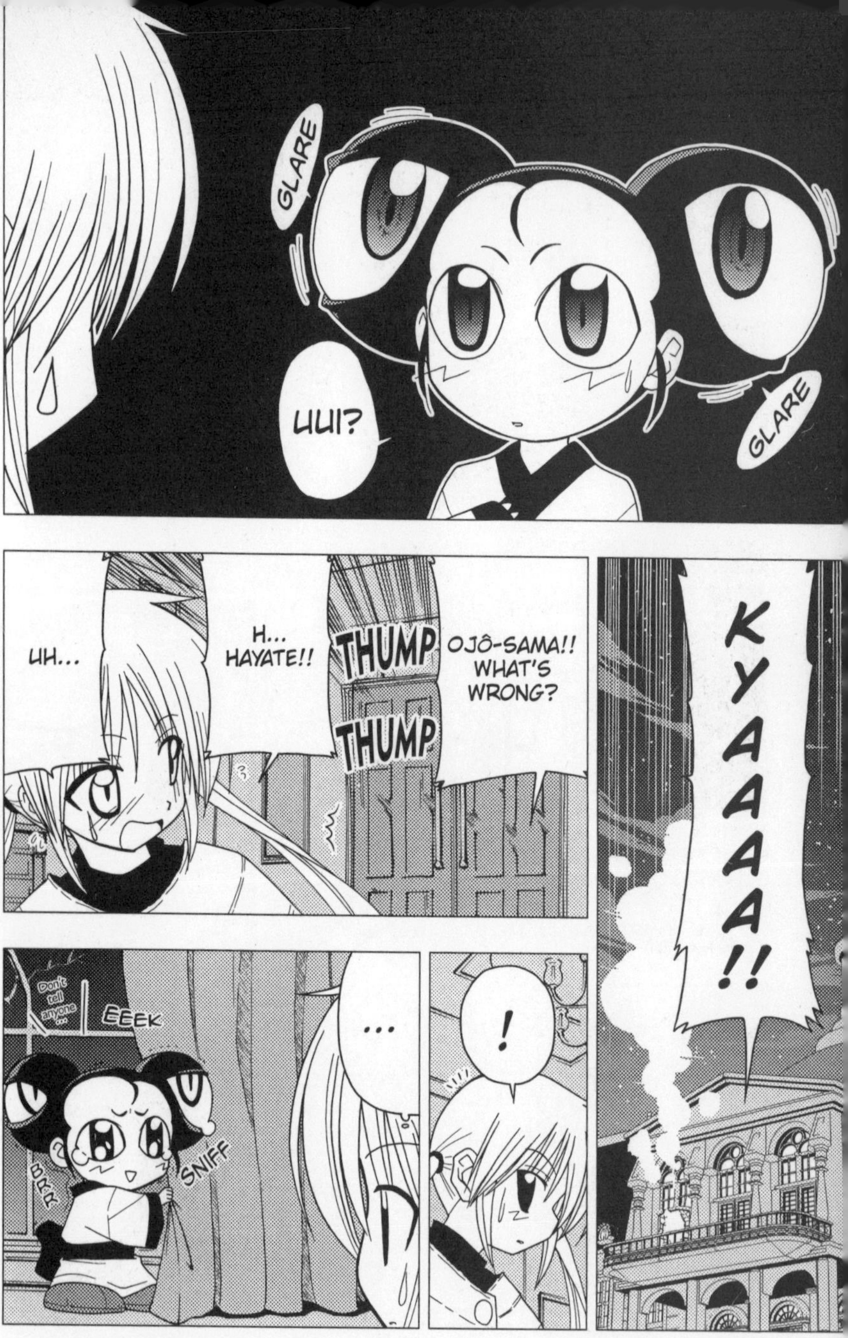
GLARE
UUI?
GLARE
KYAAAAA!!
OJÔ-SAMA!! WHAT'S WRONG?
THUMP
THUMP
H... HAYATE!!
UH...
!
...
Don't tell anyone...
EEEK
SNIFF
BRR

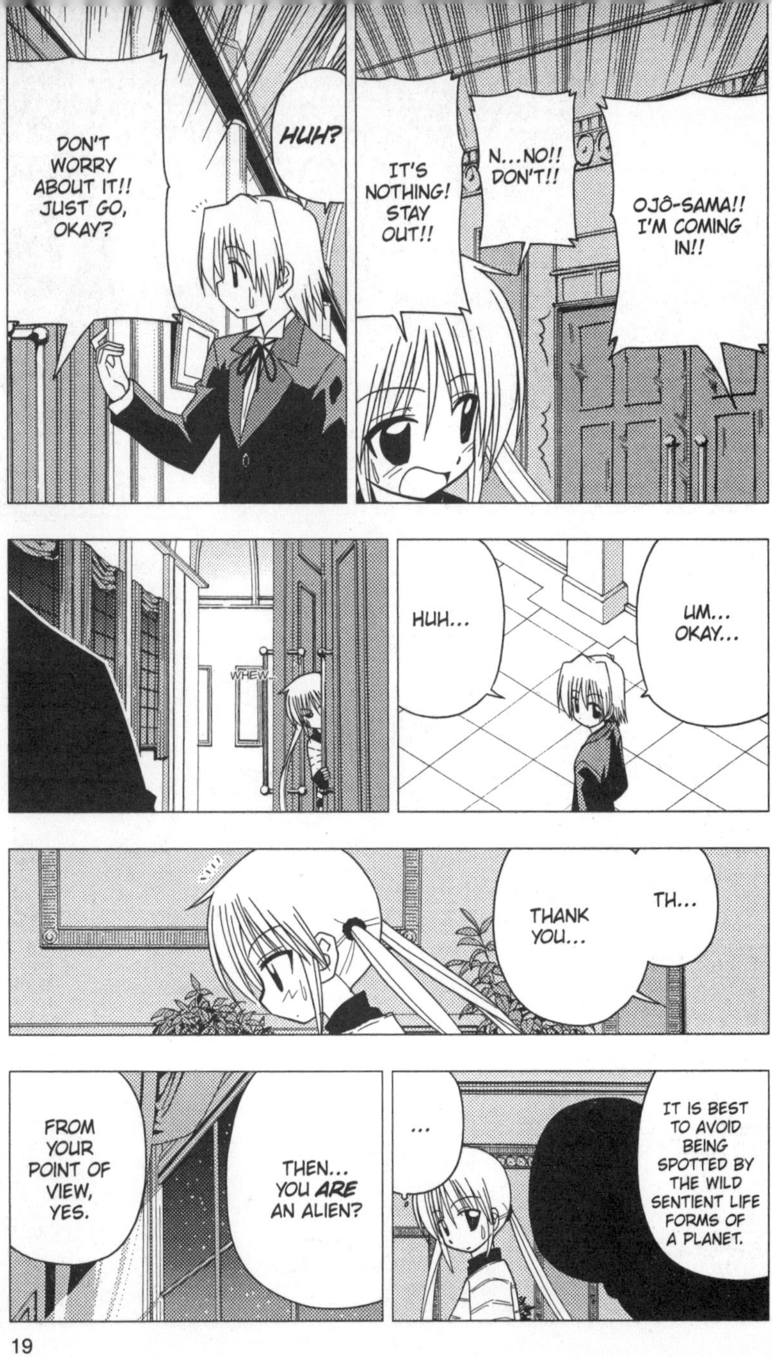
OJÔ-SAMA!! I'M COMING IN!!
N...NO!! DON'T!!
IT'S NOTHING! STAY OUT!!
HUH?
DON'T WORRY ABOUT IT!! JUST GO, OKAY?
UM... OKAY...
HUH...
WHEW...
TH...
THANK YOU...
IT IS BEST TO AVOID BEING SPOTTED BY THE WILD SENTIENT LIFE FORMS OF A PLANET.
...
THEN... YOU ARE AN ALIEN?
FROM YOUR POINT OF VIEW, YES.

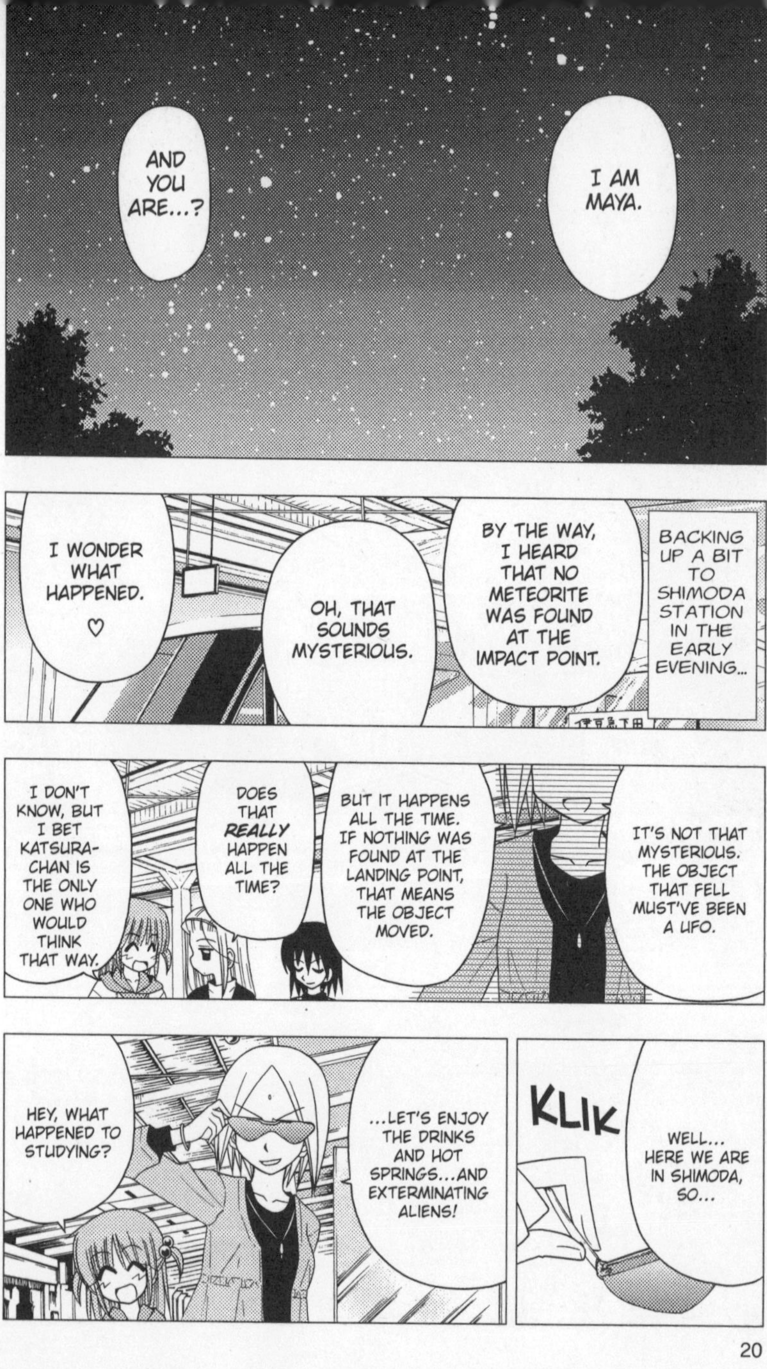
I AM MAYA.
AND YOU ARE...?
BACKING UP A BIT TO SHIMODA STATION IN THE EARLY EVENING...
伊豆急下田
BY THE WAY, I HEARD THAT NO METEORITE WAS FOUND AT THE IMPACT POINT.
OH, THAT SOUNDS MYSTERIOUS.
I WONDER WHAT HAPPENED. ♡
IT'S NOT THAT MYSTERIOUS. THE OBJECT THAT FELL MUST'VE BEEN A UFO.
BUT IT HAPPENS ALL THE TIME. IF NOTHING WAS FOUND AT THE LANDING POINT, THAT MEANS THE OBJECT MOVED.
DOES THAT *REALLY* HAPPEN ALL THE TIME?
I DON'T KNOW, BUT I BET KATSURA-CHAN IS THE ONLY ONE WHO WOULD THINK THAT WAY.
KLIK
WELL... HERE WE ARE IN SHIMODA, SO...
...LET'S ENJOY THE DRINKS AND HOT SPRINGS...AND EXTERMINATING ALIENS!
HEY, WHAT HAPPENED TO STUDYING?

Episode 2: "It Was Momoi Who Was Referred to as Having Skin like an Eggshell After a Bath"

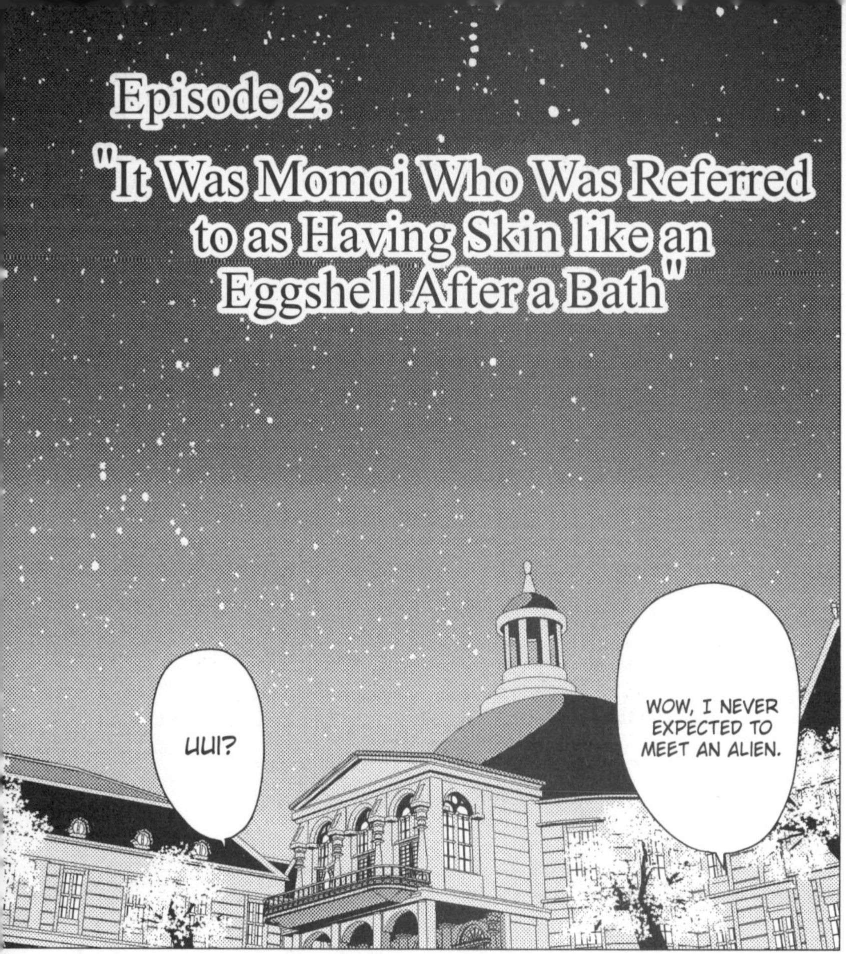

WOW, I NEVER EXPECTED TO MEET AN ALIEN.
UUI?

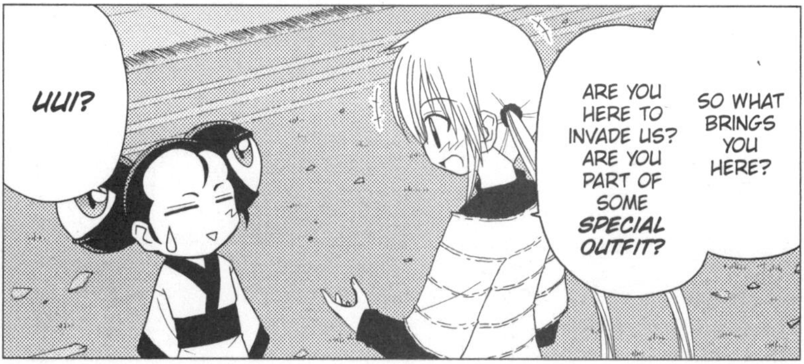

SO WHAT BRINGS YOU HERE?
ARE YOU HERE TO INVADE US? ARE YOU PART OF SOME *SPECIAL OUTFIT?*
UUI?

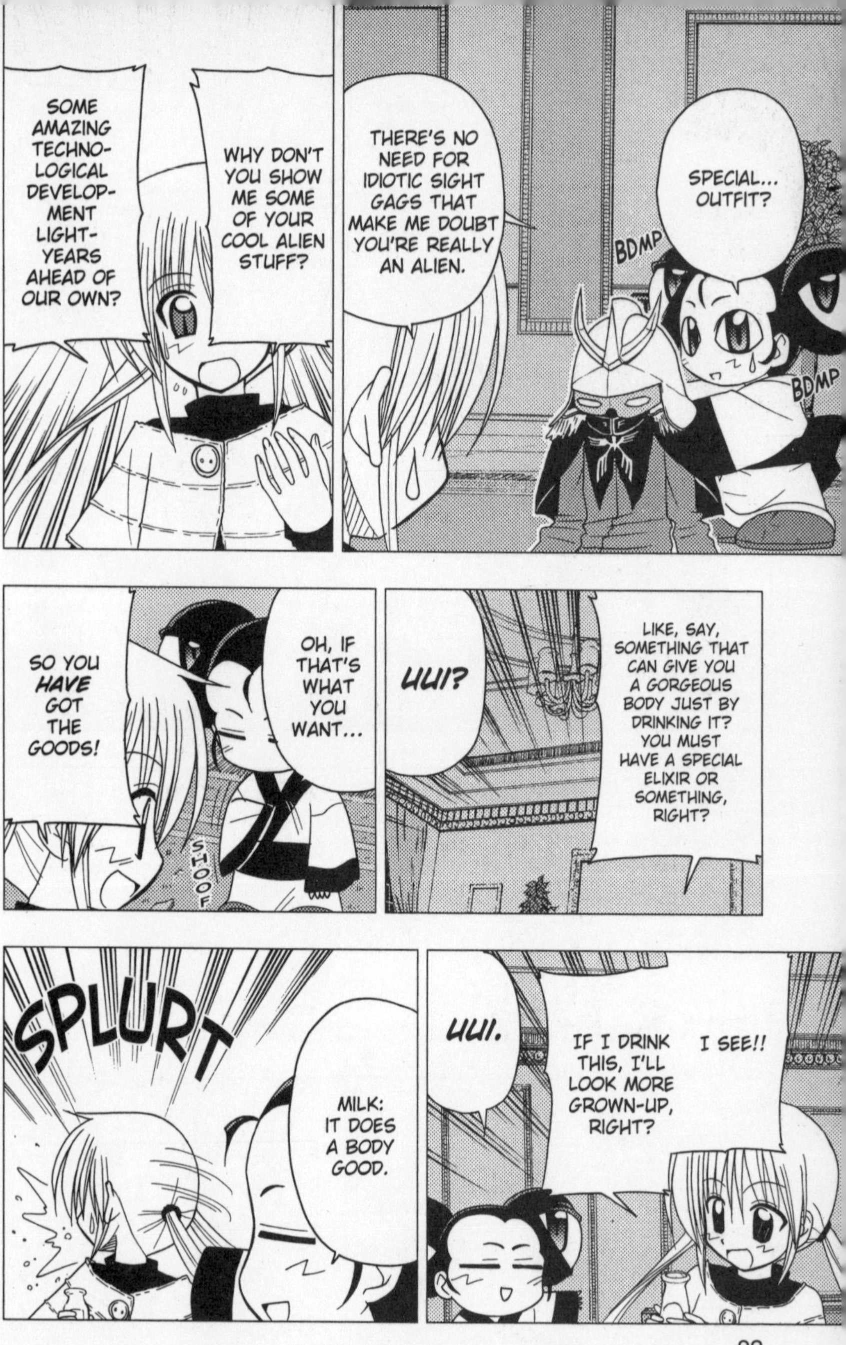
SPECIAL... OUTFIT?
BDMP
BDMP
THERE'S NO NEED FOR IDIOTIC SIGHT GAGS THAT MAKE ME DOUBT YOU'RE REALLY AN ALIEN.
WHY DON'T YOU SHOW ME SOME OF YOUR COOL ALIEN STUFF?
SOME AMAZING TECHNO-LOGICAL DEVELOP-MENT LIGHT-YEARS AHEAD OF OUR OWN?
LIKE, SAY, SOMETHING THAT CAN GIVE YOU A GORGEOUS BODY JUST BY DRINKING IT? YOU MUST HAVE A SPECIAL ELIXIR OR SOMETHING, RIGHT?
UUI?
OH, IF THAT'S WHAT YOU WANT...
SO YOU HAVE GOT THE GOODS!
SHOOF
I SEE!!
IF I DRINK THIS, I'LL LOOK MORE GROWN-UP, RIGHT?
UUI.
MILK: IT DOES A BODY GOOD.
SPLURT

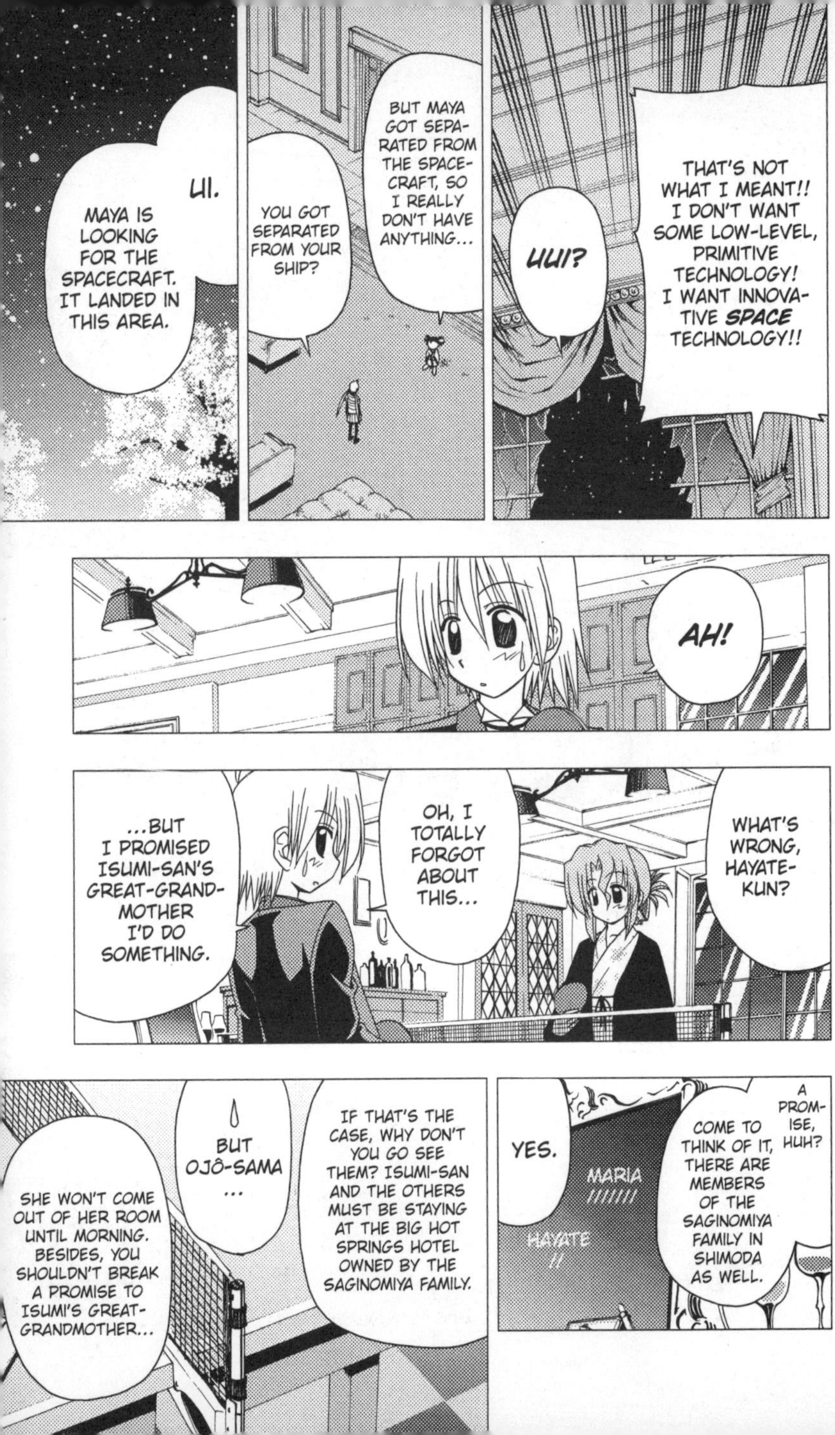
THAT'S NOT WHAT I MEANT!! I DON'T WANT SOME LOW-LEVEL, PRIMITIVE TECHNOLOGY! I WANT INNOVATIVE SPACE TECHNOLOGY!!
UUI?
BUT MAYA GOT SEPARATED FROM THE SPACECRAFT, SO I REALLY DON'T HAVE ANYTHING...
YOU GOT SEPARATED FROM YOUR SHIP?
UI.
MAYA IS LOOKING FOR THE SPACECRAFT. IT LANDED IN THIS AREA.
AH!
WHAT'S WRONG, HAYATE-KUN?
OH, I TOTALLY FORGOT ABOUT THIS...
...BUT I PROMISED ISUMI-SAN'S GREAT-GRANDMOTHER I'D DO SOMETHING.
A PROMISE, HUH?
COME TO THINK OF IT, THERE ARE MEMBERS OF THE SAGINOMIYA FAMILY IN SHIMODA AS WELL.
YES.
MARIA //////
HAYATE //
IF THAT'S THE CASE, WHY DON'T YOU GO SEE THEM? ISUMI-SAN AND THE OTHERS MUST BE STAYING AT THE BIG HOT SPRINGS HOTEL OWNED BY THE SAGINOMIYA FAMILY.
BUT OJÔ-SAMA ...
SHE WON'T COME OUT OF HER ROOM UNTIL MORNING. BESIDES, YOU SHOULDN'T BREAK A PROMISE TO ISUMI'S GREAT-GRANDMOTHER...

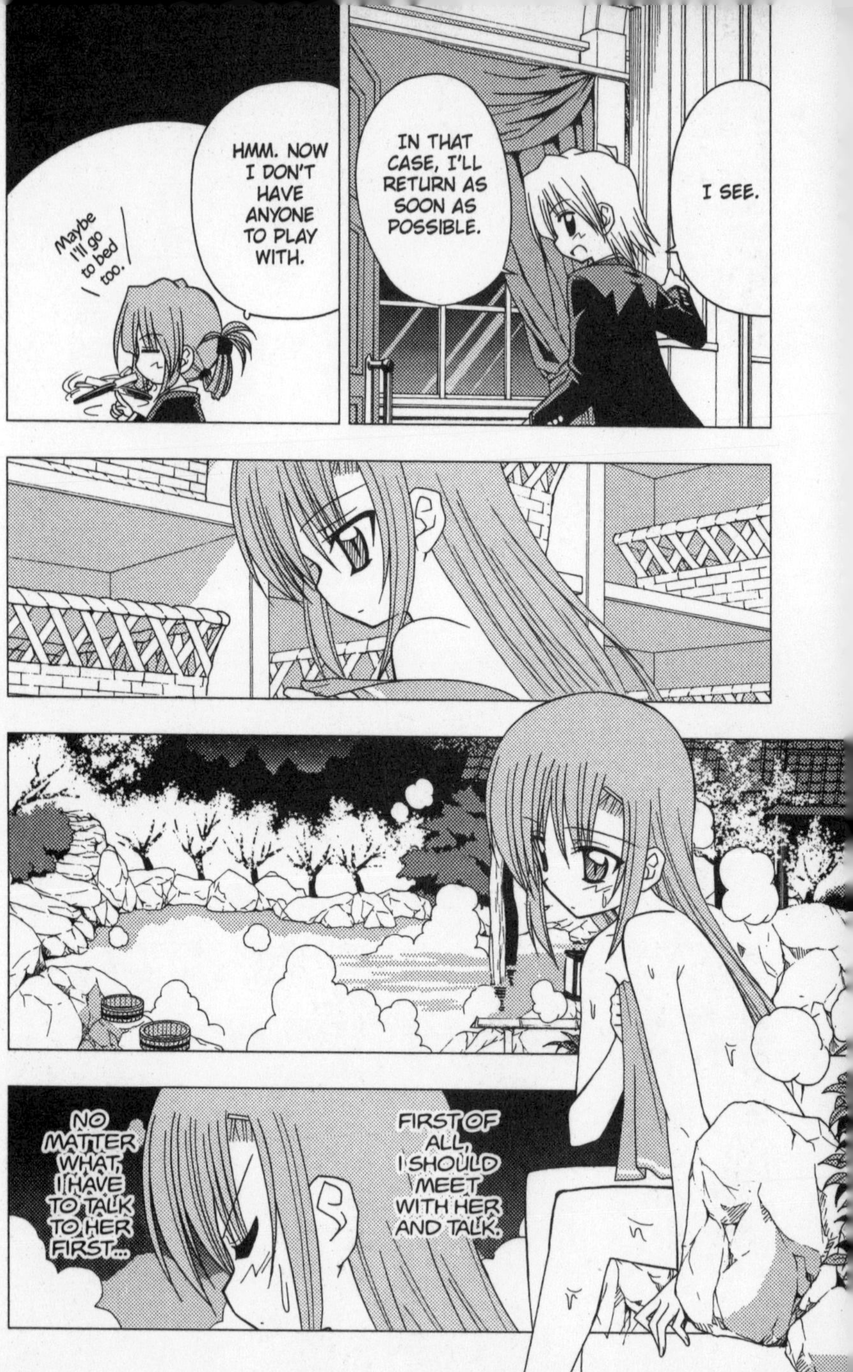
I SEE.
IN THAT CASE, I'LL RETURN AS SOON AS POSSIBLE.
HMM. NOW I DON'T HAVE ANYONE TO PLAY WITH.
Maybe I'll go to bed too.
FIRST OF ALL, I SHOULD MEET WITH HER AND TALK.
NO MATTER WHAT, I HAVE TO TALK TO HER FIRST...

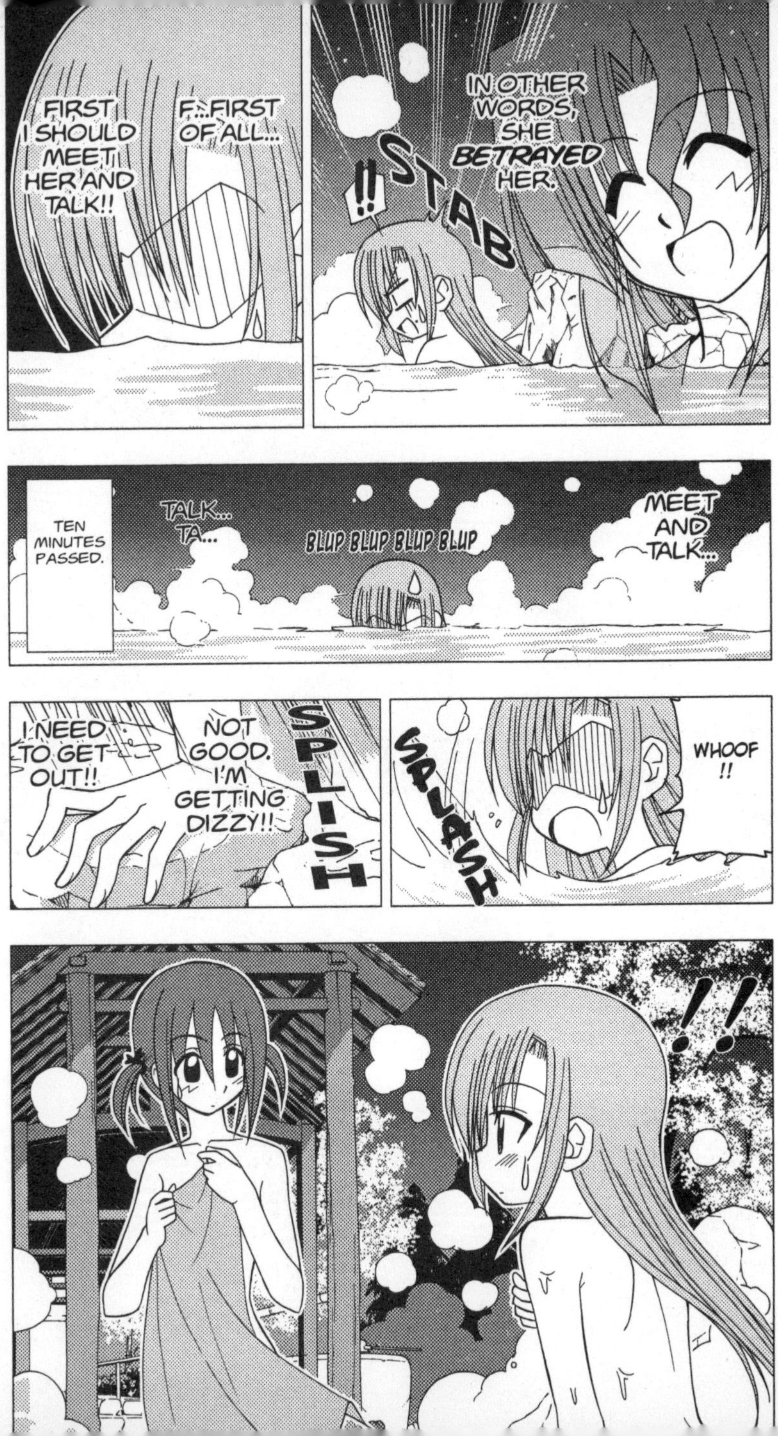
IN OTHER WORDS, SHE BETRAYED HER.
STAB
!!
F...FIRST OF ALL...
FIRST I SHOULD MEET HER AND TALK!!
MEET AND TALK...
BLUP BLUP BLUP BLUP
TALK... TA...
TEN MINUTES PASSED.
WHOOF !!
SPLASH
SPLISH
NOT GOOD. I'M GETTING DIZZY!!
I NEED TO GET OUT!!
!!

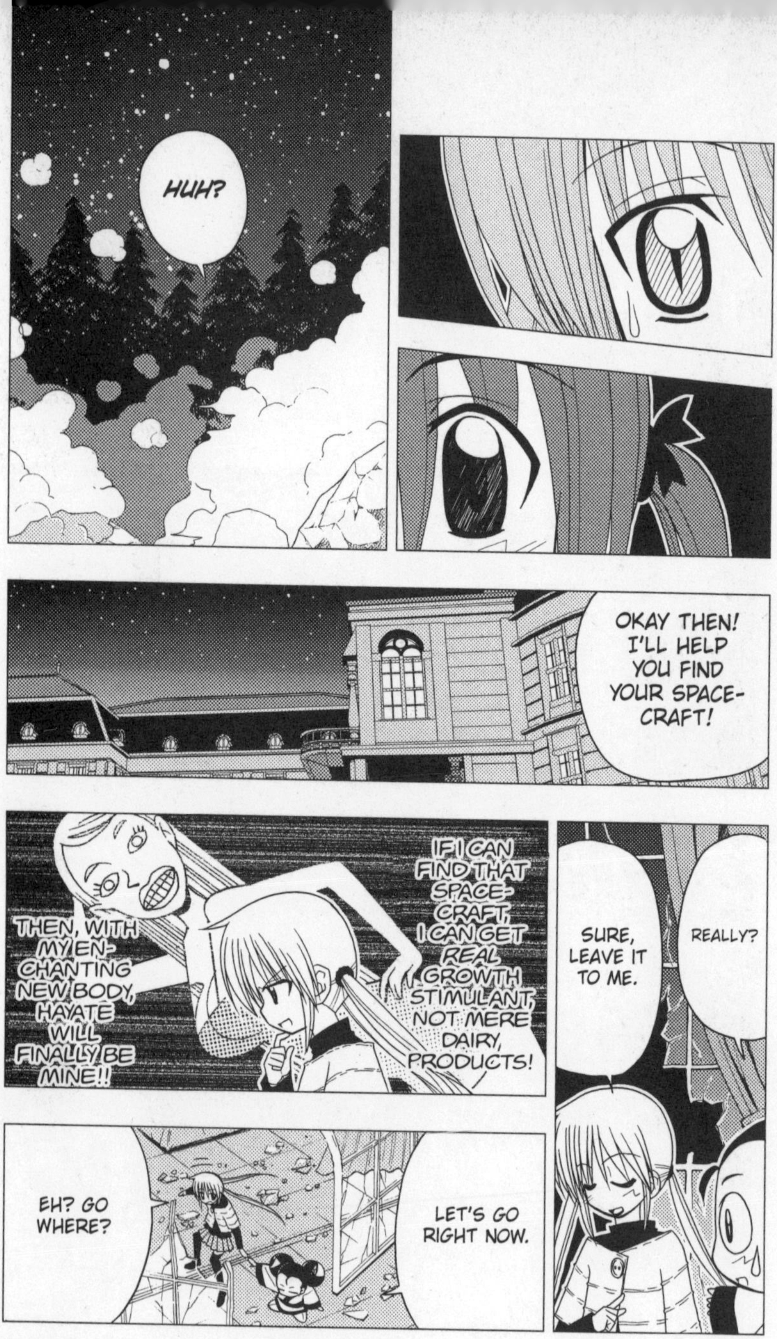
HUH?
OKAY THEN! I'LL HELP YOU FIND YOUR SPACE-CRAFT!
REALLY?
SURE, LEAVE IT TO ME.
IF I CAN FIND THAT SPACE-CRAFT, I CAN GET REAL GROWTH STIMULANT, NOT MERE DAIRY PRODUCTS!
THEN, WITH MY EN-CHANTING NEW BODY, HAYATE WILL FINALLY BE MINE!!
LET'S GO RIGHT NOW.
EH? GO WHERE?

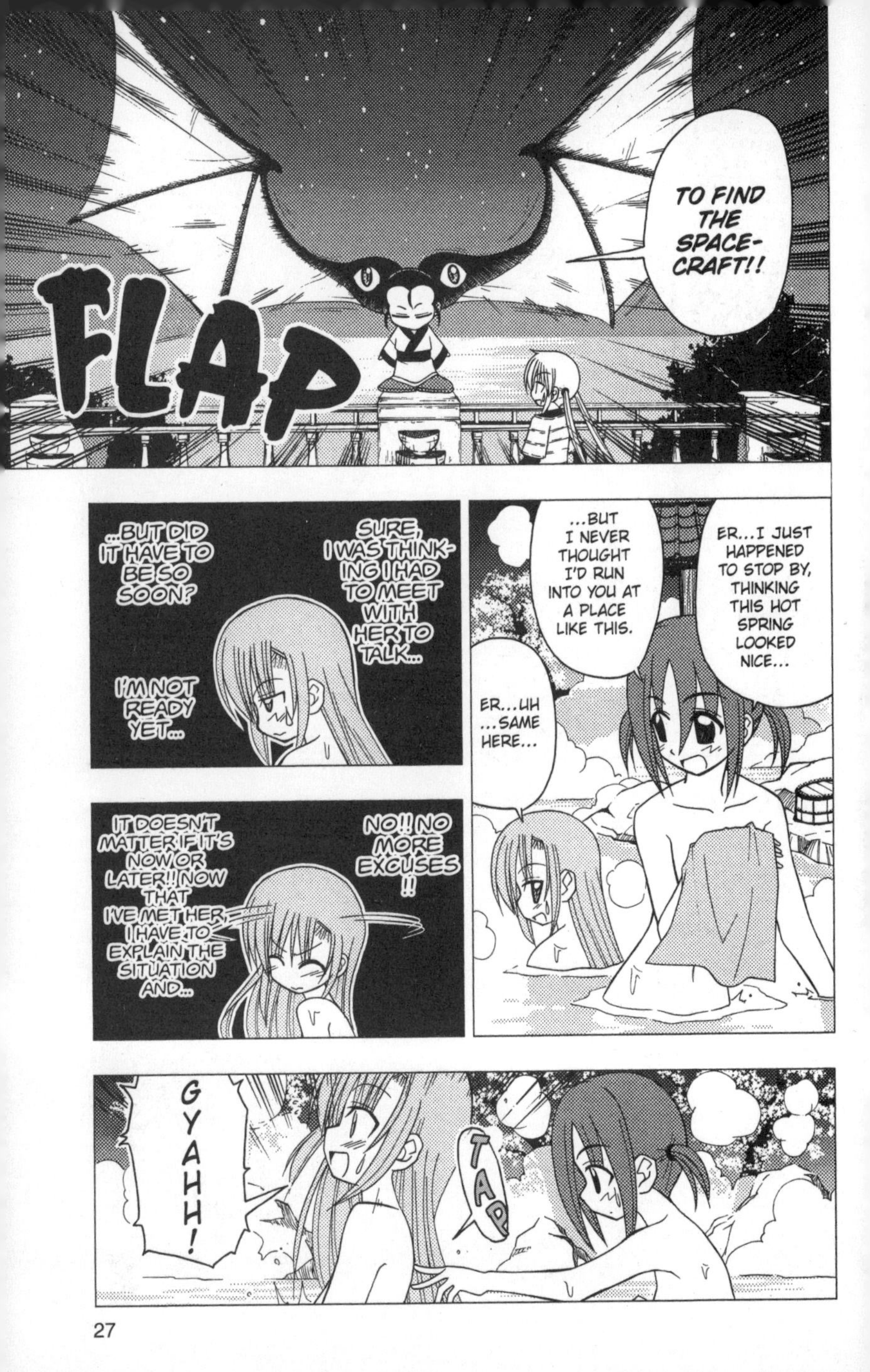
TO FIND THE SPACE-CRAFT!!
FLAP
ER...I JUST HAPPENED TO STOP BY, THINKING THIS HOT SPRING LOOKED NICE...
...BUT I NEVER THOUGHT I'D RUN INTO YOU AT A PLACE LIKE THIS.
ER...UH ...SAME HERE...
SURE, I WAS THINKING I HAD TO MEET WITH HER TO TALK...
...BUT DID IT HAVE TO BE SO SOON?
I'M NOT READY YET...
NO!! NO MORE EXCUSES!!
IT DOESN'T MATTER IF IT'S NOW OR LATER!! NOW THAT I'VE MET HER, I HAVE TO EXPLAIN THE SITUATION AND...
TAP
GYAHH!

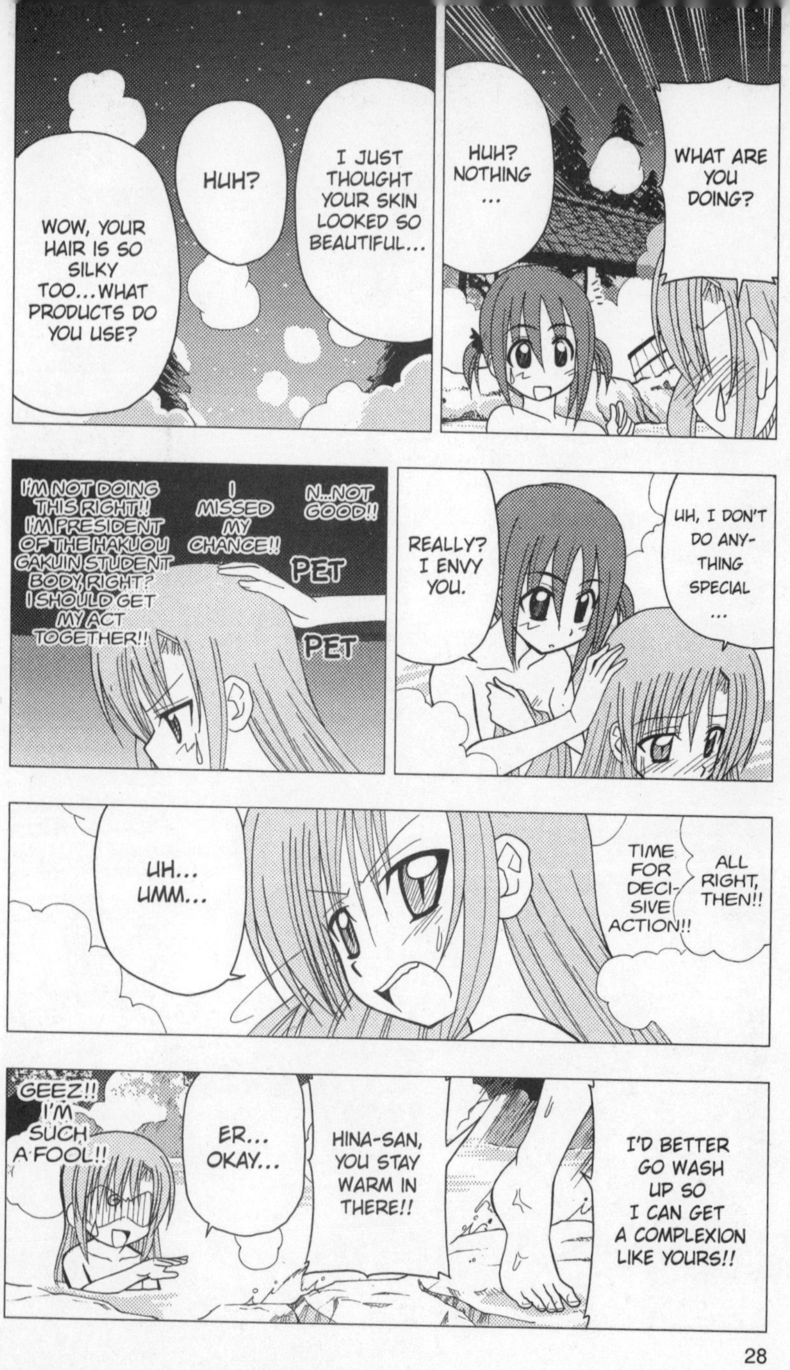
WHAT ARE YOU DOING?
HUH? NOTHING ...
I JUST THOUGHT YOUR SKIN LOOKED SO BEAUTIFUL...
HUH?
WOW, YOUR HAIR IS SO SILKY TOO...WHAT PRODUCTS DO YOU USE?
UH, I DON'T DO ANY-THING SPECIAL ...
REALLY? I ENVY YOU.
N...NOT GOOD!!
PET
PET
I MISSED MY CHANCE!!
I'M NOT DOING THIS RIGHT!! I'M PRESIDENT OF THE HAKUOU GAKUIN STUDENT BODY, RIGHT? I SHOULD GET MY ACT TOGETHER!!
ALL RIGHT, THEN!!
TIME FOR DECI-SIVE ACTION!!
UH... UMM...
I'D BETTER GO WASH UP SO I CAN GET A COMPLEXION LIKE YOURS!!
HINA-SAN, YOU STAY WARM IN THERE!!
ER... OKAY...
GEEZ!! I'M SUCH A FOOL!!

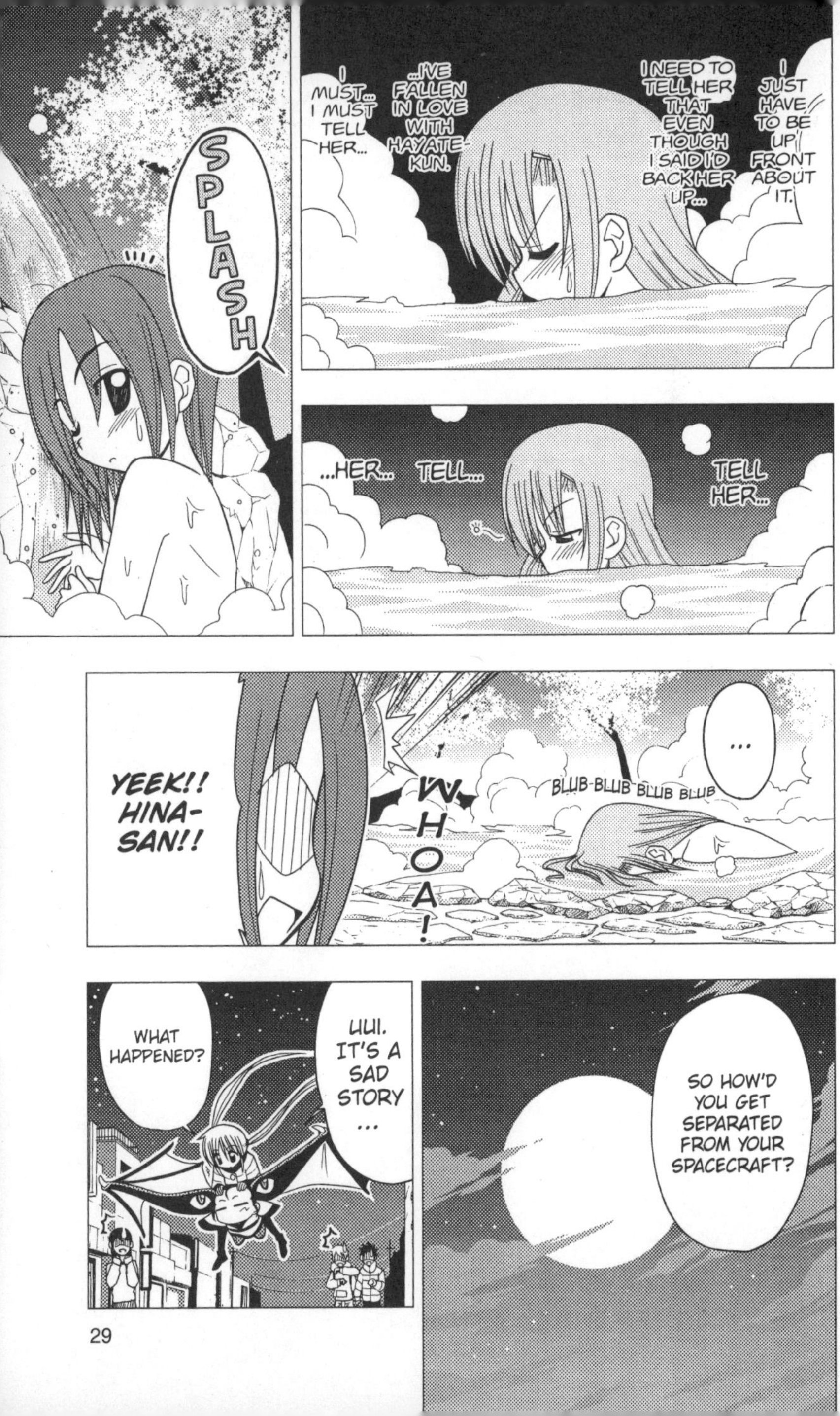
I JUST HAVE TO BE UP FRONT ABOUT IT.
I NEED TO TELL HER THAT EVEN THOUGH I SAID I'D BACK HER UP...
...I'VE FALLEN IN LOVE WITH HAYATE-KUN.
I MUST... I MUST TELL HER...
TELL HER...
TELL...
...HER...
SPLASH
...
BLUB-BLUB BLUB BLUB
WHOA!
YEEK!! HINA-SAN!!
SO HOW'D YOU GET SEPARATED FROM YOUR SPACECRAFT?
UUI. IT'S A SAD STORY ...
WHAT HAPPENED?

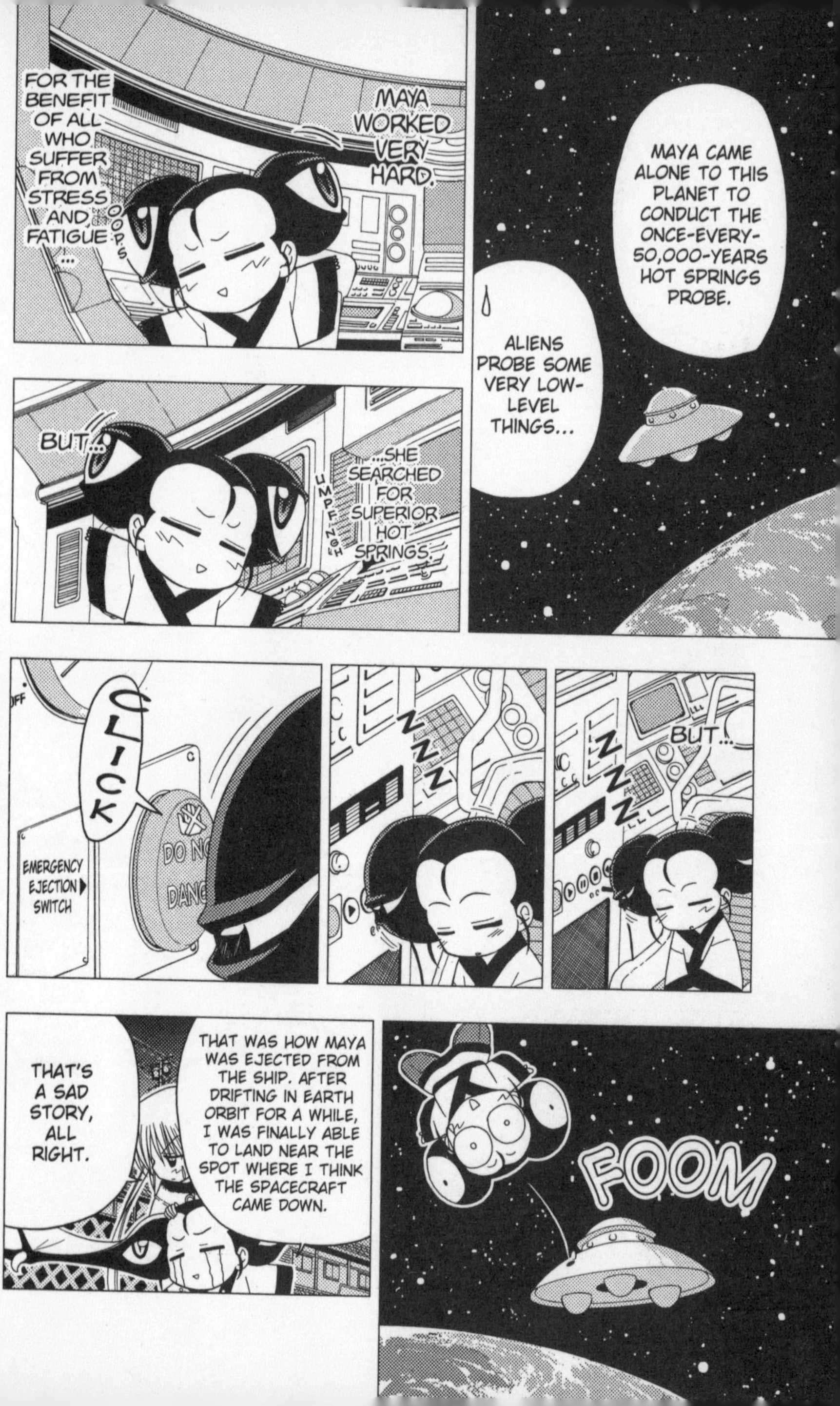
MAYA CAME ALONE TO THIS PLANET TO CONDUCT THE ONCE-EVERY-50,000-YEARS HOT SPRINGS PROBE.
ALIENS PROBE SOME VERY LOW-LEVEL THINGS...
MAYA WORKED VERY HARD.
FOR THE BENEFIT OF ALL WHO SUFFER FROM STRESS AND FATIGUE...
OOPS
...SHE SEARCHED FOR SUPERIOR HOT SPRINGS.
BUT...
UMPFINGH
BUT...
ZZZ
ZZZ
CLICK
OFF
DO NO
DANG
EMERGENCY EJECTION SWITCH
FOOM
THAT WAS HOW MAYA WAS EJECTED FROM THE SHIP. AFTER DRIFTING IN EARTH ORBIT FOR A WHILE, I WAS FINALLY ABLE TO LAND NEAR THE SPOT WHERE I THINK THE SPACECRAFT CAME DOWN.
THAT'S A SAD STORY, ALL RIGHT.

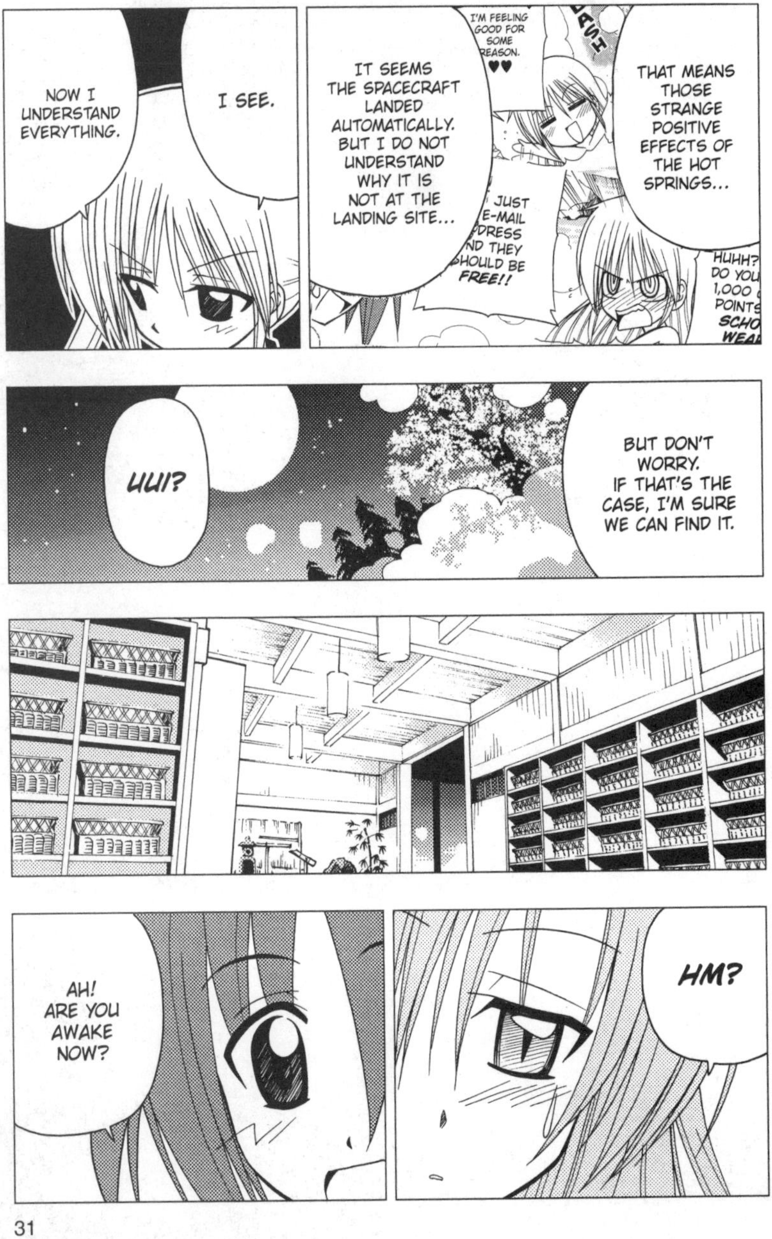
THAT MEANS THOSE STRANGE POSITIVE EFFECTS OF THE HOT SPRINGS...
I'M FEELING GOOD FOR SOME REASON. ♥♥
IT SEEMS THE SPACECRAFT LANDED AUTOMATICALLY. BUT I DO NOT UNDERSTAND WHY IT IS NOT AT THE LANDING SITE...
I SEE.
NOW I UNDERSTAND EVERYTHING.
BUT DON'T WORRY. IF THAT'S THE CASE, I'M SURE WE CAN FIND IT.
UUI?
HM?
AH! ARE YOU AWAKE NOW?

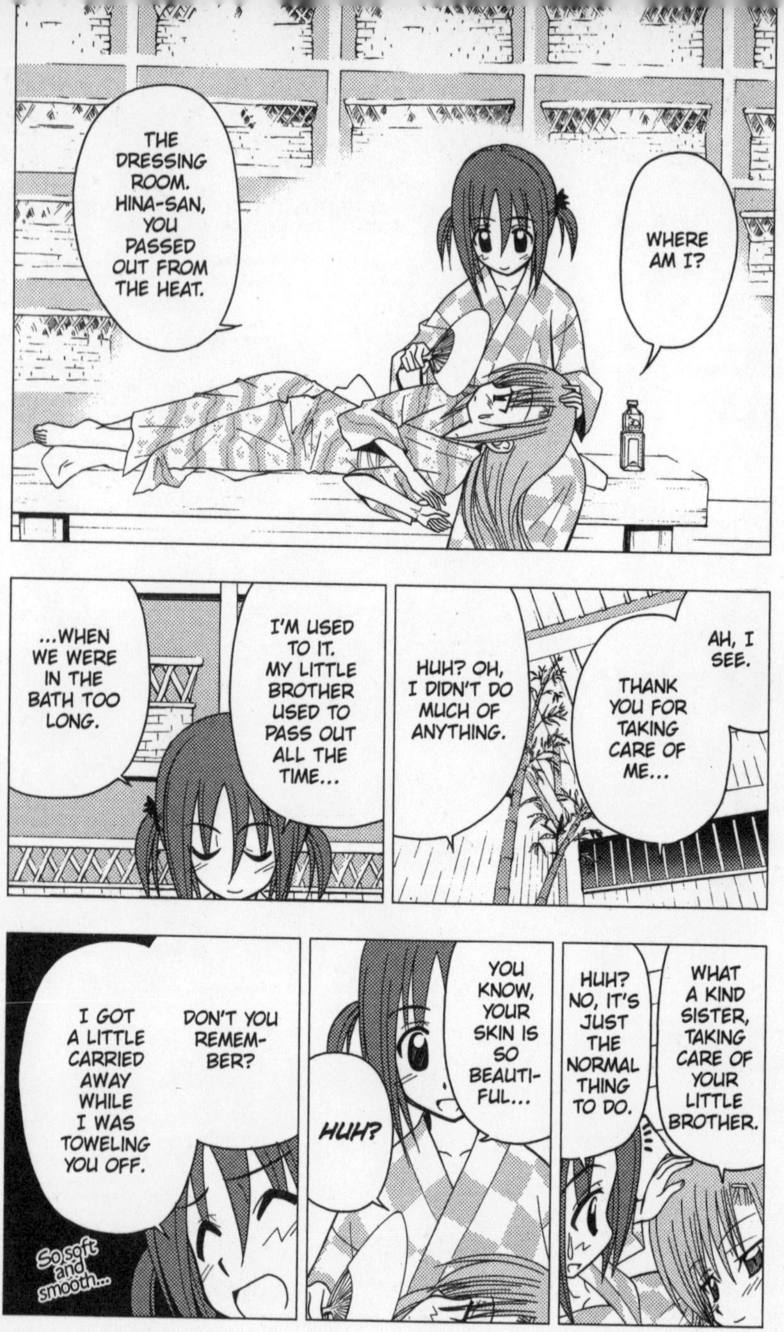
WHERE AM I?
THE DRESSING ROOM. HINA-SAN, YOU PASSED OUT FROM THE HEAT.
AH, I SEE.
THANK YOU FOR TAKING CARE OF ME...
HUH? OH, I DIDN'T DO MUCH OF ANYTHING.
I'M USED TO IT. MY LITTLE BROTHER USED TO PASS OUT ALL THE TIME...
...WHEN WE WERE IN THE BATH TOO LONG.
WHAT A KIND SISTER, TAKING CARE OF YOUR LITTLE BROTHER.
HUH? NO, IT'S JUST THE NORMAL THING TO DO.
YOU KNOW, YOUR SKIN IS SO BEAUTIFUL...
HUH?
DON'T YOU REMEMBER?
I GOT A LITTLE CARRIED AWAY WHILE I WAS TOWELING YOU OFF.
So soft and smooth...

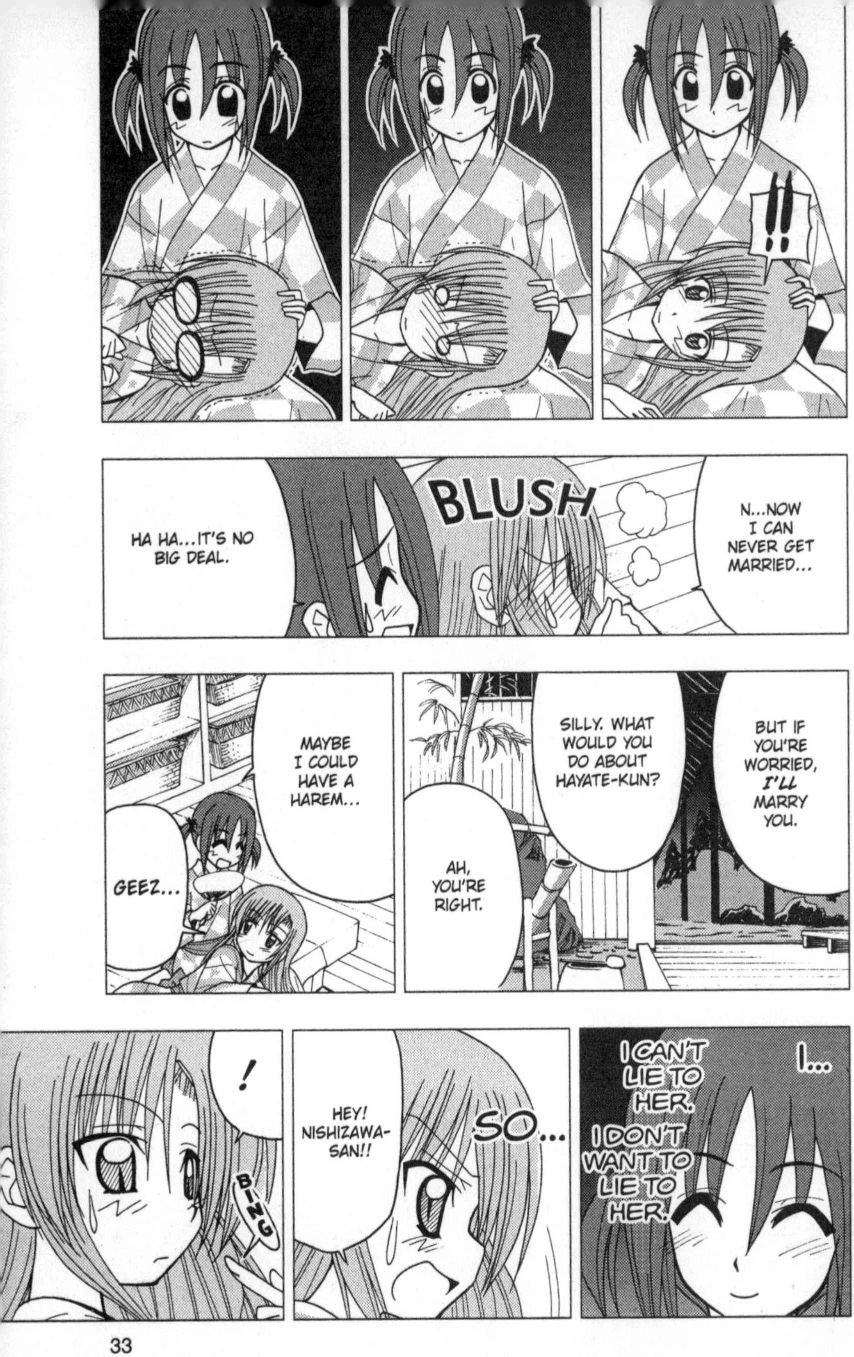
!!
N...NOW I CAN NEVER GET MARRIED...
BLUSH
HA HA...IT'S NO BIG DEAL.
BUT IF YOU'RE WORRIED, *I'LL* MARRY YOU.
SILLY. WHAT WOULD YOU DO ABOUT HAYATE-KUN?
AH, YOU'RE RIGHT.
MAYBE I COULD HAVE A HAREM...
GEEZ...
I...
I CAN'T LIE TO HER.
I DON'T WANT TO LIE TO HER.
SO...
HEY! NISHIZAWA-SAN!!
!
BING

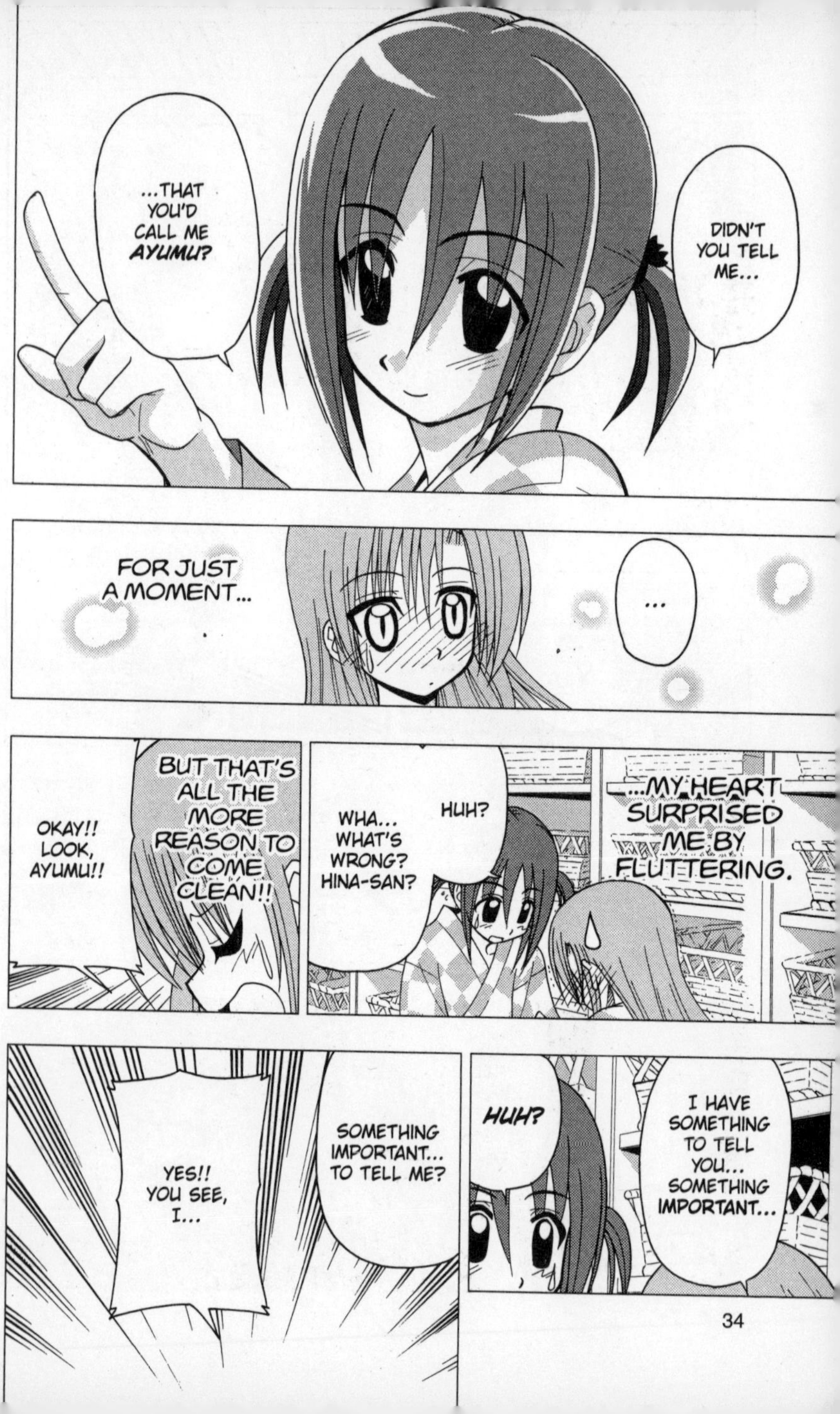
DIDN'T YOU TELL ME...
...THAT YOU'D CALL ME *AYUMU?*
...
FOR JUST A MOMENT...
...MY HEART SURPRISED ME BY FLUTTERING.
HUH?
WHA... WHAT'S WRONG? HINA-SAN?
BUT THAT'S ALL THE MORE REASON TO COME CLEAN!!
OKAY!! LOOK, AYUMU!!
I HAVE SOMETHING TO TELL YOU... SOMETHING IMPORTANT...
HUH?
SOMETHING IMPORTANT... TO TELL ME?
YES!! YOU SEE, I...

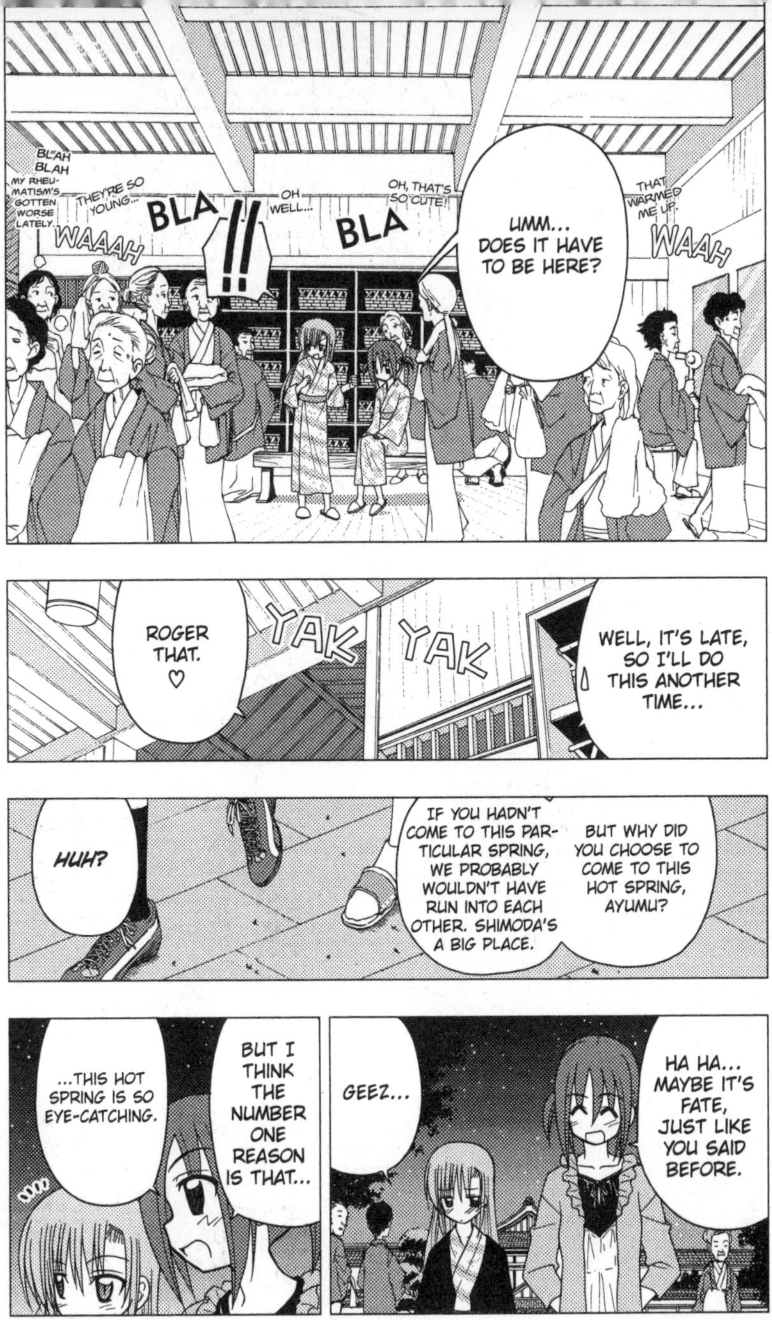
WAAH
THAT WARMED ME UP.
UMM... DOES IT HAVE TO BE HERE?
OH, THAT'S SO CUTE!
BLA
OH WELL...
!!
BLA
THEY'RE SO YOUNG...
MY RHEUMATISM'S GOTTEN WORSE LATELY.
BLAH BLAH
WAAAH
WELL, IT'S LATE, SO I'LL DO THIS ANOTHER TIME...
YAK YAK
ROGER THAT. ♡
BUT WHY DID YOU CHOOSE TO COME TO THIS HOT SPRING, AYUMU?
IF YOU HADN'T COME TO THIS PARTICULAR SPRING, WE PROBABLY WOULDN'T HAVE RUN INTO EACH OTHER. SHIMODA'S A BIG PLACE.
HUH?
HA HA... MAYBE IT'S FATE, JUST LIKE YOU SAID BEFORE.
GEEZ...
BUT I THINK THE NUMBER ONE REASON IS THAT...
...THIS HOT SPRING IS SO EYE-CATCHING.

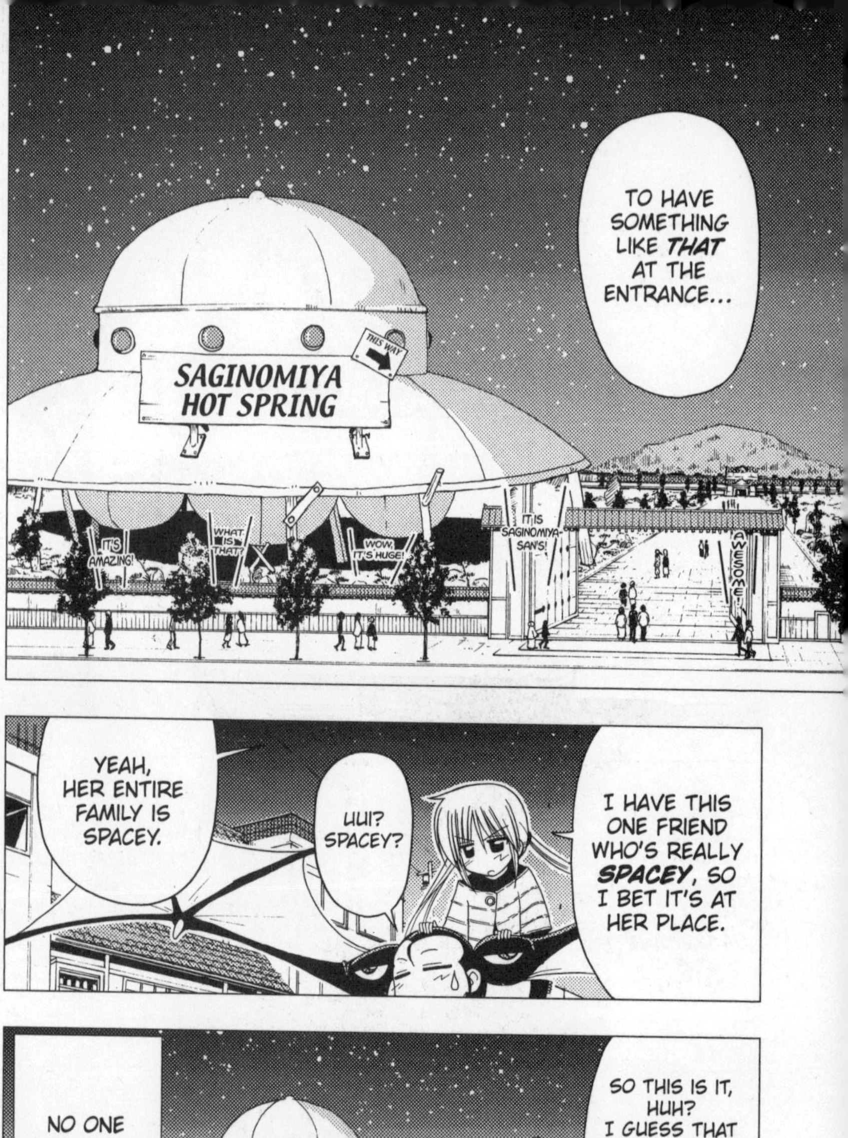
TO HAVE SOMETHING LIKE *THAT* AT THE ENTRANCE...
THIS WAY
SAGINOMIYA HOT SPRING
AWESOME!
IT IS SAGINOMIYA-SAN'S!
WOW, IT'S HUGE!
WHAT IS THAT?
IT'S AMAZING!
I HAVE THIS ONE FRIEND WHO'S REALLY ***SPACEY***, SO I BET IT'S AT HER PLACE.
UUI? SPACEY?
YEAH, HER ENTIRE FAMILY IS SPACEY.
SO THIS IS IT, HUH? I GUESS THAT *OBJET D'ART* IS JUST WHAT I'D EXPECT FROM ISUMI-SAN'S FAMILY...
SAGINOMIYA HOT SPRING
AMAZING!
IT'S HUGE!!
NO ONE QUESTIONS THOSE WHO ACT BOLDLY.

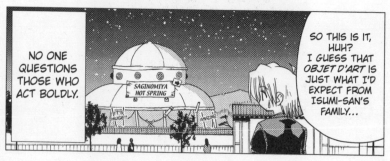

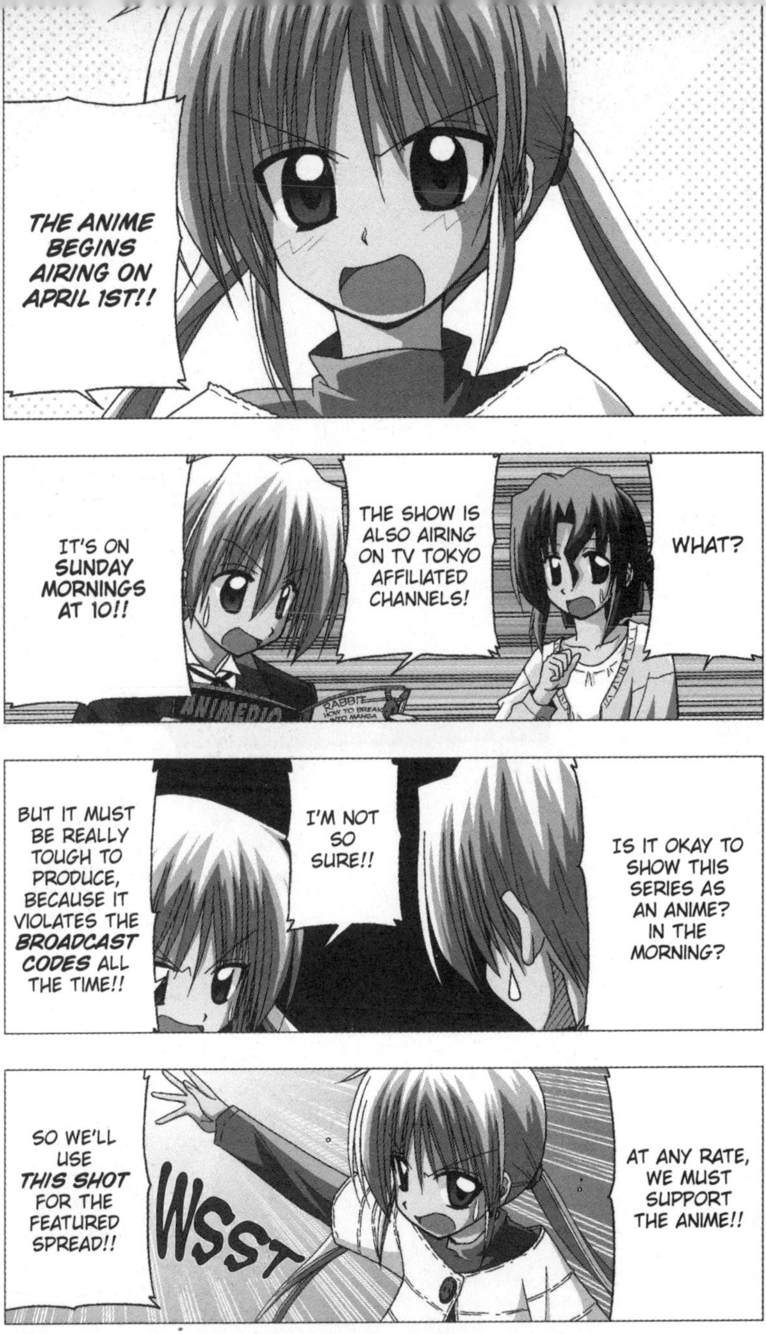
THE ANIME BEGINS AIRING ON APRIL 1ST!!
WHAT?
THE SHOW IS ALSO AIRING ON TV TOKYO AFFILIATED CHANNELS!
IT'S ON SUNDAY MORNINGS AT 10!!
ANIMEDIA
IS IT OKAY TO SHOW THIS SERIES AS AN ANIME? IN THE MORNING?
I'M NOT SO SURE!!
BUT IT MUST BE REALLY TOUGH TO PRODUCE, BECAUSE IT VIOLATES THE BROADCAST CODES ALL THE TIME!!
AT ANY RATE, WE MUST SUPPORT THE ANIME!!
WSST
SO WE'LL USE THIS SHOT FOR THE FEATURED SPREAD!!

Episode 3: "Goodbye, Mankind (Only Me)"

※ The anime aired in Japan beginning on April 1, 2007.

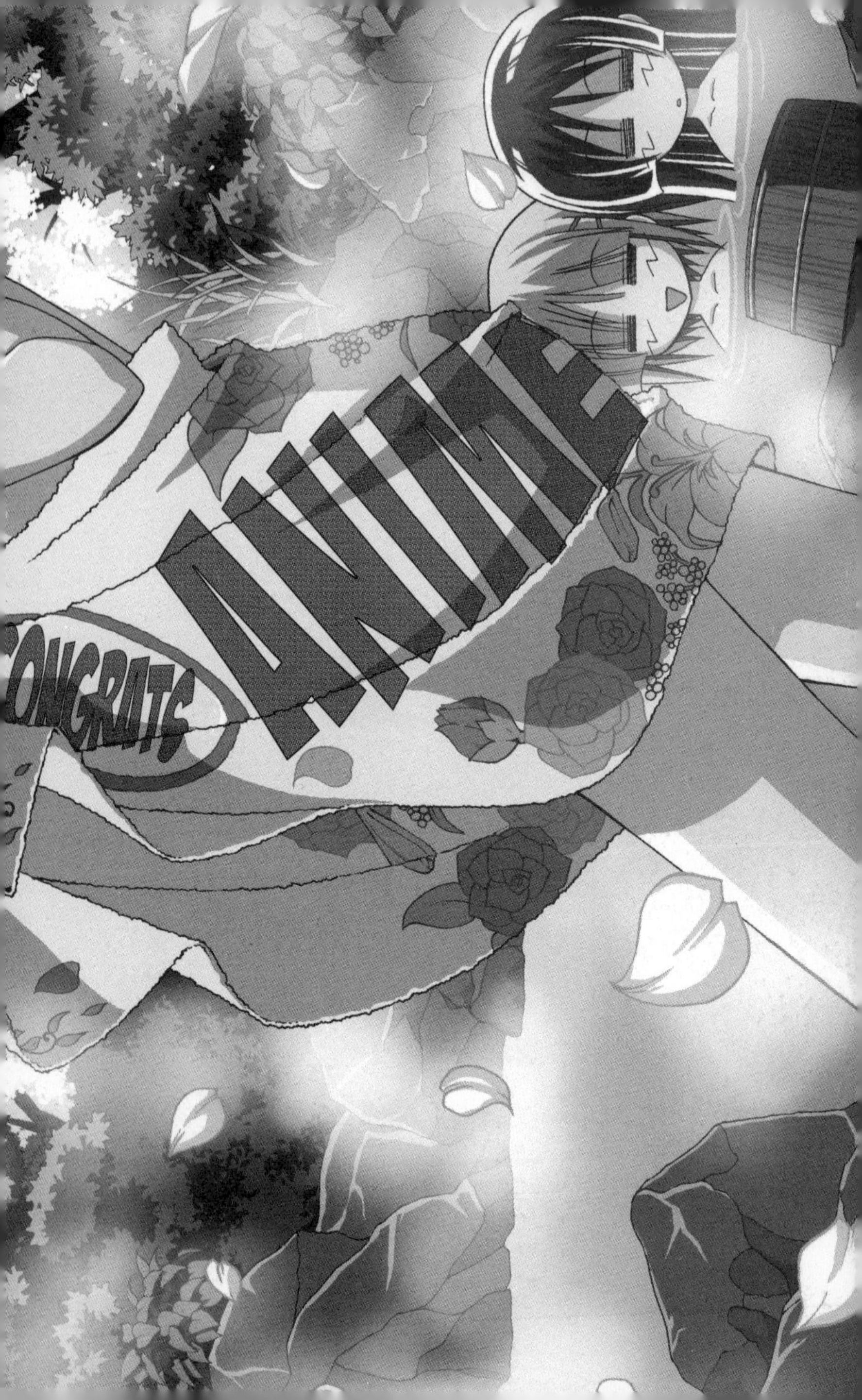
CONGRATS
ANIME

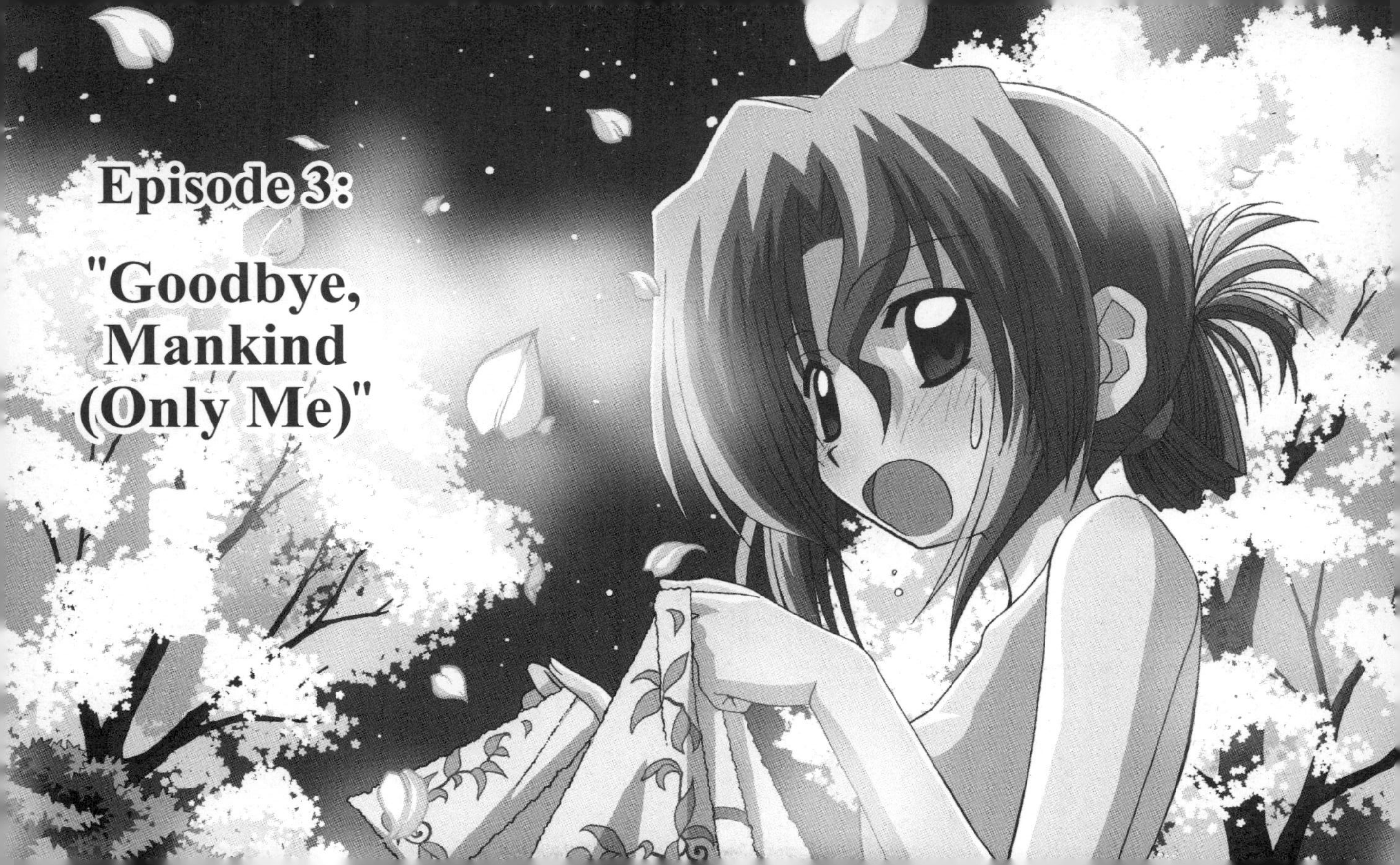
Episode 3:
"Goodbye, Mankind (Only Me)"

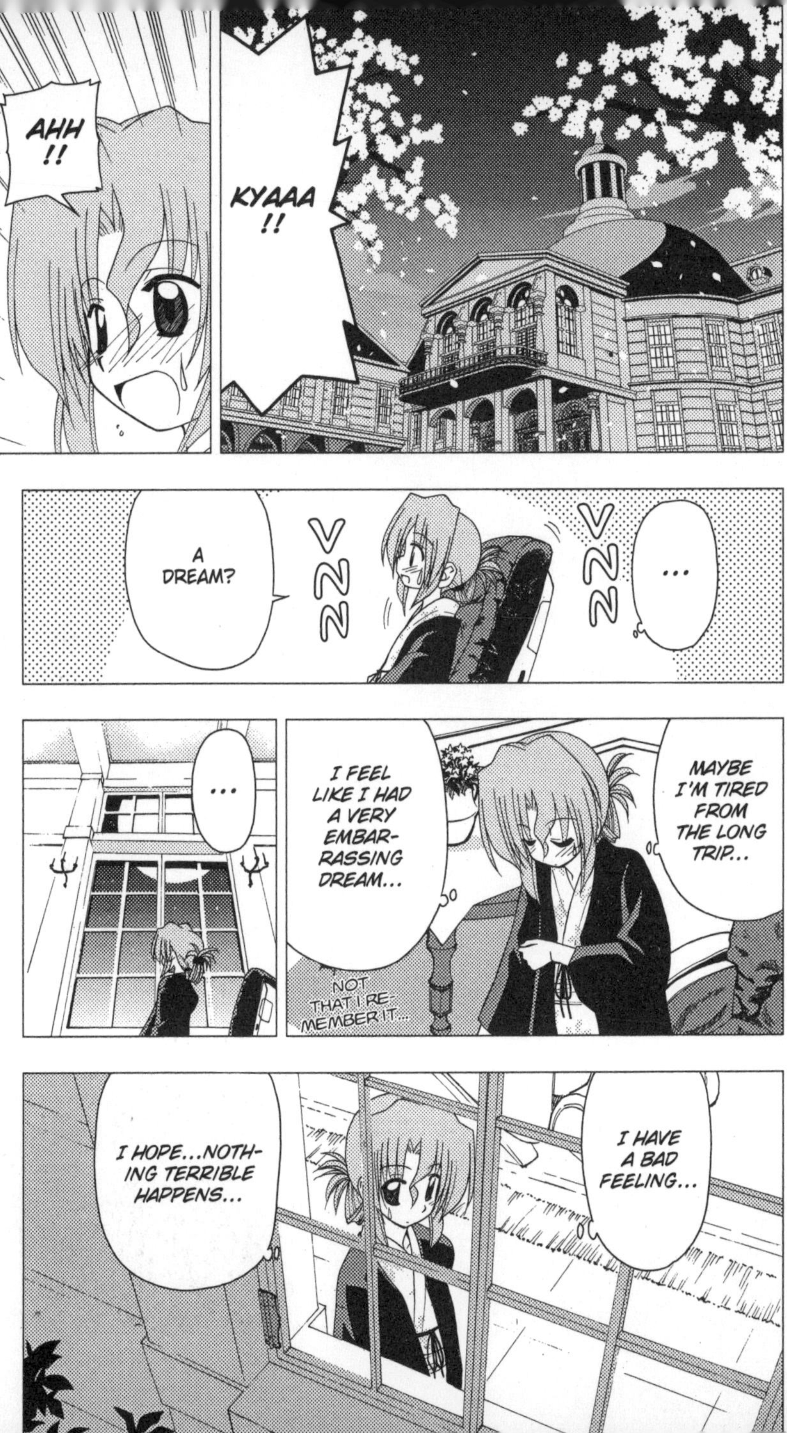
KYAAA !!
AHH !!
...
ZZZ
ZZZ
A DREAM?
MAYBE I'M TIRED FROM THE LONG TRIP...
I FEEL LIKE I HAD A VERY EMBAR-RASSING DREAM...
NOT THAT I RE-MEMBER IT...
...
I HAVE A BAD FEELING...
I HOPE...NOTH-ING TERRIBLE HAPPENS...

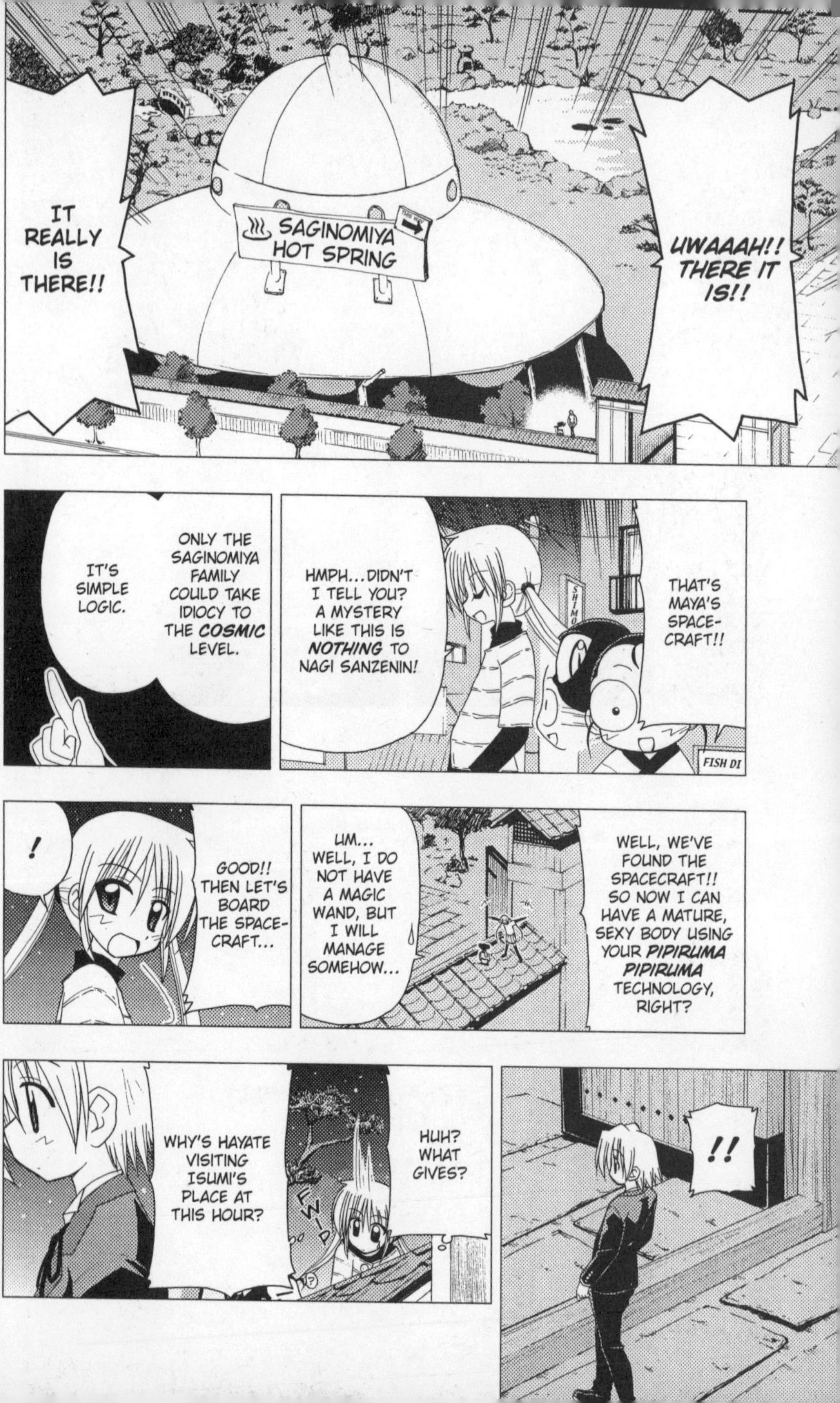
UWAAAH!! THERE IT IS!!
SAGINOMIYA HOT SPRING
IT REALLY IS THERE!!
THAT'S MAYA'S SPACE-CRAFT!!
HMPH...DIDN'T I TELL YOU? A MYSTERY LIKE THIS IS NOTHING TO NAGI SANZENIN!
FISH DI
ONLY THE SAGINOMIYA FAMILY COULD TAKE IDIOCY TO THE COSMIC LEVEL.
IT'S SIMPLE LOGIC.
WELL, WE'VE FOUND THE SPACECRAFT!! SO NOW I CAN HAVE A MATURE, SEXY BODY USING YOUR PIPIRUMA PIPIRUMA TECHNOLOGY, RIGHT?
UM... WELL, I DO NOT HAVE A MAGIC WAND, BUT I WILL MANAGE SOMEHOW...
GOOD!! THEN LET'S BOARD THE SPACE-CRAFT...
!
!!
HUH? WHAT GIVES?
FWIP
WHY'S HAYATE VISITING ISUMI'S PLACE AT THIS HOUR?

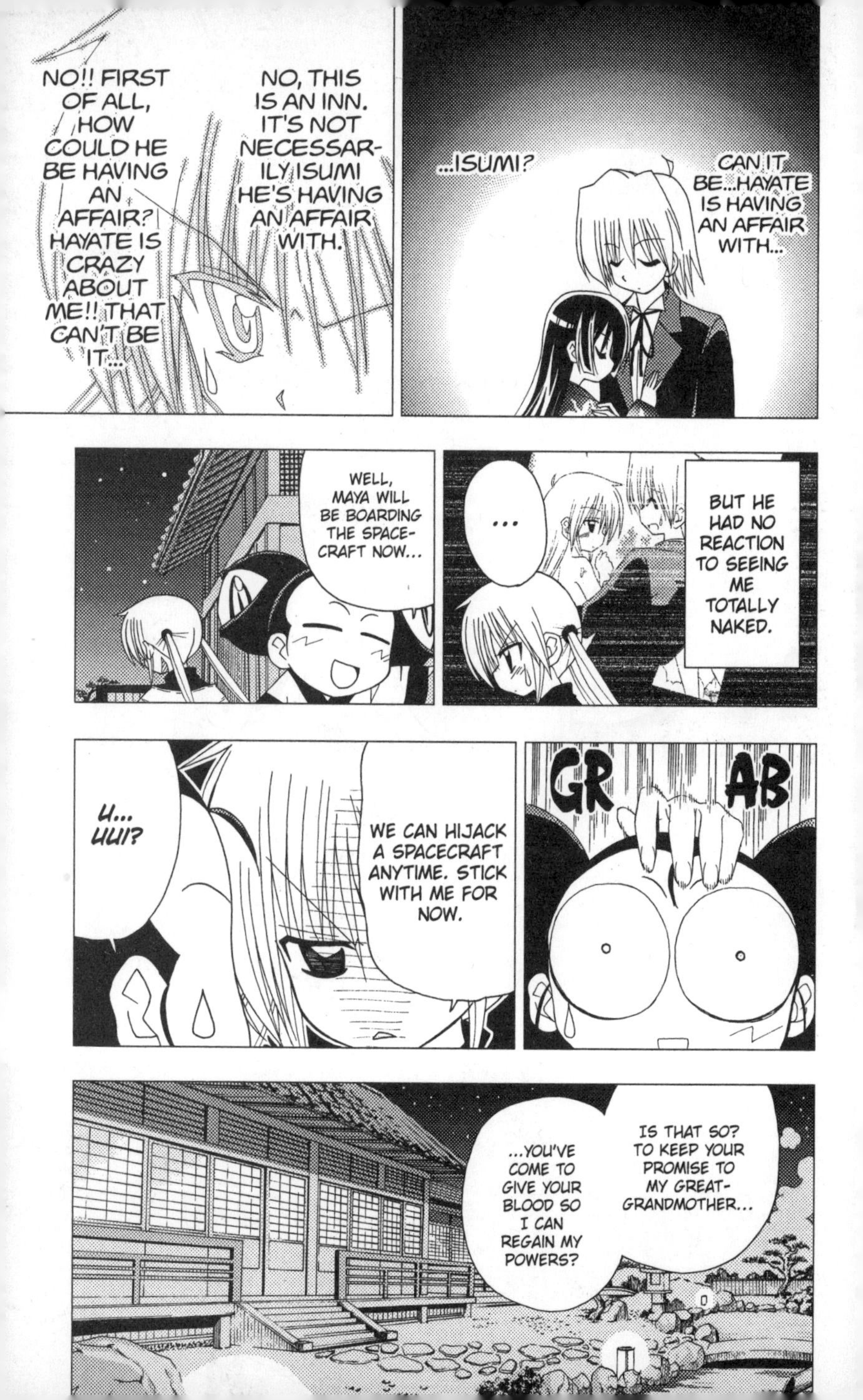
CAN IT BE...HAYATE IS HAVING AN AFFAIR WITH...
...ISUMI?
NO, THIS IS AN INN. IT'S NOT NECESSAR-ILY ISUMI HE'S HAVING AN AFFAIR WITH.
NO!! FIRST OF ALL, HOW COULD HE BE HAVING AN AFFAIR? HAYATE IS CRAZY ABOUT ME!! THAT CAN'T BE IT...
BUT HE HAD NO REACTION TO SEEING ME TOTALLY NAKED.
...
WELL, MAYA WILL BE BOARDING THE SPACE-CRAFT NOW...
GR AB
WE CAN HIJACK A SPACECRAFT ANYTIME. STICK WITH ME FOR NOW.
U... UUI?
IS THAT SO? TO KEEP YOUR PROMISE TO MY GREAT-GRANDMOTHER...
...YOU'VE COME TO GIVE YOUR BLOOD SO I CAN REGAIN MY POWERS?

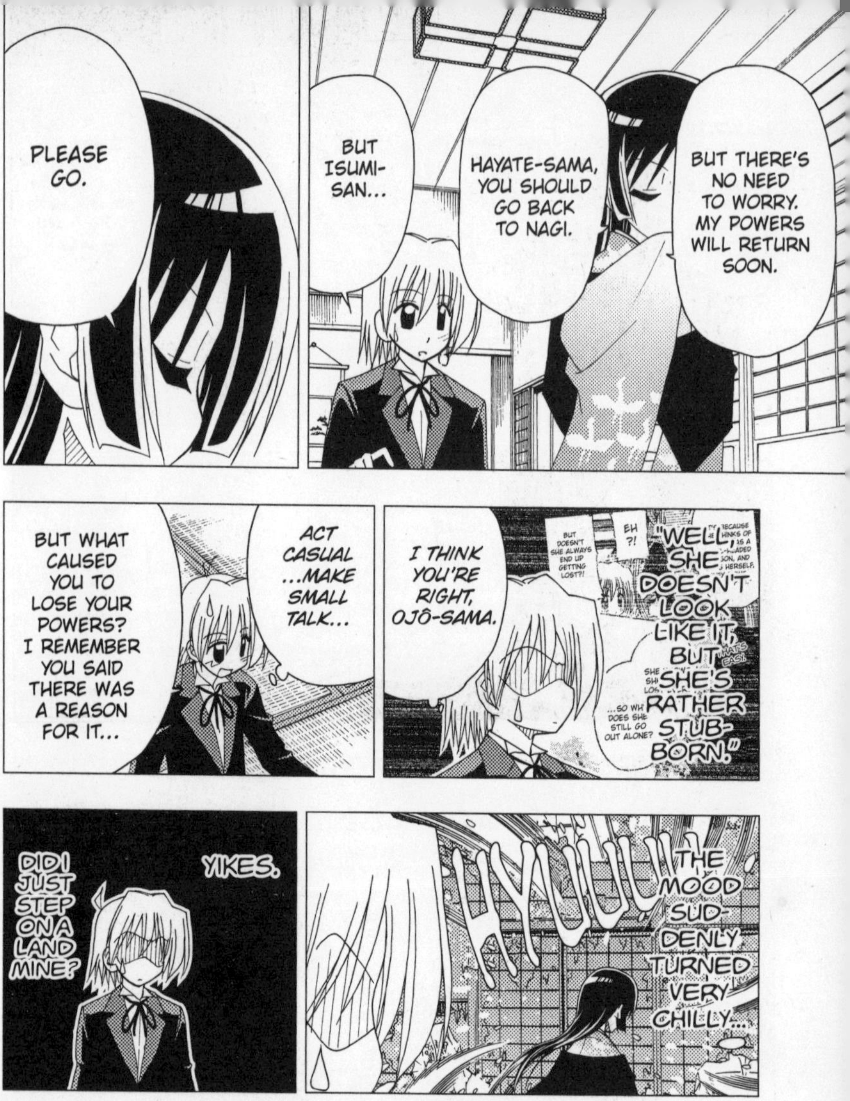
BUT THERE'S NO NEED TO WORRY. MY POWERS WILL RETURN SOON.
HAYATE-SAMA, YOU SHOULD GO BACK TO NAGI.
BUT ISUMI-SAN...
PLEASE GO.
BUT DOESN'T SHE ALWAYS END UP GETTING LOST?!
EH ?!
"WELL, SHE DOESN'T LOOK LIKE IT, BUT SHE'S RATHER STUB-BORN."
I THINK YOU'RE RIGHT, OJÔ-SAMA.
ACT CASUAL ...MAKE SMALL TALK...
BUT WHAT CAUSED YOU TO LOSE YOUR POWERS? I REMEMBER YOU SAID THERE WAS A REASON FOR IT...
HYUUU
THE MOOD SUD-DENLY TURNED VERY CHILLY...
YIKES.
DID I JUST STEP ON A LAND MINE?
EIGHT YEARS AGO, IN JANUARY...
...I MADE MY VERY FIRST FRIEND.
HUH?

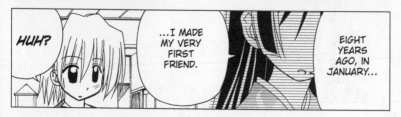

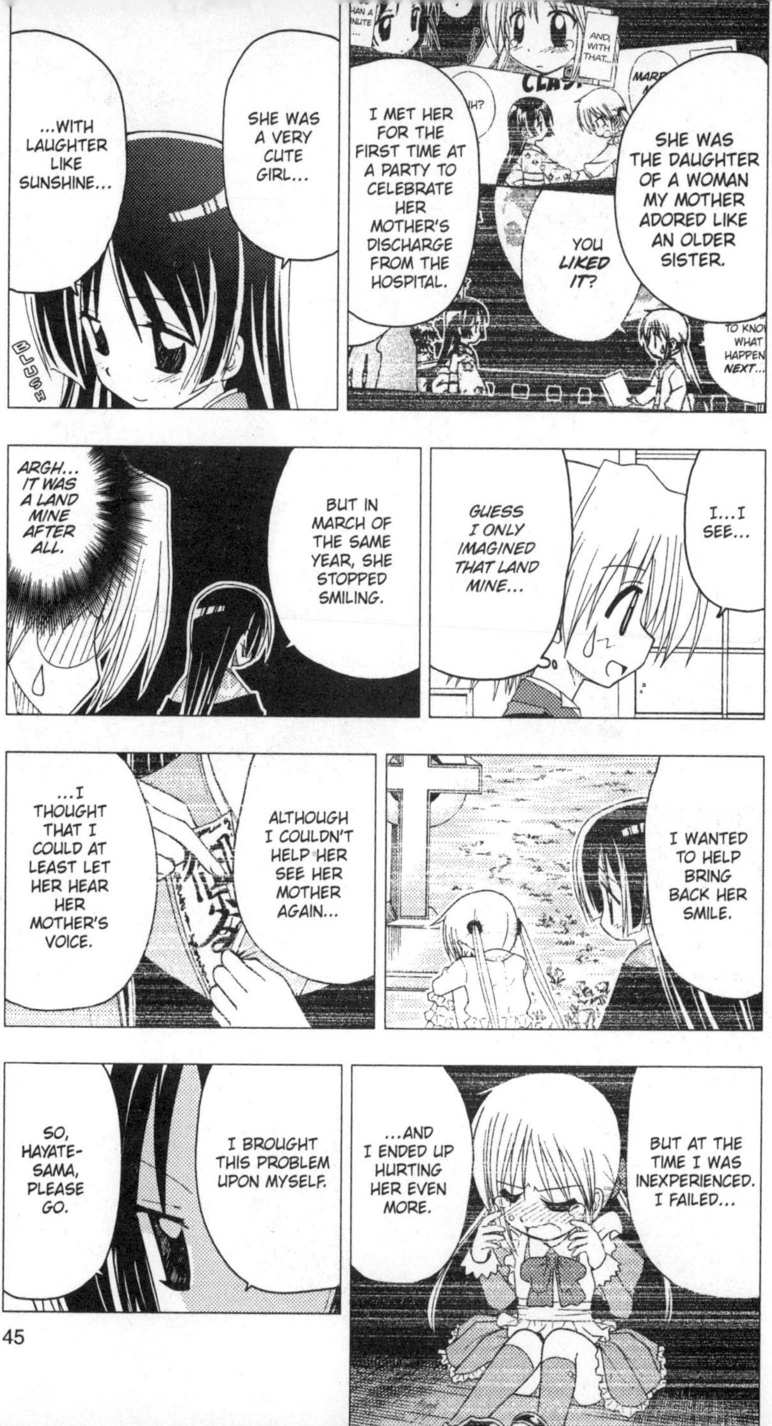
AND, WITH THAT...
SHE WAS THE DAUGHTER OF A WOMAN MY MOTHER ADORED LIKE AN OLDER SISTER.
YOU *LIKED* IT?
I MET HER FOR THE FIRST TIME AT A PARTY TO CELEBRATE HER MOTHER'S DISCHARGE FROM THE HOSPITAL.
SHE WAS A VERY CUTE GIRL...
...WITH LAUGHTER LIKE SUNSHINE...
BLUSH
I...I SEE...
GUESS I ONLY IMAGINED THAT LAND MINE...
BUT IN MARCH OF THE SAME YEAR, SHE STOPPED SMILING.
ARGH... IT WAS A LAND MINE AFTER ALL.
I WANTED TO HELP BRING BACK HER SMILE.
ALTHOUGH I COULDN'T HELP HER SEE HER MOTHER AGAIN...
...I THOUGHT THAT I COULD AT LEAST LET HER HEAR HER MOTHER'S VOICE.
BUT AT THE TIME I WAS INEXPERIENCED. I FAILED...
...AND I ENDED UP HURTING HER EVEN MORE.
I BROUGHT THIS PROBLEM UPON MYSELF.
SO, HAYATE-SAMA, PLEASE GO.

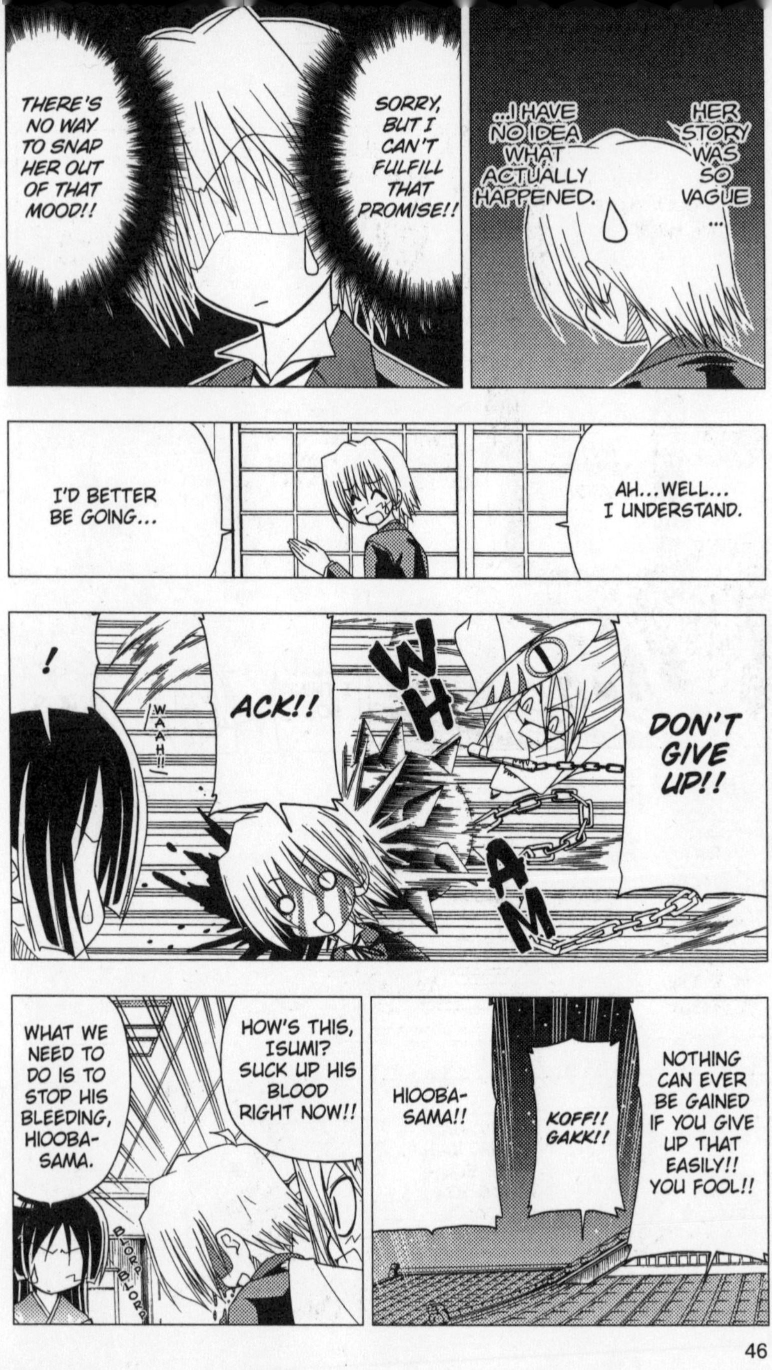
HER STORY WAS SO VAGUE...
...I HAVE NO IDEA WHAT ACTUALLY HAPPENED.
SORRY, BUT I CAN'T FULFILL THAT PROMISE!!
THERE'S NO WAY TO SNAP HER OUT OF THAT MOOD!!
AH...WELL... I UNDERSTAND.
I'D BETTER BE GOING...
DON'T GIVE UP!!
WHAM
ACK!!
WAAH!!
!
NOTHING CAN EVER BE GAINED IF YOU GIVE UP THAT EASILY!! YOU FOOL!!
KOFF!! GAKK!!
HIOOBA-SAMA!!
HOW'S THIS, ISUMI? SUCK UP HIS BLOOD RIGHT NOW!!
WHAT WE NEED TO DO IS TO STOP HIS BLEEDING, HIOOBA-SAMA.
BLORP BLORP

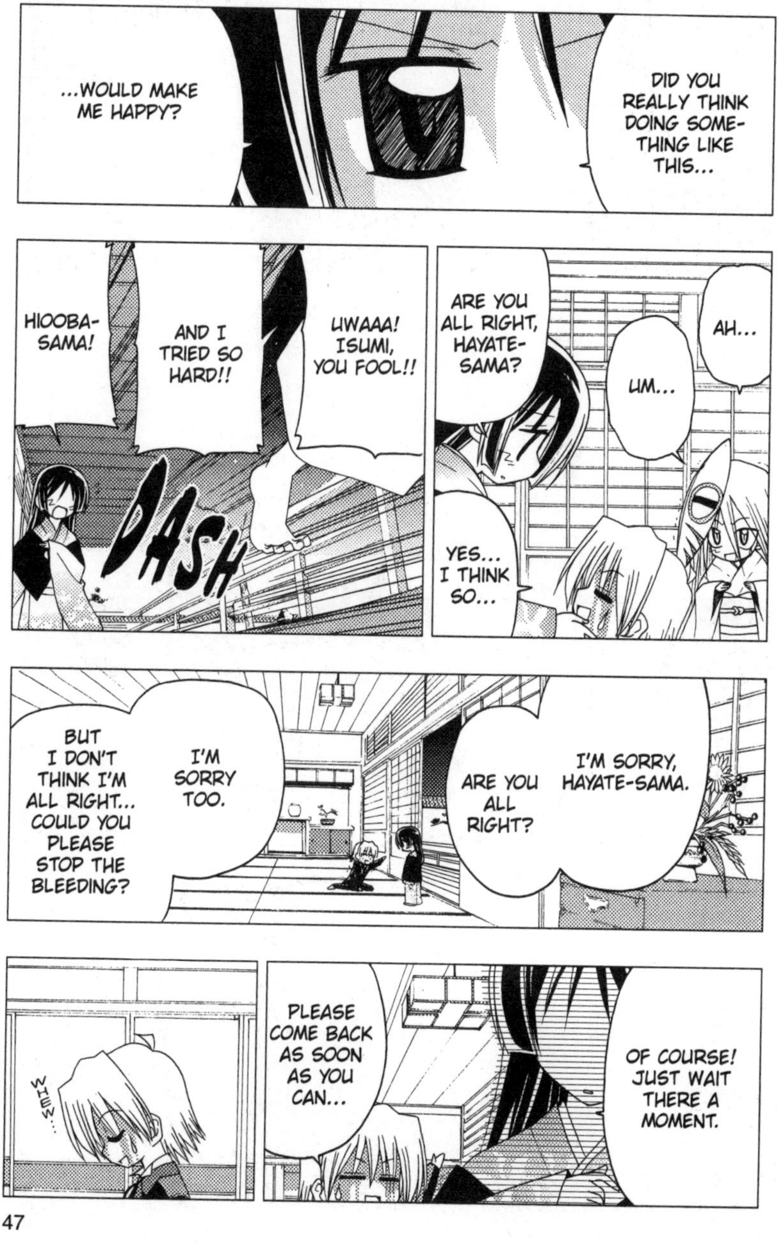
DID YOU REALLY THINK DOING SOME-THING LIKE THIS...
...WOULD MAKE ME HAPPY?
AH...
UM...
ARE YOU ALL RIGHT, HAYATE-SAMA?
YES... I THINK SO...
UWAAA! ISUMI, YOU FOOL!!
AND I TRIED SO HARD!!
HIOOBA-SAMA!
DASH
I'M SORRY, HAYATE-SAMA.
ARE YOU ALL RIGHT?
I'M SORRY TOO.
BUT I DON'T THINK I'M ALL RIGHT... COULD YOU PLEASE STOP THE BLEEDING?
OF COURSE! JUST WAIT THERE A MOMENT.
PLEASE COME BACK AS SOON AS YOU CAN...
WHEW...

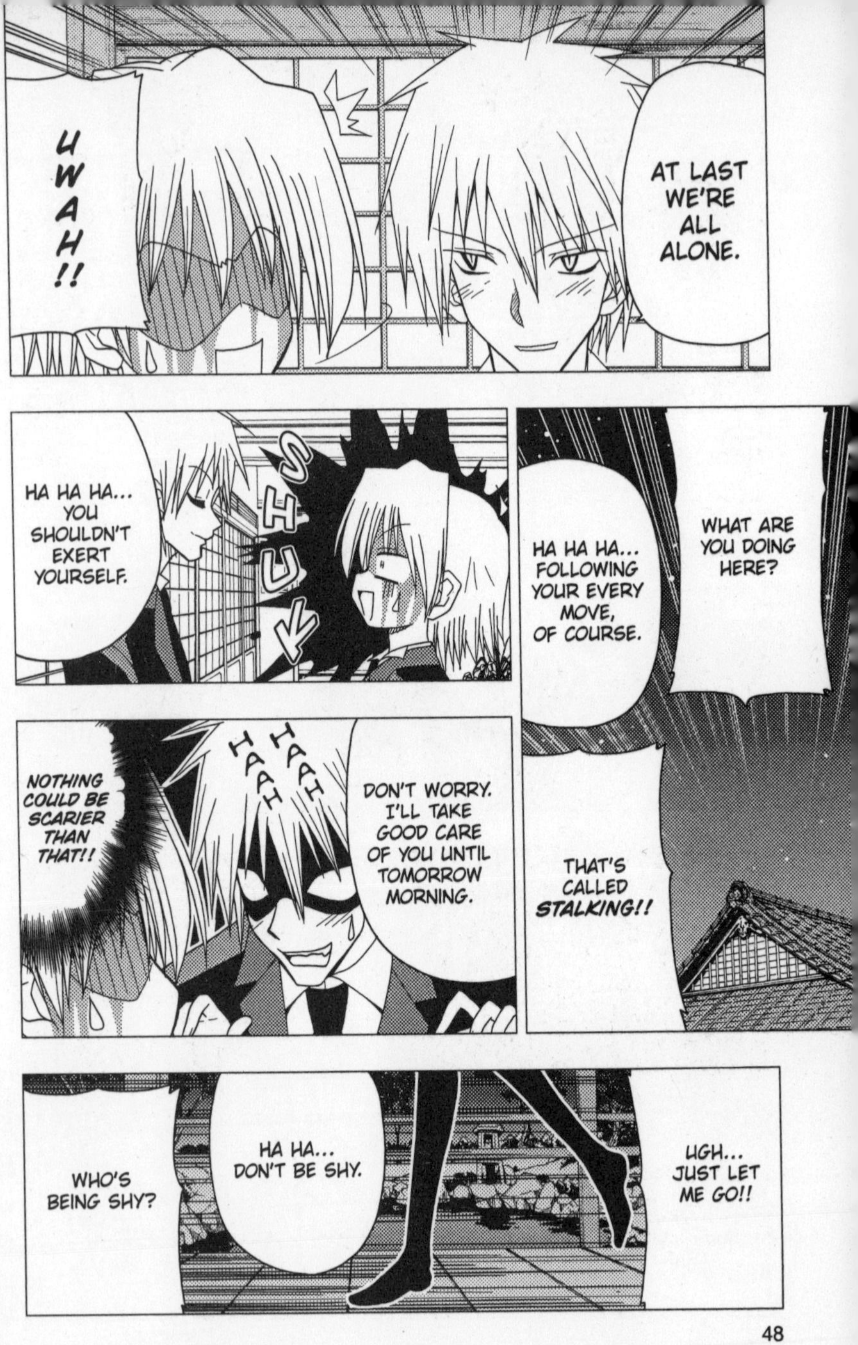
AT LAST WE'RE ALL ALONE.
UWAH!!
WHAT ARE YOU DOING HERE?
HA HA HA... FOLLOWING YOUR EVERY MOVE, OF COURSE.
THAT'S CALLED STALKING!!
SHUK
HA HA HA... YOU SHOULDN'T EXERT YOURSELF.
HAAH HAAH
DON'T WORRY. I'LL TAKE GOOD CARE OF YOU UNTIL TOMORROW MORNING.
NOTHING COULD BE SCARIER THAN THAT!!
UGH... JUST LET ME GO!!
HA HA... DON'T BE SHY.
WHO'S BEING SHY?

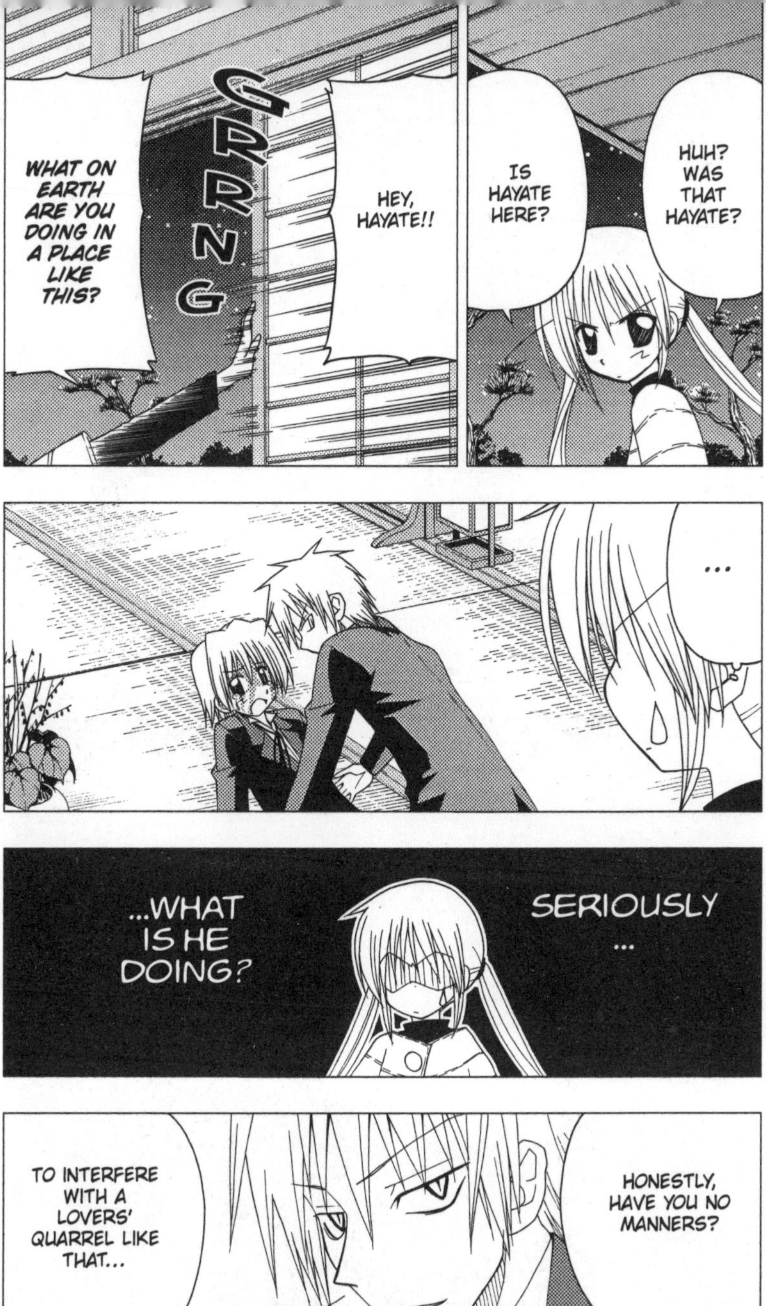
HUH? WAS THAT HAYATE?
IS HAYATE HERE?
HEY, HAYATE!!
GRRNG
WHAT ON EARTH ARE YOU DOING IN A PLACE LIKE THIS?
...
SERIOUSLY ...
...WHAT IS HE DOING?
HONESTLY, HAVE YOU NO MANNERS?
TO INTERFERE WITH A LOVERS' QUARREL LIKE THAT...

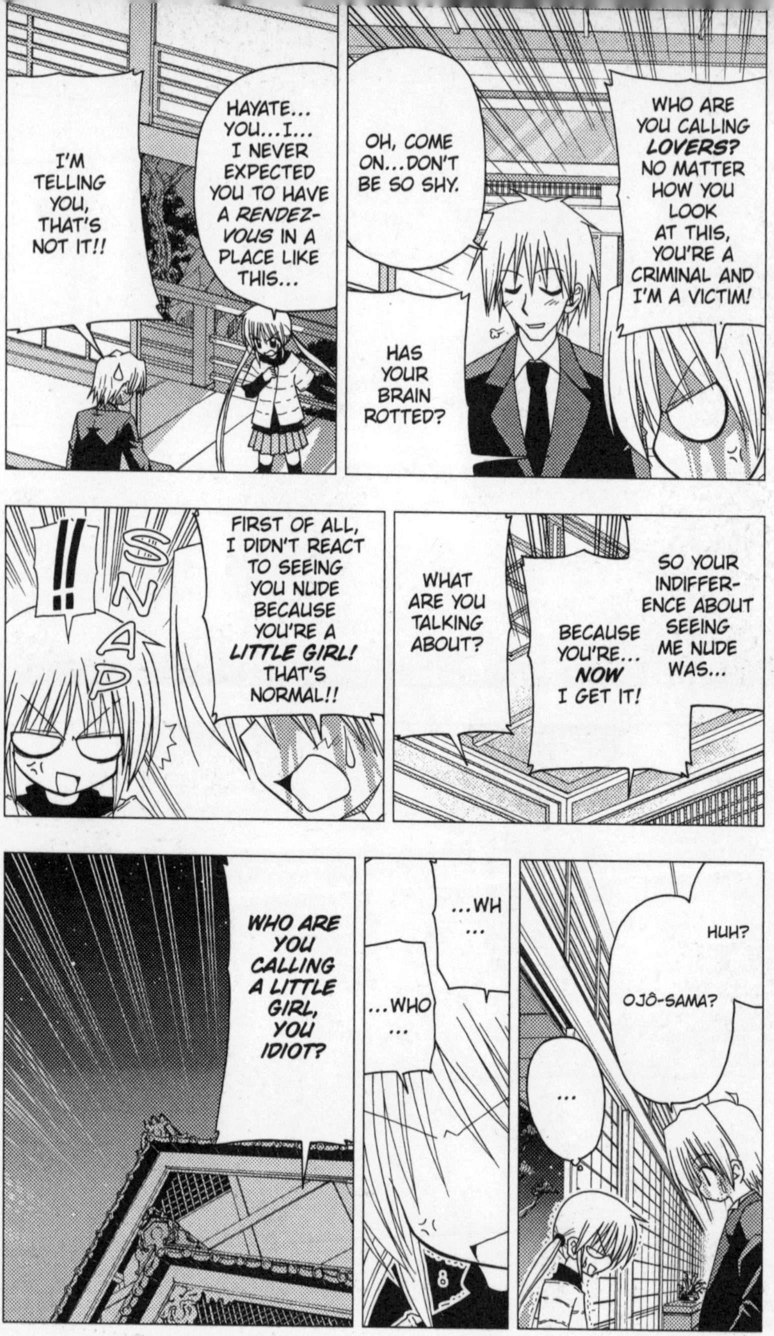
WHO ARE YOU CALLING *LOVERS?* NO MATTER HOW YOU LOOK AT THIS, YOU'RE A CRIMINAL AND I'M A VICTIM!
OH, COME ON...DON'T BE SO SHY.
HAS YOUR BRAIN ROTTED?
HAYATE... YOU...I... I NEVER EXPECTED YOU TO HAVE A *RENDEZ-VOUS* IN A PLACE LIKE THIS...
I'M TELLING YOU, THAT'S NOT IT!!
SO YOUR INDIFFER-ENCE ABOUT SEEING ME NUDE WAS...
BECAUSE YOU'RE... *NOW* I GET IT!
WHAT ARE YOU TALKING ABOUT?
FIRST OF ALL, I DIDN'T REACT TO SEEING YOU NUDE BECAUSE YOU'RE A *LITTLE GIRL!* THAT'S NORMAL!!
SNAP
!!
HUH?
OJÔ-SAMA?
...
...WH ...
...WHO ...
WHO ARE YOU CALLING A LITTLE GIRL, YOU IDIOT?

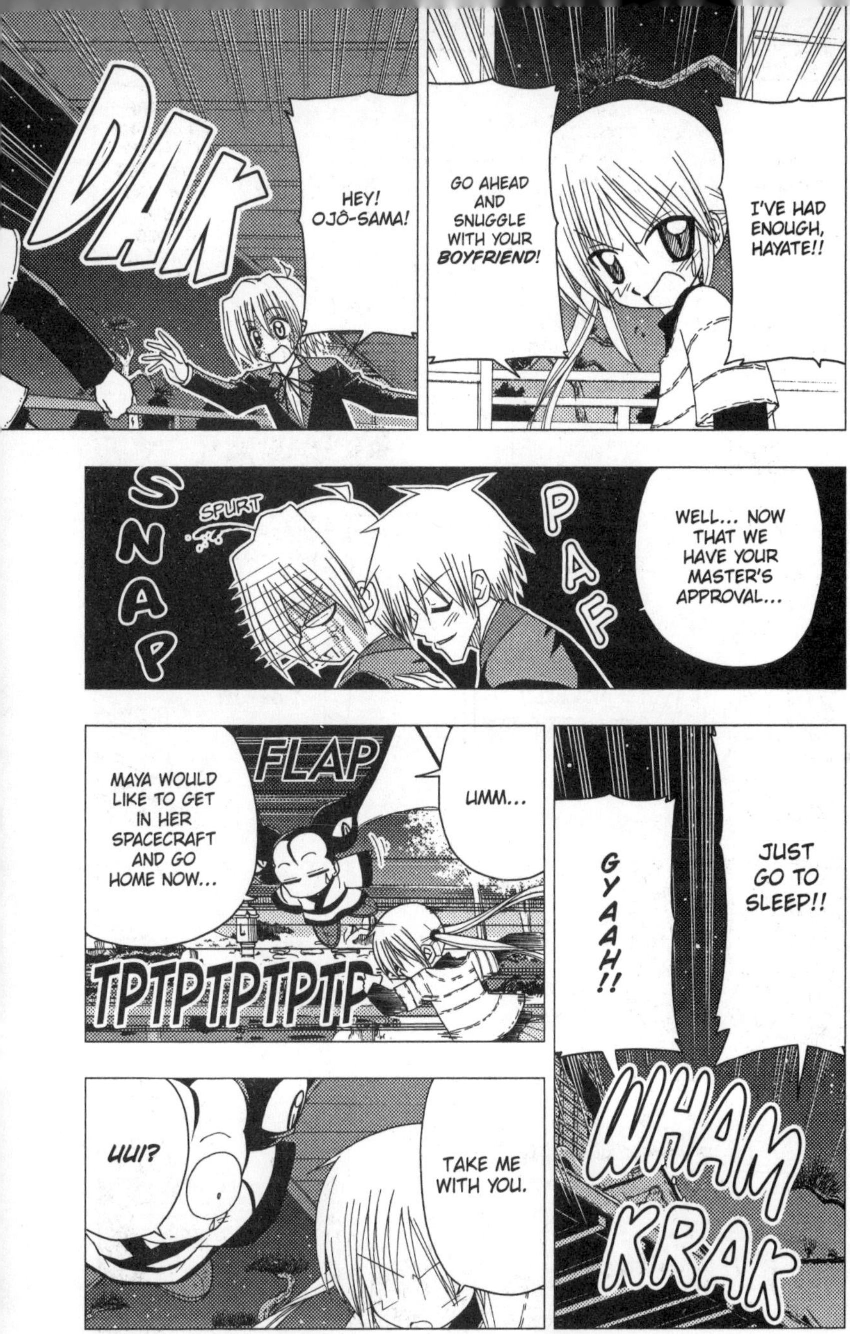
I'VE HAD ENOUGH, HAYATE!!
GO AHEAD AND SNUGGLE WITH YOUR BOYFRIEND!
HEY! OJÔ-SAMA!
DAK
WELL... NOW THAT WE HAVE YOUR MASTER'S APPROVAL...
PAF
SPURT
SNAP
JUST GO TO SLEEP!!
GYAAAH!!
WHAM
KRAK
UMM...
FLAP
MAYA WOULD LIKE TO GET IN HER SPACECRAFT AND GO HOME NOW...
TPTPTPTPTP
TAKE ME WITH YOU.
UUI?

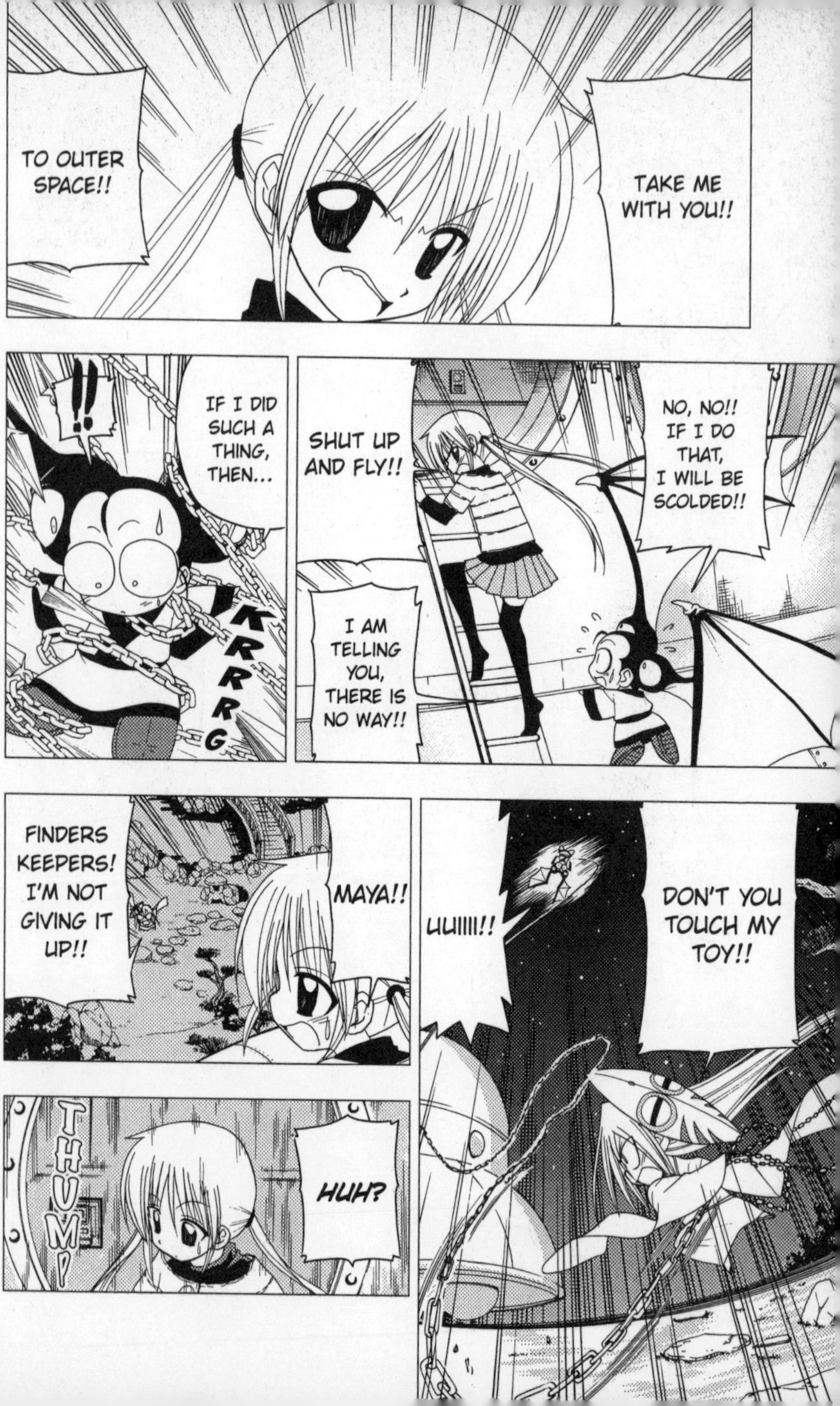
TAKE ME WITH YOU!!
TO OUTER SPACE!!
NO, NO!! IF I DO THAT, I WILL BE SCOLDED!!
SHUT UP AND FLY!!
I AM TELLING YOU, THERE IS NO WAY!!
!!
IF I DID SUCH A THING, THEN...
KRRRRG
DON'T YOU TOUCH MY TOY!!
UUIIII!!
MAYA!!
FINDERS KEEPERS! I'M NOT GIVING IT UP!!
HUH?
THUMP

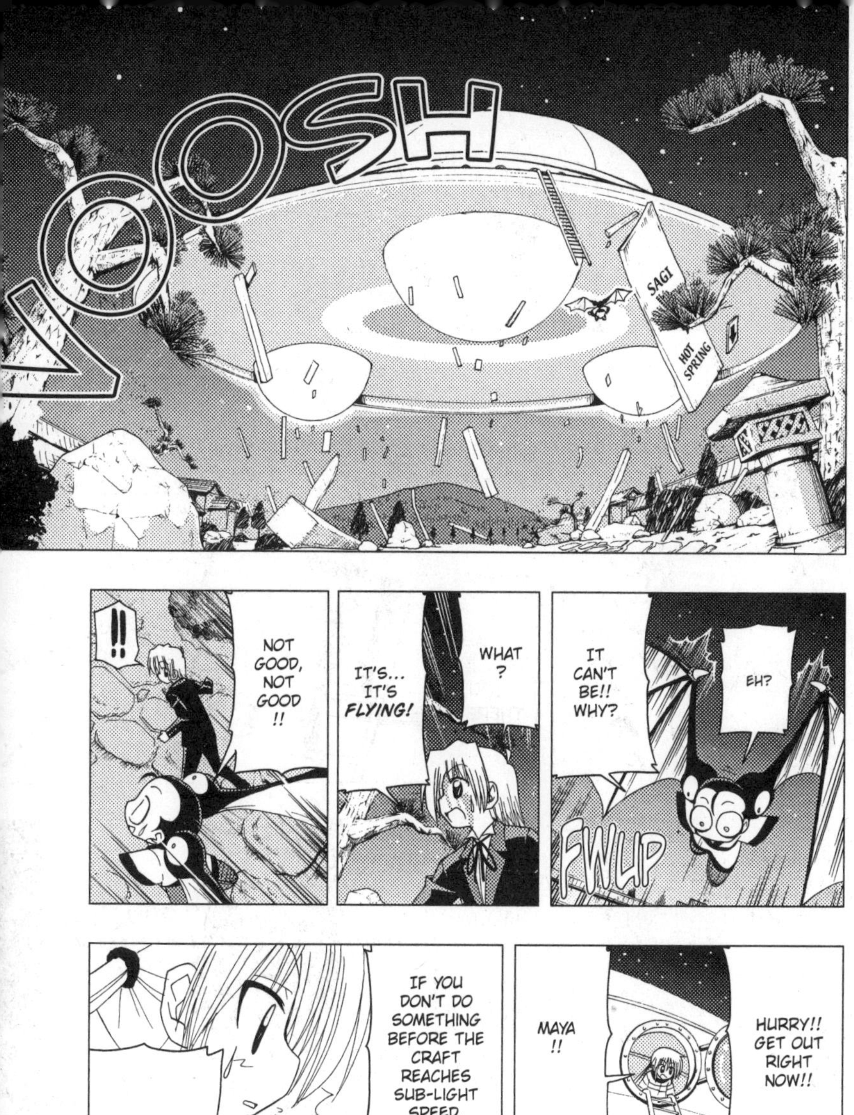
VOOSH
SAGI
HOT SPRING
EH?
IT CAN'T BE!! WHY?
FWUP
WHAT ?
IT'S... IT'S *FLYING!*
NOT GOOD, NOT GOOD !!
!!
HURRY!! GET OUT RIGHT NOW!!
MAYA !!
IF YOU DON'T DO SOMETHING BEFORE THE CRAFT REACHES SUB-LIGHT SPEED, THEN NAGI...
...WILL BE UNABLE TO RETURN TO EARTH!!

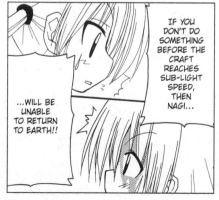

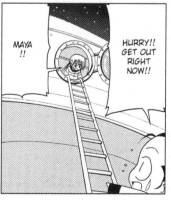

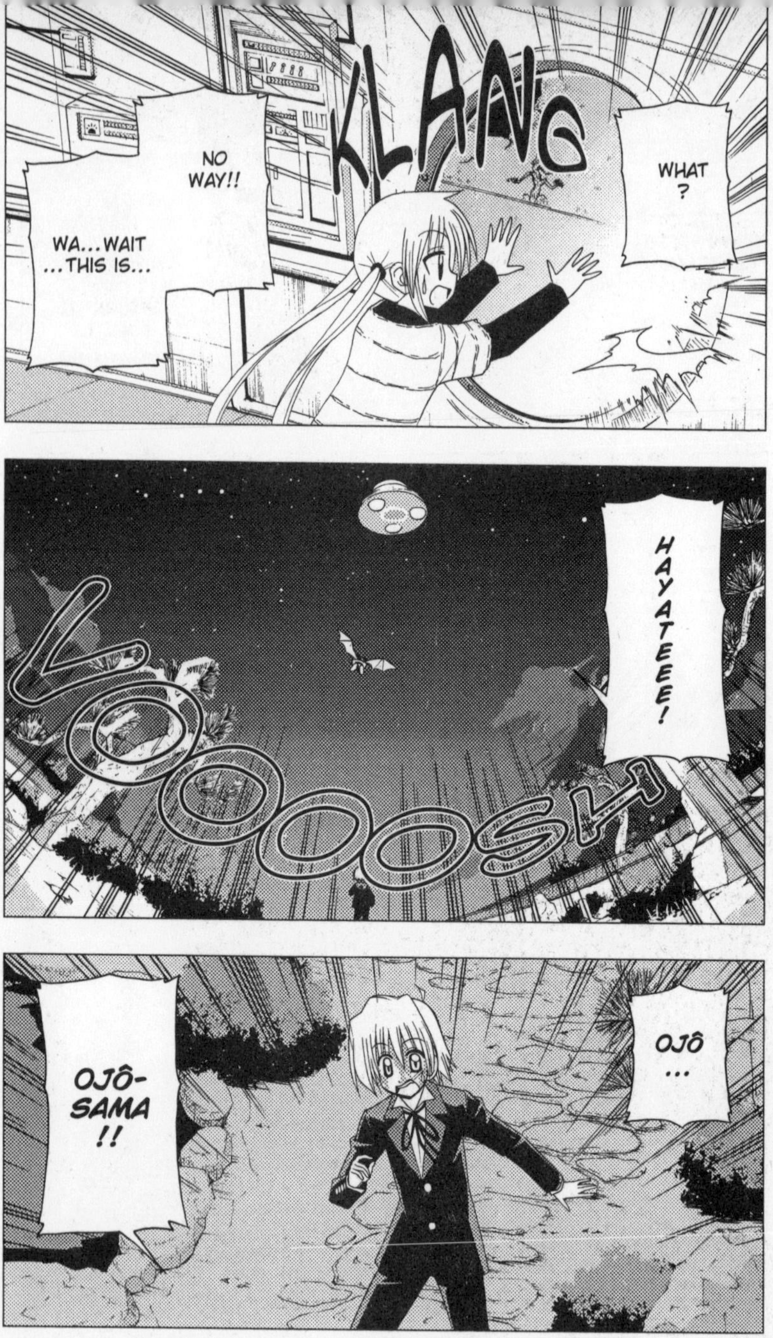
WHAT ?
KLANG
NO WAY!!
WA...WAIT ...THIS IS...
HAYATEEE!
VOOOOSH
OJÔ ...
OJÔ-SAMA !!

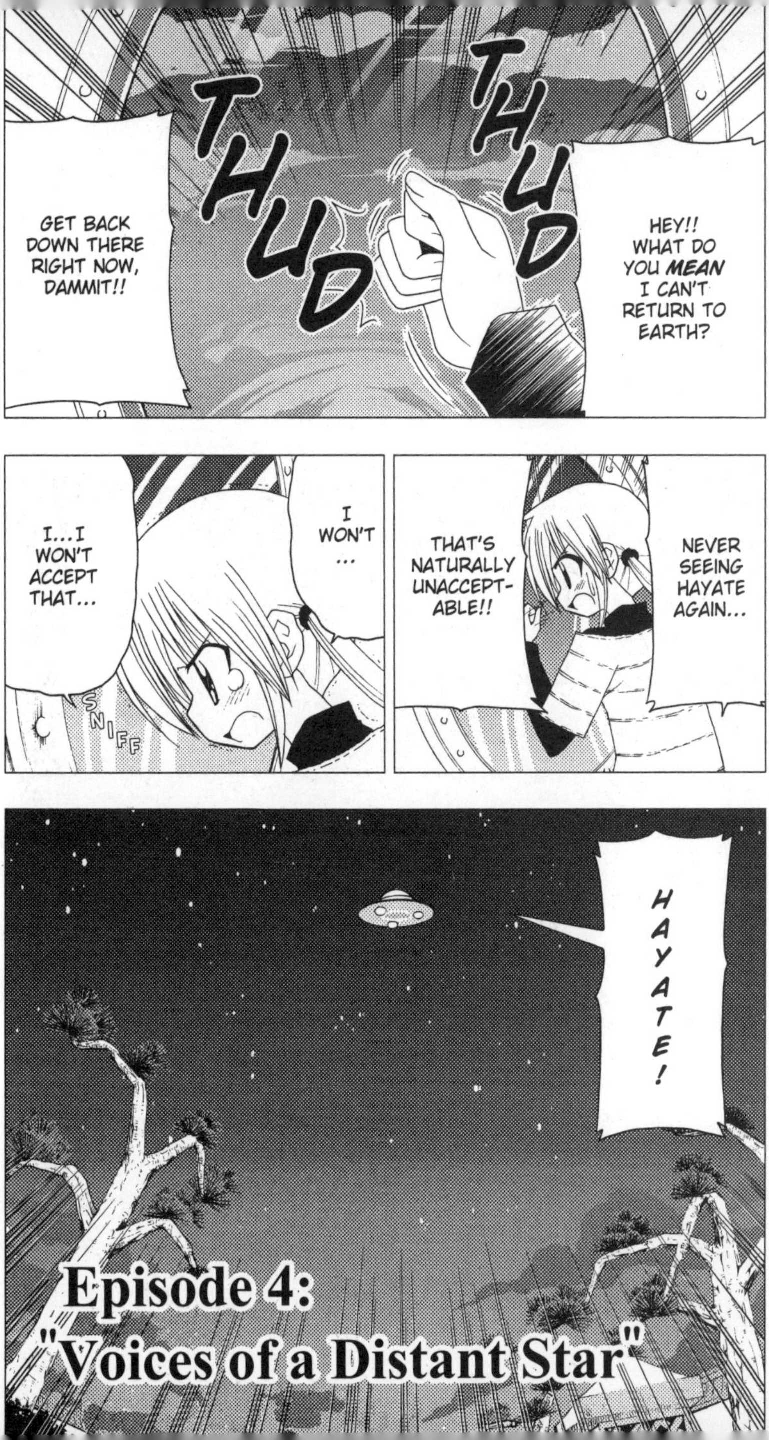
HEY!! WHAT DO YOU MEAN I CAN'T RETURN TO EARTH?
THUD
THUD
GET BACK DOWN THERE RIGHT NOW, DAMMIT!!
NEVER SEEING HAYATE AGAIN...
THAT'S NATURALLY UNACCEPTABLE!!
I WON'T ...
I...I WON'T ACCEPT THAT...
SNIFF
HAYATE!
Episode 4: "Voices of a Distant Star"

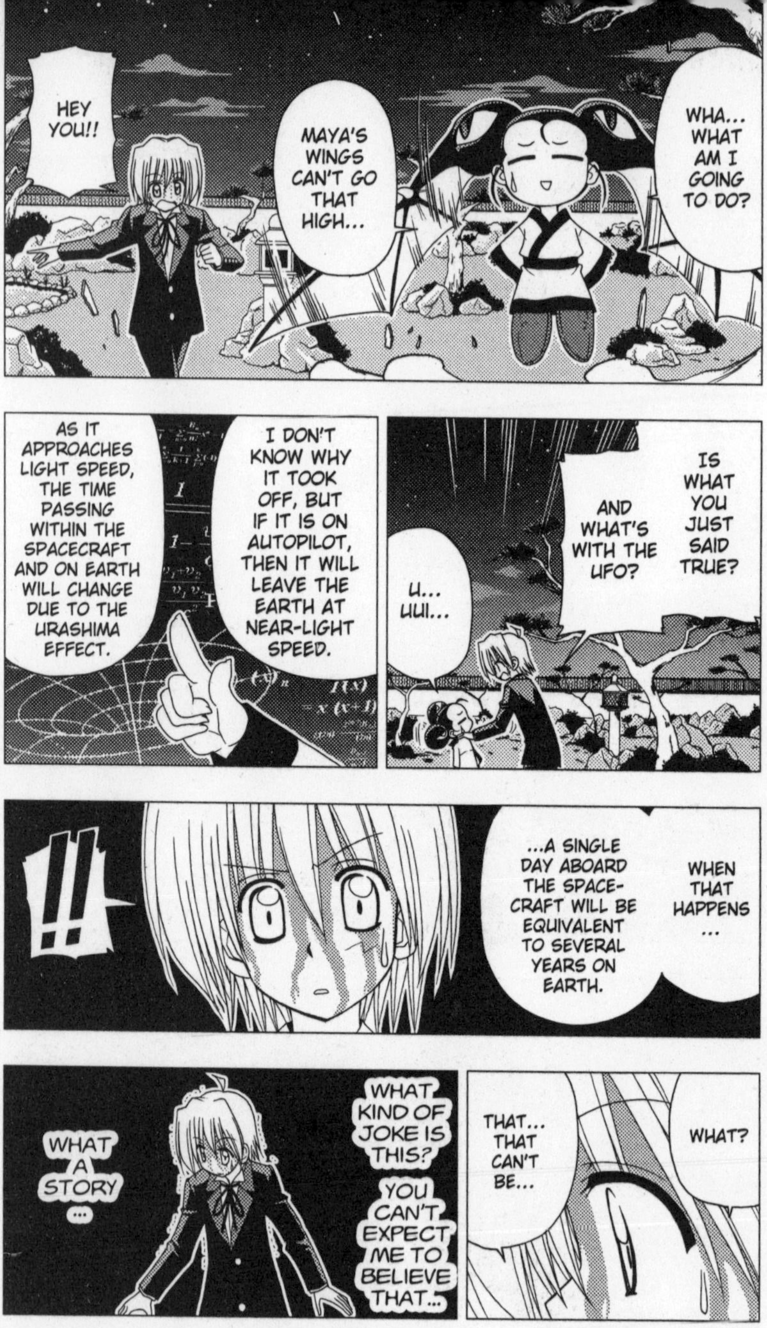
WHA... WHAT AM I GOING TO DO?
MAYA'S WINGS CAN'T GO THAT HIGH...
HEY YOU!!
IS WHAT YOU JUST SAID TRUE?
AND WHAT'S WITH THE UFO?
U... UUI...
I DON'T KNOW WHY IT TOOK OFF, BUT IF IT IS ON AUTOPILOT, THEN IT WILL LEAVE THE EARTH AT NEAR-LIGHT SPEED.
AS IT APPROACHES LIGHT SPEED, THE TIME PASSING WITHIN THE SPACECRAFT AND ON EARTH WILL CHANGE DUE TO THE URASHIMA EFFECT.
WHEN THAT HAPPENS...
...A SINGLE DAY ABOARD THE SPACE-CRAFT WILL BE EQUIVALENT TO SEVERAL YEARS ON EARTH.
!!
WHAT?
THAT... THAT CAN'T BE...
WHAT KIND OF JOKE IS THIS?
YOU CAN'T EXPECT ME TO BELIEVE THAT...
WHAT A STORY...

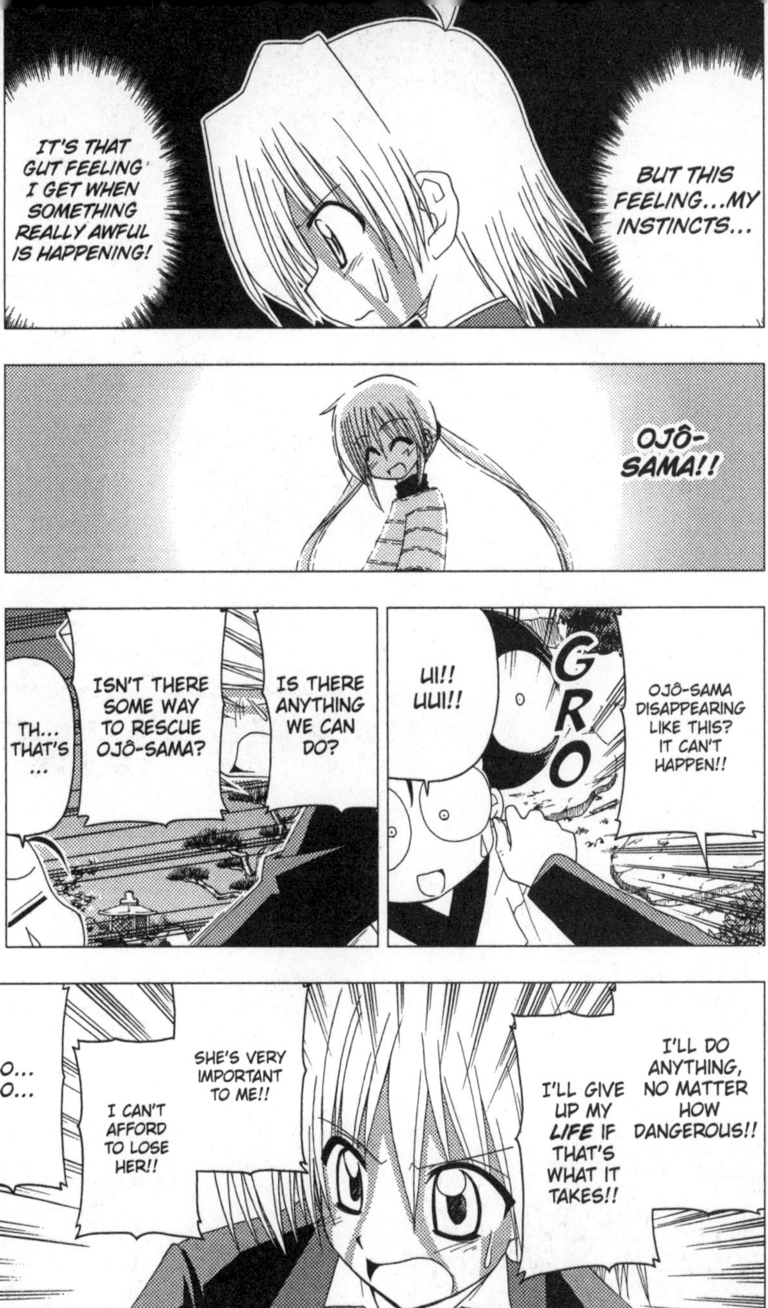
BUT THIS FEELING...MY INSTINCTS...
IT'S THAT GUT FEELING I GET WHEN SOMETHING REALLY AWFUL IS HAPPENING!
OJÔ-SAMA!!
OJÔ-SAMA DISAPPEARING LIKE THIS? IT CAN'T HAPPEN!!
GRO
UI!! UUI!!
IS THERE ANYTHING WE CAN DO?
ISN'T THERE SOME WAY TO RESCUE OJÔ-SAMA?
TH... THAT'S ...
I'LL DO ANYTHING, NO MATTER HOW DANGEROUS!!
I'LL GIVE UP MY *LIFE* IF THAT'S WHAT IT TAKES!!
SHE'S VERY IMPORTANT TO ME!!
I CAN'T AFFORD TO LOSE HER!!
SO... SO...

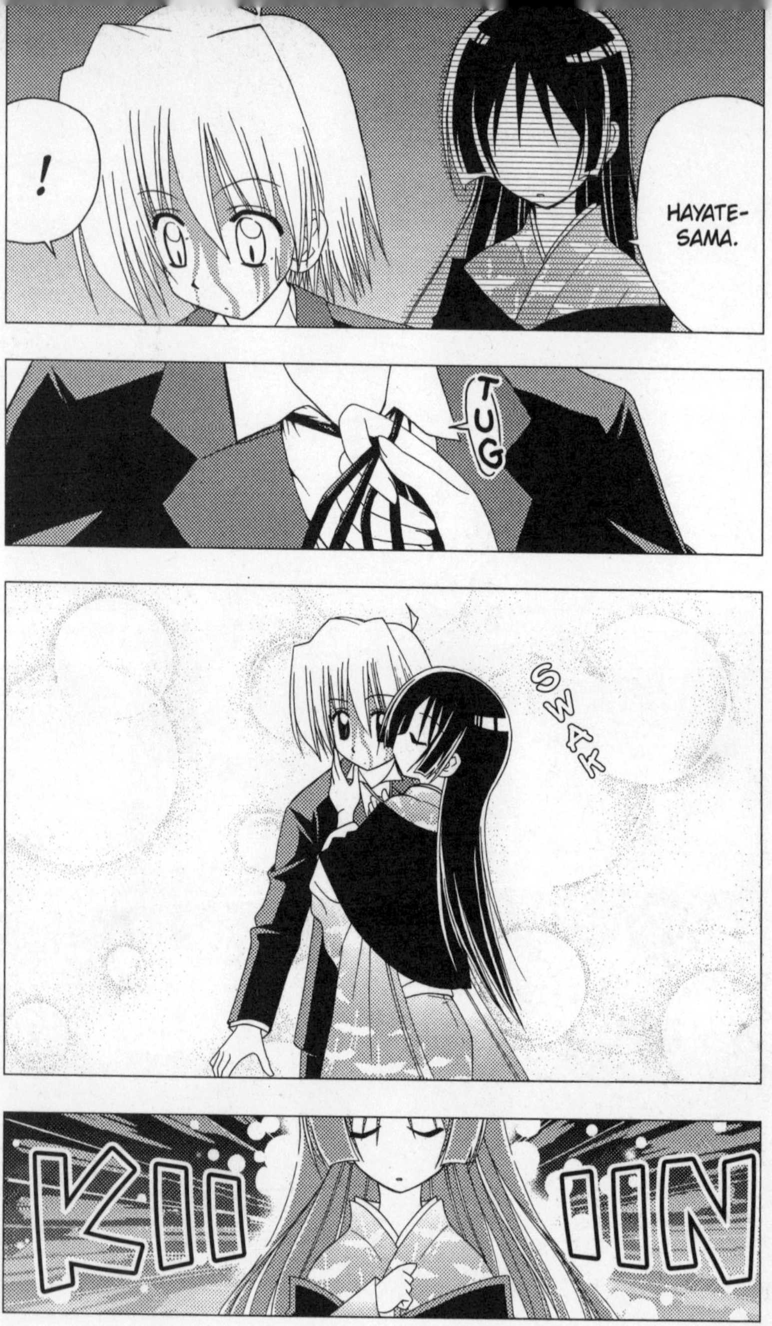
HAYATE-SAMA.
!
TUG
SWAK
KII IIN

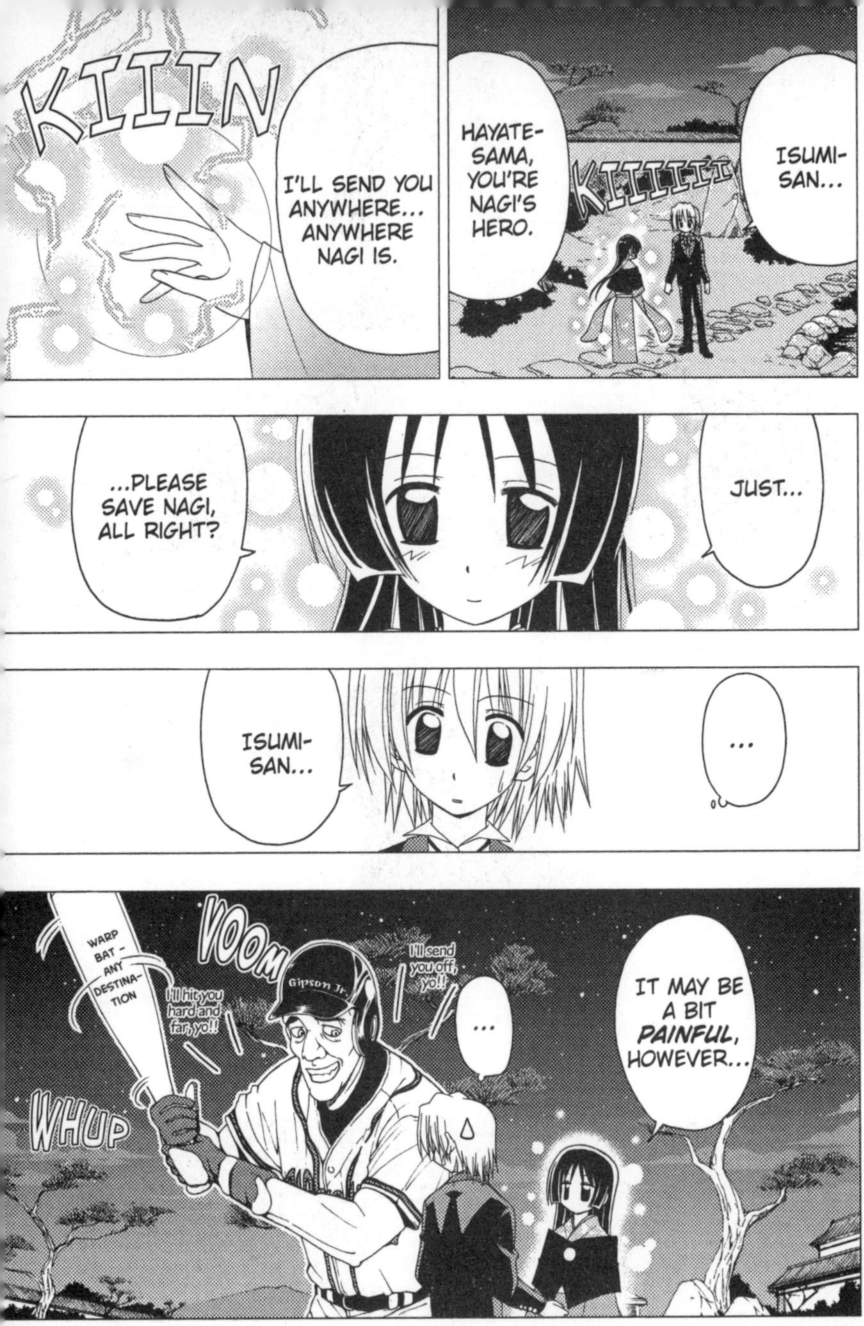
ISUMI-SAN...
KIIIIII
HAYATE-SAMA, YOU'RE NAGI'S HERO.
I'LL SEND YOU ANYWHERE... ANYWHERE NAGI IS.
KIIIN
JUST...
...PLEASE SAVE NAGI, ALL RIGHT?
...
ISUMI-SAN...
IT MAY BE A BIT PAINFUL, HOWEVER...
...
I'll send you off, yo!!
VOOM
I'll hit you hard and far, yo!!
Gipson Jr.
WARP BAT - ANY DESTINATION
WHUP

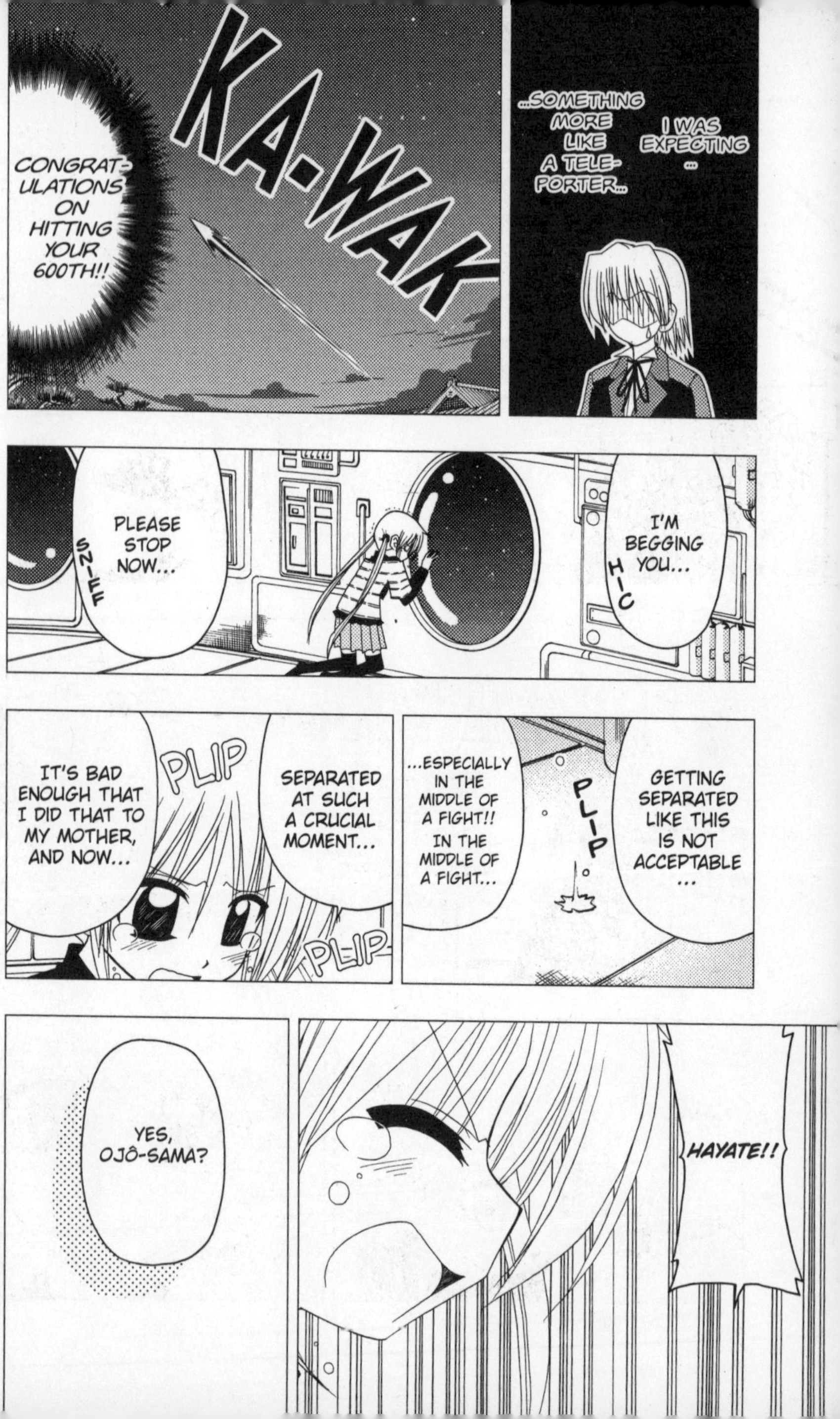
I WAS EXPECTING ...
...SOMETHING MORE LIKE A TELE-PORTER...
KA-WAK
CONGRAT-ULATIONS ON HITTING YOUR 600TH!!
I'M BEGGING YOU...
HIC
PLEASE STOP NOW...
SNIFF
GETTING SEPARATED LIKE THIS IS NOT ACCEPTABLE ...
PLIP
...ESPECIALLY IN THE MIDDLE OF A FIGHT!! IN THE MIDDLE OF A FIGHT...
SEPARATED AT SUCH A CRUCIAL MOMENT...
PLIP
IT'S BAD ENOUGH THAT I DID THAT TO MY MOTHER, AND NOW...
PLIP
HAYATE!!
YES, OJÔ-SAMA?

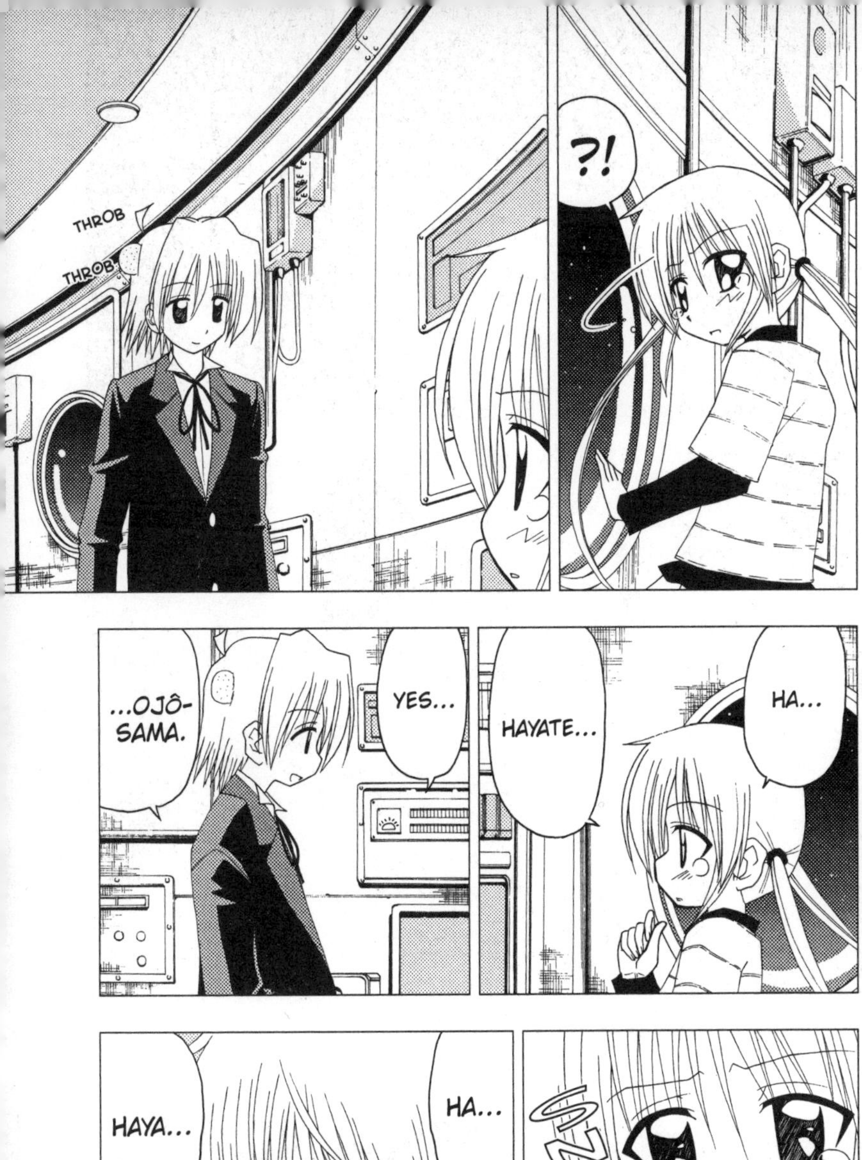
?!
THROB
THROB
HA...
HAYATE...
YES...
...OJÔ-SAMA.
SNIFF
HA...
HAYA...
T.P

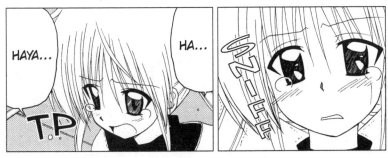

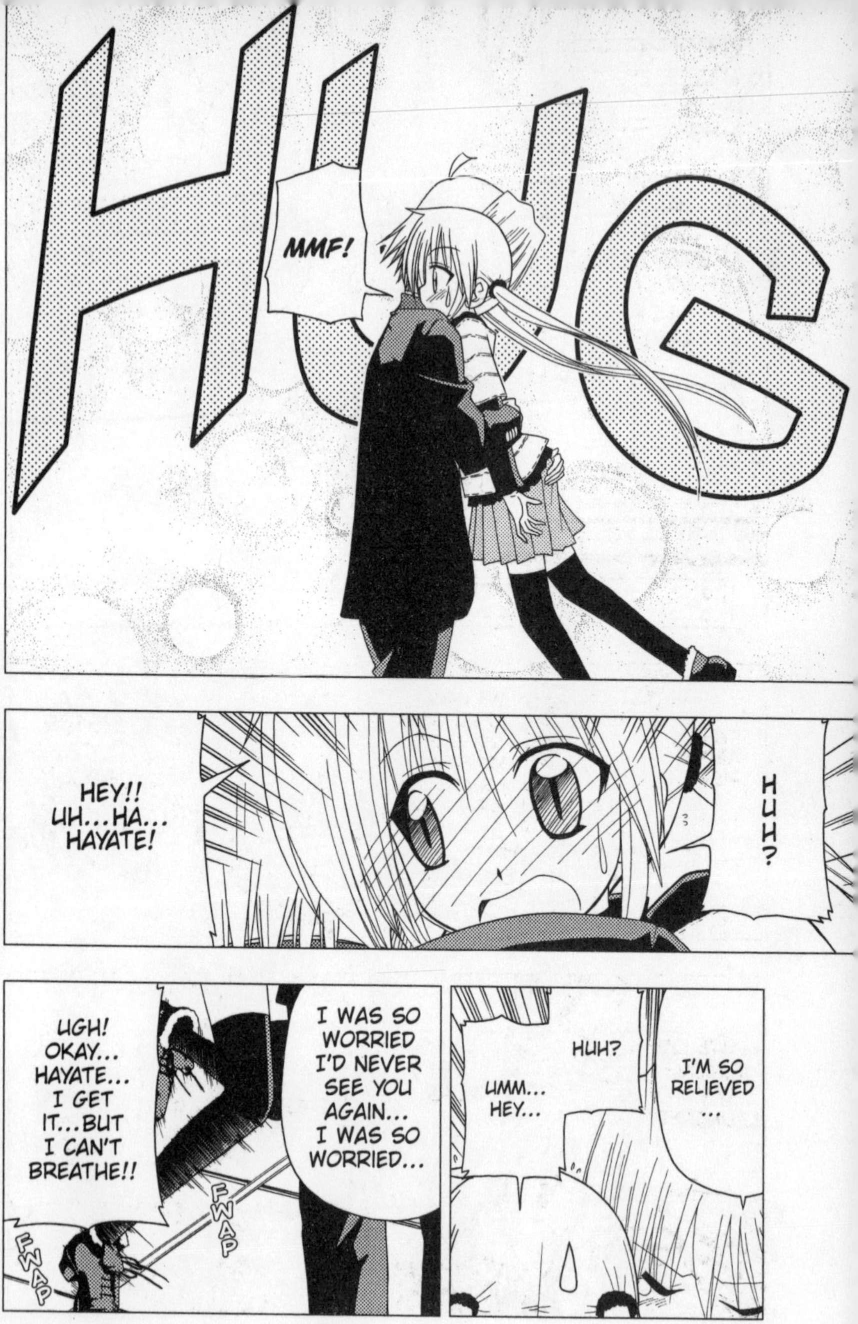
HUG
MMF!
HUH?
HEY!! UH...HA... HAYATE!
I'M SO RELIEVED ...
HUH?
UMM... HEY...
I WAS SO WORRIED I'D NEVER SEE YOU AGAIN... I WAS SO WORRIED...
UGH! OKAY... HAYATE... I GET IT...BUT I CAN'T BREATHE!!
FWAP
FWAP

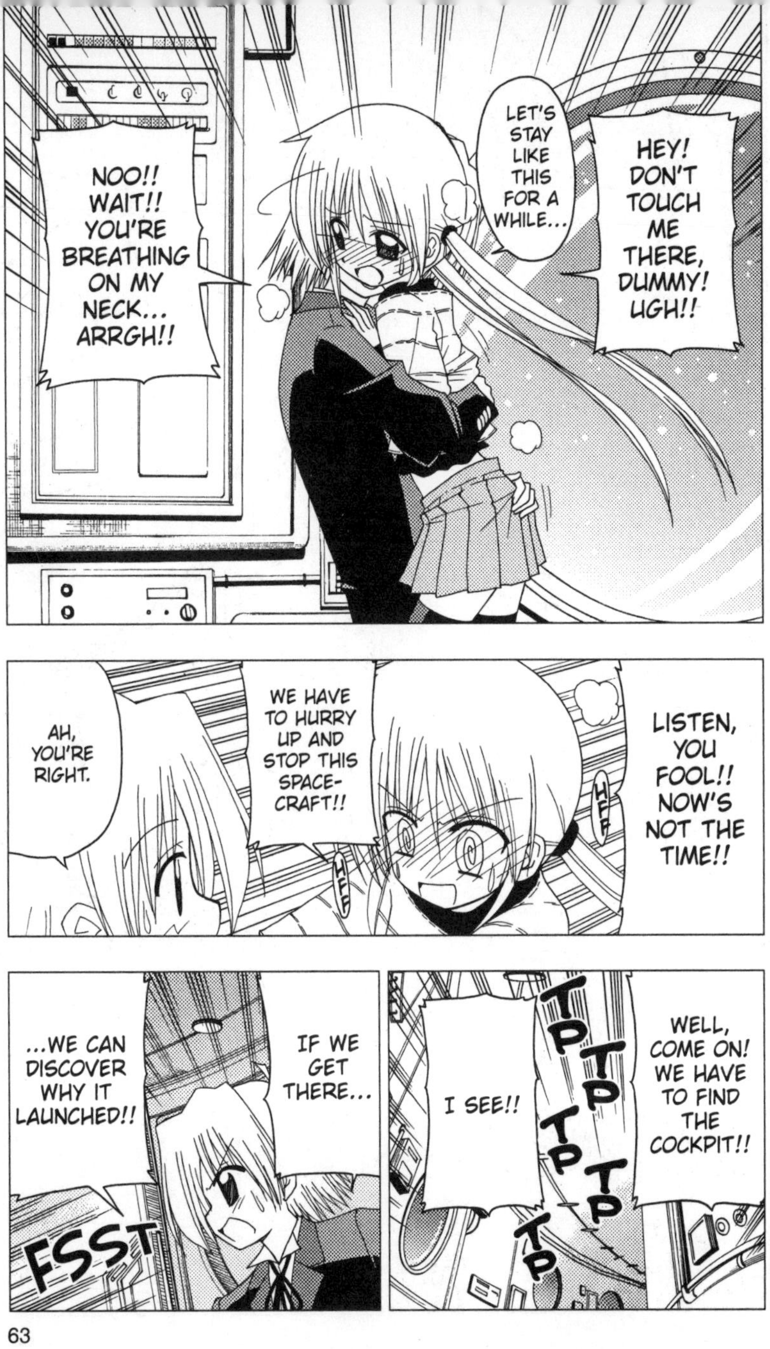
HEY! DON'T TOUCH ME THERE, DUMMY! UGH!!
LET'S STAY LIKE THIS FOR A WHILE...
NOO!! WAIT!! YOU'RE BREATHING ON MY NECK... ARRGH!!
LISTEN, YOU FOOL!! NOW'S NOT THE TIME!!
HFF
HFF
WE HAVE TO HURRY UP AND STOP THIS SPACE-CRAFT!!
AH, YOU'RE RIGHT.
WELL, COME ON! WE HAVE TO FIND THE COCKPIT!!
TP TP TP TP TP TP TP TP TP
I SEE!!
IF WE GET THERE...
...WE CAN DISCOVER WHY IT LAUNCHED!!
FSST

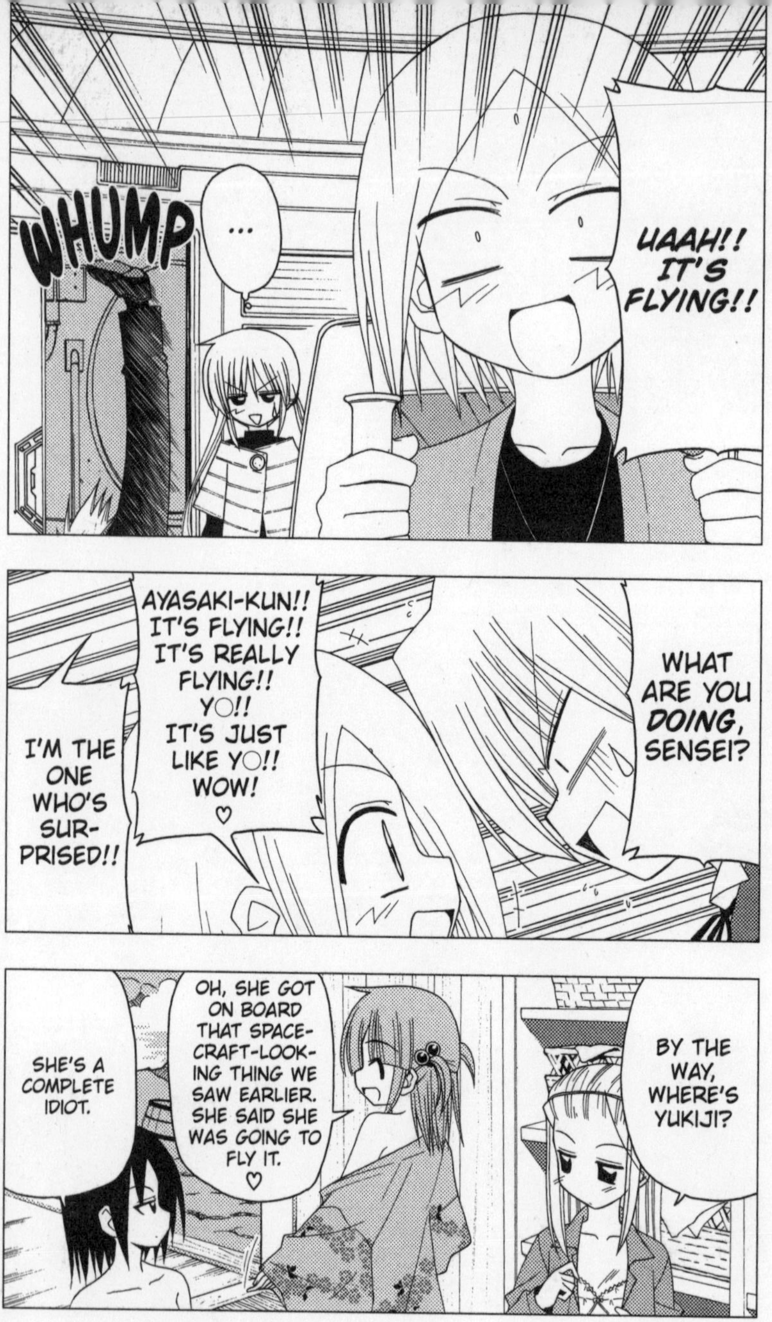
UAAH!! IT'S FLYING!!
...
WHUMP
WHAT ARE YOU DOING, SENSEI?
AYASAKI-KUN!! IT'S FLYING!! IT'S REALLY FLYING!! Y○!! IT'S JUST LIKE Y○!! WOW! ♡
I'M THE ONE WHO'S SUR-PRISED!!
BY THE WAY, WHERE'S YUKIJI?
OH, SHE GOT ON BOARD THAT SPACE-CRAFT-LOOK-ING THING WE SAW EARLIER. SHE SAID SHE WAS GOING TO FLY IT. ♡
SHE'S A COMPLETE IDIOT.

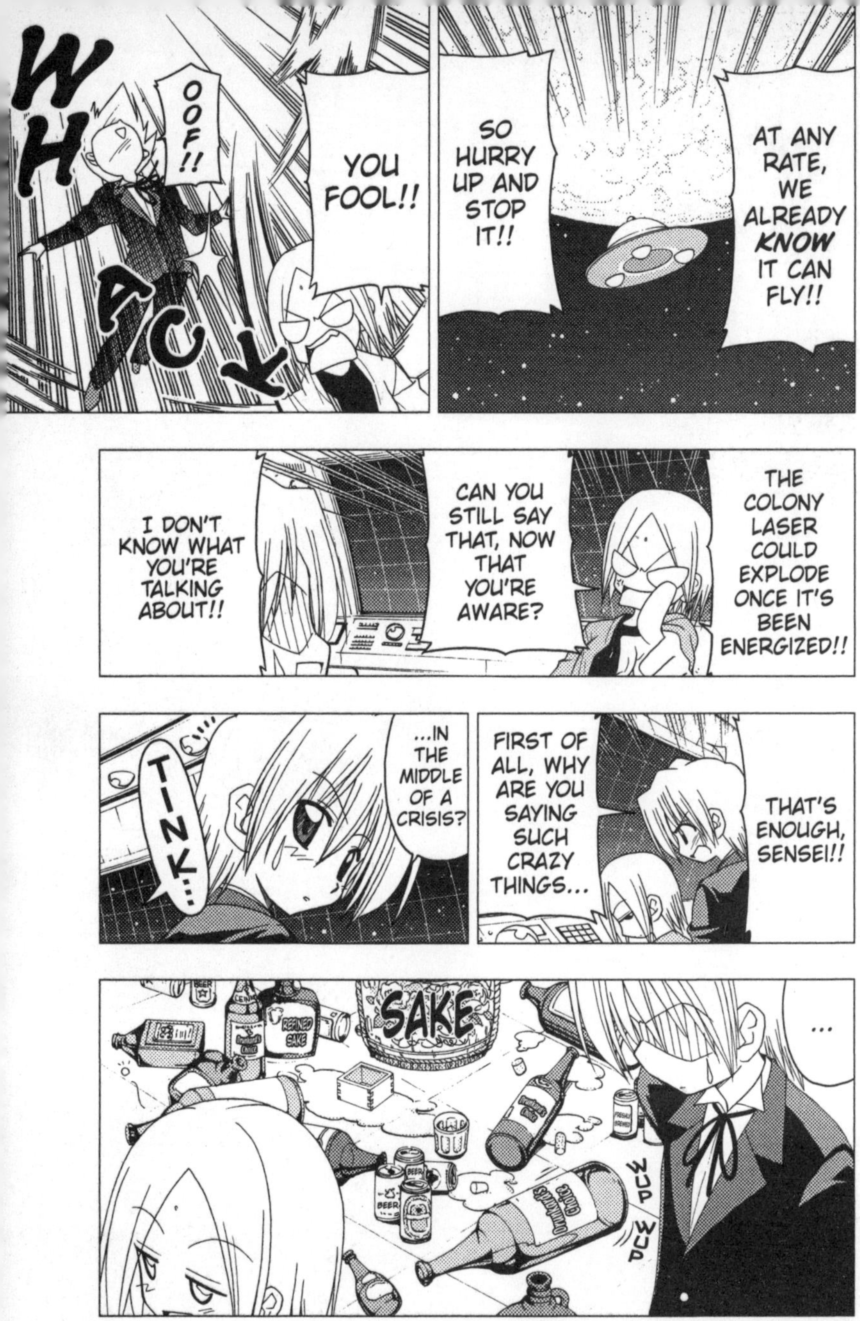
AT ANY RATE, WE ALREADY **KNOW** IT CAN FLY!!
SO HURRY UP AND STOP IT!!
YOU FOOL!!
OOF!!
WHACK
THE COLONY LASER COULD EXPLODE ONCE IT'S BEEN ENERGIZED!!
CAN YOU STILL SAY THAT, NOW THAT YOU'RE AWARE?
I DON'T KNOW WHAT YOU'RE TALKING ABOUT!!
THAT'S ENOUGH, SENSEI!!
FIRST OF ALL, WHY ARE YOU SAYING SUCH CRAZY THINGS...
...IN THE MIDDLE OF A CRISIS?
TINK...
...
WUP WUP
SAKE
REFINED SAKE

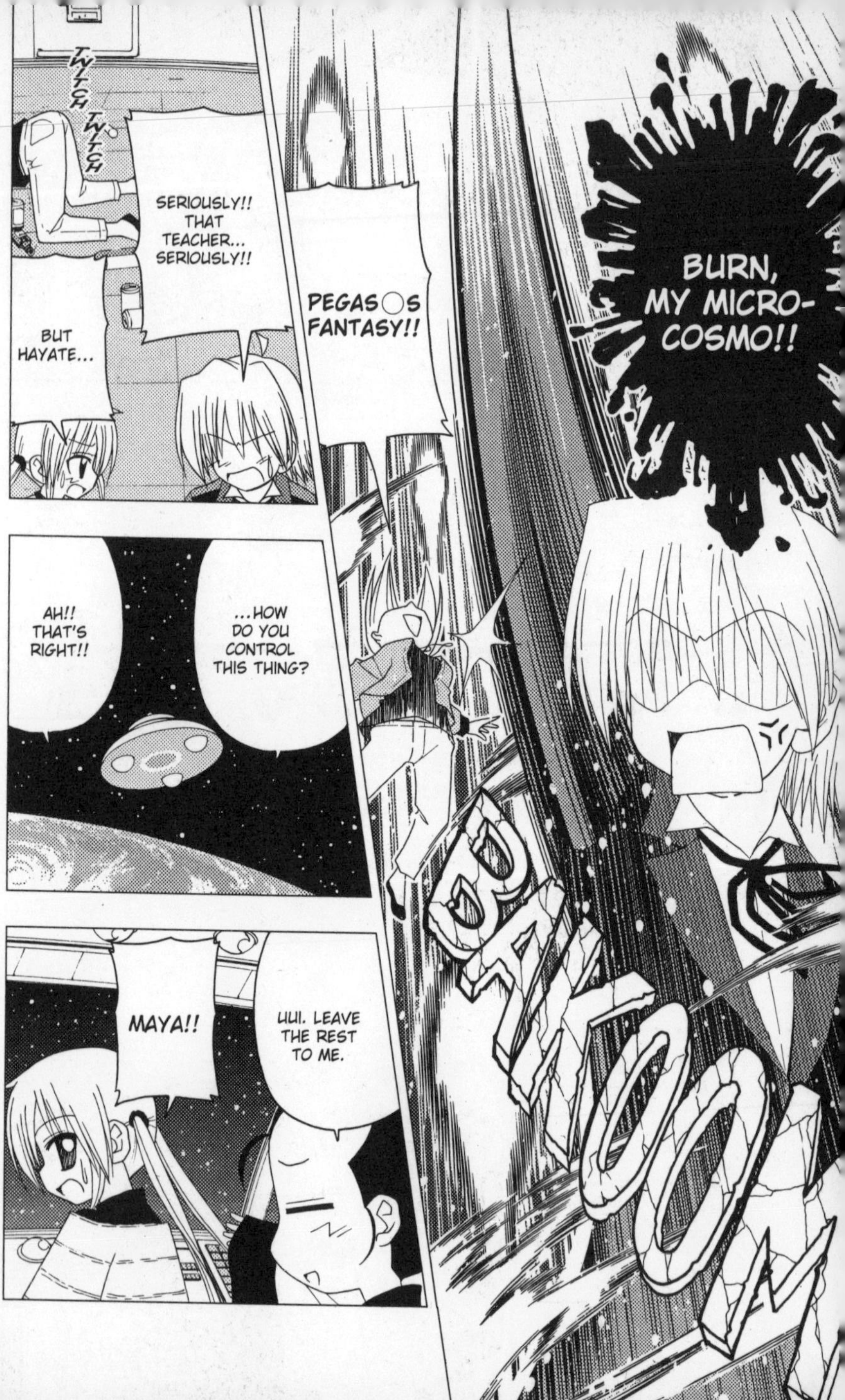
BURN, MY MICRO-COSMO!!
BKOOM
PEGAS○S FANTASY!!
TWITCH TWITCH
SERIOUSLY!! THAT TEACHER... SERIOUSLY!!
BUT HAYATE...
...HOW DO YOU CONTROL THIS THING?
AH!! THAT'S RIGHT!!
UUI. LEAVE THE REST TO ME.
MAYA!!

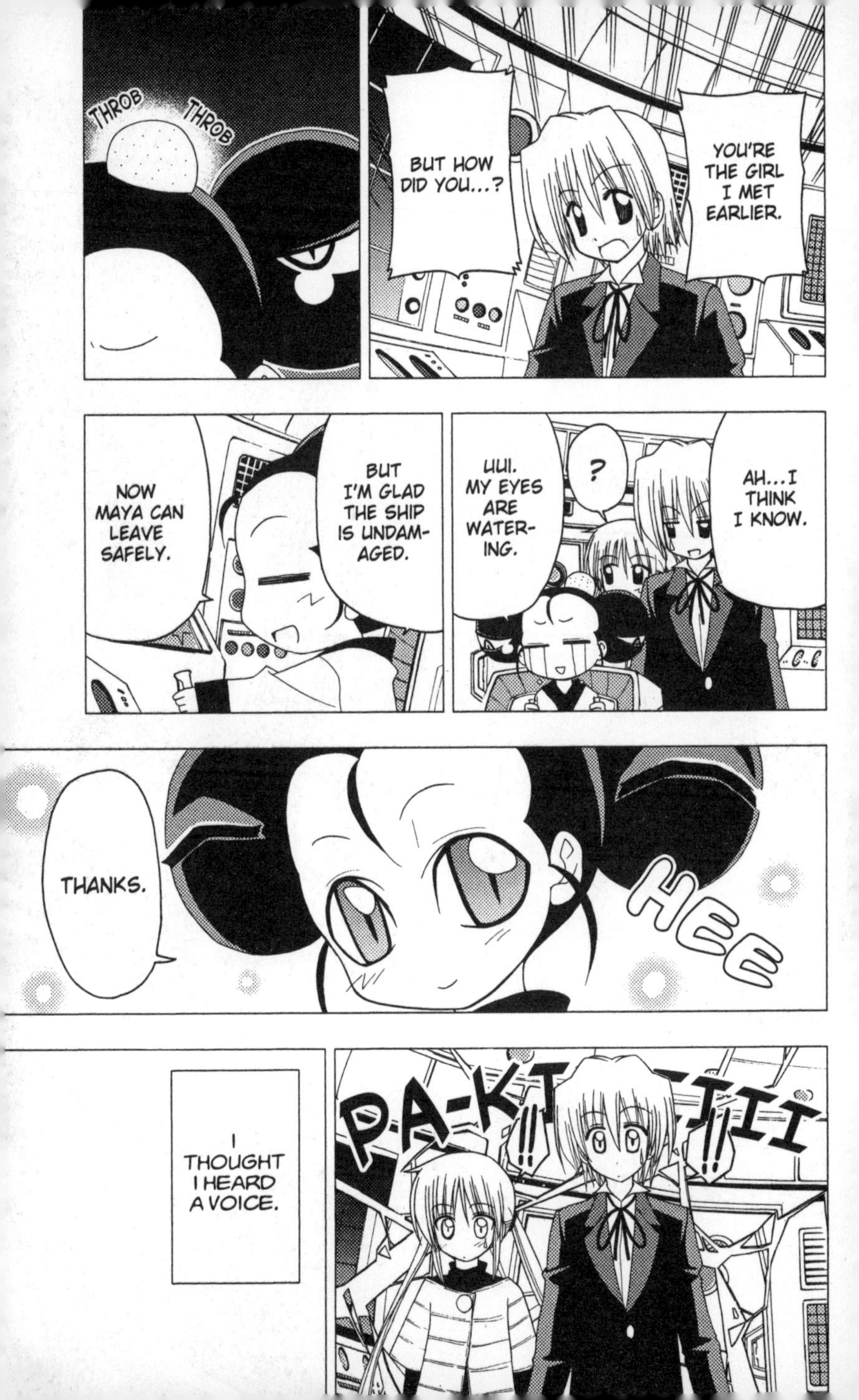
YOU'RE THE GIRL I MET EARLIER.
BUT HOW DID YOU...?
THROB
THROB
AH...I THINK I KNOW.
?
UUI. MY EYES ARE WATERING.
BUT I'M GLAD THE SHIP IS UNDAMAGED.
NOW MAYA CAN LEAVE SAFELY.
HEE
THANKS.
PA-KI——III
!!
!!
I THOUGHT I HEARD A VOICE.

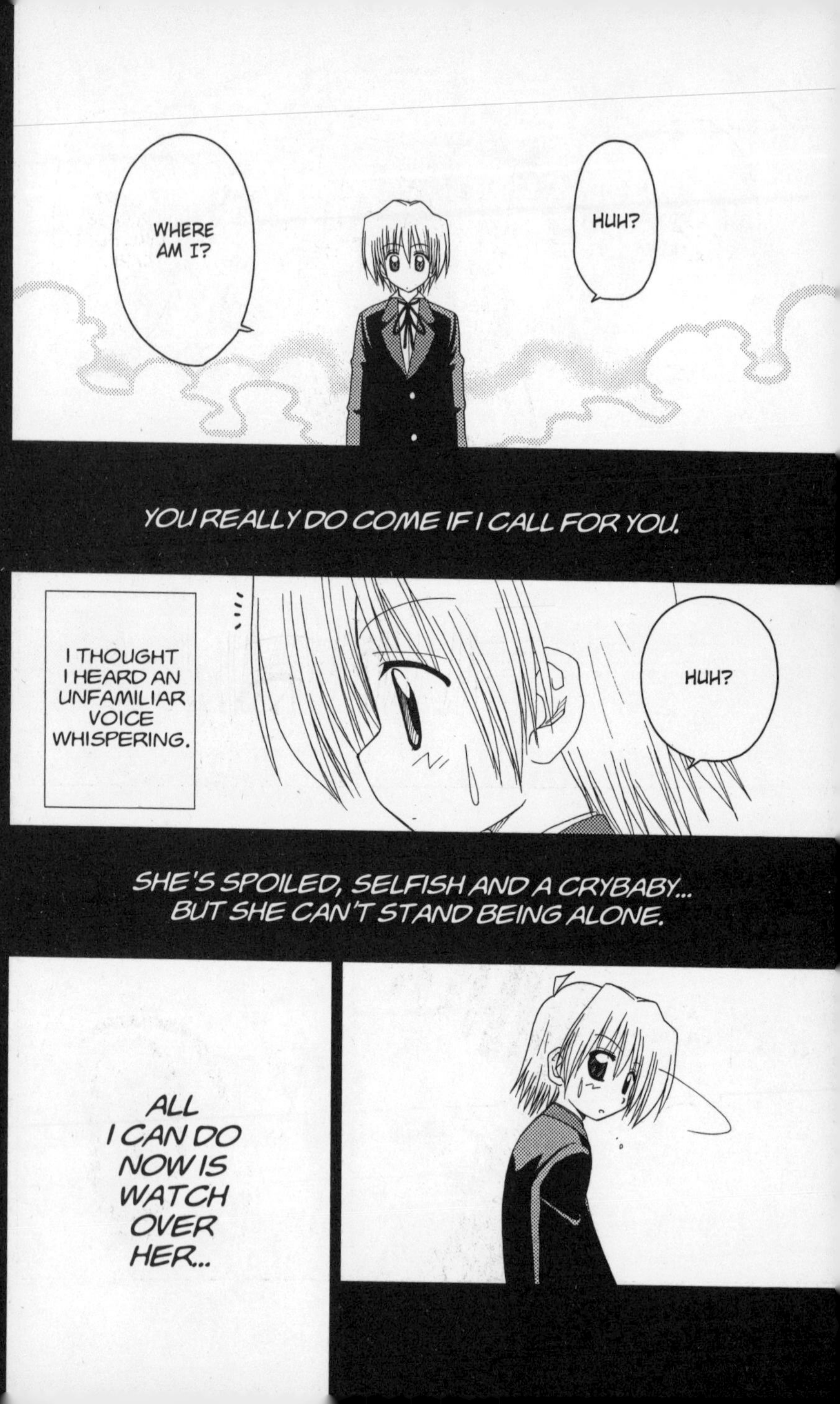
HUH?
WHERE AM I?
YOU REALLY DO COME IF I CALL FOR YOU.
HUH?
I THOUGHT I HEARD AN UNFAMILIAR VOICE WHISPERING.
SHE'S SPOILED, SELFISH AND A CRYBABY... BUT SHE CAN'T STAND BEING ALONE.
ALL I CAN DO NOW IS WATCH OVER HER...

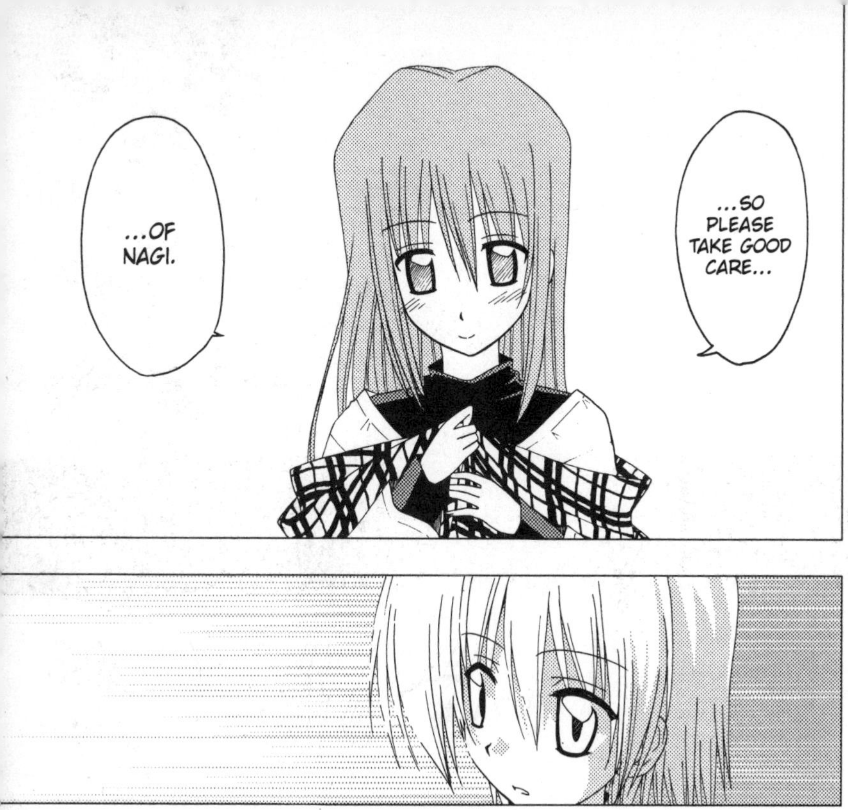
...SO PLEASE TAKE GOOD CARE...
...OF NAGI.

IN MY DREAM, I THOUGHT I SAW THE SMILE OF A GROWN-UP OJÔ-SAMA.

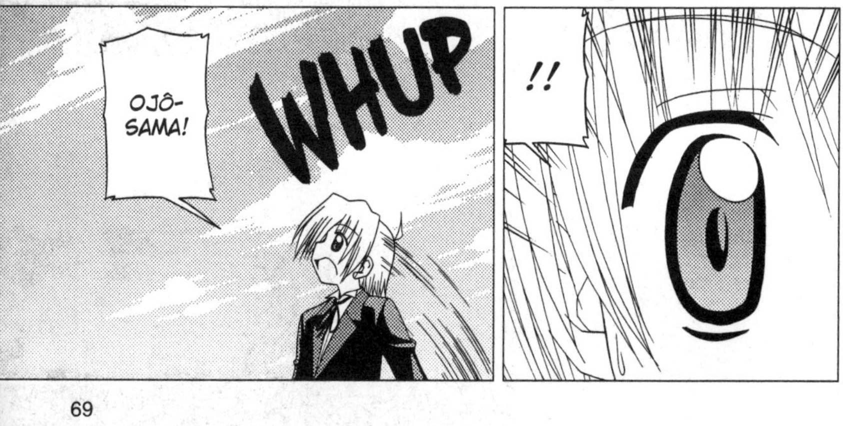
!!
OJÔ-SAMA!
WHUP

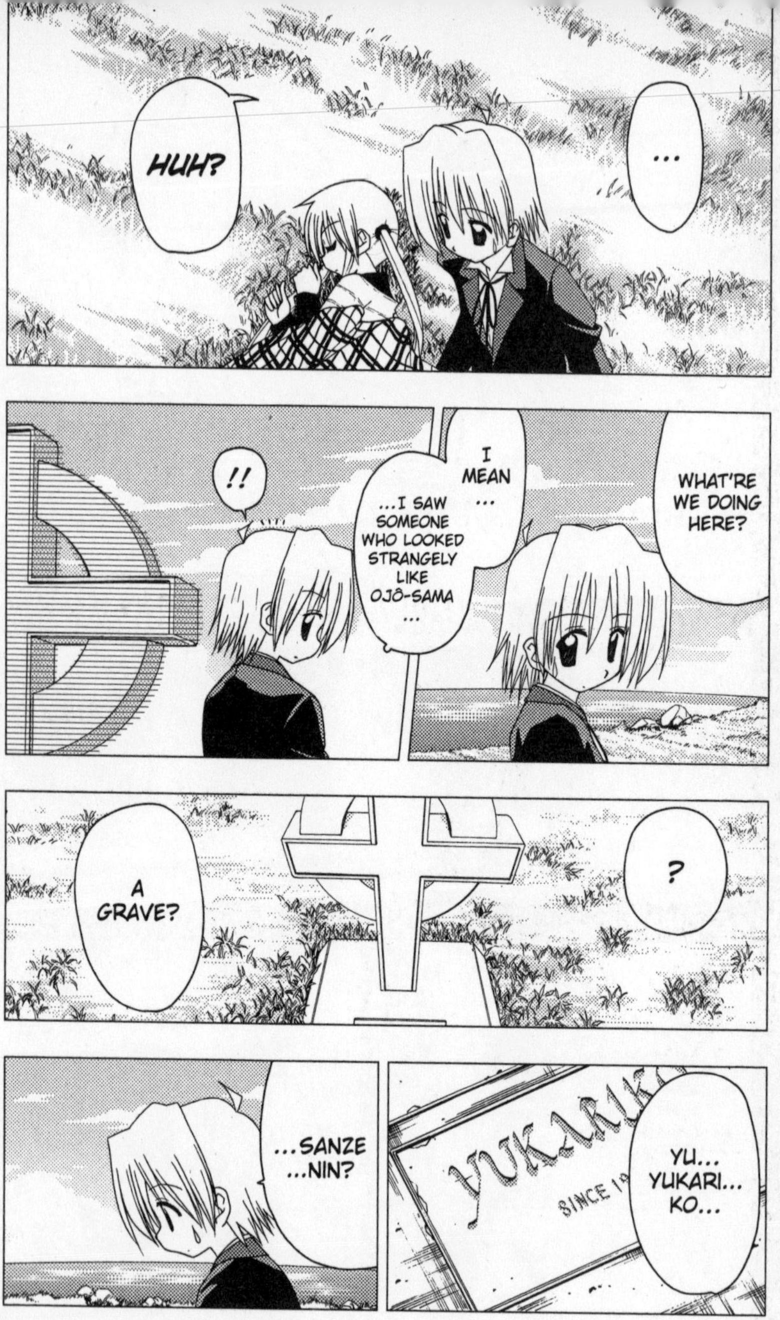
...
HUH?
WHAT'RE WE DOING HERE?
I MEAN ...
...I SAW SOMEONE WHO LOOKED STRANGELY LIKE OJÔ-SAMA ...
!!
?
A GRAVE?
YU... YUKARI... KO...
...SANZE ...NIN?

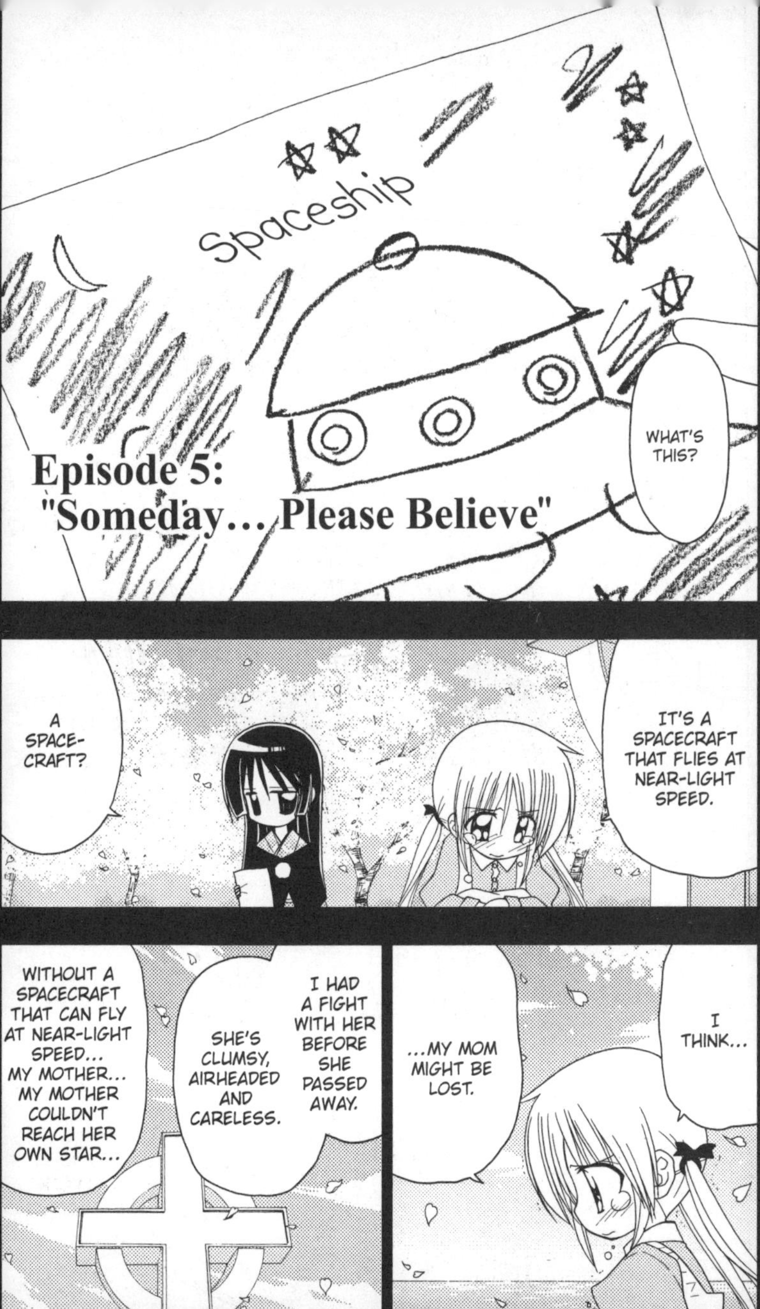
Spaceship
WHAT'S THIS?
Episode 5: "Someday… Please Believe"
IT'S A SPACECRAFT THAT FLIES AT NEAR-LIGHT SPEED.
A SPACE-CRAFT?
I THINK…
…MY MOM MIGHT BE LOST.
I HAD A FIGHT WITH HER BEFORE SHE PASSED AWAY.
SHE'S CLUMSY, AIRHEADED AND CARELESS.
WITHOUT A SPACECRAFT THAT CAN FLY AT NEAR-LIGHT SPEED… MY MOTHER… MY MOTHER COULDN'T REACH HER OWN STAR…

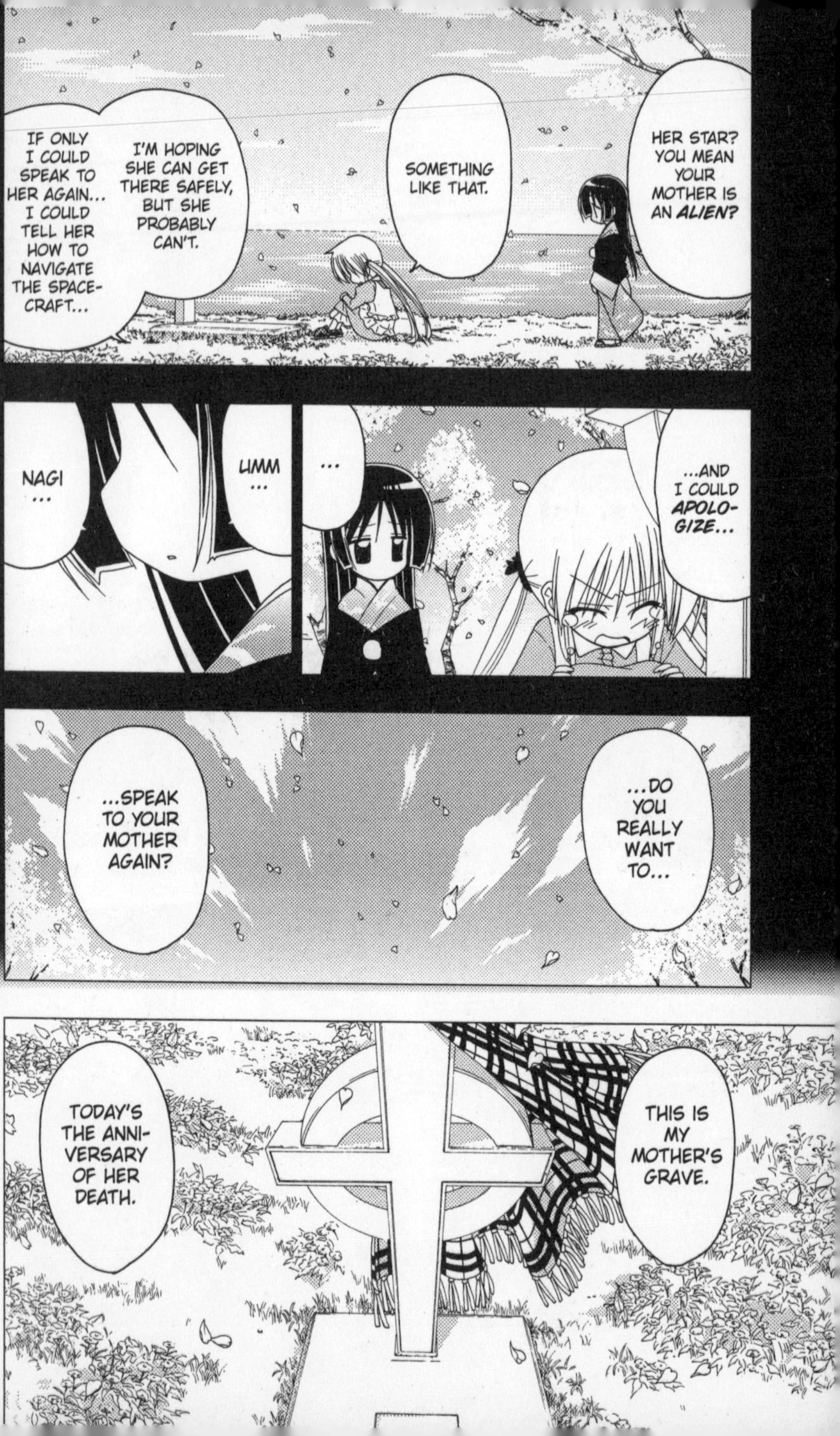
HER STAR? YOU MEAN YOUR MOTHER IS AN *ALIEN?*
SOMETHING LIKE THAT.
I'M HOPING SHE CAN GET THERE SAFELY, BUT SHE PROBABLY CAN'T.
IF ONLY I COULD SPEAK TO HER AGAIN... I COULD TELL HER HOW TO NAVIGATE THE SPACE-CRAFT...
...AND I COULD *APOLO-GIZE...*
...
UMM ...
NAGI ...
...DO YOU REALLY WANT TO...
...SPEAK TO YOUR MOTHER AGAIN?
THIS IS MY MOTHER'S GRAVE.
TODAY'S THE ANNI-VERSARY OF HER DEATH.

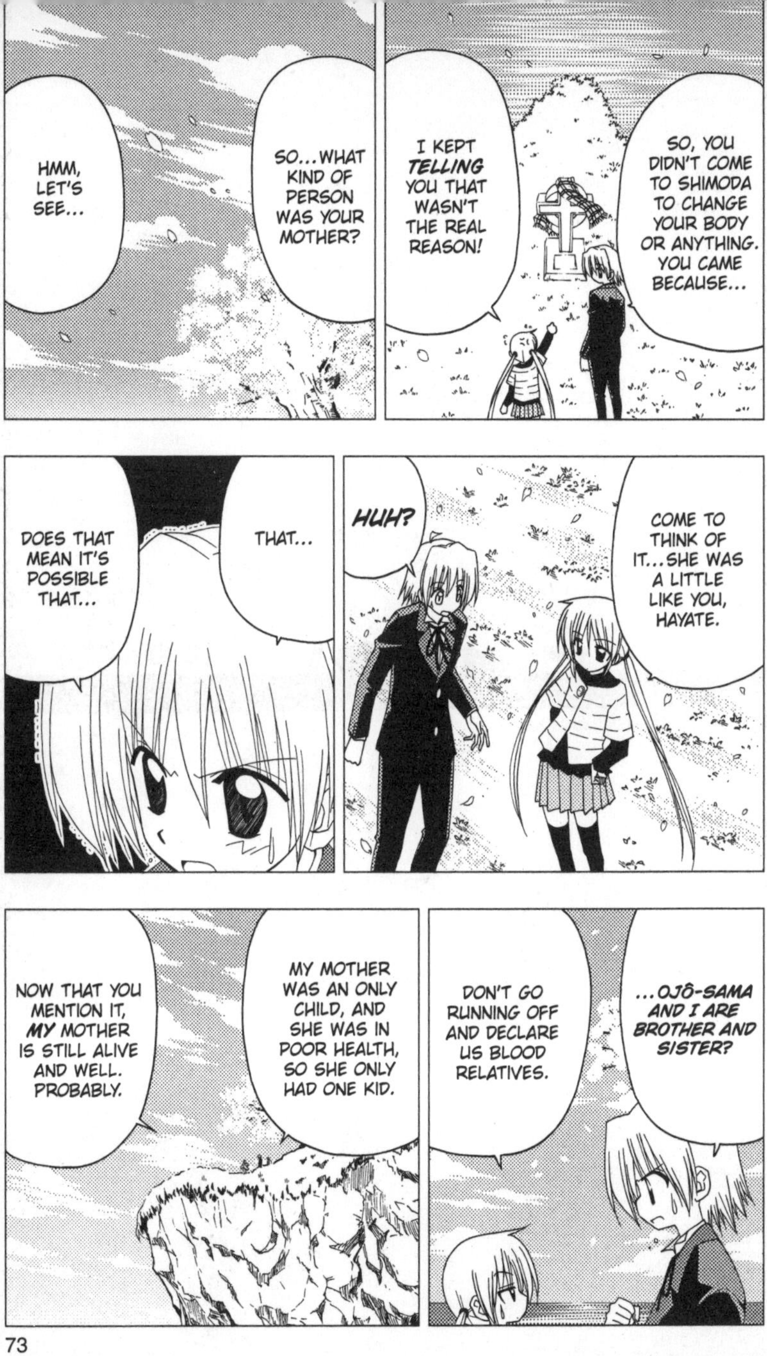
SO, YOU DIDN'T COME TO SHIMODA TO CHANGE YOUR BODY OR ANYTHING. YOU CAME BECAUSE...
I KEPT *TELLING* YOU THAT WASN'T THE REAL REASON!
SO...WHAT KIND OF PERSON WAS YOUR MOTHER?
HMM, LET'S SEE...
COME TO THINK OF IT...SHE WAS A LITTLE LIKE YOU, HAYATE.
HUH?
THAT...
DOES THAT MEAN IT'S POSSIBLE THAT...
...OJÔ-SAMA AND I ARE BROTHER AND SISTER?
DON'T GO RUNNING OFF AND DECLARE US BLOOD RELATIVES.
MY MOTHER WAS AN ONLY CHILD, AND SHE WAS IN POOR HEALTH, SO SHE ONLY HAD ONE KID.
NOW THAT YOU MENTION IT, *MY* MOTHER IS STILL ALIVE AND WELL. PROBABLY.

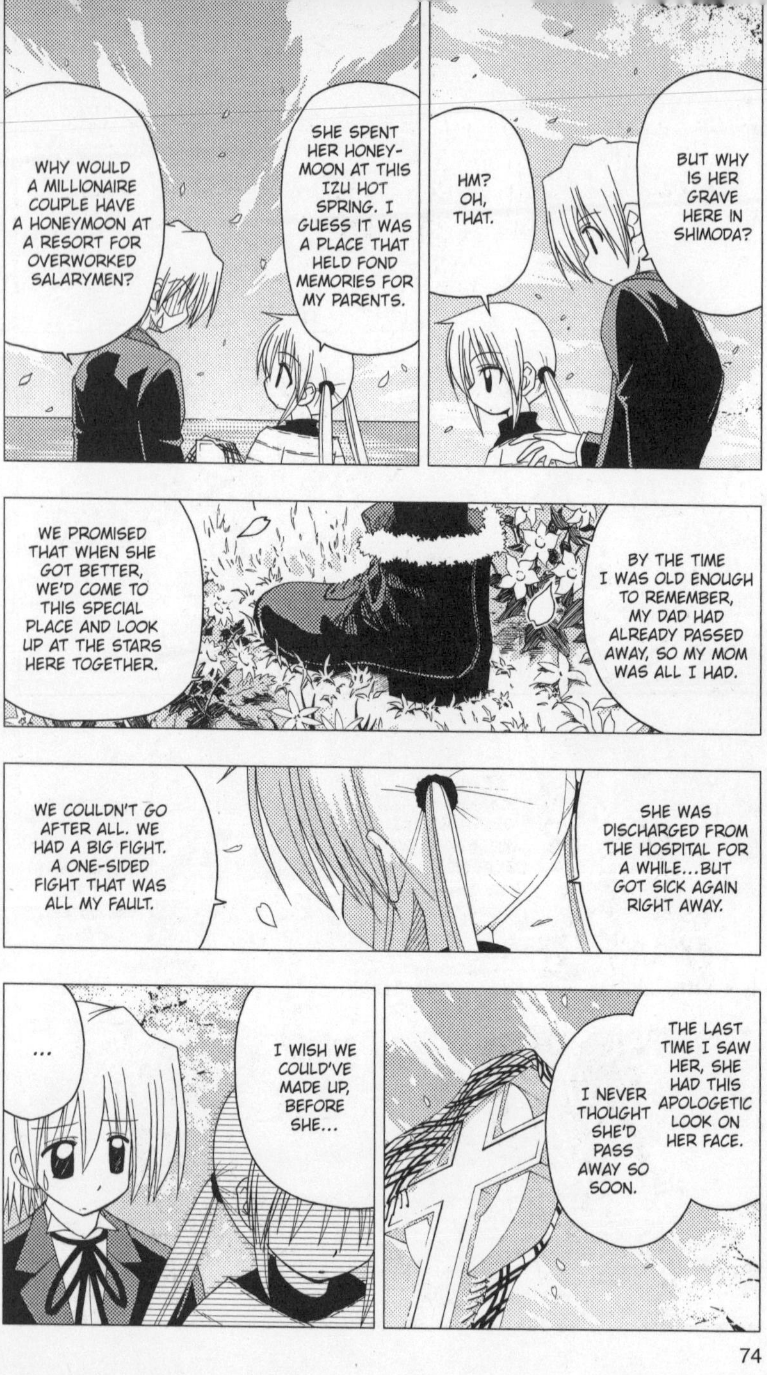
BUT WHY IS HER GRAVE HERE IN SHIMODA?
HM? OH, THAT.
SHE SPENT HER HONEY-MOON AT THIS IZU HOT SPRING. I GUESS IT WAS A PLACE THAT HELD FOND MEMORIES FOR MY PARENTS.
WHY WOULD A MILLIONAIRE COUPLE HAVE A HONEYMOON AT A RESORT FOR OVERWORKED SALARYMEN?
BY THE TIME I WAS OLD ENOUGH TO REMEMBER, MY DAD HAD ALREADY PASSED AWAY, SO MY MOM WAS ALL I HAD.
WE PROMISED THAT WHEN SHE GOT BETTER, WE'D COME TO THIS SPECIAL PLACE AND LOOK UP AT THE STARS HERE TOGETHER.
SHE WAS DISCHARGED FROM THE HOSPITAL FOR A WHILE...BUT GOT SICK AGAIN RIGHT AWAY.
WE COULDN'T GO AFTER ALL. WE HAD A BIG FIGHT. A ONE-SIDED FIGHT THAT WAS ALL MY FAULT.
THE LAST TIME I SAW HER, SHE HAD THIS APOLOGETIC LOOK ON HER FACE.
I NEVER THOUGHT SHE'D PASS AWAY SO SOON.
I WISH WE COULD'VE MADE UP, BEFORE SHE...
...

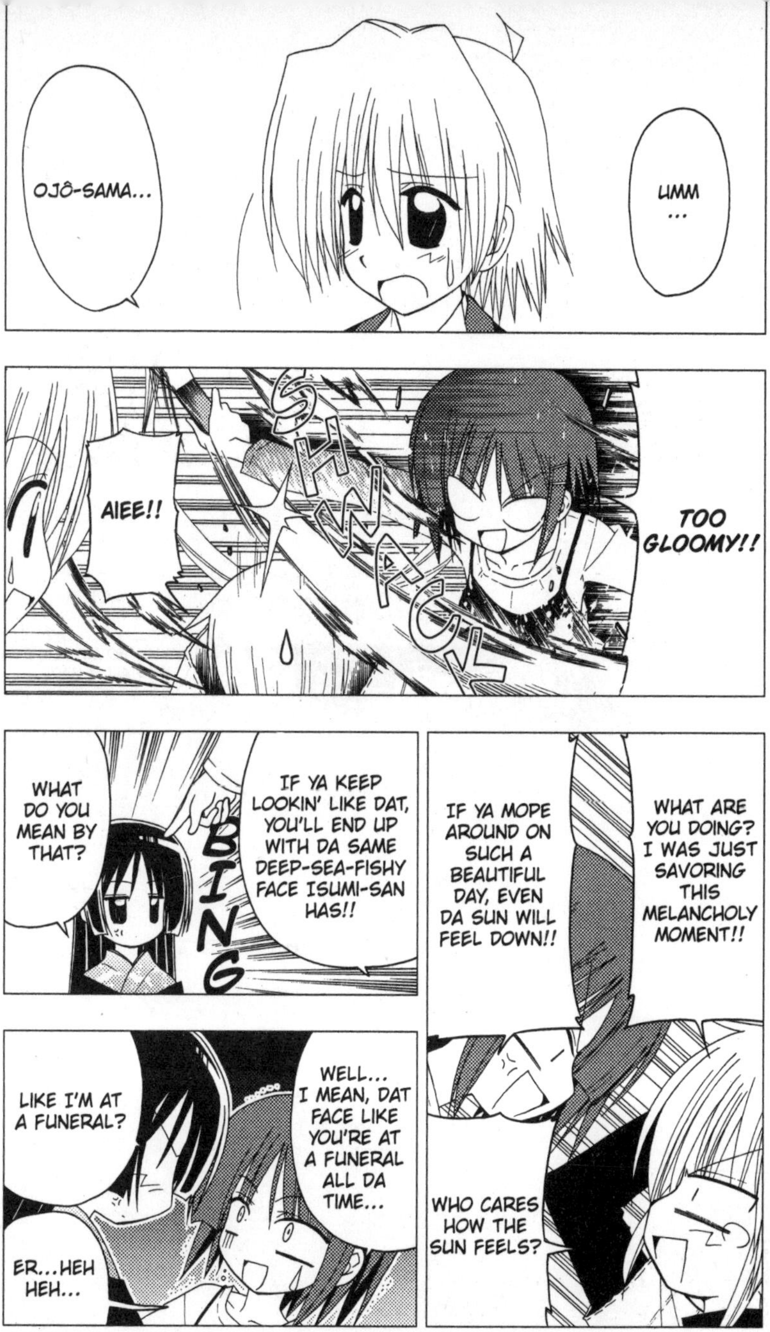
UMM ...
OJÔ-SAMA...
TOO GLOOMY!!
SHWACK
AIEE!!
WHAT ARE YOU DOING? I WAS JUST SAVORING THIS MELANCHOLY MOMENT!!
IF YA MOPE AROUND ON SUCH A BEAUTIFUL DAY, EVEN DA SUN WILL FEEL DOWN!!
WHO CARES HOW THE SUN FEELS?
IF YA KEEP LOOKIN' LIKE DAT, YOU'LL END UP WITH DA SAME DEEP-SEA-FISHY FACE ISUMI-SAN HAS!!
BING
WHAT DO YOU MEAN BY THAT?
WELL... I MEAN, DAT FACE LIKE YOU'RE AT A FUNERAL ALL DA TIME...
LIKE I'M AT A FUNERAL?
ER...HEH HEH...

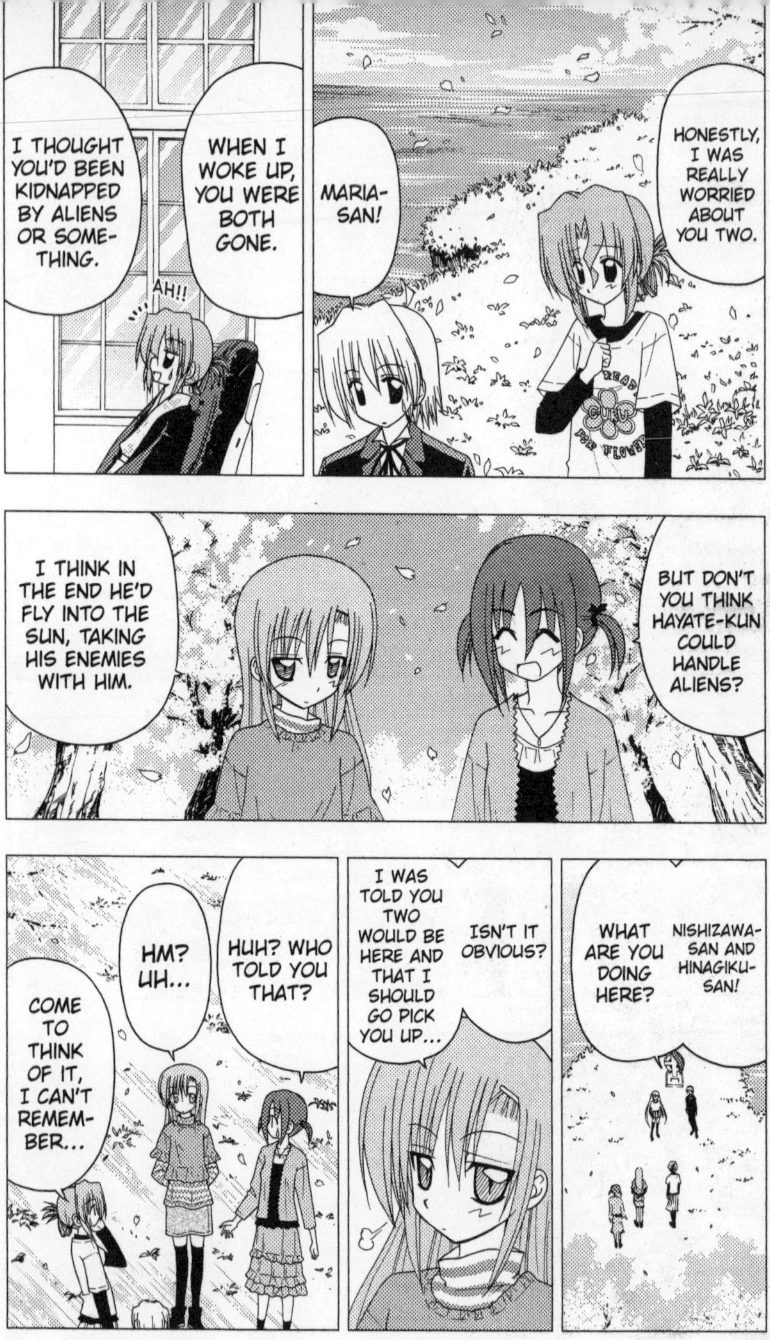
HONESTLY, I WAS REALLY WORRIED ABOUT YOU TWO.
MARIA-SAN!
WHEN I WOKE UP, YOU WERE BOTH GONE.
I THOUGHT YOU'D BEEN KIDNAPPED BY ALIENS OR SOME-THING.
AH!!
BUT DON'T YOU THINK HAYATE-KUN COULD HANDLE ALIENS?
I THINK IN THE END HE'D FLY INTO THE SUN, TAKING HIS ENEMIES WITH HIM.
NISHIZAWA-SAN AND HINAGIKU-SAN!
WHAT ARE YOU DOING HERE?
ISN'T IT OBVIOUS?
I WAS TOLD YOU TWO WOULD BE HERE AND THAT I SHOULD GO PICK YOU UP...
HUH? WHO TOLD YOU THAT?
HM? UH...
COME TO THINK OF IT, I CAN'T REMEM-BER...

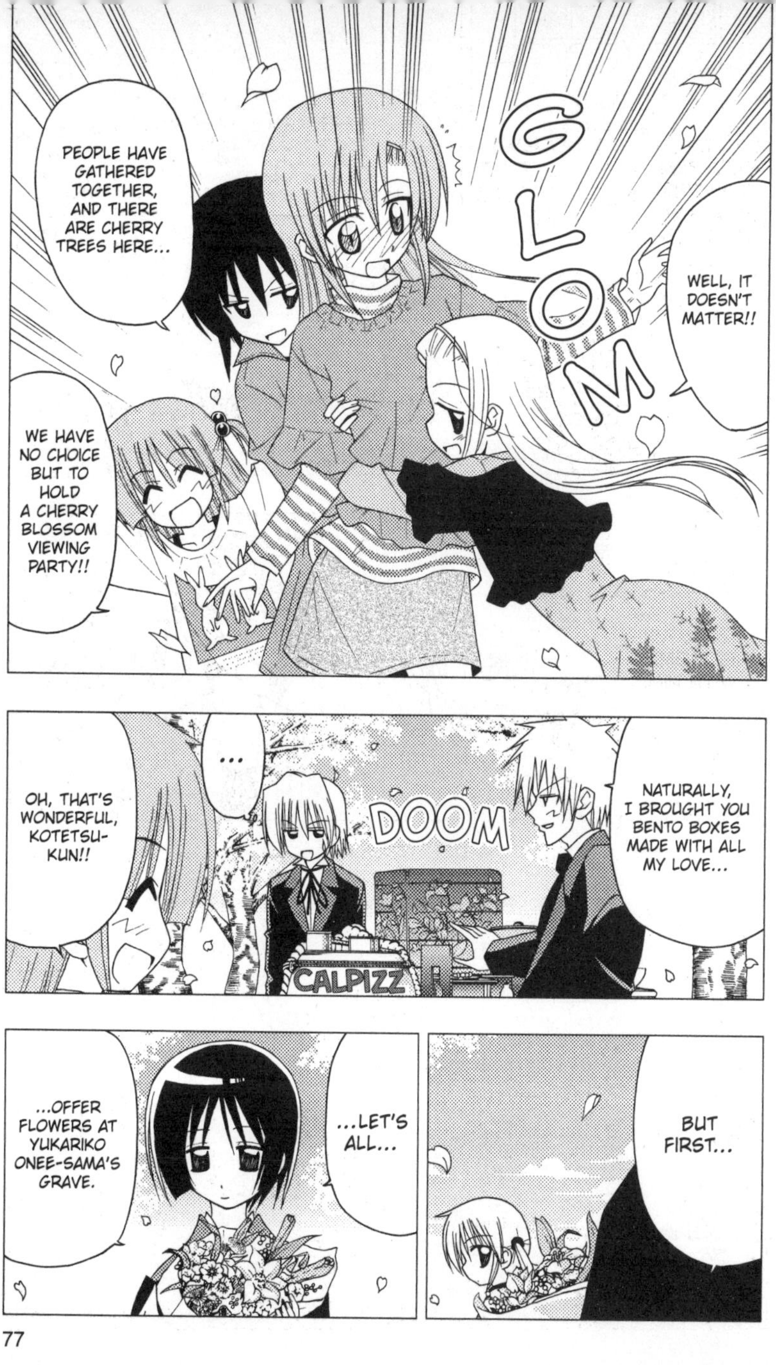
WELL, IT DOESN'T MATTER!!
GLOM
PEOPLE HAVE GATHERED TOGETHER, AND THERE ARE CHERRY TREES HERE...
WE HAVE NO CHOICE BUT TO HOLD A CHERRY BLOSSOM VIEWING PARTY!!
NATURALLY, I BROUGHT YOU BENTO BOXES MADE WITH ALL MY LOVE...
DOOM
...
OH, THAT'S WONDERFUL, KOTETSU-KUN!!
CALPIZZ
BUT FIRST...
...LET'S ALL...
...OFFER FLOWERS AT YUKARIKO ONEE-SAMA'S GRAVE.

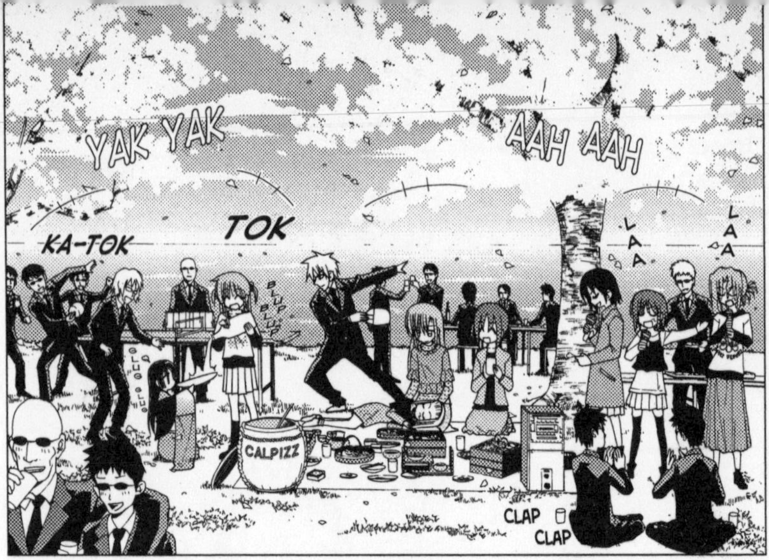
AAH AAH
LA LA
LA A A
YAK YAK
TOK
KA-TOK
BLUP BLUP
GLUG GLUG
CALPIZZ
CLAP
CLAP

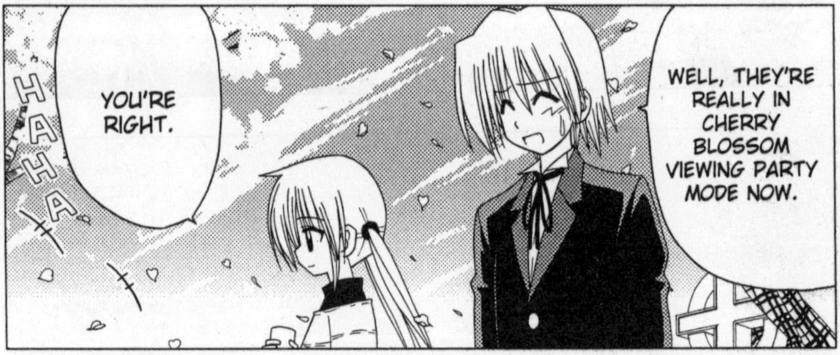
WELL, THEY'RE REALLY IN CHERRY BLOSSOM VIEWING PARTY MODE NOW.
YOU'RE RIGHT.
HAHAHA

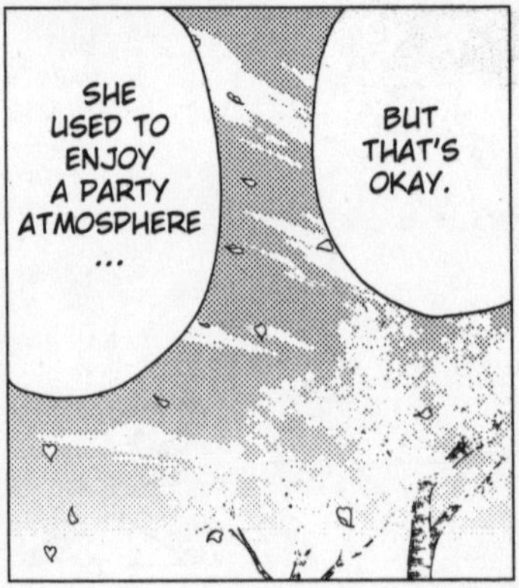
BUT THAT'S OKAY.
SHE USED TO ENJOY A PARTY ATMOSPHERE ...

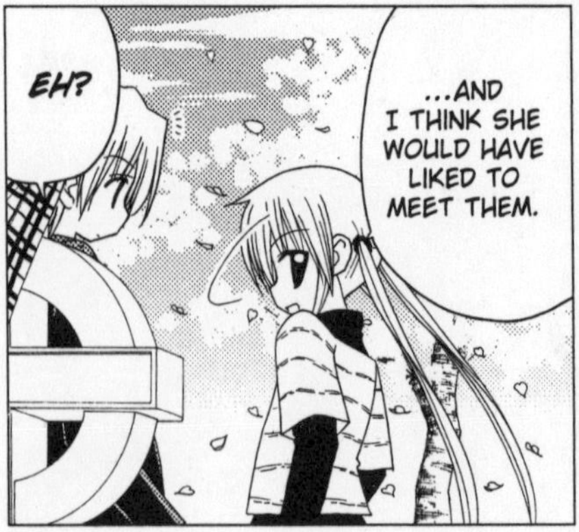
...AND I THINK SHE WOULD HAVE LIKED TO MEET THEM.
EH?

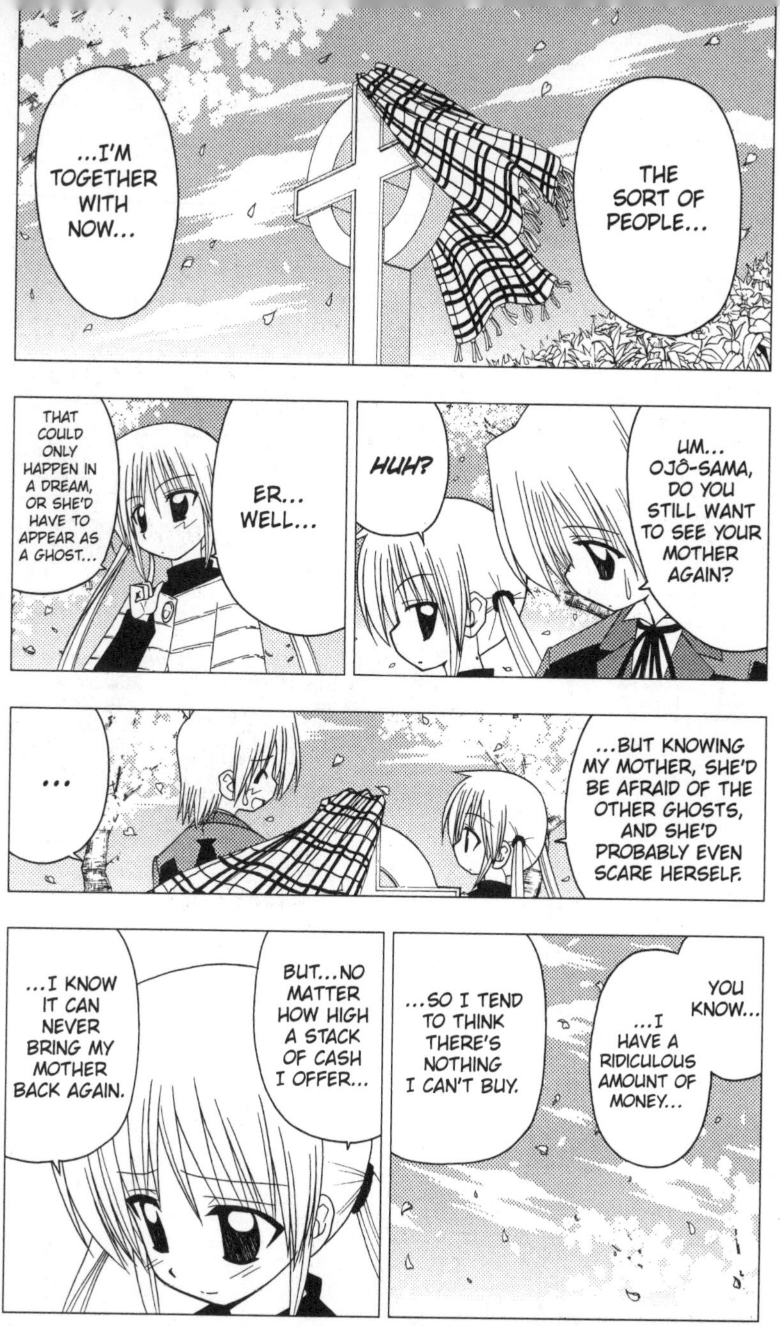

THE SORT OF PEOPLE...
...I'M TOGETHER WITH NOW...
UM... OJÔ-SAMA, DO YOU STILL WANT TO SEE YOUR MOTHER AGAIN?
HUH?
ER... WELL...
THAT COULD ONLY HAPPEN IN A DREAM, OR SHE'D HAVE TO APPEAR AS A GHOST...
...BUT KNOWING MY MOTHER, SHE'D BE AFRAID OF THE OTHER GHOSTS, AND SHE'D PROBABLY EVEN SCARE HERSELF.
...
YOU KNOW...
...I HAVE A RIDICULOUS AMOUNT OF MONEY...
...SO I TEND TO THINK THERE'S NOTHING I CAN'T BUY.
BUT...NO MATTER HOW HIGH A STACK OF CASH I OFFER...
...I KNOW IT CAN NEVER BRING MY MOTHER BACK AGAIN.

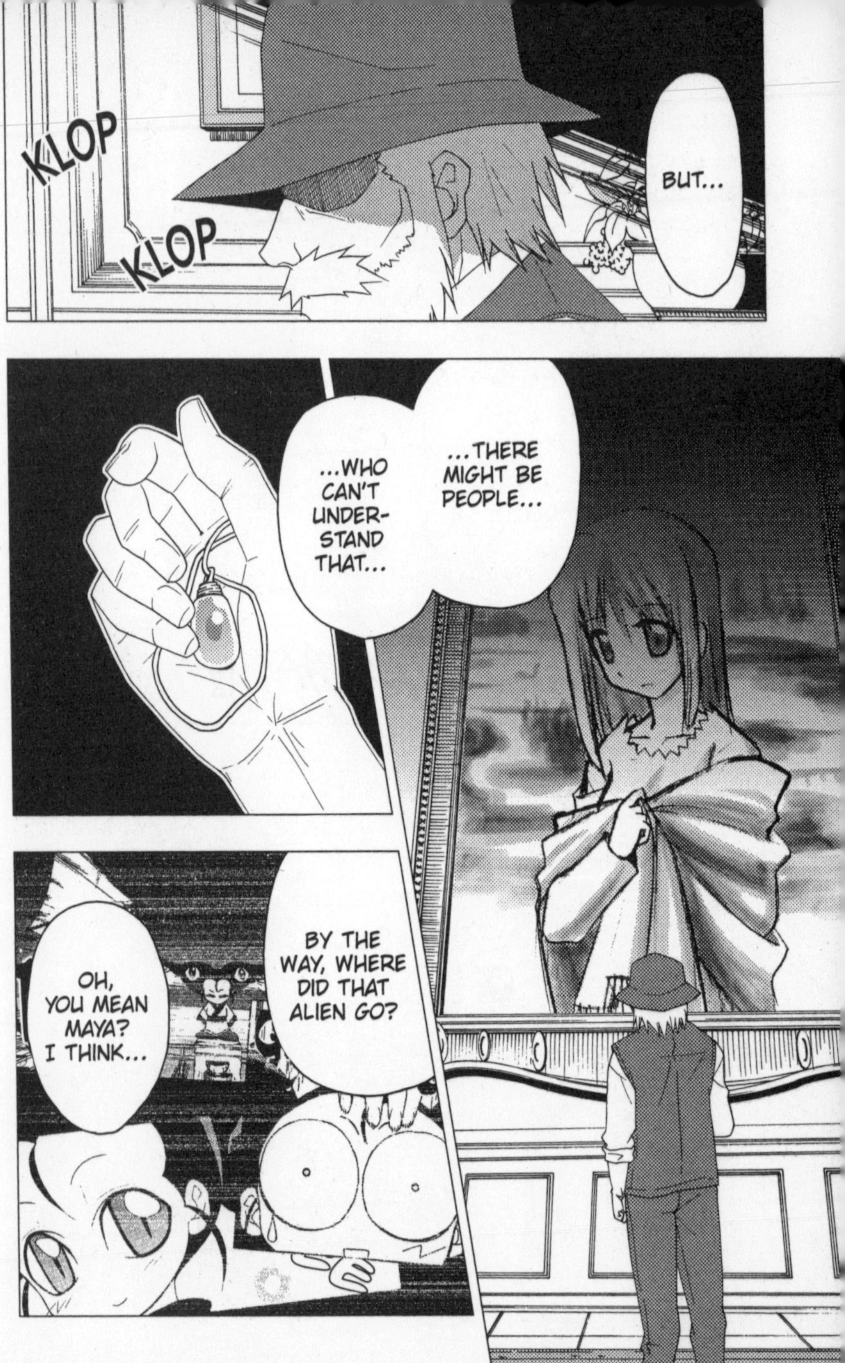
BUT...
KLOP
KLOP
...THERE MIGHT BE PEOPLE...
...WHO CAN'T UNDER-STAND THAT...
BY THE WAY, WHERE DID THAT ALIEN GO?
OH, YOU MEAN MAYA? I THINK...

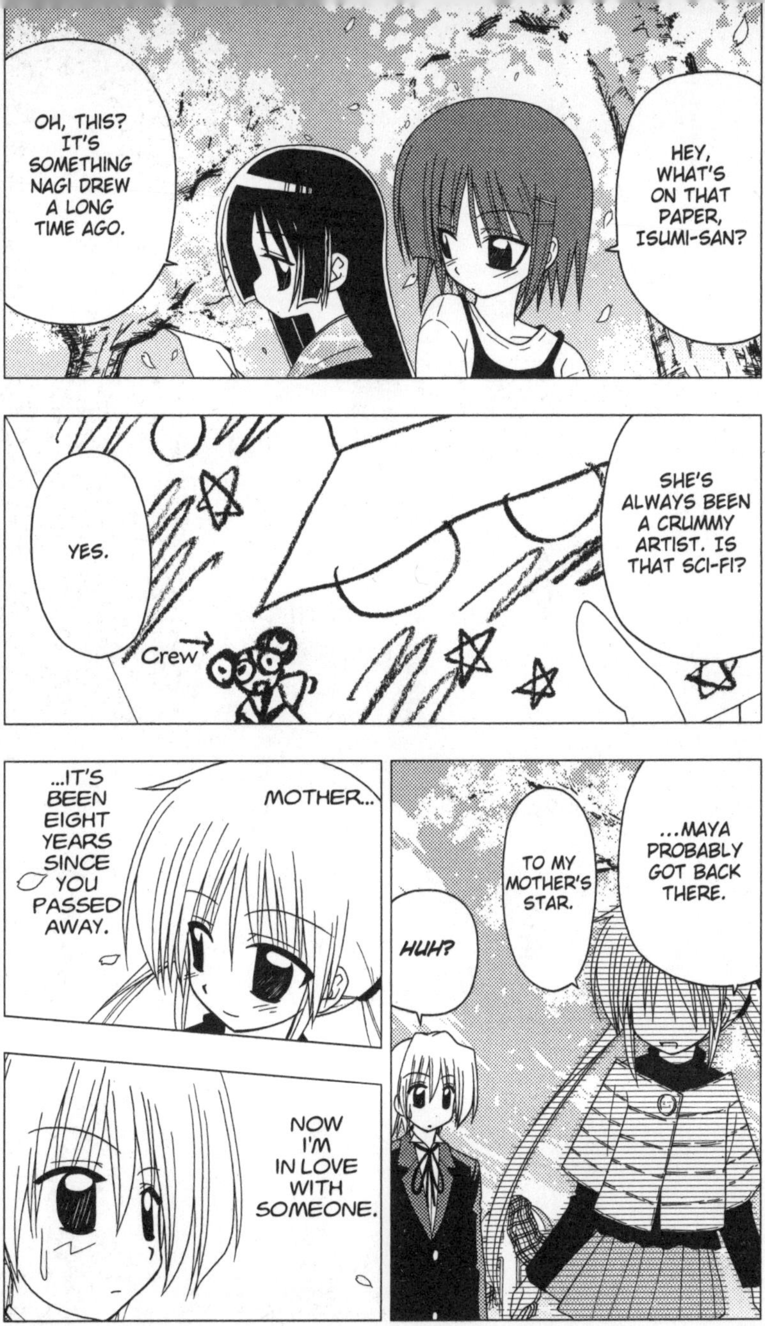
HEY, WHAT'S ON THAT PAPER, ISUMI-SAN?
OH, THIS? IT'S SOMETHING NAGI DREW A LONG TIME AGO.
SHE'S ALWAYS BEEN A CRUMMY ARTIST. IS THAT SCI-FI?
YES.
Crew
...MAYA PROBABLY GOT BACK THERE.
TO MY MOTHER'S STAR.
HUH?
MOTHER...
...IT'S BEEN EIGHT YEARS SINCE YOU PASSED AWAY.
NOW I'M IN LOVE WITH SOMEONE.

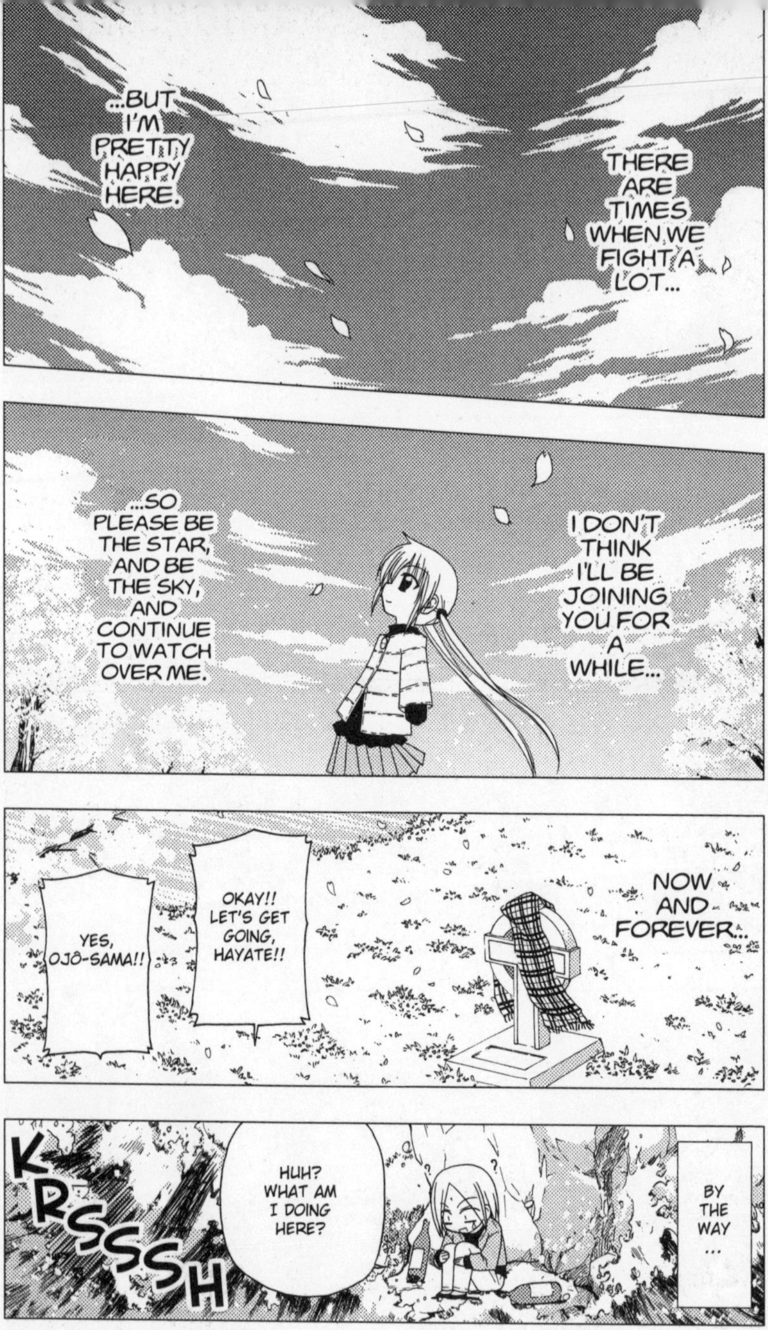
THERE ARE TIMES WHEN WE FIGHT A LOT...
...BUT I'M PRETTY HAPPY HERE.
I DON'T THINK I'LL BE JOINING YOU FOR A WHILE...
...SO PLEASE BE THE STAR, AND BE THE SKY, AND CONTINUE TO WATCH OVER ME.
NOW AND FOREVER...
OKAY!! LET'S GET GOING, HAYATE!!
YES, OJÔ-SAMA!!
BY THE WAY ...
HUH? WHAT AM I DOING HERE?
KRSSSH

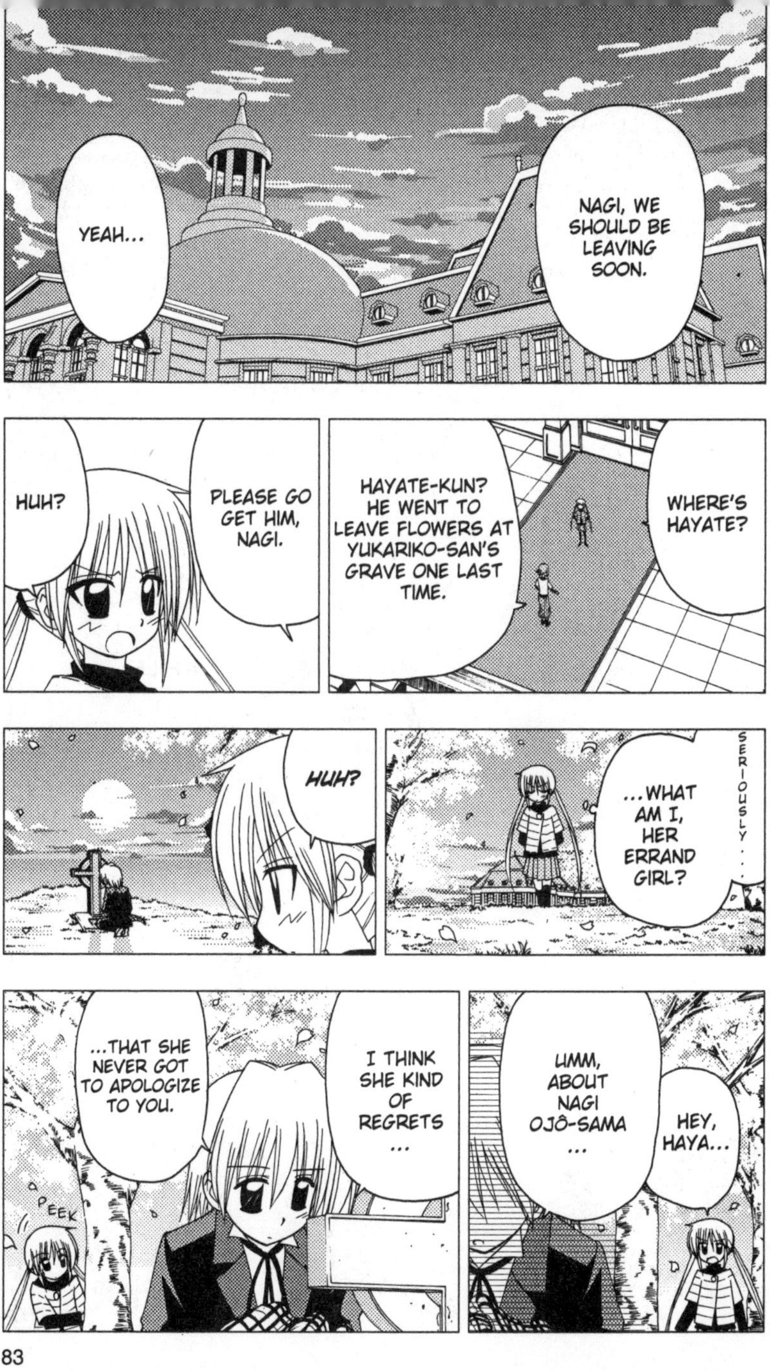
NAGI, WE SHOULD BE LEAVING SOON.
YEAH...
WHERE'S HAYATE?
HAYATE-KUN? HE WENT TO LEAVE FLOWERS AT YUKARIKO-SAN'S GRAVE ONE LAST TIME.
PLEASE GO GET HIM, NAGI.
HUH?
SERIOUSLY...
...WHAT AM I, HER ERRAND GIRL?
HUH?
HEY, HAYA...
UMM, ABOUT NAGI OJÔ-SAMA...
I THINK SHE KIND OF REGRETS...
...THAT SHE NEVER GOT TO APOLOGIZE TO YOU.
PEEK

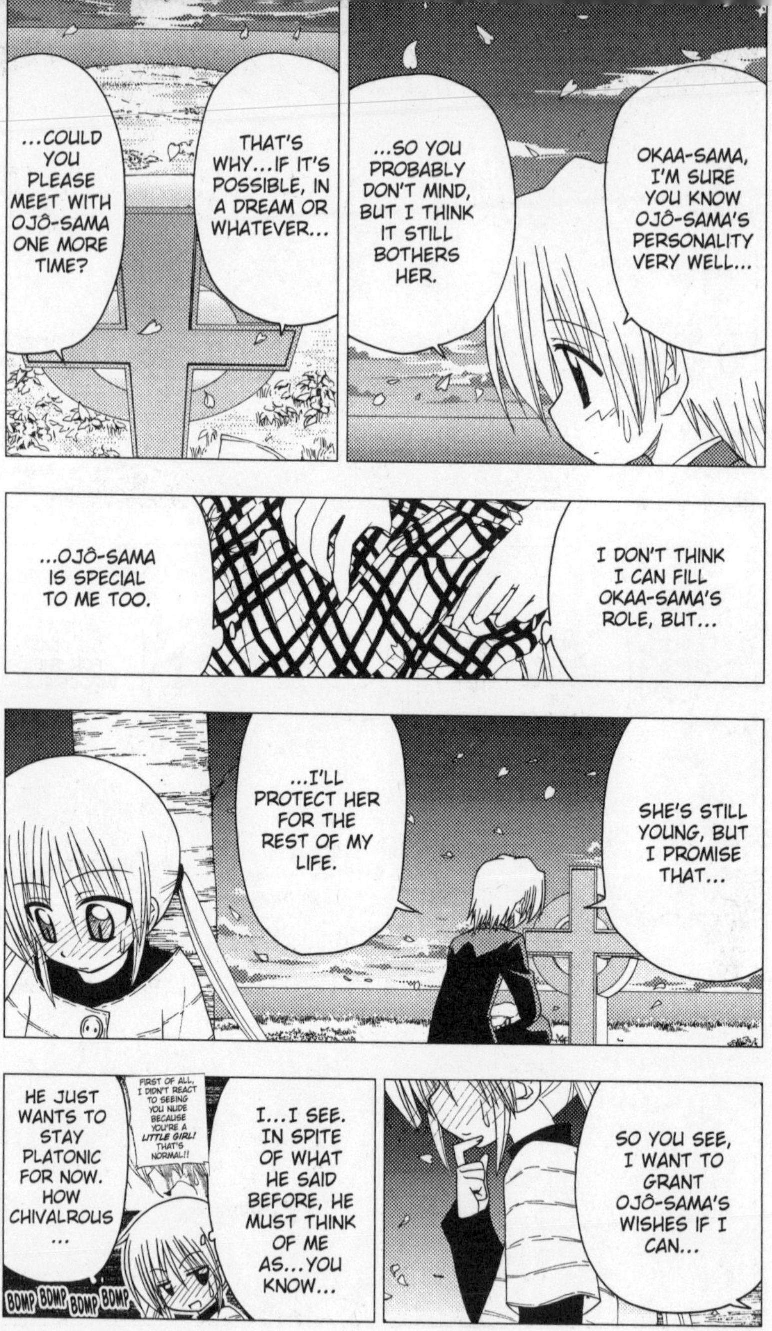
OKAA-SAMA, I'M SURE YOU KNOW OJÔ-SAMA'S PERSONALITY VERY WELL...
...SO YOU PROBABLY DON'T MIND, BUT I THINK IT STILL BOTHERS HER.
THAT'S WHY...IF IT'S POSSIBLE, IN A DREAM OR WHATEVER...
...COULD YOU PLEASE MEET WITH OJÔ-SAMA ONE MORE TIME?
I DON'T THINK I CAN FILL OKAA-SAMA'S ROLE, BUT...
...OJÔ-SAMA IS SPECIAL TO ME TOO.
SHE'S STILL YOUNG, BUT I PROMISE THAT...
...I'LL PROTECT HER FOR THE REST OF MY LIFE.
SO YOU SEE, I WANT TO GRANT OJÔ-SAMA'S WISHES IF I CAN...
I...I SEE. IN SPITE OF WHAT HE SAID BEFORE, HE MUST THINK OF ME AS...YOU KNOW...
FIRST OF ALL, I DIDN'T REACT TO SEEING YOU NUDE BECAUSE YOU'RE A *LITTLE GIRL!* THAT'S NORMAL!!
HE JUST WANTS TO STAY PLATONIC FOR NOW. HOW CHIVALROUS...
BDMP BDMP BDMP BDMP

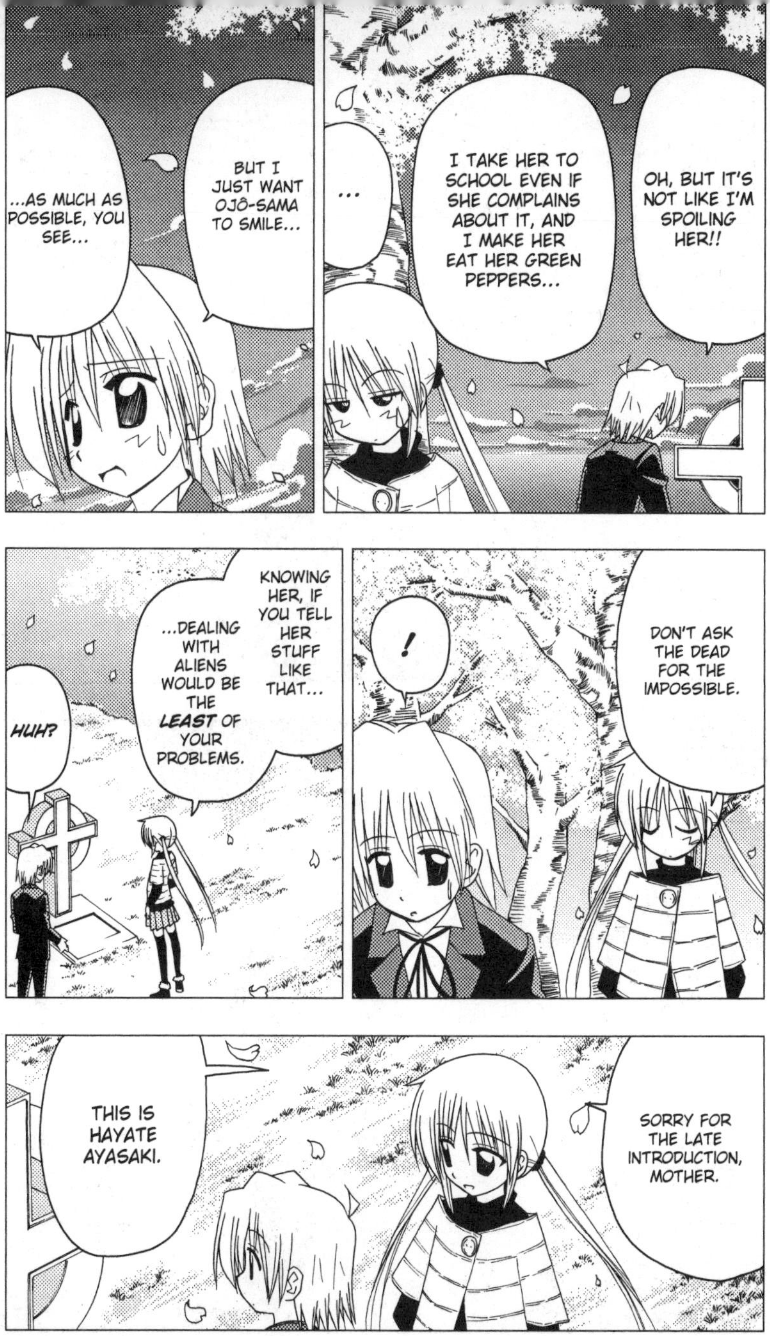
OH, BUT IT'S NOT LIKE I'M SPOILING HER!!
I TAKE HER TO SCHOOL EVEN IF SHE COMPLAINS ABOUT IT, AND I MAKE HER EAT HER GREEN PEPPERS...
...
BUT I JUST WANT OJÔ-SAMA TO SMILE...
...AS MUCH AS POSSIBLE, YOU SEE...
DON'T ASK THE DEAD FOR THE IMPOSSIBLE.
!
KNOWING HER, IF YOU TELL HER STUFF LIKE THAT...
...DEALING WITH ALIENS WOULD BE THE LEAST OF YOUR PROBLEMS.
HUH?
SORRY FOR THE LATE INTRODUCTION, MOTHER.
THIS IS HAYATE AYASAKI.

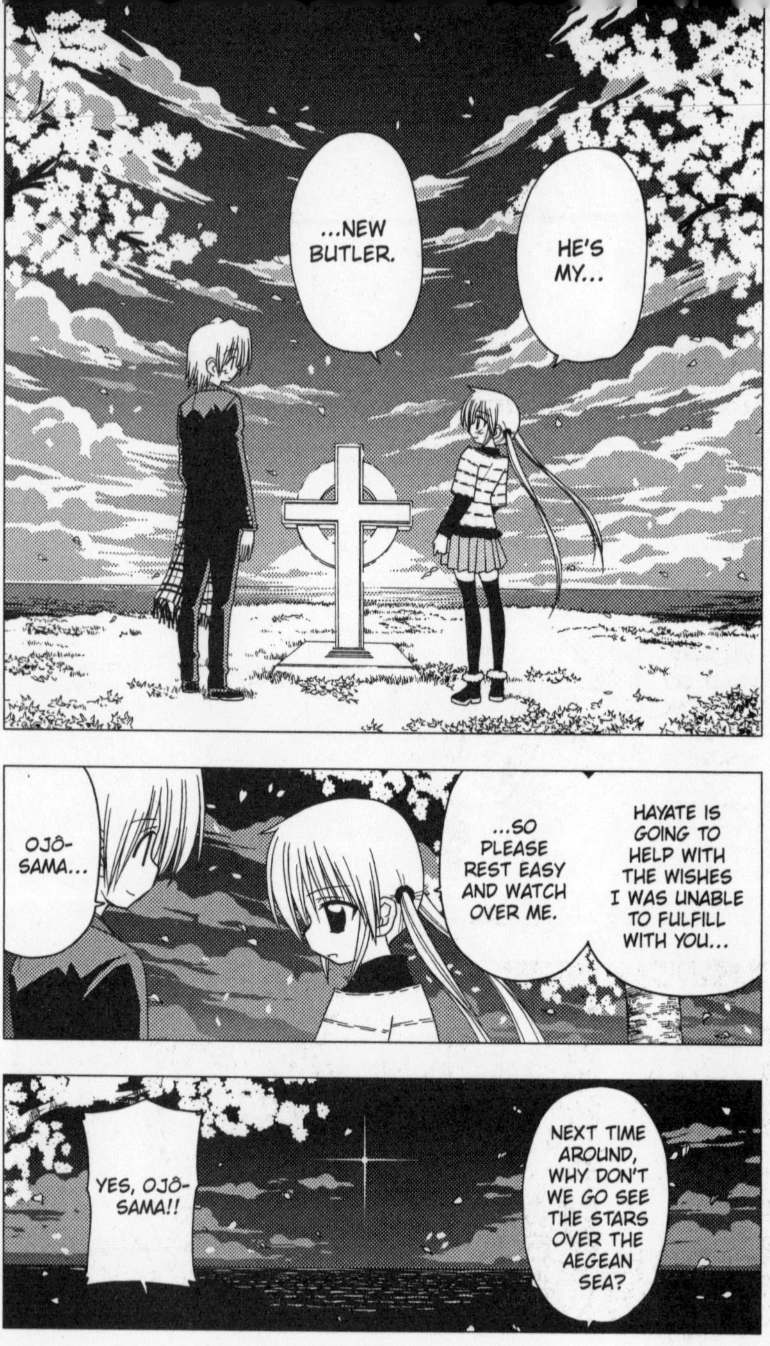
HE'S MY...
...NEW BUTLER.
HAYATE IS GOING TO HELP WITH THE WISHES I WAS UNABLE TO FULFILL WITH YOU...
...SO PLEASE REST EASY AND WATCH OVER ME.
OJÔ-SAMA...
NEXT TIME AROUND, WHY DON'T WE GO SEE THE STARS OVER THE AEGEAN SEA?
YES, OJÔ-SAMA!!

Episode 6: "Just as Sp◯der-Man Spends His Day Saving Human Lives Instead of Fighting Monsters like in the Movies, a Butler's Daily Life Is Much the Same"

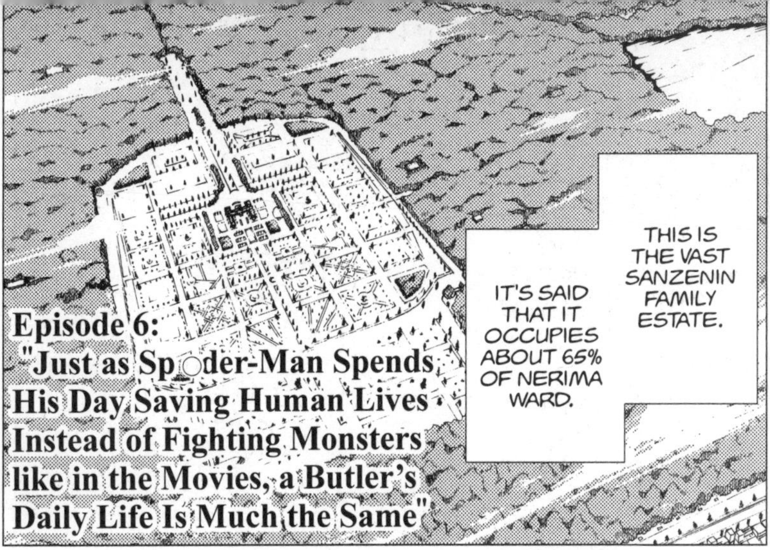
THIS IS THE VAST SANZENIN FAMILY ESTATE.
IT'S SAID THAT IT OCCUPIES ABOUT 65% OF NERIMA WARD.

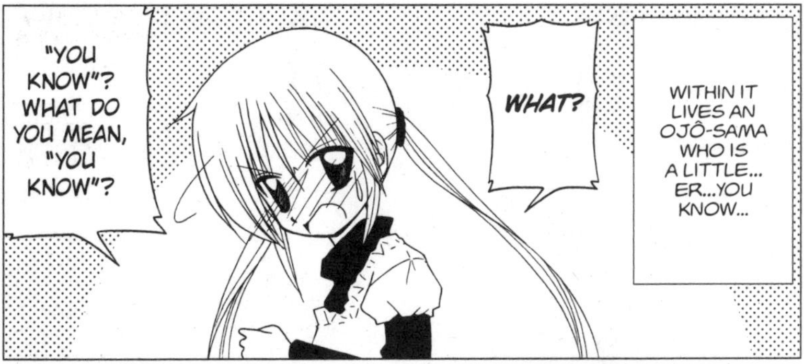
WITHIN IT LIVES AN OJÔ-SAMA WHO IS A LITTLE... ER...YOU KNOW...
WHAT?
"YOU KNOW"? WHAT DO YOU MEAN, "YOU KNOW"?

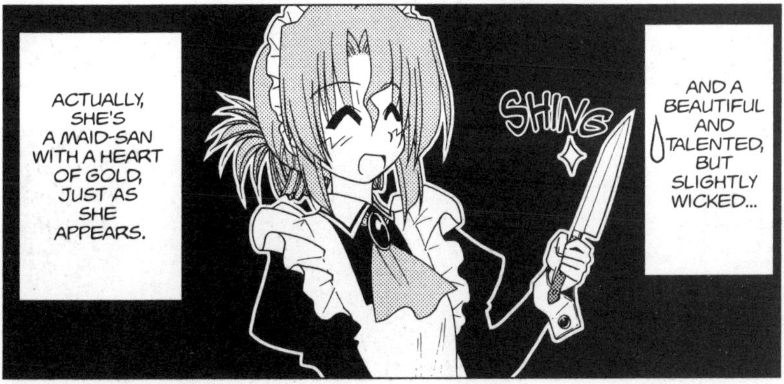
AND A BEAUTIFUL AND TALENTED, BUT SLIGHTLY WICKED...
SHING
ACTUALLY, SHE'S A MAID-SAN WITH A HEART OF GOLD, JUST AS SHE APPEARS.

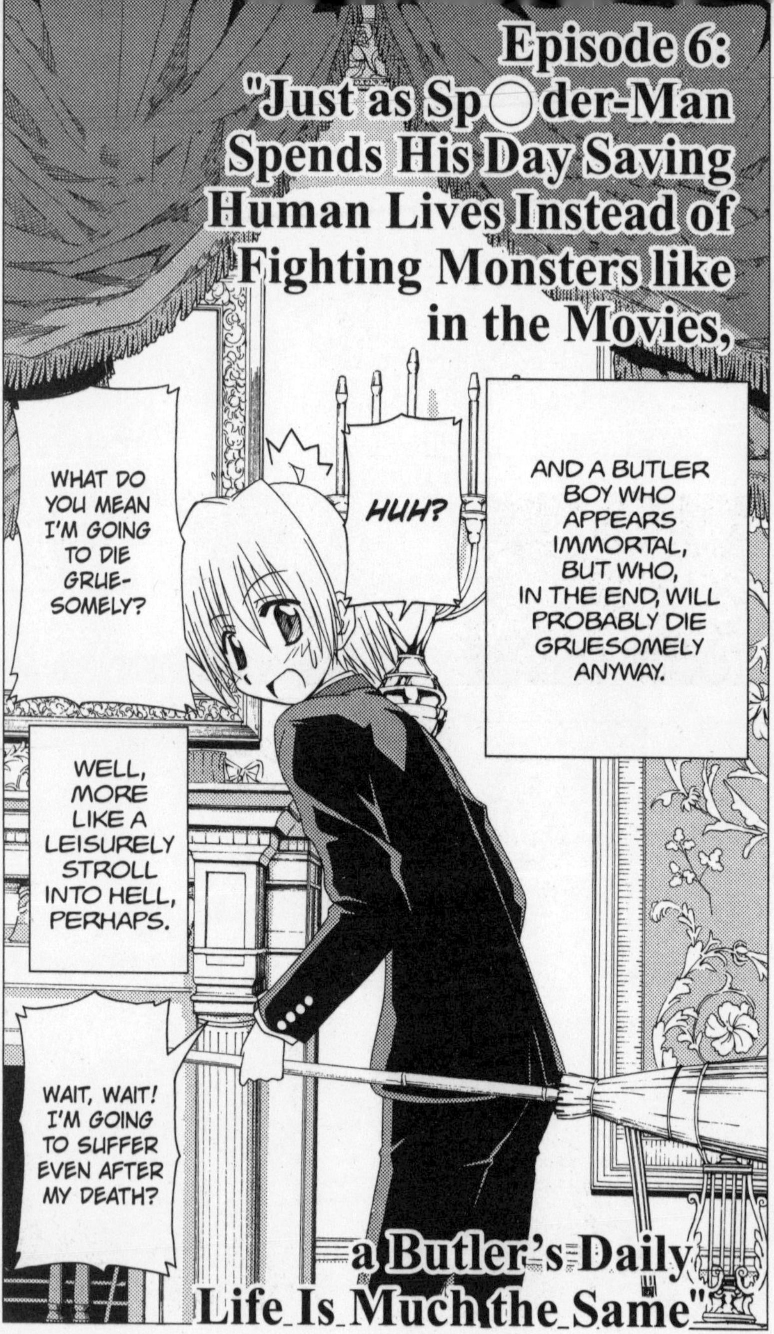
Episode 6:
"Just as Sp○der-Man Spends His Day Saving Human Lives Instead of Fighting Monsters like in the Movies,
AND A BUTLER BOY WHO APPEARS IMMORTAL, BUT WHO, IN THE END, WILL PROBABLY DIE GRUESOMELY ANYWAY.
HUH?
WHAT DO YOU MEAN I'M GOING TO DIE GRUE-SOMELY?
WELL, MORE LIKE A LEISURELY STROLL INTO HELL, PERHAPS.
WAIT, WAIT! I'M GOING TO SUFFER EVEN AFTER MY DEATH?
a Butler's Daily Life Is Much the Same"

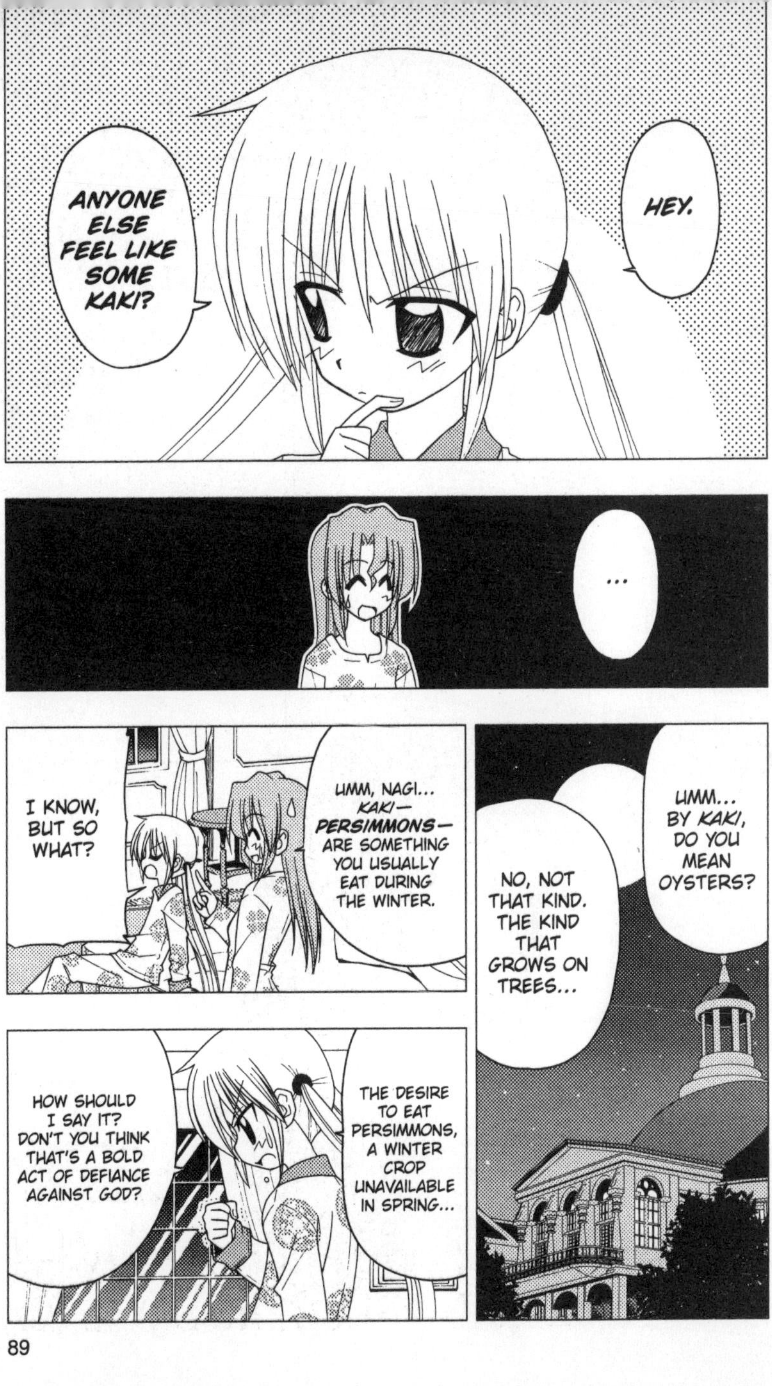
HEY.
ANYONE ELSE FEEL LIKE SOME KAKI?
...
UMM... BY KAKI, DO YOU MEAN OYSTERS?
NO, NOT THAT KIND. THE KIND THAT GROWS ON TREES...
UMM, NAGI... KAKI—PERSIMMONS—ARE SOMETHING YOU USUALLY EAT DURING THE WINTER.
I KNOW, BUT SO WHAT?
THE DESIRE TO EAT PERSIMMONS, A WINTER CROP UNAVAILABLE IN SPRING...
HOW SHOULD I SAY IT? DON'T YOU THINK THAT'S A BOLD ACT OF DEFIANCE AGAINST GOD?

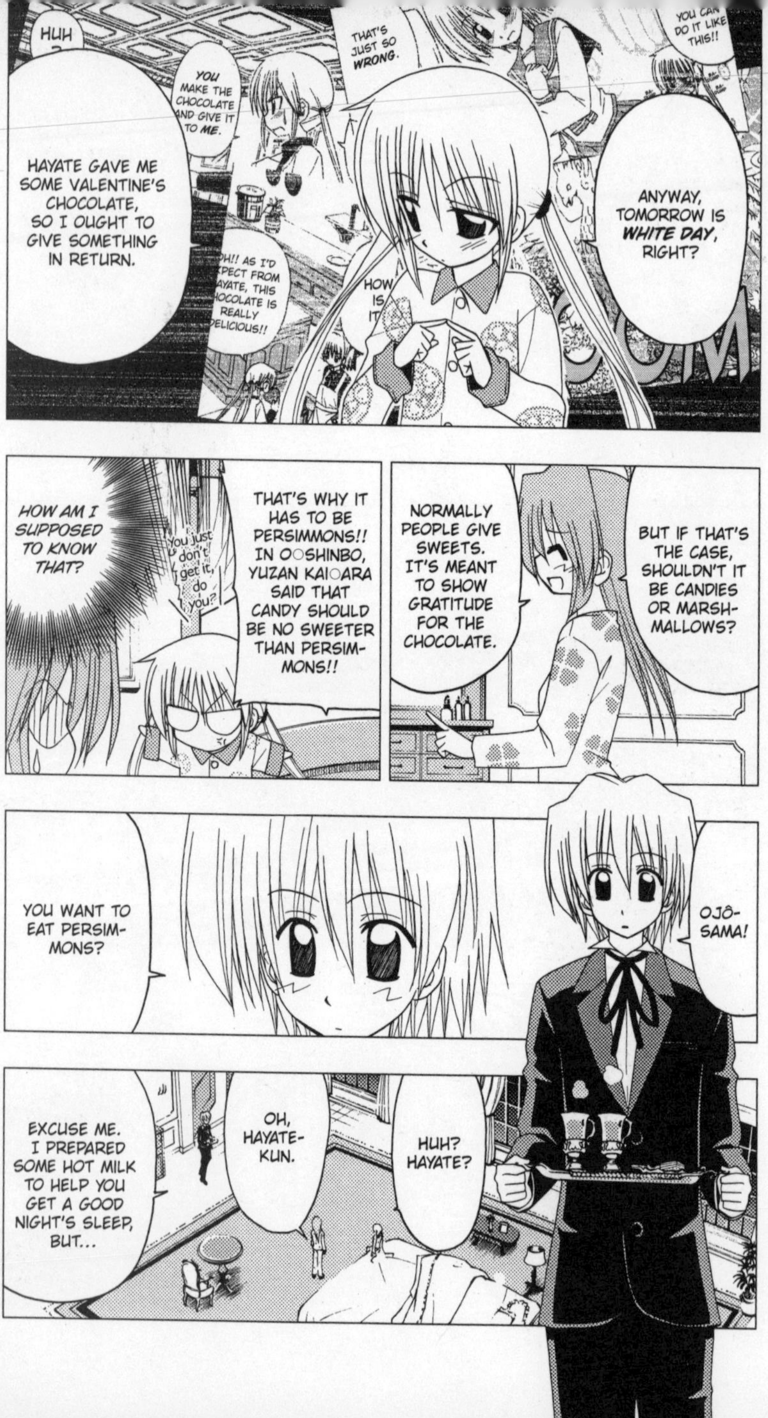

ANYWAY, TOMORROW IS WHITE DAY, RIGHT?
YOU CAN DO IT LIKE THIS!!
THAT'S JUST SO WRONG.
HOW IS IT
H!! AS I'D XPECT FROM AYATE, THIS HOCOLATE IS REALLY ELICIOUS!!
YOU MAKE THE CHOCOLATE AND GIVE IT TO ME.
HUH
HAYATE GAVE ME SOME VALENTINE'S CHOCOLATE, SO I OUGHT TO GIVE SOMETHING IN RETURN.
BUT IF THAT'S THE CASE, SHOULDN'T IT BE CANDIES OR MARSH-MALLOWS?
NORMALLY PEOPLE GIVE SWEETS. IT'S MEANT TO SHOW GRATITUDE FOR THE CHOCOLATE.
THAT'S WHY IT HAS TO BE PERSIMMONS!! IN O○SHINBO, YUZAN KAI○ARA SAID THAT CANDY SHOULD BE NO SWEETER THAN PERSIM-MONS!!
You just don't get it, do you?
HOW AM I SUPPOSED TO KNOW THAT?
OJÔ-SAMA!
YOU WANT TO EAT PERSIM-MONS?
HUH? HAYATE?
OH, HAYATE-KUN.
EXCUSE ME. I PREPARED SOME HOT MILK TO HELP YOU GET A GOOD NIGHT'S SLEEP, BUT...

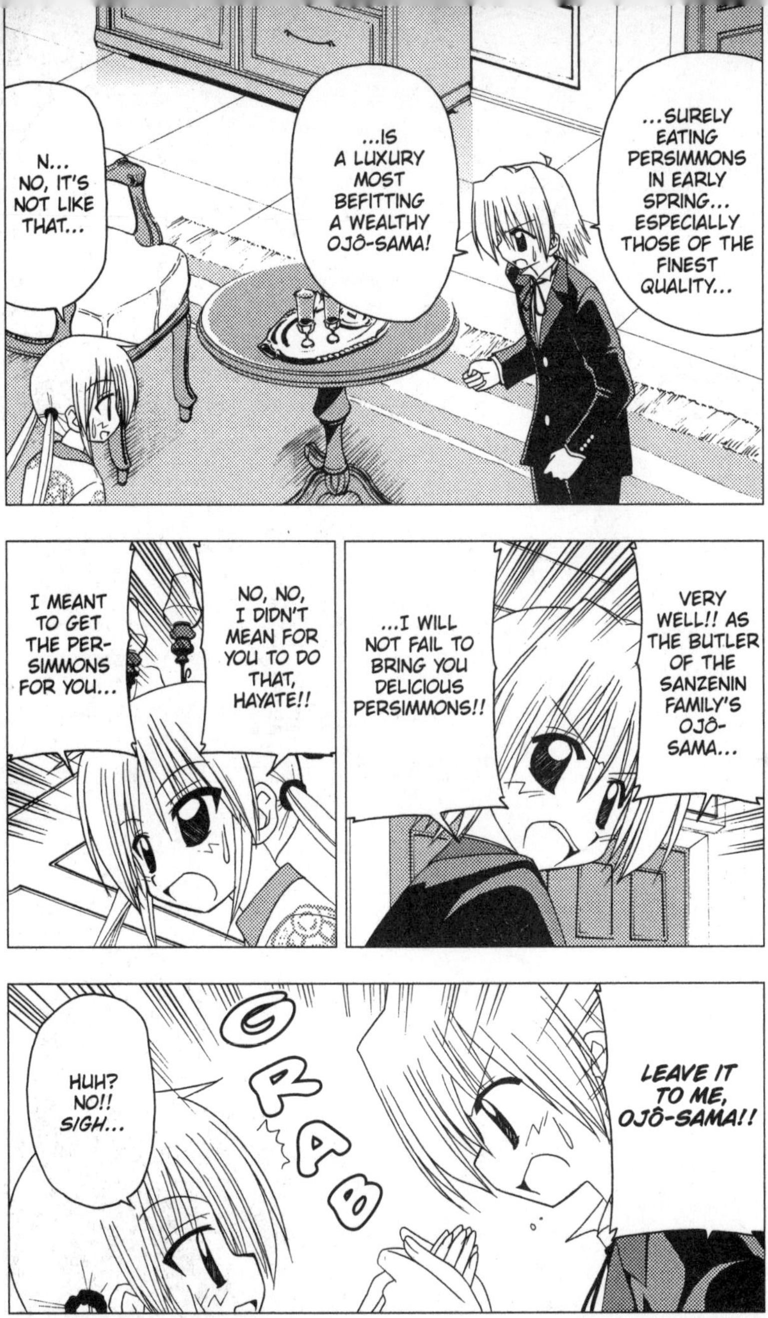
...SURELY EATING PERSIMMONS IN EARLY SPRING... ESPECIALLY THOSE OF THE FINEST QUALITY...
...IS A LUXURY MOST BEFITTING A WEALTHY OJÔ-SAMA!
N... NO, IT'S NOT LIKE THAT...
VERY WELL!! AS THE BUTLER OF THE SANZENIN FAMILY'S OJÔ-SAMA...
...I WILL NOT FAIL TO BRING YOU DELICIOUS PERSIMMONS!!
NO, NO, I DIDN'T MEAN FOR YOU TO DO THAT, HAYATE!!
I MEANT TO GET THE PER-SIMMONS FOR YOU...
LEAVE IT TO ME, OJÔ-SAMA!!
GRAB
HUH? NO!! SIGH...

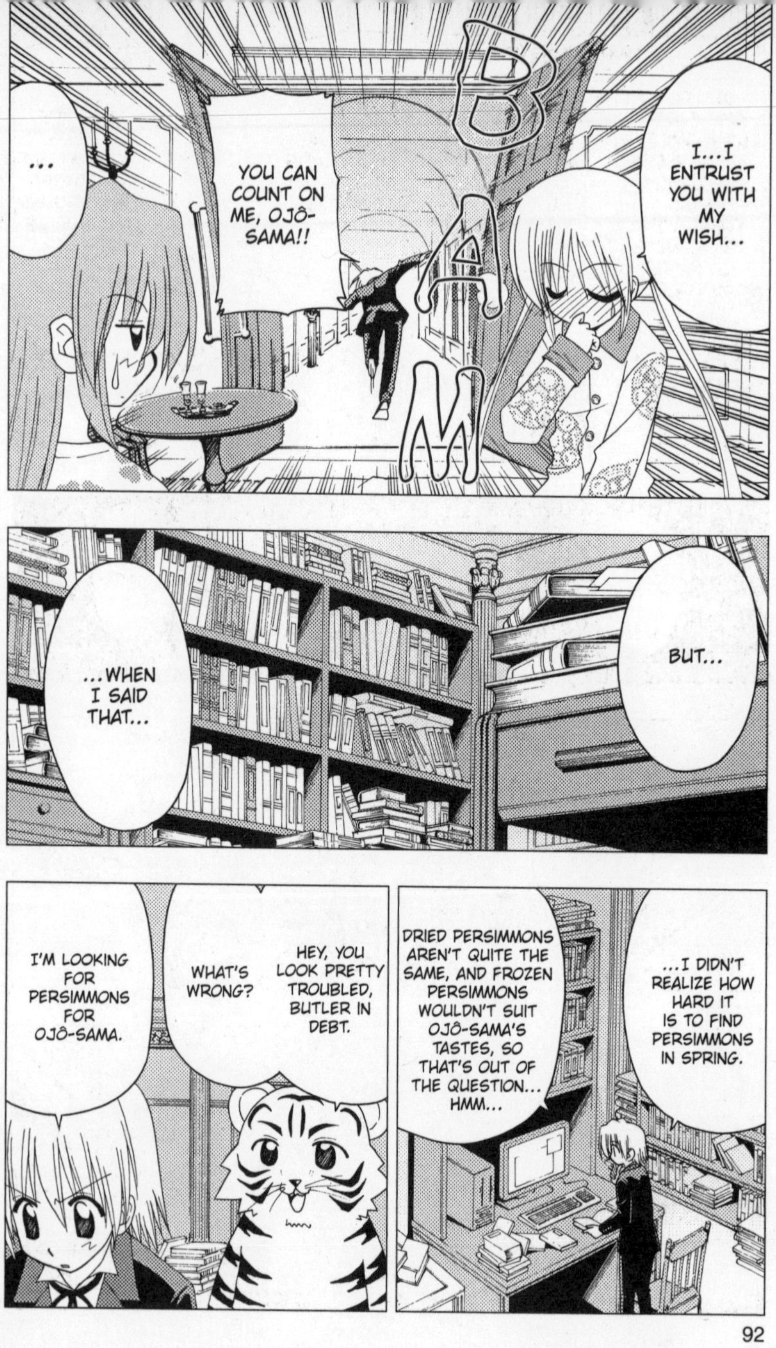
I...I ENTRUST YOU WITH MY WISH...
YOU CAN COUNT ON ME, OJÔ-SAMA!!
BAM
...
BUT...
...WHEN I SAID THAT...
...I DIDN'T REALIZE HOW HARD IT IS TO FIND PERSIMMONS IN SPRING.
DRIED PERSIMMONS AREN'T QUITE THE SAME, AND FROZEN PERSIMMONS WOULDN'T SUIT OJÔ-SAMA'S TASTES, SO THAT'S OUT OF THE QUESTION... HMM...
HEY, YOU LOOK PRETTY TROUBLED, BUTLER IN DEBT.
WHAT'S WRONG?
I'M LOOKING FOR PERSIMMONS FOR OJÔ-SAMA.

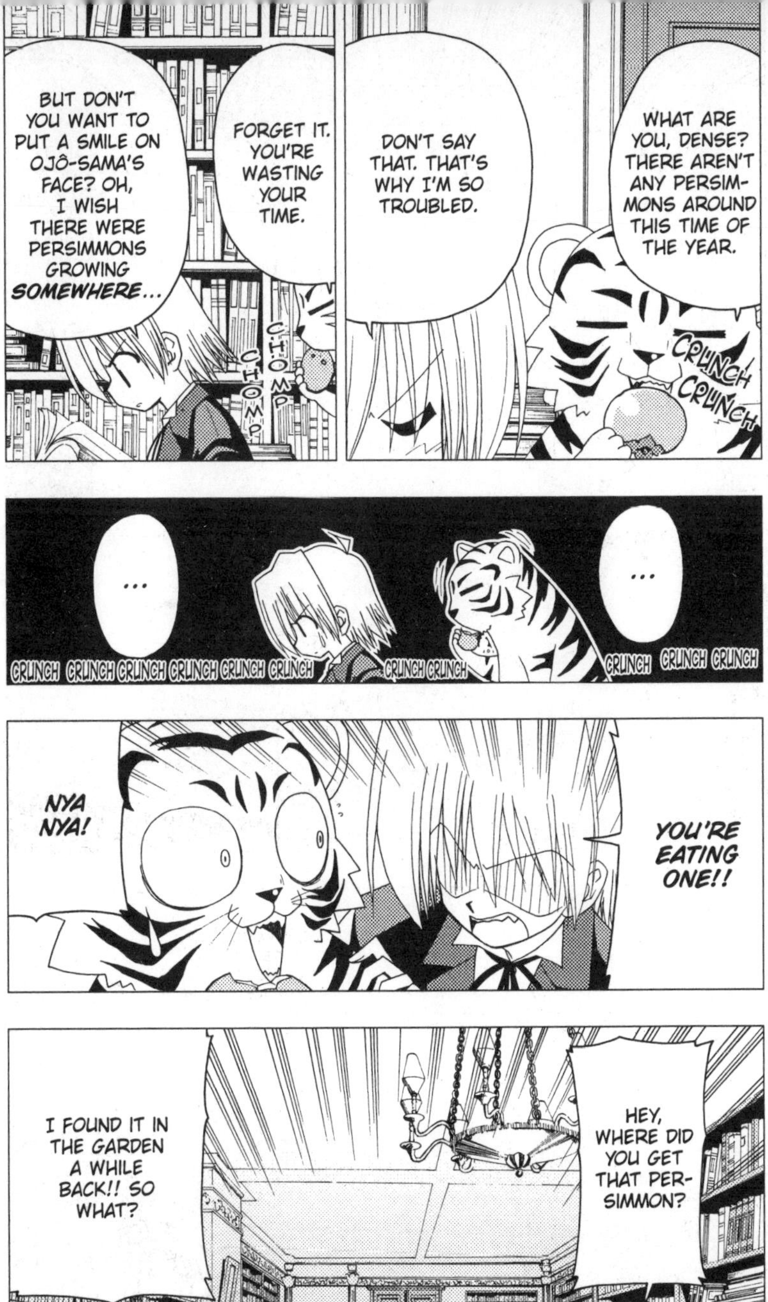
WHAT ARE YOU, DENSE? THERE AREN'T ANY PERSIM-MONS AROUND THIS TIME OF THE YEAR.
DON'T SAY THAT. THAT'S WHY I'M SO TROUBLED.
CRUNCH CRUNCH
FORGET IT. YOU'RE WASTING YOUR TIME.
BUT DON'T YOU WANT TO PUT A SMILE ON OJÔ-SAMA'S FACE? OH, I WISH THERE WERE PERSIMMONS GROWING **SOMEWHERE**...
CHOMP CHOMP
...
...
CRUNCH CRUNCH CRUNCH CRUNCH CRUNCH CRUNCH CRUNCH CRUNCH CRUNCH CRUNCH CRUNCH CRUNCH
YOU'RE EATING ONE!!
NYA NYA!
HEY, WHERE DID YOU GET THAT PER-SIMMON?
I FOUND IT IN THE GARDEN A WHILE BACK!! SO WHAT?

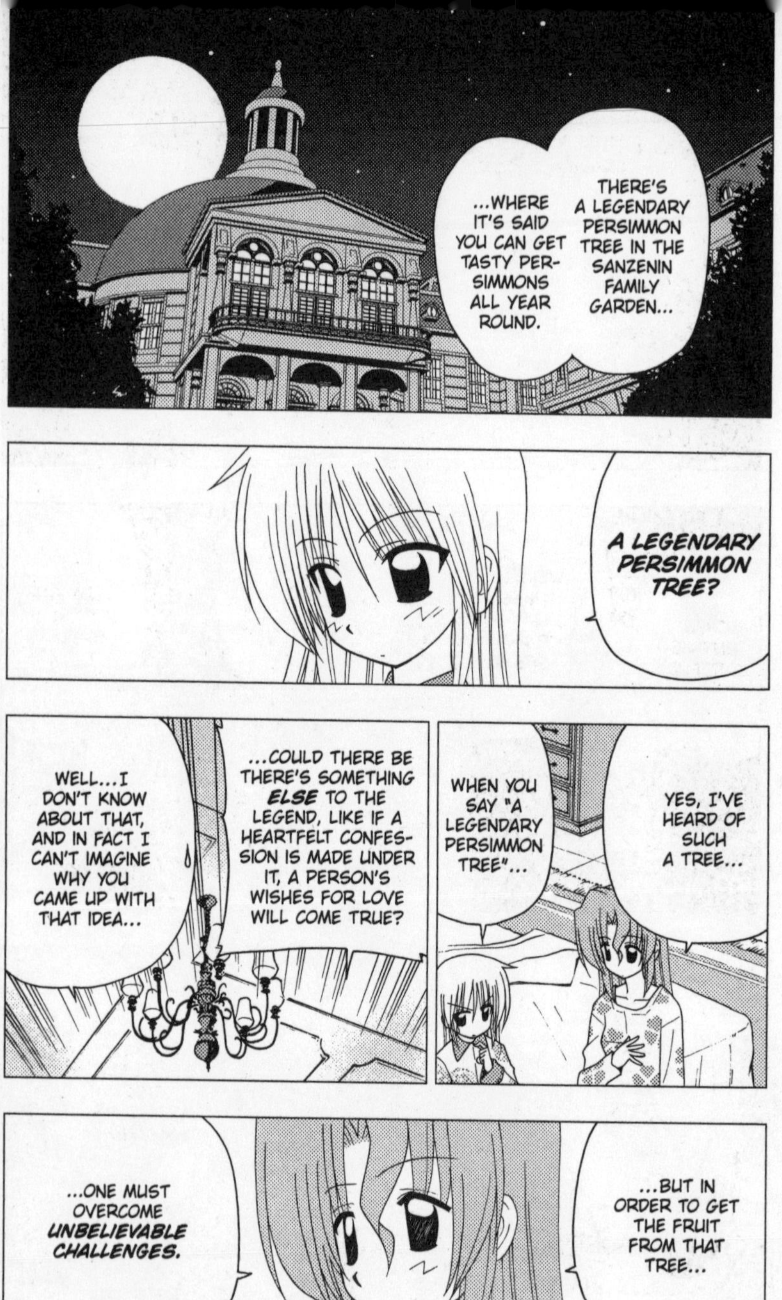
THERE'S A LEGENDARY PERSIMMON TREE IN THE SANZENIN FAMILY GARDEN...
...WHERE IT'S SAID YOU CAN GET TASTY PERSIMMONS ALL YEAR ROUND.
A LEGENDARY PERSIMMON TREE?
YES, I'VE HEARD OF SUCH A TREE...
WHEN YOU SAY "A LEGENDARY PERSIMMON TREE"...
...COULD THERE BE THERE'S SOMETHING ELSE TO THE LEGEND, LIKE IF A HEARTFELT CONFESSION IS MADE UNDER IT, A PERSON'S WISHES FOR LOVE WILL COME TRUE?
WELL...I DON'T KNOW ABOUT THAT, AND IN FACT I CAN'T IMAGINE WHY YOU CAME UP WITH THAT IDEA...
...BUT IN ORDER TO GET THE FRUIT FROM THAT TREE...
...ONE MUST OVERCOME UNBELIEVABLE CHALLENGES.

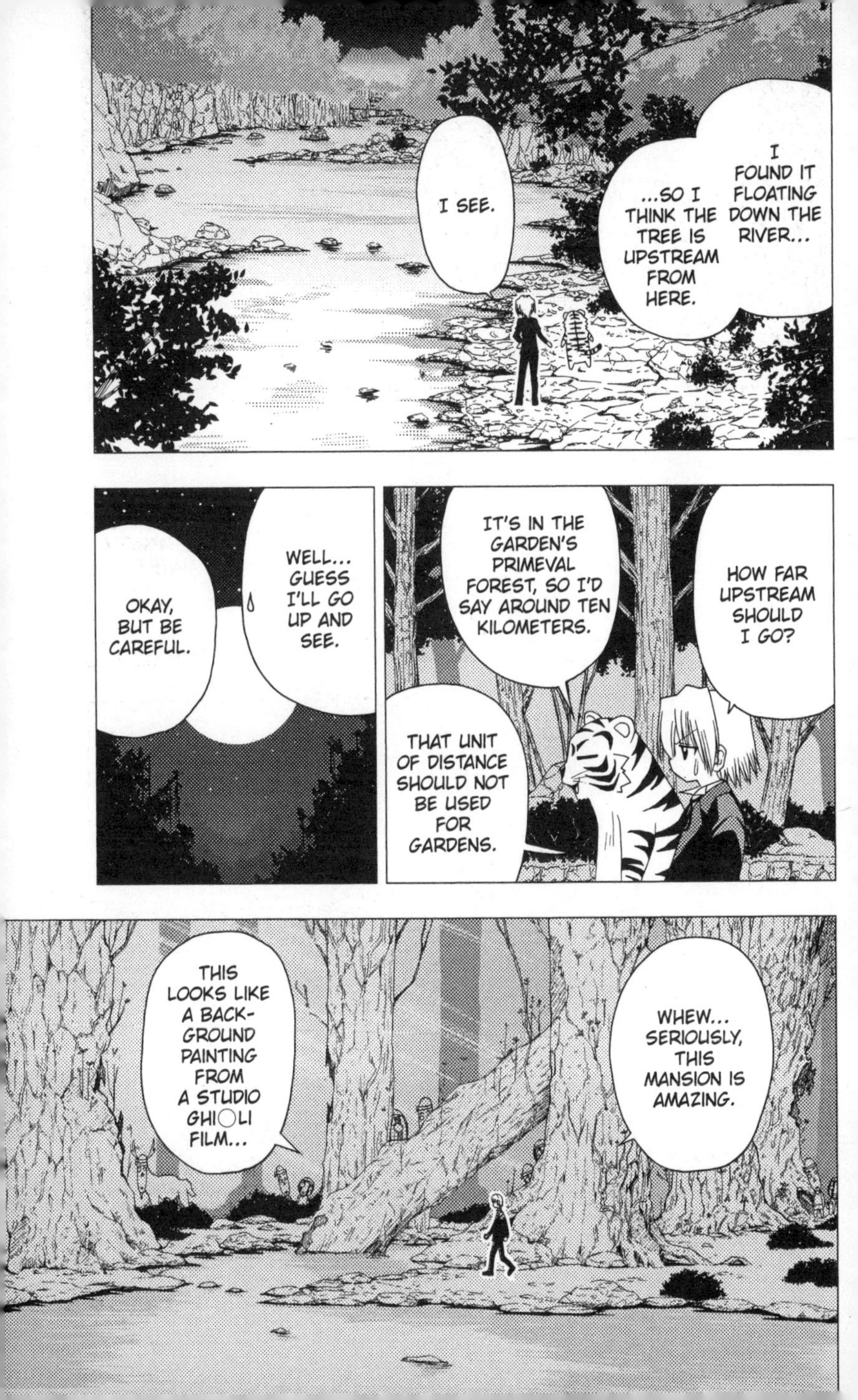I FOUND IT FLOATING DOWN THE RIVER...
...SO I THINK THE TREE IS UPSTREAM FROM HERE.
I SEE.
HOW FAR UPSTREAM SHOULD I GO?
IT'S IN THE GARDEN'S PRIMEVAL FOREST, SO I'D SAY AROUND TEN KILOMETERS.
THAT UNIT OF DISTANCE SHOULD NOT BE USED FOR GARDENS.
WELL... GUESS I'LL GO UP AND SEE.
OKAY, BUT BE CAREFUL.
WHEW... SERIOUSLY, THIS MANSION IS AMAZING.
THIS LOOKS LIKE A BACK-GROUND PAINTING FROM A STUDIO GHI◯LI FILM...

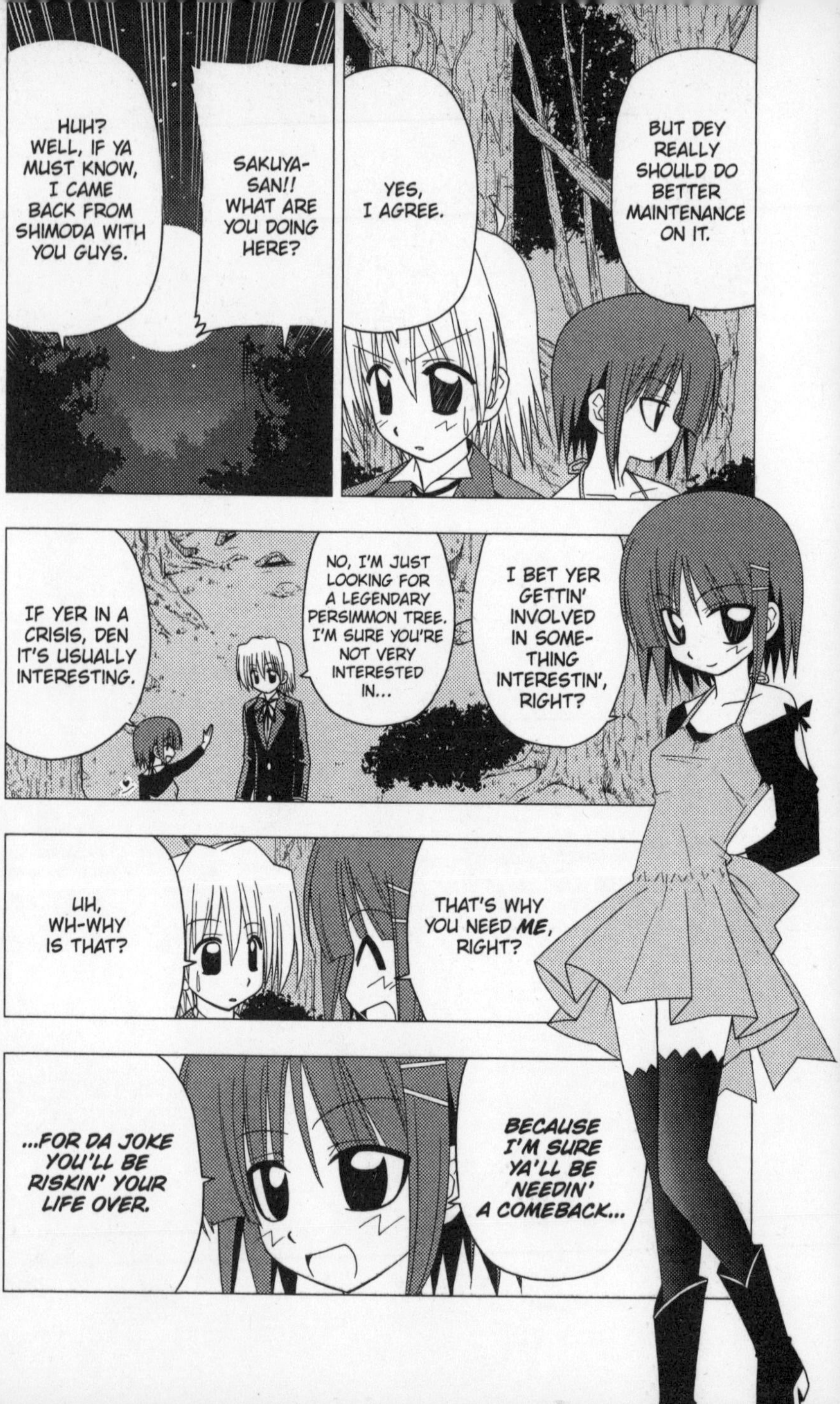
BUT DEY REALLY SHOULD DO BETTER MAINTENANCE ON IT.
YES, I AGREE.
SAKUYA-SAN!! WHAT ARE YOU DOING HERE?
HUH? WELL, IF YA MUST KNOW, I CAME BACK FROM SHIMODA WITH YOU GUYS.
I BET YER GETTIN' INVOLVED IN SOME-THING INTERESTIN', RIGHT?
NO, I'M JUST LOOKING FOR A LEGENDARY PERSIMMON TREE. I'M SURE YOU'RE NOT VERY INTERESTED IN...
IF YER IN A CRISIS, DEN IT'S USUALLY INTERESTING.
THAT'S WHY YOU NEED *ME*, RIGHT?
UH, WH-WHY IS THAT?
BECAUSE I'M SURE YA'LL BE NEEDIN' A COMEBACK...
...FOR DA JOKE YOU'LL BE RISKIN' YOUR LIFE OVER.

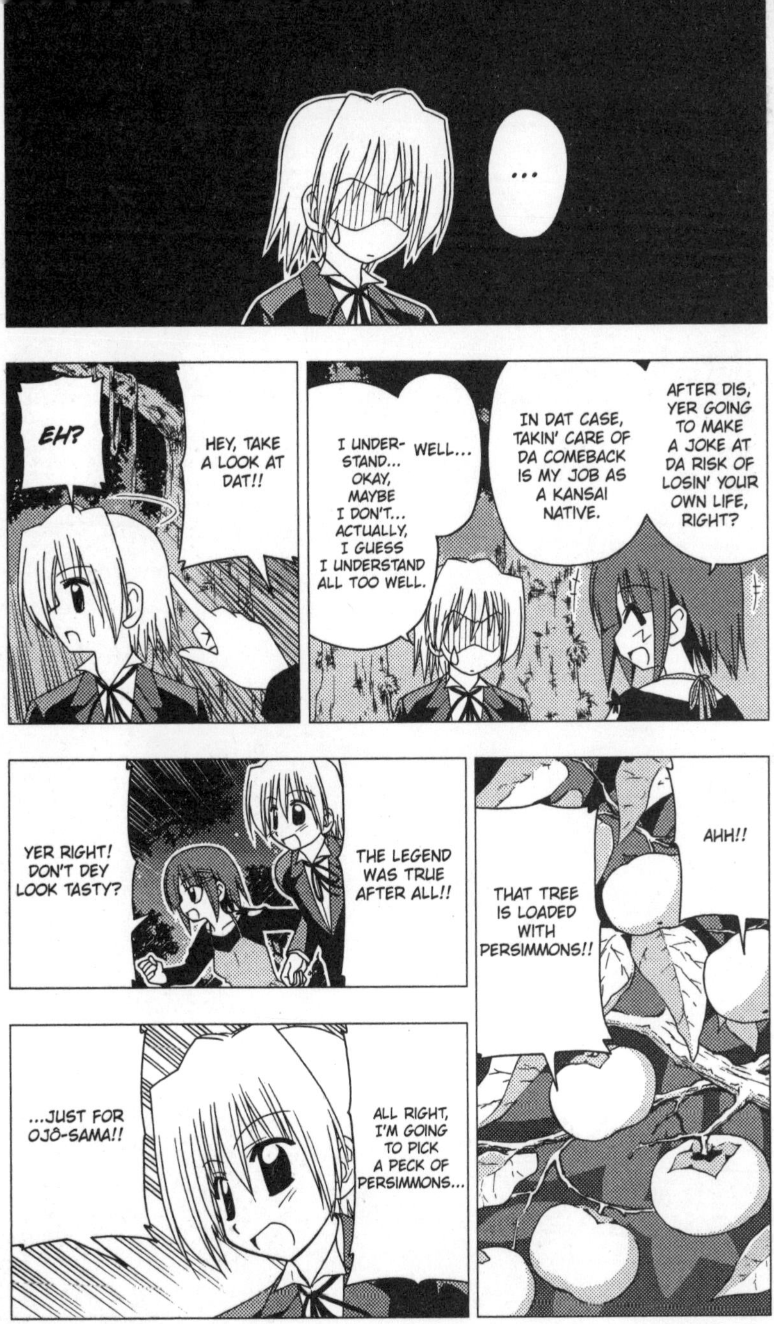
...
AFTER DIS, YER GOING TO MAKE A JOKE AT DA RISK OF LOSIN' YOUR OWN LIFE, RIGHT?
IN DAT CASE, TAKIN' CARE OF DA COMEBACK IS MY JOB AS A KANSAI NATIVE.
WELL...
I UNDER-STAND... OKAY, MAYBE I DON'T... ACTUALLY, I GUESS I UNDERSTAND ALL TOO WELL.
HEY, TAKE A LOOK AT DAT!!
EH?
AHH!!
THAT TREE IS LOADED WITH PERSIMMONS!!
THE LEGEND WAS TRUE AFTER ALL!!
YER RIGHT! DON'T DEY LOOK TASTY?
ALL RIGHT, I'M GOING TO PICK A PECK OF PERSIMMONS...
...JUST FOR OJŌ-SAMA!!

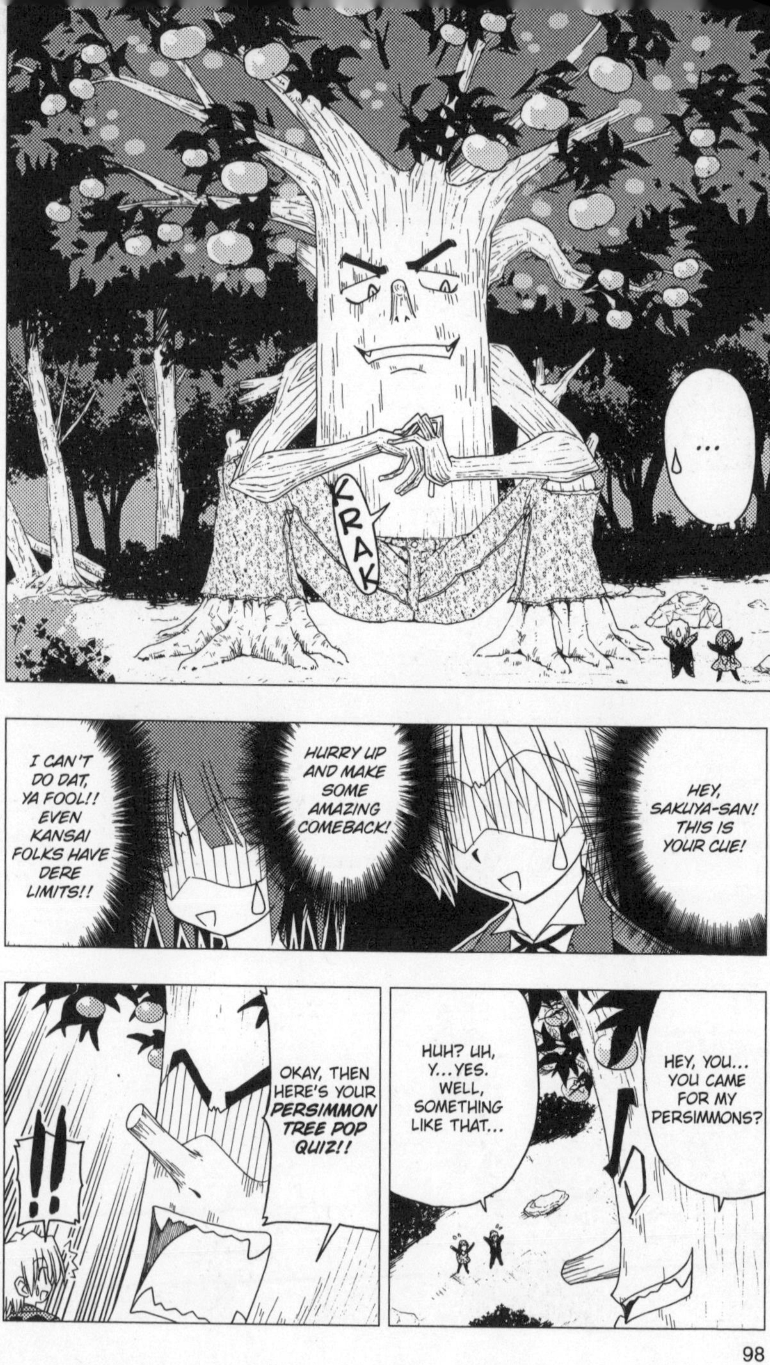
...
KRAK
HEY, SAKUYA-SAN! THIS IS YOUR CUE!
HURRY UP AND MAKE SOME AMAZING COMEBACK!
I CAN'T DO DAT, YA FOOL!! EVEN KANSAI FOLKS HAVE DERE LIMITS!!
HEY, YOU... YOU CAME FOR MY PERSIMMONS?
HUH? UH, Y...YES. WELL, SOMETHING LIKE THAT...
OKAY, THEN HERE'S YOUR PERSIMMON TREE POP QUIZ!!
!!

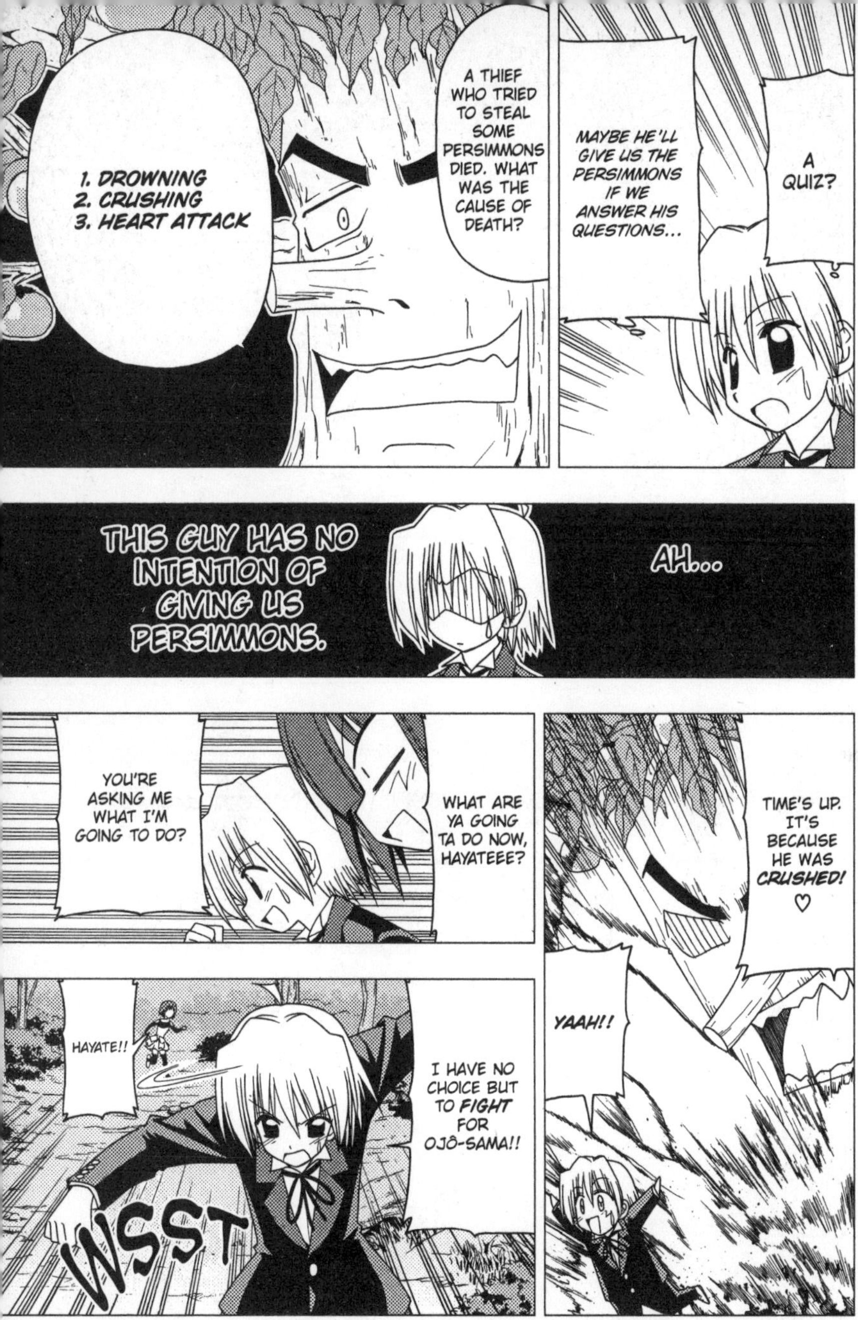
A QUIZ?
MAYBE HE'LL GIVE US THE PERSIMMONS IF WE ANSWER HIS QUESTIONS...
A THIEF WHO TRIED TO STEAL SOME PERSIMMONS DIED. WHAT WAS THE CAUSE OF DEATH?
1. DROWNING 2. CRUSHING 3. HEART ATTACK
AH...
THIS GUY HAS NO INTENTION OF GIVING US PERSIMMONS.
TIME'S UP. IT'S BECAUSE HE WAS **CRUSHED!** ♡
YAAH!!
WHAT ARE YA GOING TA DO NOW, HAYATEEE?
YOU'RE ASKING ME WHAT I'M GOING TO DO?
I HAVE NO CHOICE BUT TO **FIGHT** FOR OJÔ-SAMA!!
HAYATE!!
WSST

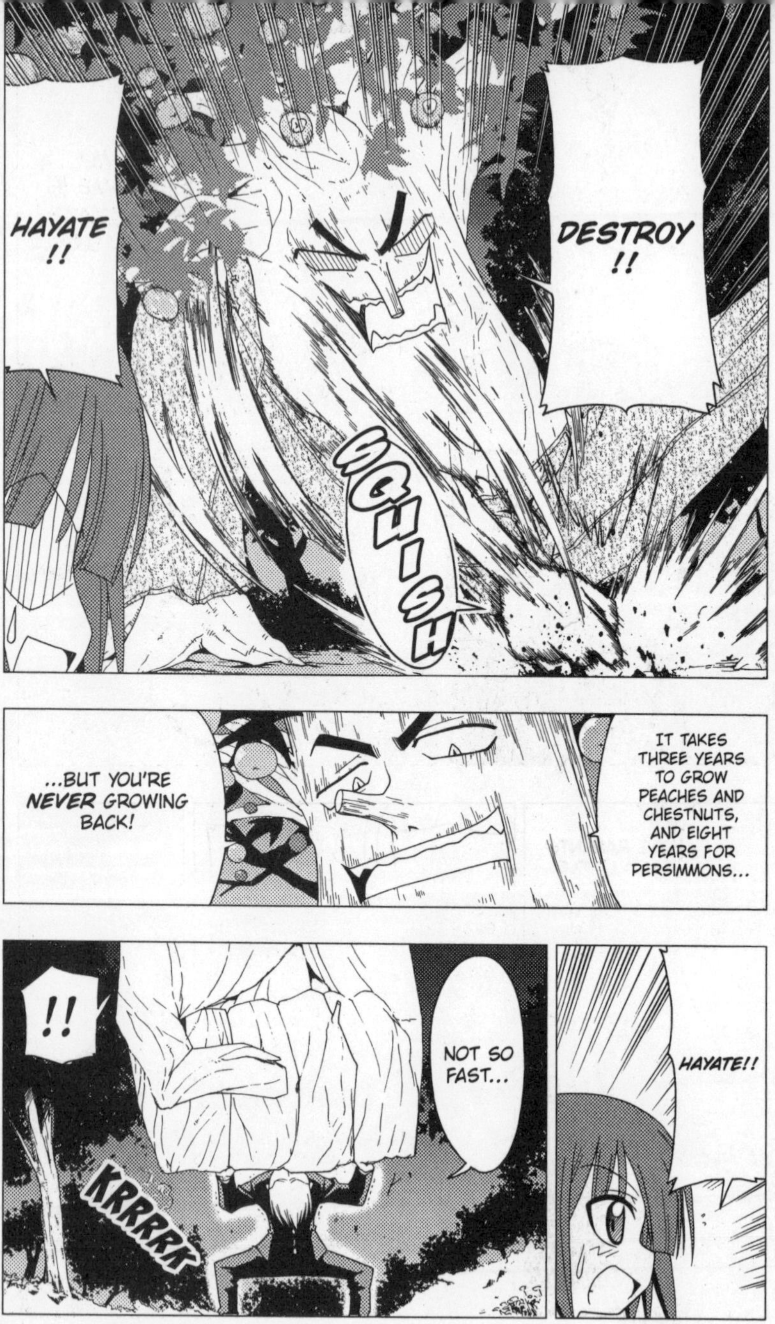
DESTROY!!
HAYATE!!
SQUISH
IT TAKES THREE YEARS TO GROW PEACHES AND CHESTNUTS, AND EIGHT YEARS FOR PERSIMMONS...
...BUT YOU'RE *NEVER* GROWING BACK!
HAYATE!!
NOT SO FAST...
!!
KRRRRK

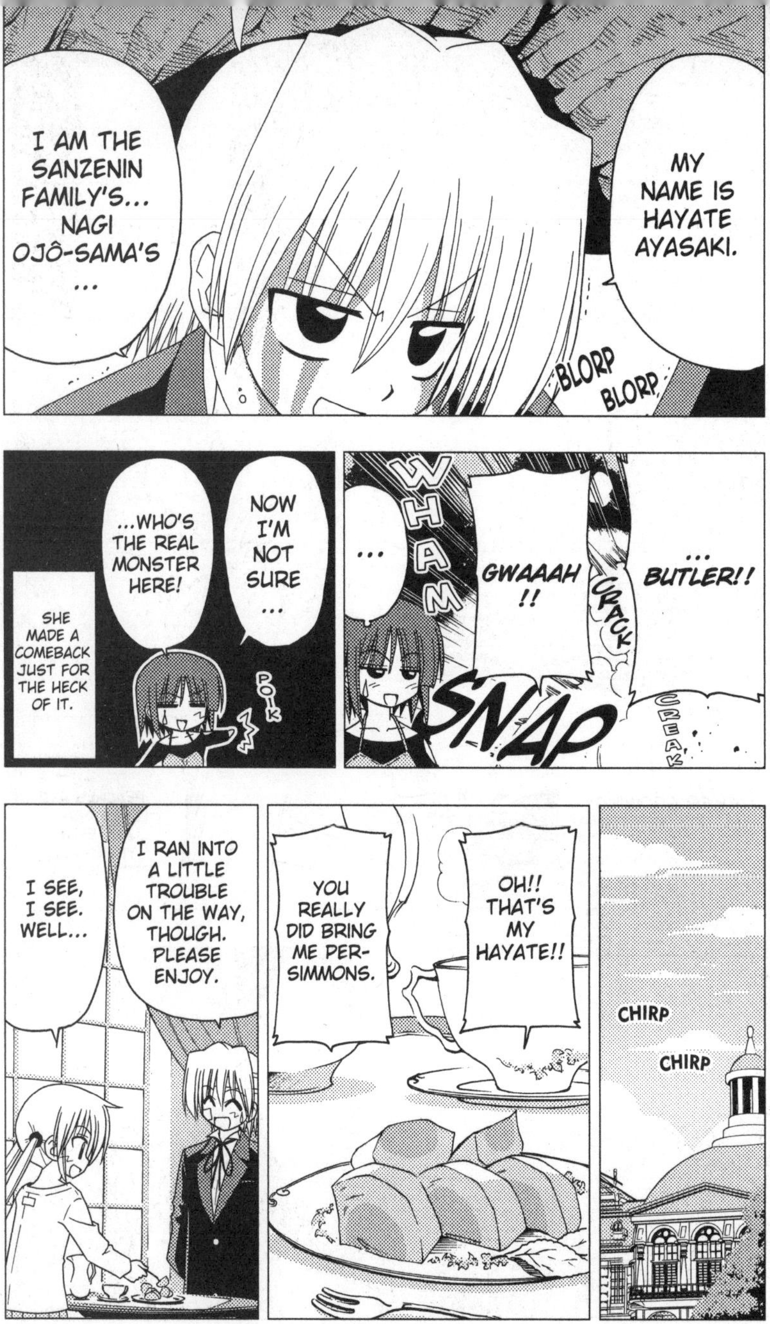
MY NAME IS HAYATE AYASAKI.
I AM THE SANZENIN FAMILY'S... NAGI OJÔ-SAMA'S ...
BLORP BLORP
... BUTLER!!
CRACK
CREAK
GWAAAH !!
WHAM
...
SNAP
NOW I'M NOT SURE ...
...WHO'S THE REAL MONSTER HERE!
POIK
SHE MADE A COMEBACK JUST FOR THE HECK OF IT.
CHIRP
CHIRP
OH!! THAT'S MY HAYATE!!
YOU REALLY DID BRING ME PER-SIMMONS.
I RAN INTO A LITTLE TROUBLE ON THE WAY, THOUGH. PLEASE ENJOY.
I SEE, I SEE. WELL...

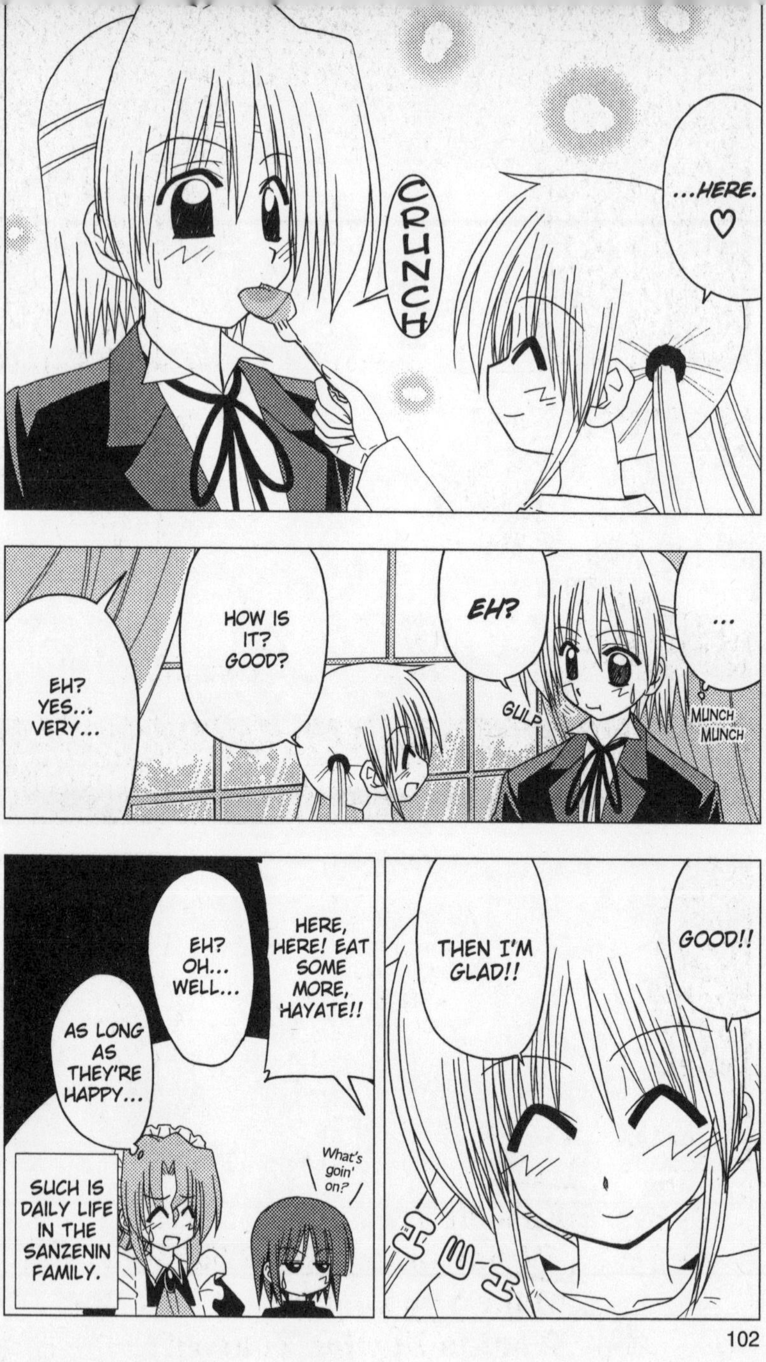
...HERE. ♡
CRUNCH
...
MUNCH MUNCH
EH?
GULP
HOW IS IT? GOOD?
EH? YES... VERY...
GOOD!!
THEN I'M GLAD!!
HERE, HERE! EAT SOME MORE, HAYATE!!
EH? OH... WELL...
AS LONG AS THEY'RE HAPPY...
What's goin' on?
SUCH IS DAILY LIFE IN THE SANZENIN FAMILY.

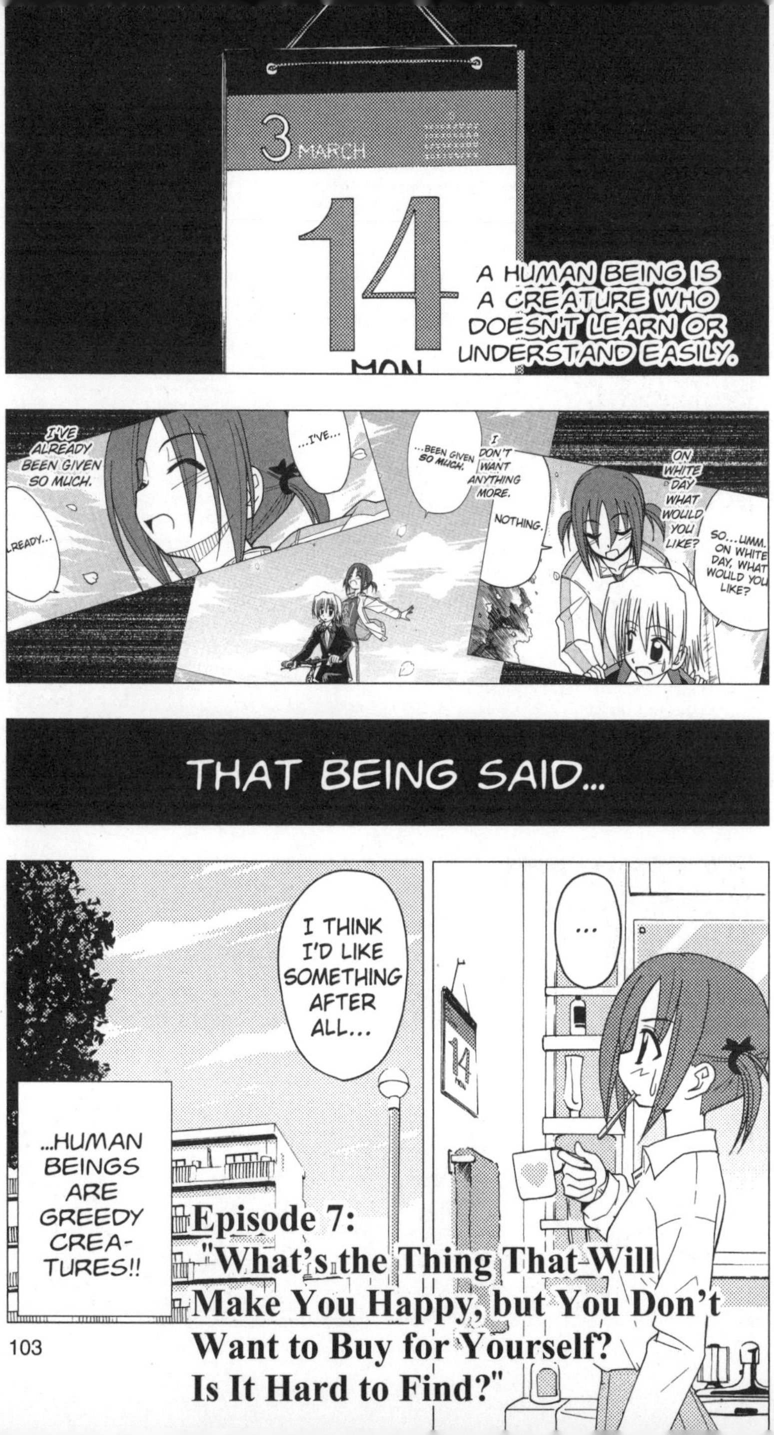
3 MARCH
14
MON
A HUMAN BEING IS A CREATURE WHO DOESN'T LEARN OR UNDERSTAND EASILY.
SO…UMM. ON WHITE DAY, WHAT WOULD YOU LIKE?
ON WHITE DAY WHAT WOULD YOU LIKE?
I DON'T WANT ANYTHING MORE.
NOTHING.
…BEEN GIVEN SO MUCH.
…I'VE…
READY…
I'VE ALREADY BEEN GIVEN SO MUCH.
THAT BEING SAID…
…
I THINK I'D LIKE SOMETHING AFTER ALL…
…HUMAN BEINGS ARE GREEDY CREATURES!!
Episode 7: "What's the Thing That Will Make You Happy, but You Don't Want to Buy for Yourself? Is It Hard to Find?"

Episode 7:
"What's the Thing That Will Make You Happy, but You Don't Want to Buy for Yourself? Is It Hard to Find?"

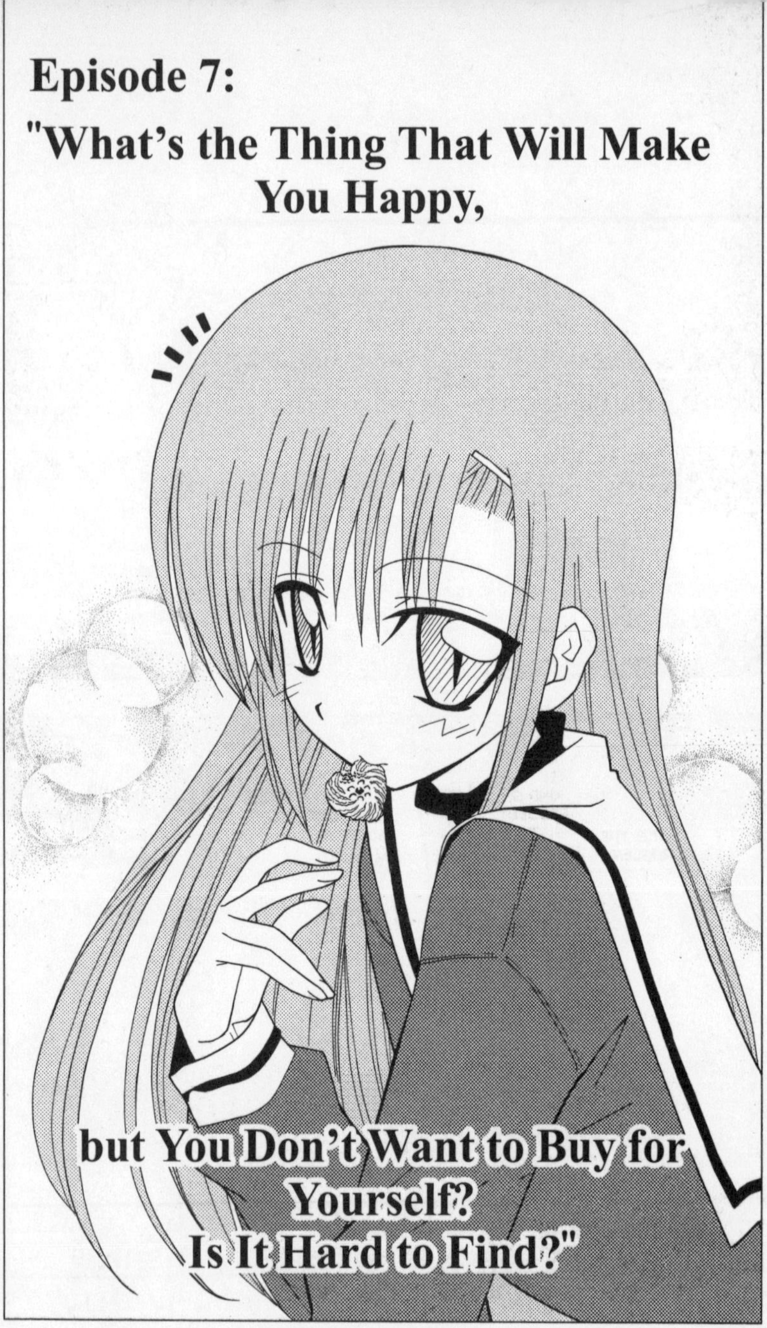

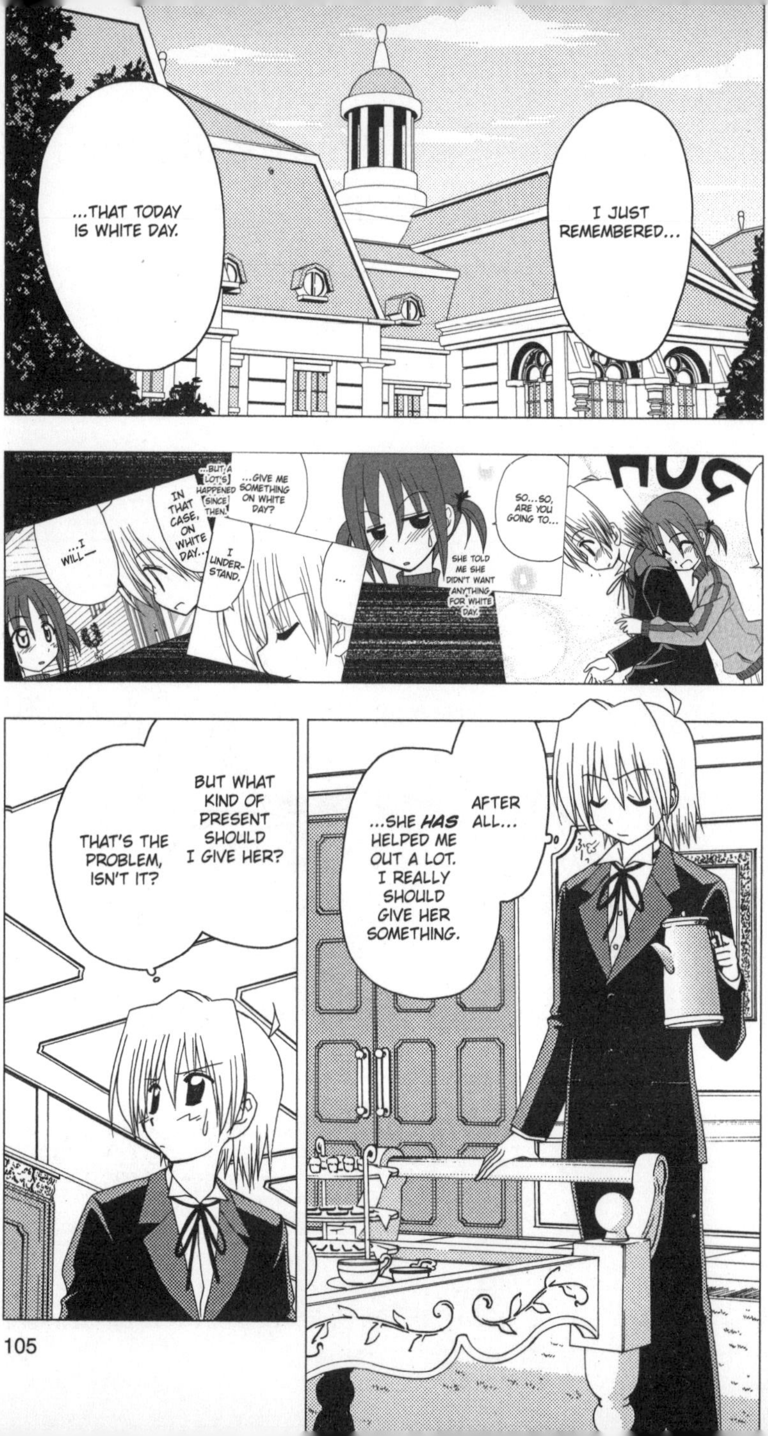
I JUST REMEMBERED...
...THAT TODAY IS WHITE DAY.
SO...SO, ARE YOU GOING TO...
SHE TOLD ME SHE DIDN'T WANT ANYTHING FOR WHITE DAY.
...GIVE ME SOMETHING ON WHITE DAY?
...
I UNDERSTAND.
...BUT A LOT'S HAPPENED SINCE THEN.
IN THAT CASE, ON WHITE DAY...
...I WILL—
AFTER ALL...
...SHE *HAS* HELPED ME OUT A LOT. I REALLY SHOULD GIVE HER SOMETHING.
BUT WHAT KIND OF PRESENT SHOULD I GIVE HER?
THAT'S THE PROBLEM, ISN'T IT?

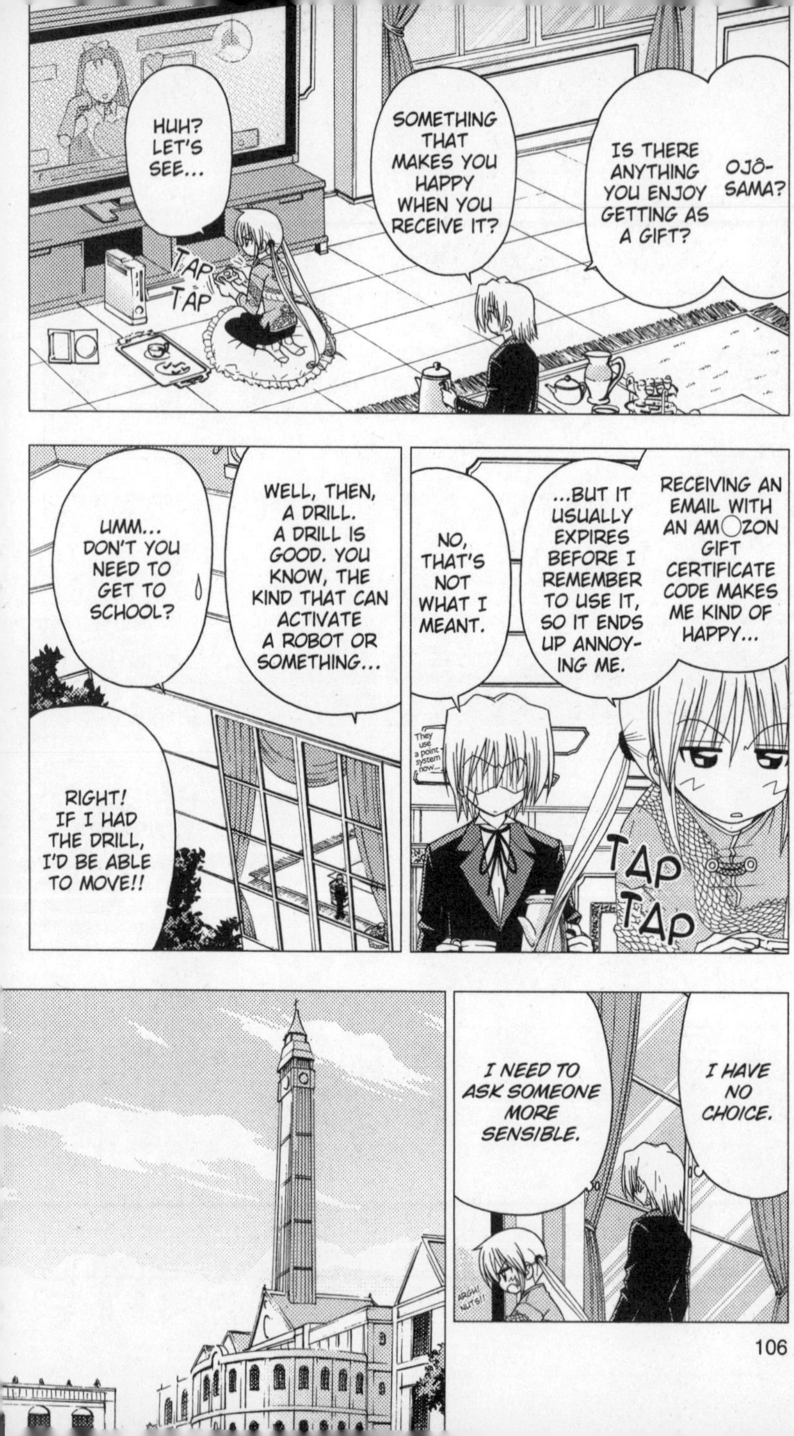
IS THERE ANYTHING YOU ENJOY GETTING AS A GIFT? OJÔ-SAMA?
SOMETHING THAT MAKES YOU HAPPY WHEN YOU RECEIVE IT?
HUH? LET'S SEE...
TAP TAP
RECEIVING AN EMAIL WITH AN AM◯ZON GIFT CERTIFICATE CODE MAKES ME KIND OF HAPPY...
...BUT IT USUALLY EXPIRES BEFORE I REMEMBER TO USE IT, SO IT ENDS UP ANNOYING ME.
NO, THAT'S NOT WHAT I MEANT.
They use a point system now...
TAP TAP
WELL, THEN, A DRILL. A DRILL IS GOOD. YOU KNOW, THE KIND THAT CAN ACTIVATE A ROBOT OR SOMETHING...
UMM... DON'T YOU NEED TO GET TO SCHOOL?
RIGHT! IF I HAD THE DRILL, I'D BE ABLE TO MOVE!!
I HAVE NO CHOICE.
I NEED TO ASK SOMEONE MORE SENSIBLE.
ARGH! NUTS!!

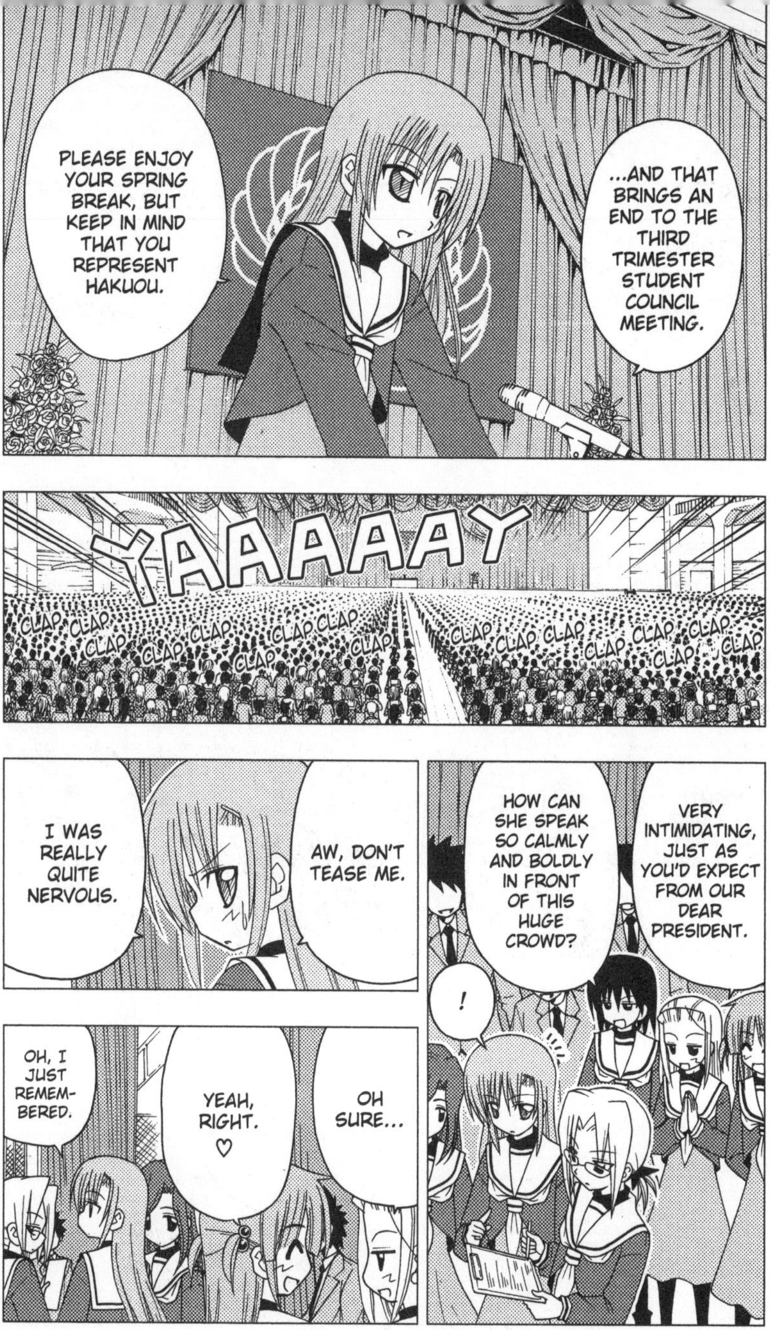
...AND THAT BRINGS AN END TO THE THIRD TRIMESTER STUDENT COUNCIL MEETING.
PLEASE ENJOY YOUR SPRING BREAK, BUT KEEP IN MIND THAT YOU REPRESENT HAKUOU.
YAAAAAY
CLAP CLAP CLAP CLAP CLAP CLAP CLAP CLAP CLAP CLAP CLAP CLAP CLAP CLAP CLAP CLAP CLAP
VERY INTIMIDATING, JUST AS YOU'D EXPECT FROM OUR DEAR PRESIDENT.
HOW CAN SHE SPEAK SO CALMLY AND BOLDLY IN FRONT OF THIS HUGE CROWD?
!
AW, DON'T TEASE ME.
I WAS REALLY QUITE NERVOUS.
OH SURE...
YEAH, RIGHT. ♡
OH, I JUST REMEMBERED.

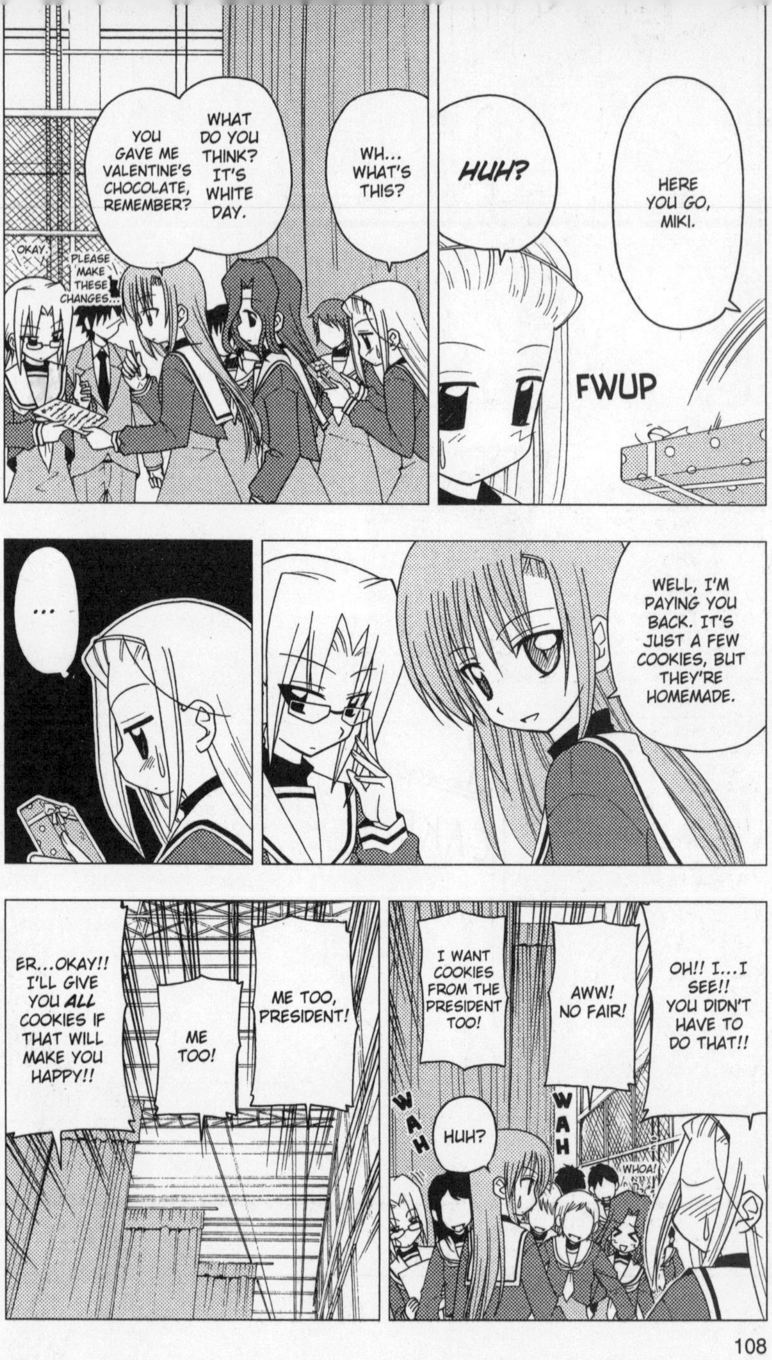
HERE YOU GO, MIKI.
FWUP
HUH?
WH... WHAT'S THIS?
WHAT DO YOU THINK? IT'S WHITE DAY.
YOU GAVE ME VALENTINE'S CHOCOLATE, REMEMBER?
PLEASE MAKE THESE CHANGES...
OKAY.
WELL, I'M PAYING YOU BACK. IT'S JUST A FEW COOKIES, BUT THEY'RE HOMEMADE.
...
OH!! I...I SEE!! YOU DIDN'T HAVE TO DO THAT!!
AWW! NO FAIR!
I WANT COOKIES FROM THE PRESIDENT TOO!
WAH
WHOA!
HUH?
WAH
ME TOO, PRESIDENT!
ME TOO!
ER...OKAY!! I'LL GIVE YOU ALL COOKIES IF THAT WILL MAKE YOU HAPPY!!

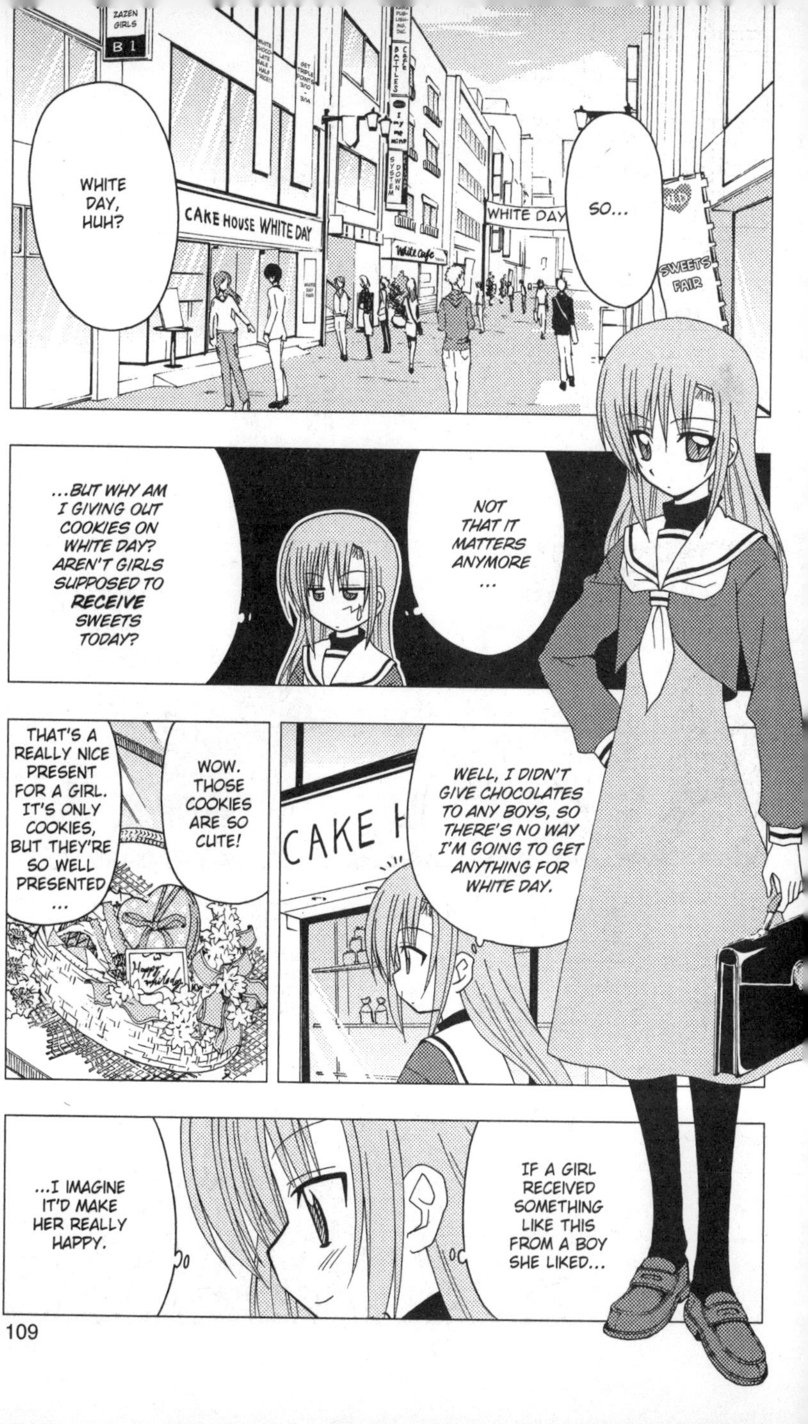
SO...
SWEETS FAIR
WHITE DAY
CAKE HOUSE WHITE DAY
WHITE DAY, HUH?
ZAZEN GIRLS B1
NOT THAT IT MATTERS ANYMORE...
...BUT WHY AM I GIVING OUT COOKIES ON WHITE DAY? AREN'T GIRLS SUPPOSED TO **RECEIVE** SWEETS TODAY?
WELL, I DIDN'T GIVE CHOCOLATES TO ANY BOYS, SO THERE'S NO WAY I'M GOING TO GET ANYTHING FOR WHITE DAY.
CAKE H
WOW. THOSE COOKIES ARE SO CUTE!
THAT'S A REALLY NICE PRESENT FOR A GIRL. IT'S ONLY COOKIES, BUT THEY'RE SO WELL PRESENTED...
IF A GIRL RECEIVED SOMETHING LIKE THIS FROM A BOY SHE LIKED...
...I IMAGINE IT'D MAKE HER REALLY HAPPY.

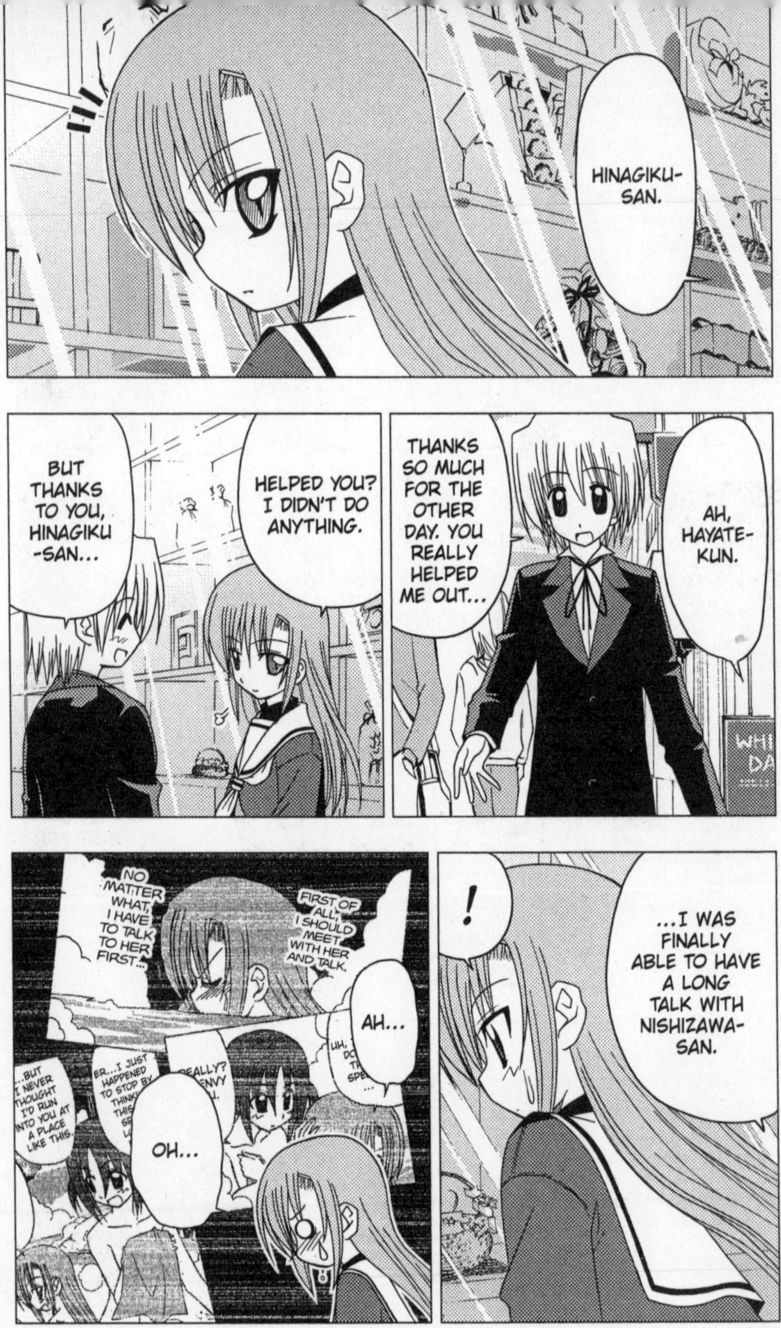
HINAGIKU-SAN.
AH, HAYATE-KUN.
THANKS SO MUCH FOR THE OTHER DAY. YOU REALLY HELPED ME OUT...
HELPED YOU? I DIDN'T DO ANYTHING.
BUT THANKS TO YOU, HINAGIKU-SAN...
...I WAS FINALLY ABLE TO HAVE A LONG TALK WITH NISHIZAWA-SAN.
!
FIRST OF ALL, I SHOULD MEET WITH HER AND TALK.
NO MATTER WHAT, I HAVE TO TALK TO HER FIRST...
AH...
...BUT I NEVER THOUGHT I'D RUN INTO YOU AT A PLACE LIKE THIS.
OH...

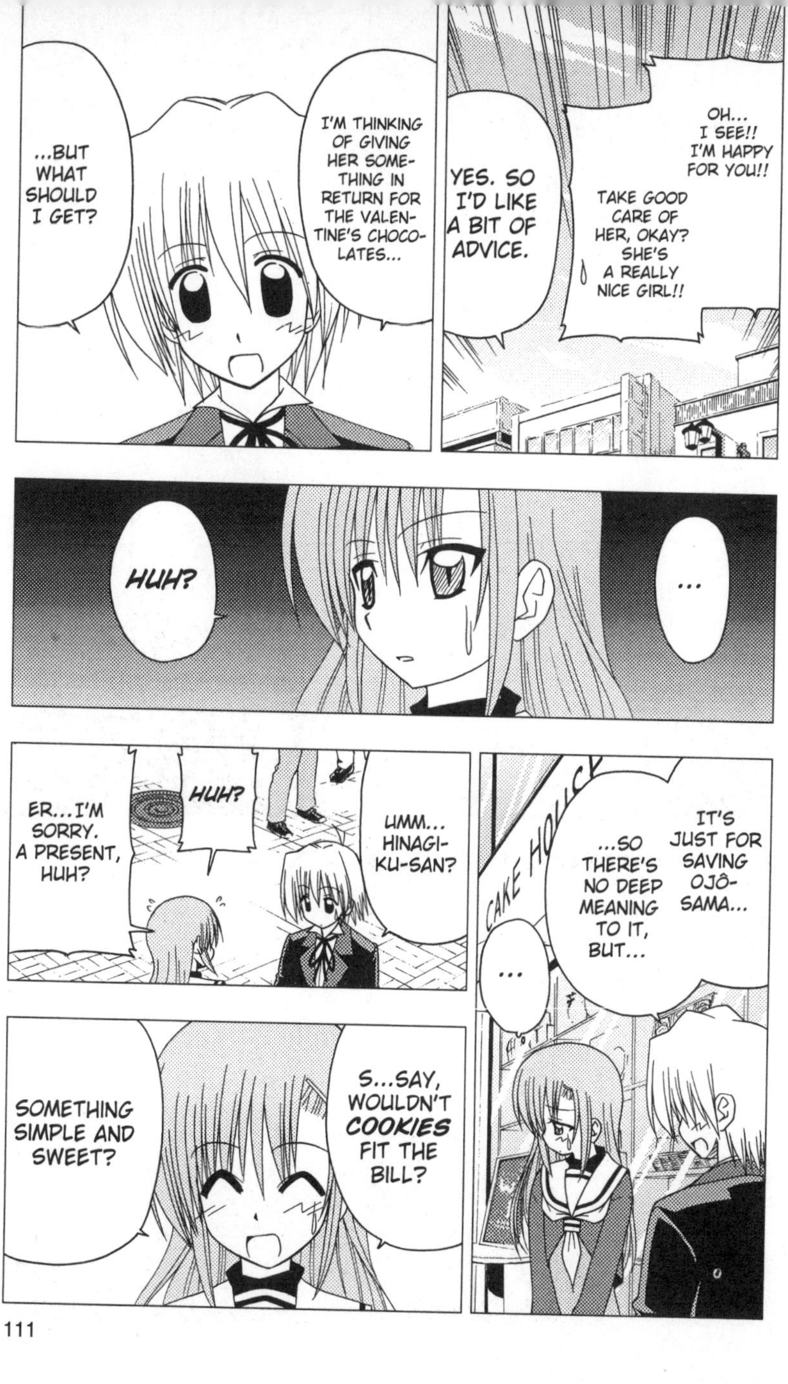
OH... I SEE!! I'M HAPPY FOR YOU!!
TAKE GOOD CARE OF HER, OKAY? SHE'S A REALLY NICE GIRL!!
YES. SO I'D LIKE A BIT OF ADVICE.
I'M THINKING OF GIVING HER SOME-THING IN RETURN FOR THE VALEN-TINE'S CHOCO-LATES...
...BUT WHAT SHOULD I GET?
...
HUH?
IT'S JUST FOR SAVING OJÔ-SAMA...
...SO THERE'S NO DEEP MEANING TO IT, BUT...
...
CAKE HOUSE
UMM... HINAGI-KU-SAN?
HUH?
ER...I'M SORRY. A PRESENT, HUH?
S...SAY, WOULDN'T COOKIES FIT THE BILL?
SOMETHING SIMPLE AND SWEET?

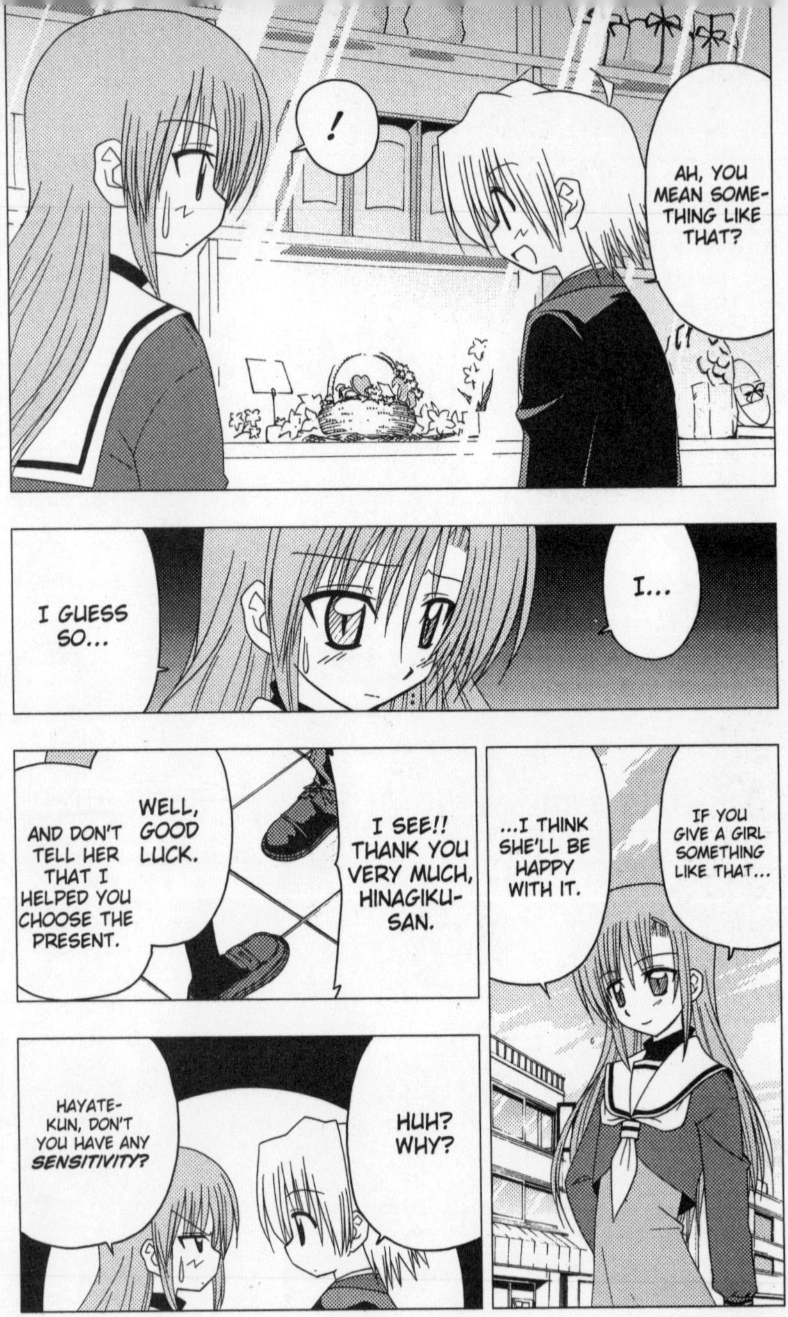
AH, YOU MEAN SOMETHING LIKE THAT?
!
I...
I GUESS SO...
IF YOU GIVE A GIRL SOMETHING LIKE THAT...
...I THINK SHE'LL BE HAPPY WITH IT.
I SEE!! THANK YOU VERY MUCH, HINAGIKU-SAN.
WELL, GOOD LUCK.
AND DON'T TELL HER THAT I HELPED YOU CHOOSE THE PRESENT.
HUH? WHY?
HAYATE-KUN, DON'T YOU HAVE ANY *SENSITIVITY?*

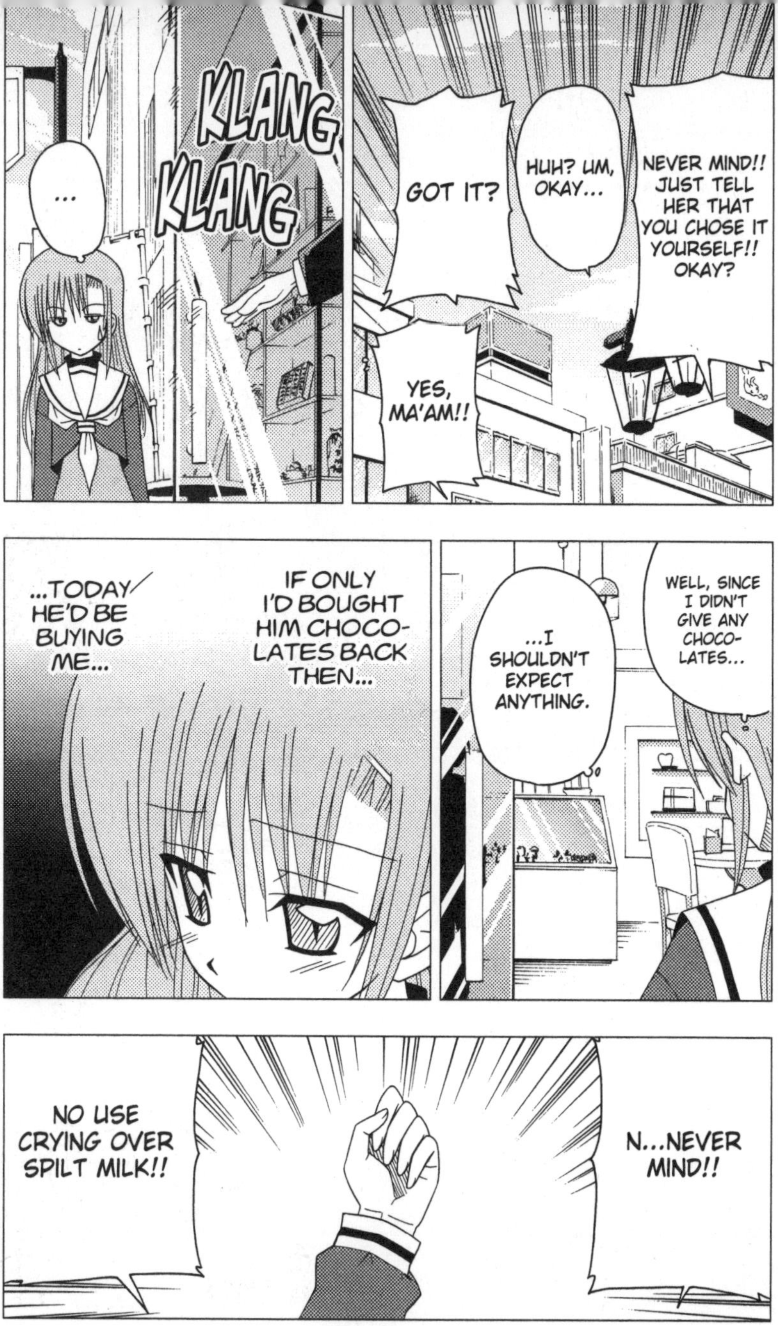

NEVER MIND!! JUST TELL HER THAT YOU CHOSE IT YOURSELF!! OKAY?
HUH? UM, OKAY...
GOT IT?
YES, MA'AM!!
KLANG KLANG
...
WELL, SINCE I DIDN'T GIVE ANY CHOCO-LATES...
...I SHOULDN'T EXPECT ANYTHING.
IF ONLY I'D BOUGHT HIM CHOCO-LATES BACK THEN...
...TODAY HE'D BE BUYING ME...
N...NEVER MIND!!
NO USE CRYING OVER SPILT MILK!!

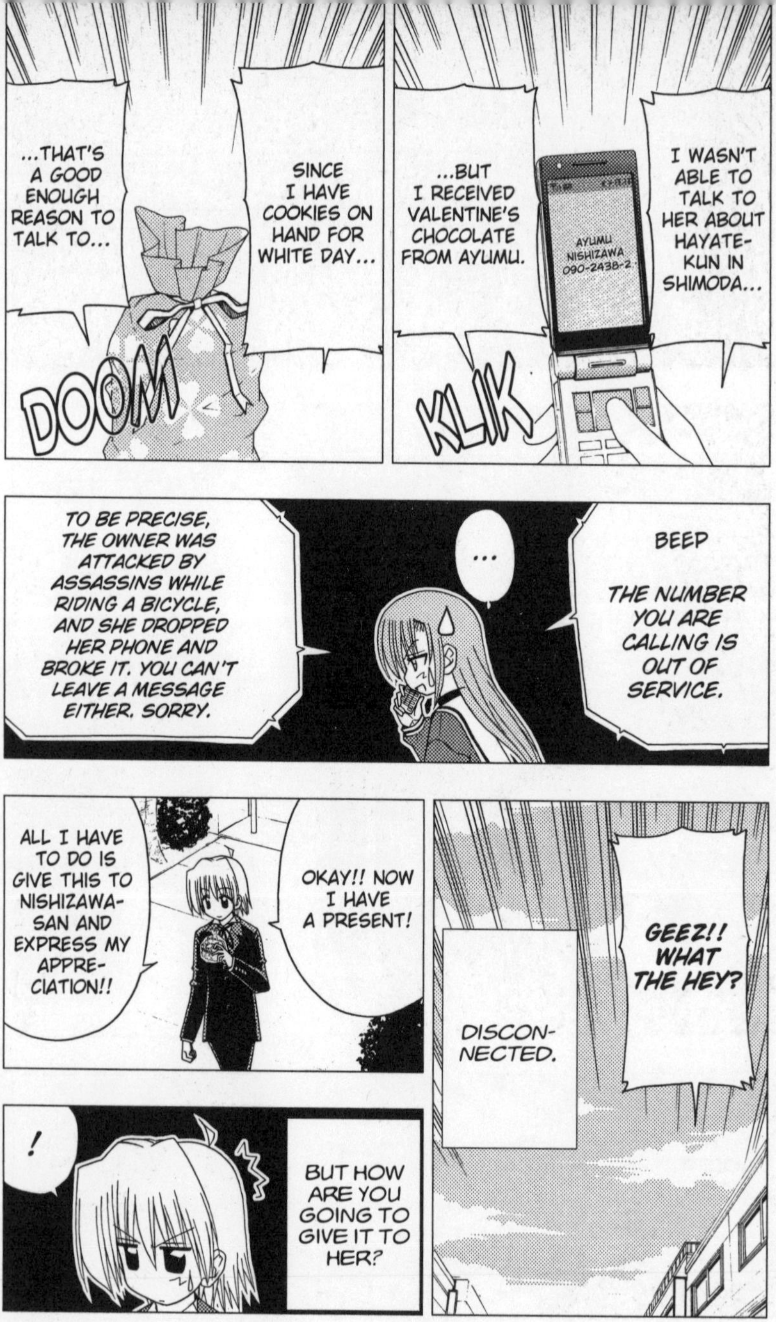
I WASN'T ABLE TO TALK TO HER ABOUT HAYATE-KUN IN SHIMODA...
AYUMU NISHIZAWA 090-2438-2
...BUT I RECEIVED VALENTINE'S CHOCOLATE FROM AYUMU.
KLIK
SINCE I HAVE COOKIES ON HAND FOR WHITE DAY...
...THAT'S A GOOD ENOUGH REASON TO TALK TO...
DOOM
BEEP
THE NUMBER YOU ARE CALLING IS OUT OF SERVICE.
...
TO BE PRECISE, THE OWNER WAS ATTACKED BY ASSASSINS WHILE RIDING A BICYCLE, AND SHE DROPPED HER PHONE AND BROKE IT. YOU CAN'T LEAVE A MESSAGE EITHER. SORRY.
GEEZ!! WHAT THE HEY?
DISCONNECTED.
OKAY!! NOW I HAVE A PRESENT!
ALL I HAVE TO DO IS GIVE THIS TO NISHIZAWA-SAN AND EXPRESS MY APPRECIATION!!
BUT HOW ARE YOU GOING TO GIVE IT TO HER?
!

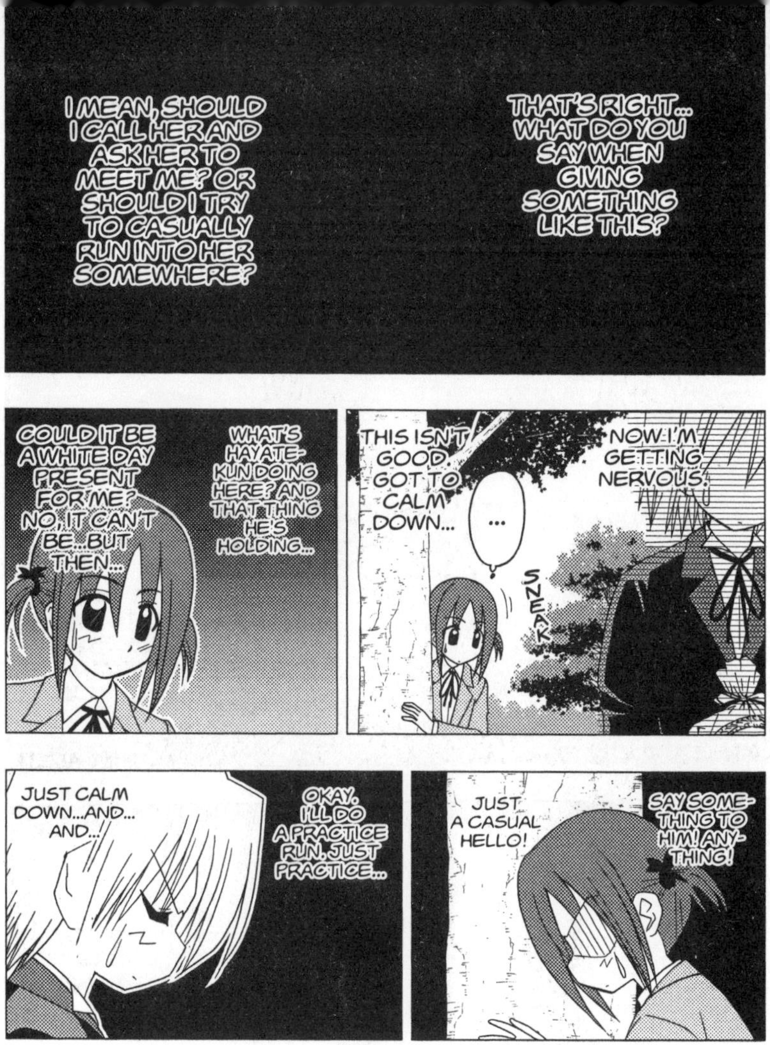

THAT'S RIGHT... WHAT DO YOU SAY WHEN GIVING SOMETHING LIKE THIS?
I MEAN, SHOULD I CALL HER AND ASK HER TO MEET ME? OR SHOULD I TRY TO CASUALLY RUN INTO HER SOMEWHERE?
NOW I'M GETTING NERVOUS.
THIS ISN'T GOOD. GOT TO CALM DOWN...
...
SNEAK
WHAT'S HAYATE-KUN DOING HERE? AND THAT THING HE'S HOLDING...
COULD IT BE A WHITE DAY PRESENT FOR ME? NO, IT CAN'T BE...BUT THEN...
SAY SOME-THING TO HIM! ANY-THING!
JUST A CASUAL HELLO!
OKAY. I'LL DO A PRACTICE RUN. JUST PRACTICE...
JUST CALM DOWN...AND... AND...!
ALL RIGHT!! LET'S DO THIS!!
TUP
PLEASE ...
...ACCEPT THIS!!

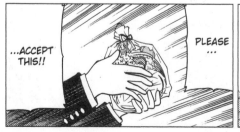

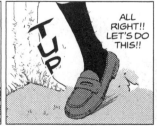

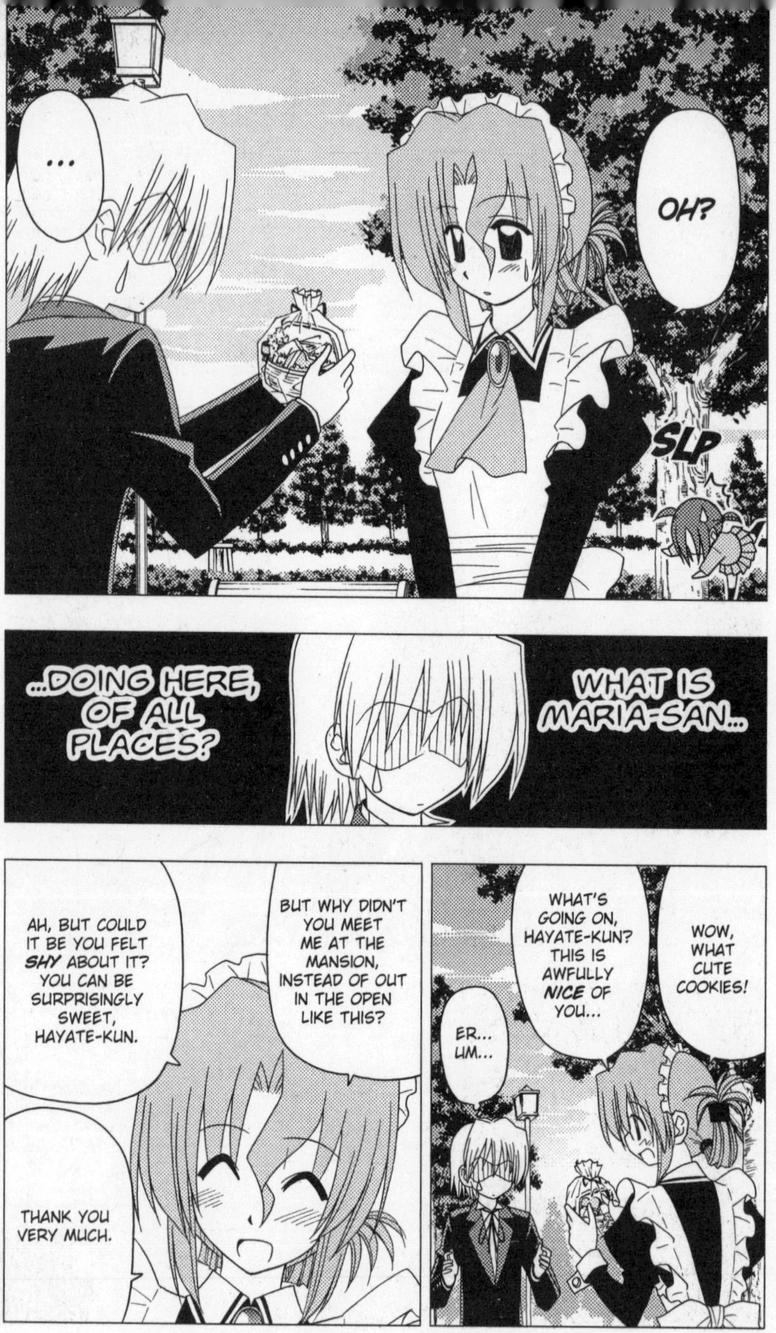
OH?
SLP
...
WHAT IS MARIA-SAN...
...DOING HERE, OF ALL PLACES?
WOW, WHAT CUTE COOKIES!
WHAT'S GOING ON, HAYATE-KUN? THIS IS AWFULLY *NICE* OF YOU...
ER... UM...
BUT WHY DIDN'T YOU MEET ME AT THE MANSION, INSTEAD OF OUT IN THE OPEN LIKE THIS?
AH, BUT COULD IT BE YOU FELT *SHY* ABOUT IT? YOU CAN BE SURPRISINGLY SWEET, HAYATE-KUN.
THANK YOU VERY MUCH.

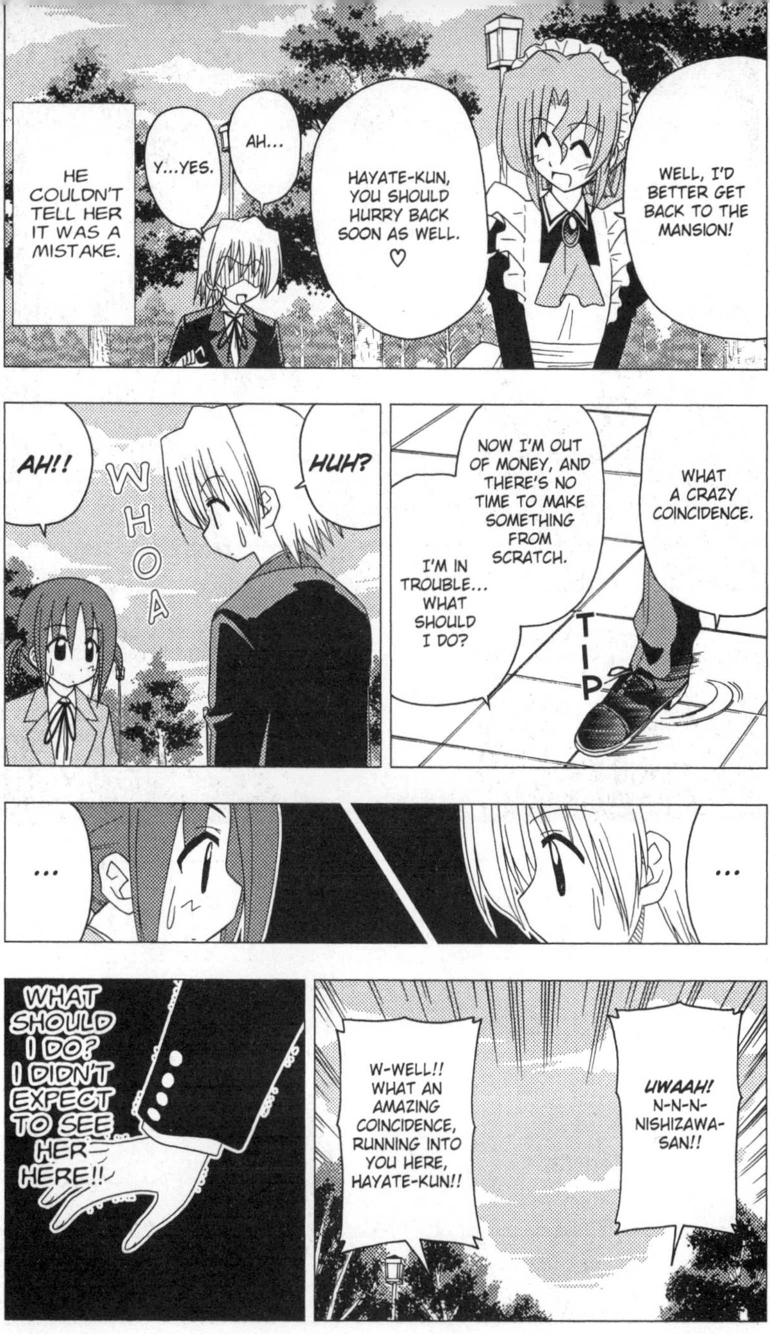
WELL, I'D BETTER GET BACK TO THE MANSION!
HAYATE-KUN, YOU SHOULD HURRY BACK SOON AS WELL. ♡
AH...
Y...YES.
HE COULDN'T TELL HER IT WAS A MISTAKE.
WHAT A CRAZY COINCIDENCE.
NOW I'M OUT OF MONEY, AND THERE'S NO TIME TO MAKE SOMETHING FROM SCRATCH.
I'M IN TROUBLE... WHAT SHOULD I DO?
TIP
HUH?
WHOA
AH!!
...
...
UWAAH! N-N-N-NISHIZAWA-SAN!!
W-WELL!! WHAT AN AMAZING COINCIDENCE, RUNNING INTO YOU HERE, HAYATE-KUN!!
WHAT SHOULD I DO? I DIDN'T EXPECT TO SEE HER HERE!!

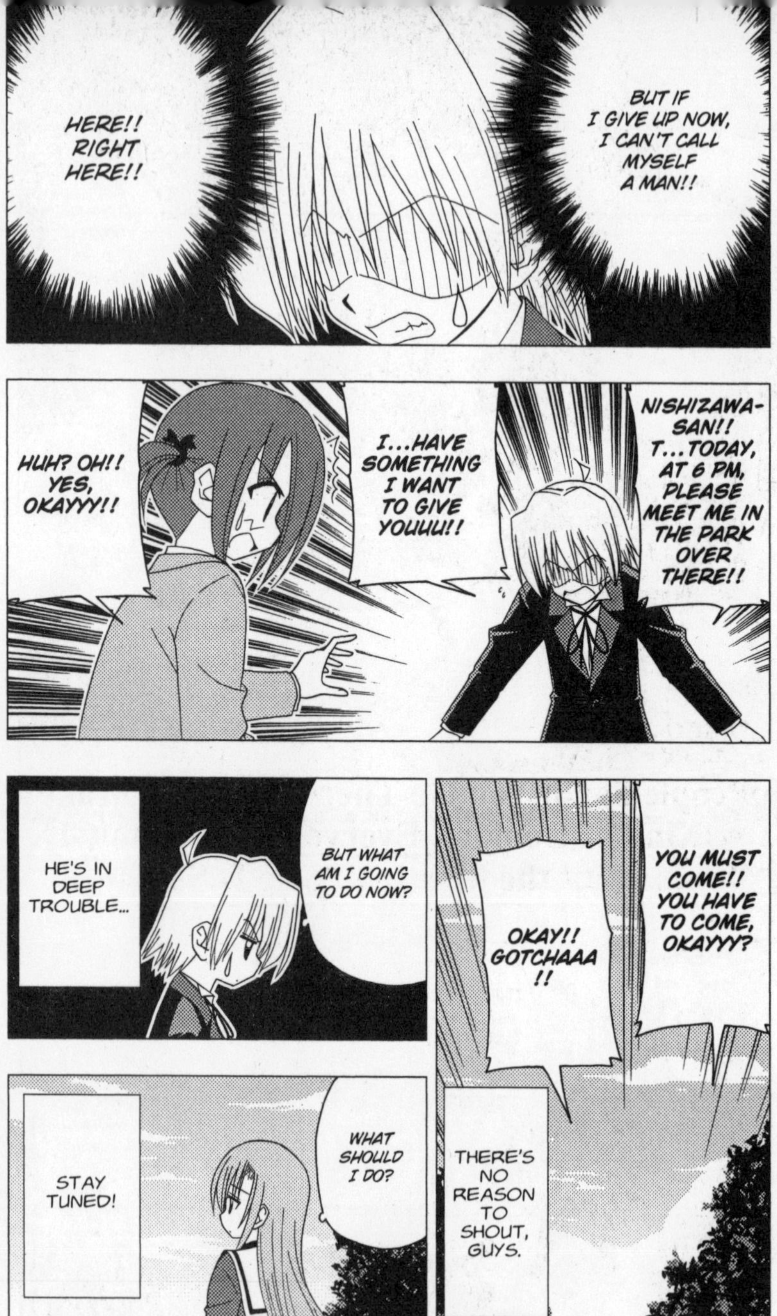
BUT IF I GIVE UP NOW, I CAN'T CALL MYSELF A MAN!!
HERE!! RIGHT HERE!!
NISHIZAWA-SAN!! T...TODAY, AT 6 PM, PLEASE MEET ME IN THE PARK OVER THERE!!
I...HAVE SOMETHING I WANT TO GIVE YOUUU!!
HUH? OH!! YES, OKAYYY!!
YOU MUST COME!! YOU HAVE TO COME, OKAYYY?
OKAY!! GOTCHAAA!!
THERE'S NO REASON TO SHOUT, GUYS.
BUT WHAT AM I GOING TO DO NOW?
HE'S IN DEEP TROUBLE...
WHAT SHOULD I DO?
STAY TUNED!

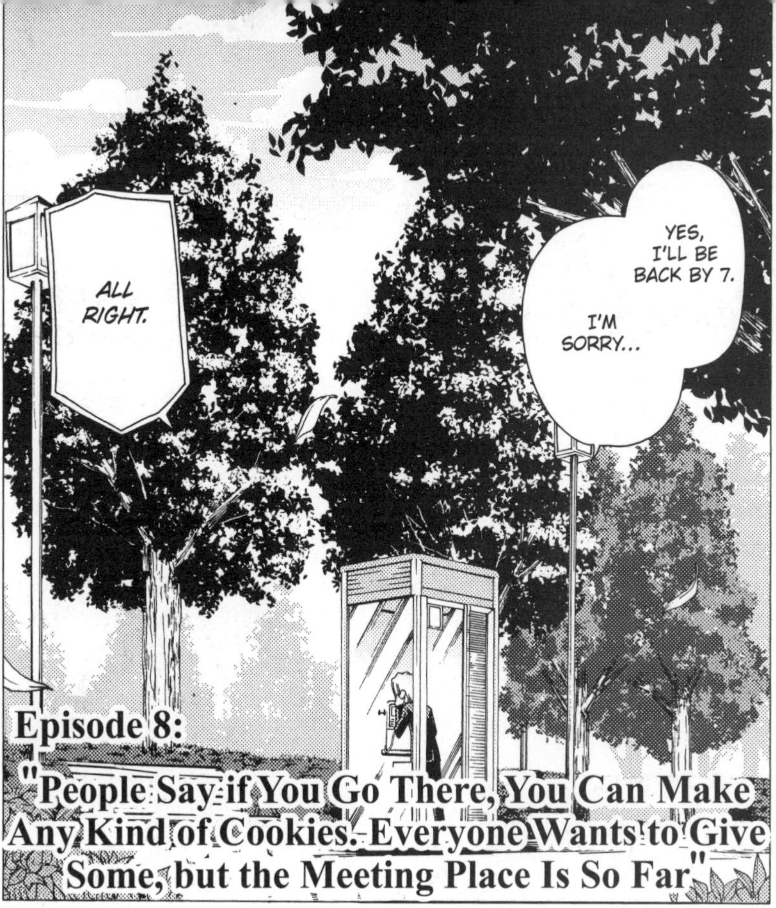
YES, I'LL BE BACK BY 7.
I'M SORRY...
ALL RIGHT.

Episode 8: "People Say if You Go There, You Can Make Any Kind of Cookies. Everyone Wants to Give Some, but the Meeting Place Is So Far"

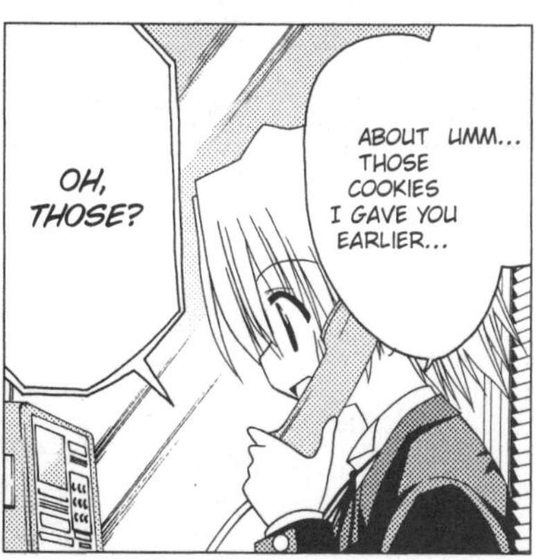
UMM...
ABOUT THOSE COOKIES I GAVE YOU EARLIER...
OH, THOSE?

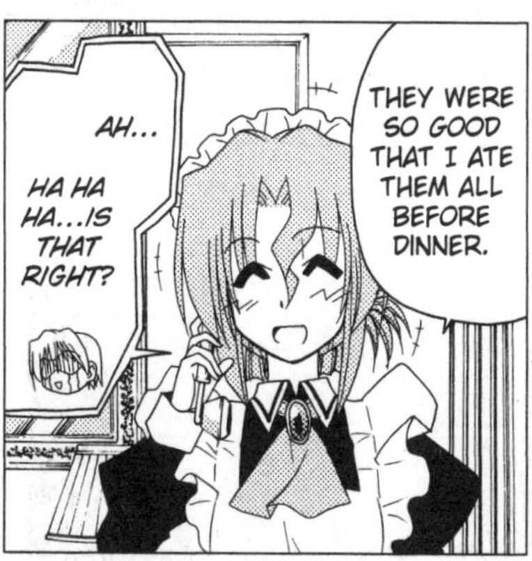
THEY WERE SO GOOD THAT I ATE THEM ALL BEFORE DINNER.
AH...
HA HA HA...IS THAT RIGHT?

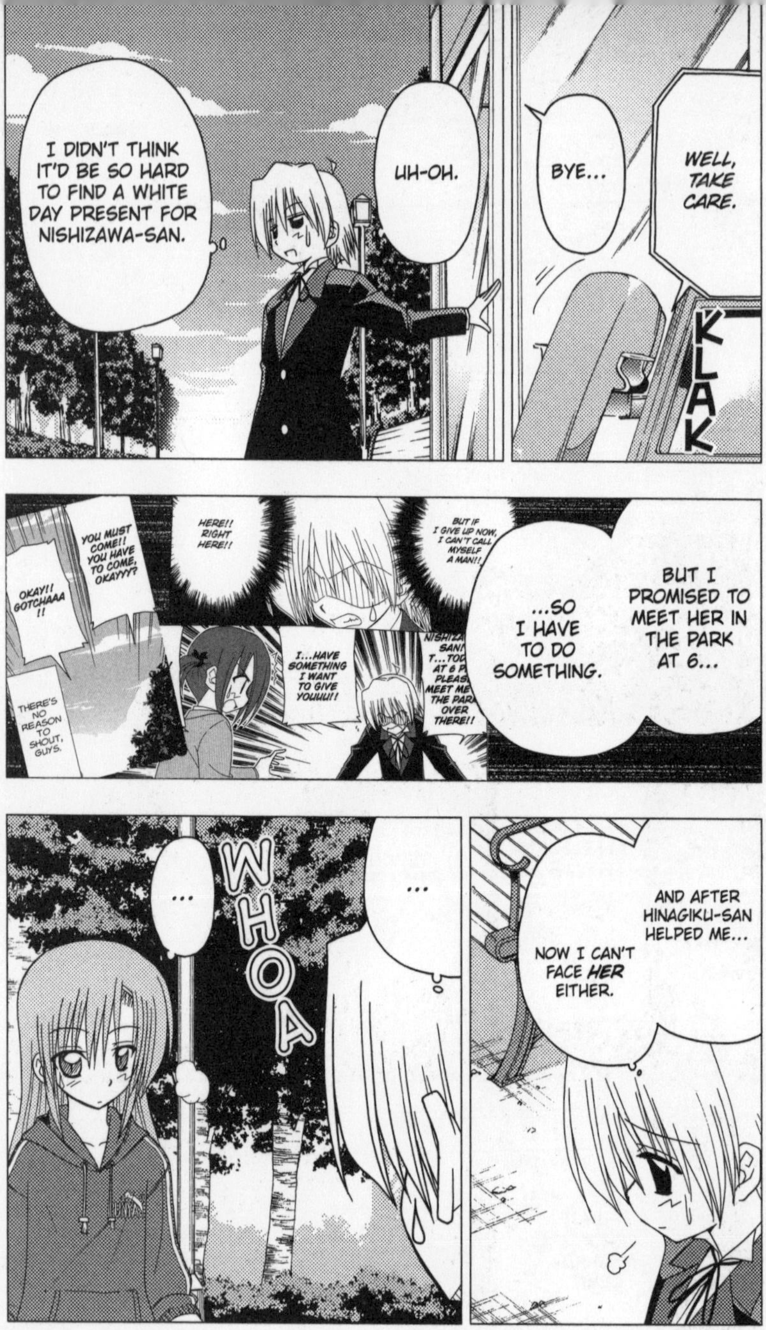
WELL, TAKE CARE.
BYE...
KLAK
UH-OH.
I DIDN'T THINK IT'D BE SO HARD TO FIND A WHITE DAY PRESENT FOR NISHIZAWA-SAN.
BUT I PROMISED TO MEET HER IN THE PARK AT 6...
...SO I HAVE TO DO SOMETHING.
BUT IF I GIVE UP NOW, I CAN'T CALL MYSELF A MAN!!
HERE!! RIGHT HERE!!
YOU MUST COME!! YOU HAVE TO COME, OKAYYY?
OKAY!! GOTCHAAA!!
NISHIZA SAN! T...TOD AT 6 P PLEAS MEET ME THE PARK OVER THERE!!
I...HAVE SOMETHING I WANT TO GIVE YOUUU!!
THERE'S NO REASON TO SHOUT, GUYS.
AND AFTER HINAGIKU-SAN HELPED ME...
NOW I CAN'T FACE *HER* EITHER.
...
WHOA
...

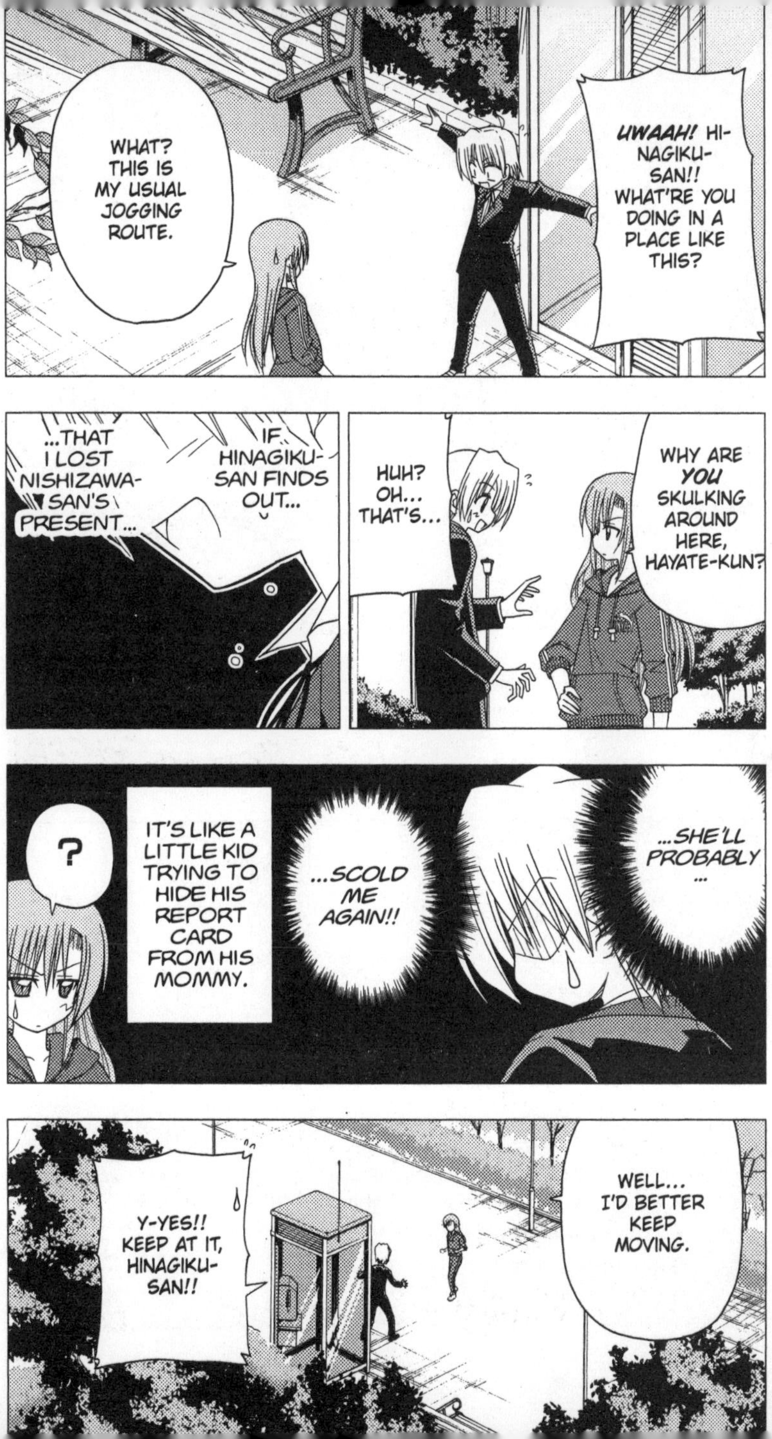
UWAAH! HI-NAGIKU-SAN!! WHAT'RE YOU DOING IN A PLACE LIKE THIS?
WHAT? THIS IS MY USUAL JOGGING ROUTE.
WHY ARE YOU SKULKING AROUND HERE, HAYATE-KUN?
HUH? OH... THAT'S...
IF HINAGIKU-SAN FINDS OUT...
...THAT I LOST NISHIZAWA-SAN'S PRESENT...
...SHE'LL PROBABLY ...
...SCOLD ME AGAIN!!
IT'S LIKE A LITTLE KID TRYING TO HIDE HIS REPORT CARD FROM HIS MOMMY.
?
WELL... I'D BETTER KEEP MOVING.
Y-YES!! KEEP AT IT, HINAGIKU-SAN!!

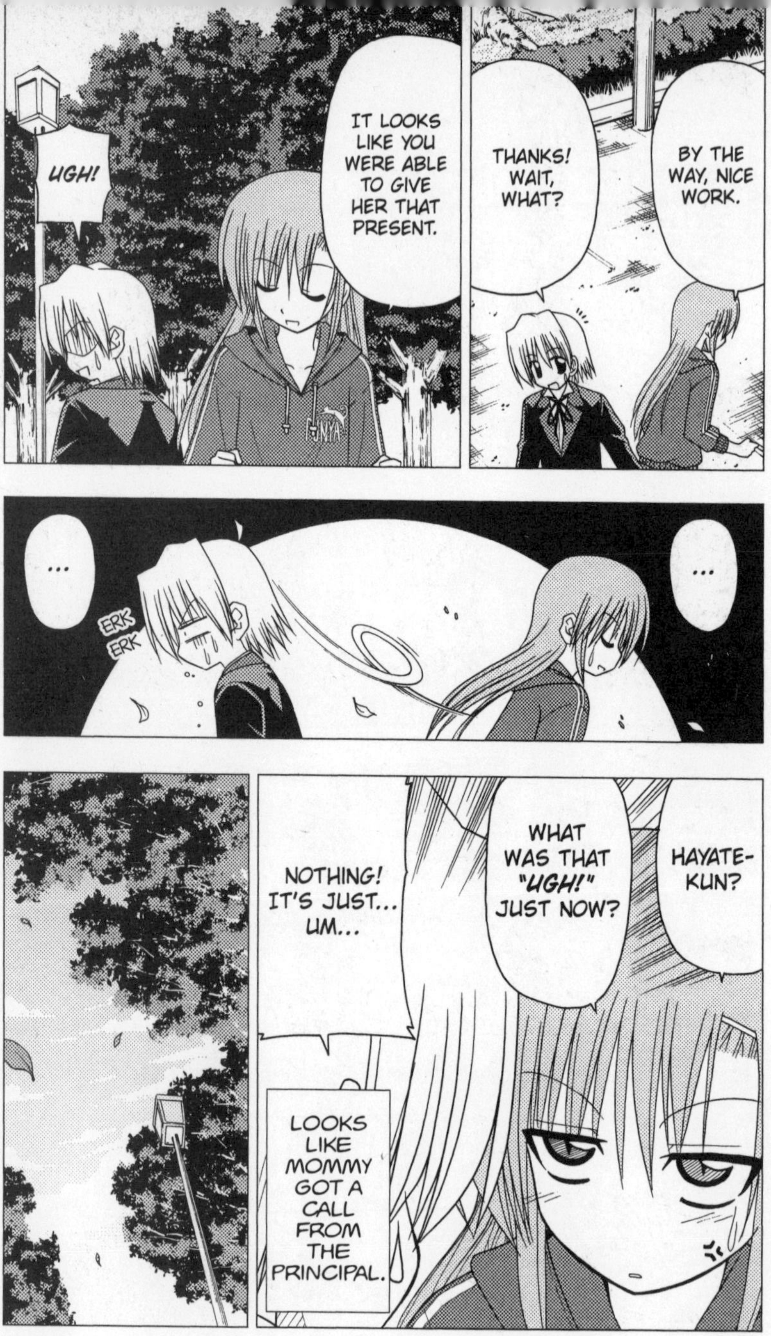
BY THE WAY, NICE WORK.
THANKS! WAIT, WHAT?
IT LOOKS LIKE YOU WERE ABLE TO GIVE HER THAT PRESENT.
UGH!
...
...
ERK ERK
HAYATE-KUN?
WHAT WAS THAT "UGH!" JUST NOW?
NOTHING! IT'S JUST... UM...
LOOKS LIKE MOMMY GOT A CALL FROM THE PRINCIPAL.

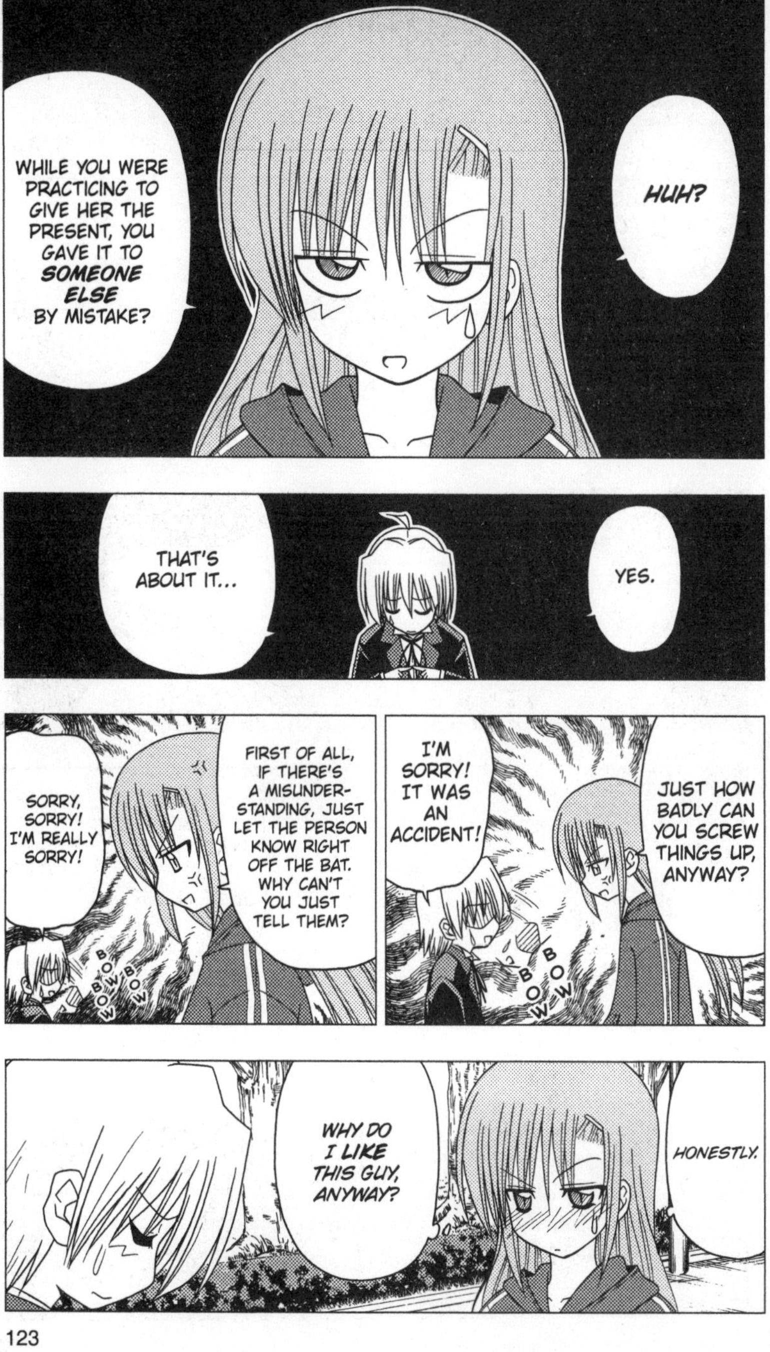
HUH?
WHILE YOU WERE PRACTICING TO GIVE HER THE PRESENT, YOU GAVE IT TO **SOMEONE ELSE** BY MISTAKE?
YES.
THAT'S ABOUT IT...
JUST HOW BADLY CAN YOU SCREW THINGS UP, ANYWAY?
I'M SORRY! IT WAS AN ACCIDENT!
BOW BOW BOW
FIRST OF ALL, IF THERE'S A MISUNDER-STANDING, JUST LET THE PERSON KNOW RIGHT OFF THE BAT. WHY CAN'T YOU JUST TELL THEM?
SORRY, SORRY! I'M REALLY SORRY!
BOW BOW BOW
HONESTLY.
*WHY DO **I LIKE** THIS GUY, ANYWAY?*

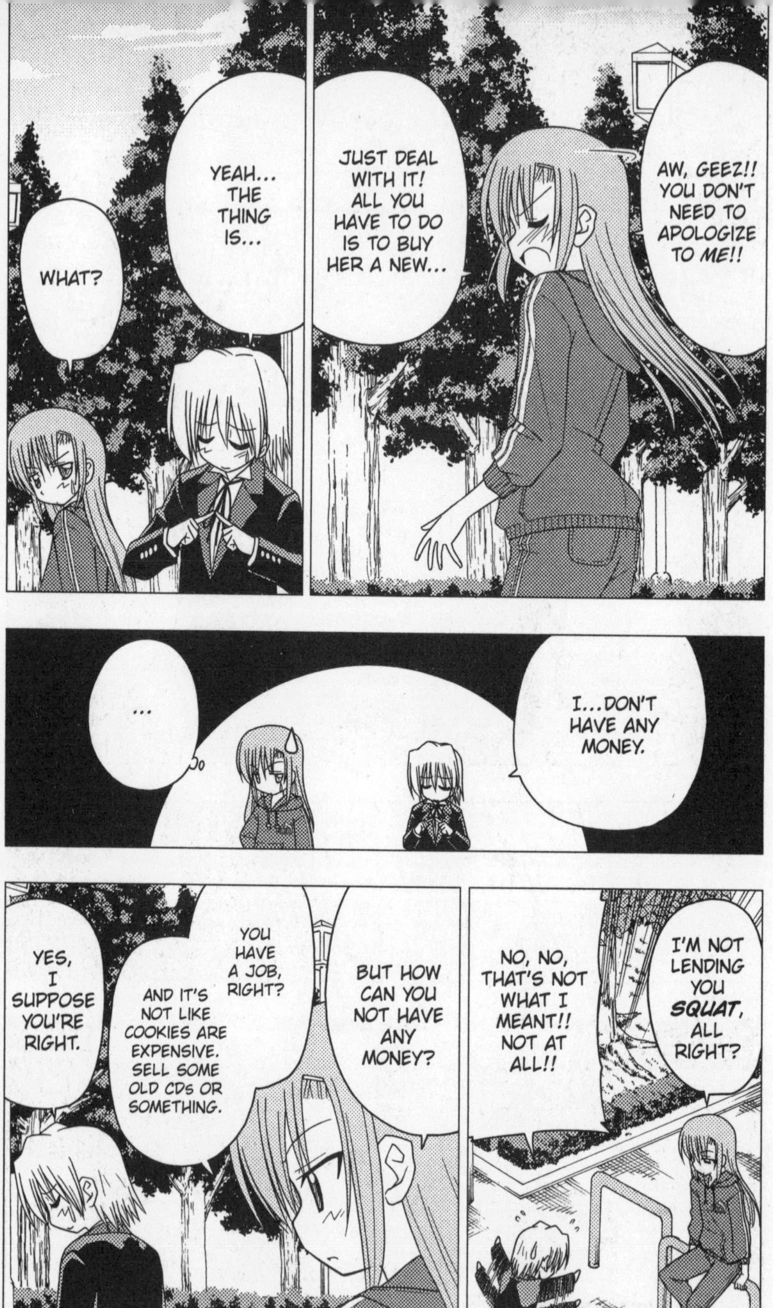
AW, GEEZ!! YOU DON'T NEED TO APOLOGIZE TO *ME*!!
JUST DEAL WITH IT! ALL YOU HAVE TO DO IS TO BUY HER A NEW...
YEAH... THE THING IS...
WHAT?
I...DON'T HAVE ANY MONEY.
...
I'M NOT LENDING YOU ***SQUAT***, ALL RIGHT?
NO, NO, THAT'S NOT WHAT I MEANT!! NOT AT ALL!!
BUT HOW CAN YOU NOT HAVE ANY MONEY?
YOU HAVE A JOB, RIGHT?
AND IT'S NOT LIKE COOKIES ARE EXPENSIVE. SELL SOME OLD CDs OR SOMETHING.
YES, I SUPPOSE YOU'RE RIGHT.

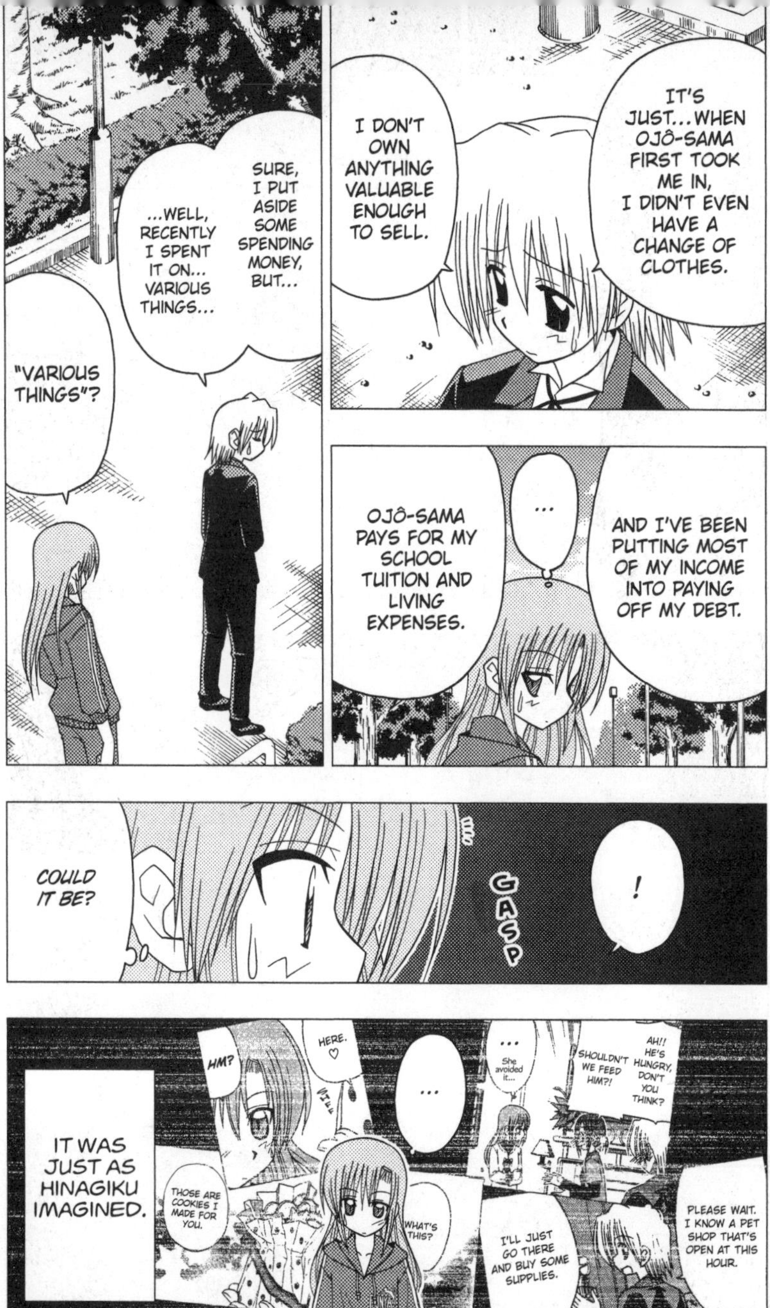
IT'S JUST...WHEN OJÔ-SAMA FIRST TOOK ME IN, I DIDN'T EVEN HAVE A CHANGE OF CLOTHES.
I DON'T OWN ANYTHING VALUABLE ENOUGH TO SELL.
AND I'VE BEEN PUTTING MOST OF MY INCOME INTO PAYING OFF MY DEBT.
...
OJÔ-SAMA PAYS FOR MY SCHOOL TUITION AND LIVING EXPENSES.
SURE, I PUT ASIDE SOME SPENDING MONEY, BUT...
...WELL, RECENTLY I SPENT IT ON... VARIOUS THINGS...
"VARIOUS THINGS"?
!
GASP
COULD IT BE?
PLEASE WAIT. I KNOW A PET SHOP THAT'S OPEN AT THIS HOUR.
I'LL JUST GO THERE AND BUY SOME SUPPLIES.
AH!! HE'S HUNGRY, DON'T YOU THINK?
SHOULDN'T WE FEED HIM?!
...
She avoided it...
...
HERE. ♡
HM?
WHAT'S THIS?
THOSE ARE COOKIES I MADE FOR YOU.
IT WAS JUST AS HINAGIKU IMAGINED.

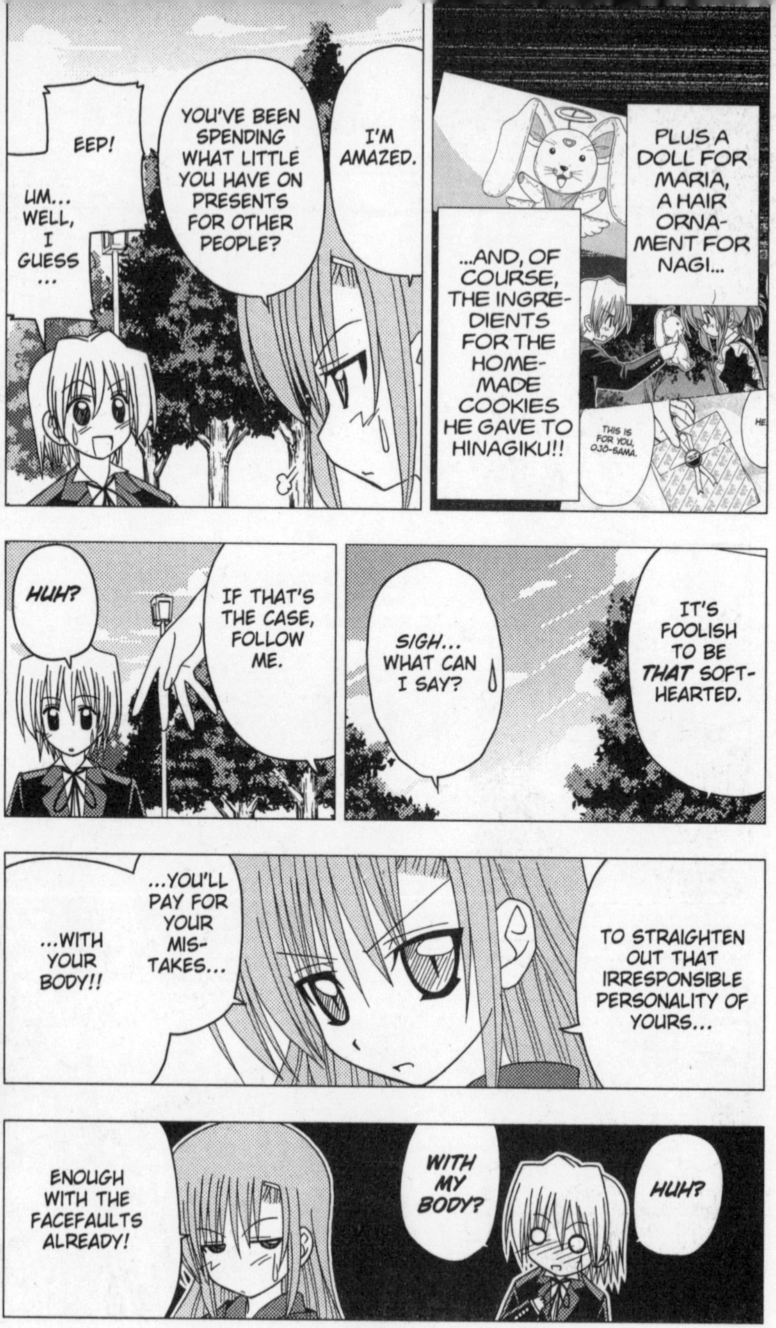
PLUS A DOLL FOR MARIA, A HAIR ORNAMENT FOR NAGI...
...AND, OF COURSE, THE INGREDIENTS FOR THE HOMEMADE COOKIES HE GAVE TO HINAGIKU!!
THIS IS FOR YOU, OJŌ-SAMA.
I'M AMAZED.
YOU'VE BEEN SPENDING WHAT LITTLE YOU HAVE ON PRESENTS FOR OTHER PEOPLE?
EEP!
UM... WELL, I GUESS...
IT'S FOOLISH TO BE *THAT* SOFT-HEARTED.
SIGH... WHAT CAN I SAY?
IF THAT'S THE CASE, FOLLOW ME.
HUH?
TO STRAIGHTEN OUT THAT IRRESPONSIBLE PERSONALITY OF YOURS...
...YOU'LL PAY FOR YOUR MISTAKES...
...WITH YOUR BODY!!
HUH?
WITH MY BODY?
ENOUGH WITH THE FACEFAULTS ALREADY!

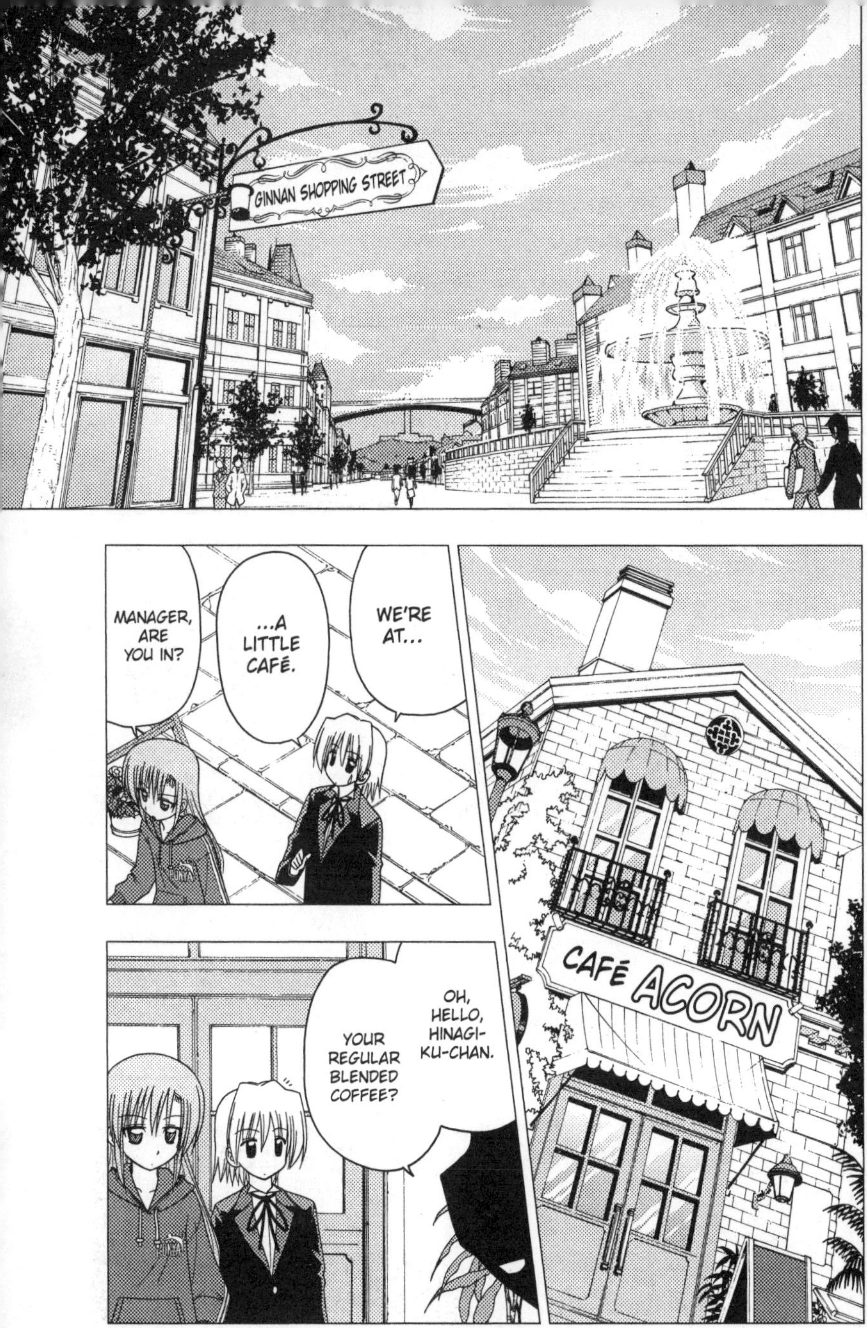
GINNAN SHOPPING STREET
CAFÉ ACORN
WE'RE AT...
...A LITTLE CAFÉ.
MANAGER, ARE YOU IN?
OH, HELLO, HINAGIKU-CHAN.
YOUR REGULAR BLENDED COFFEE?

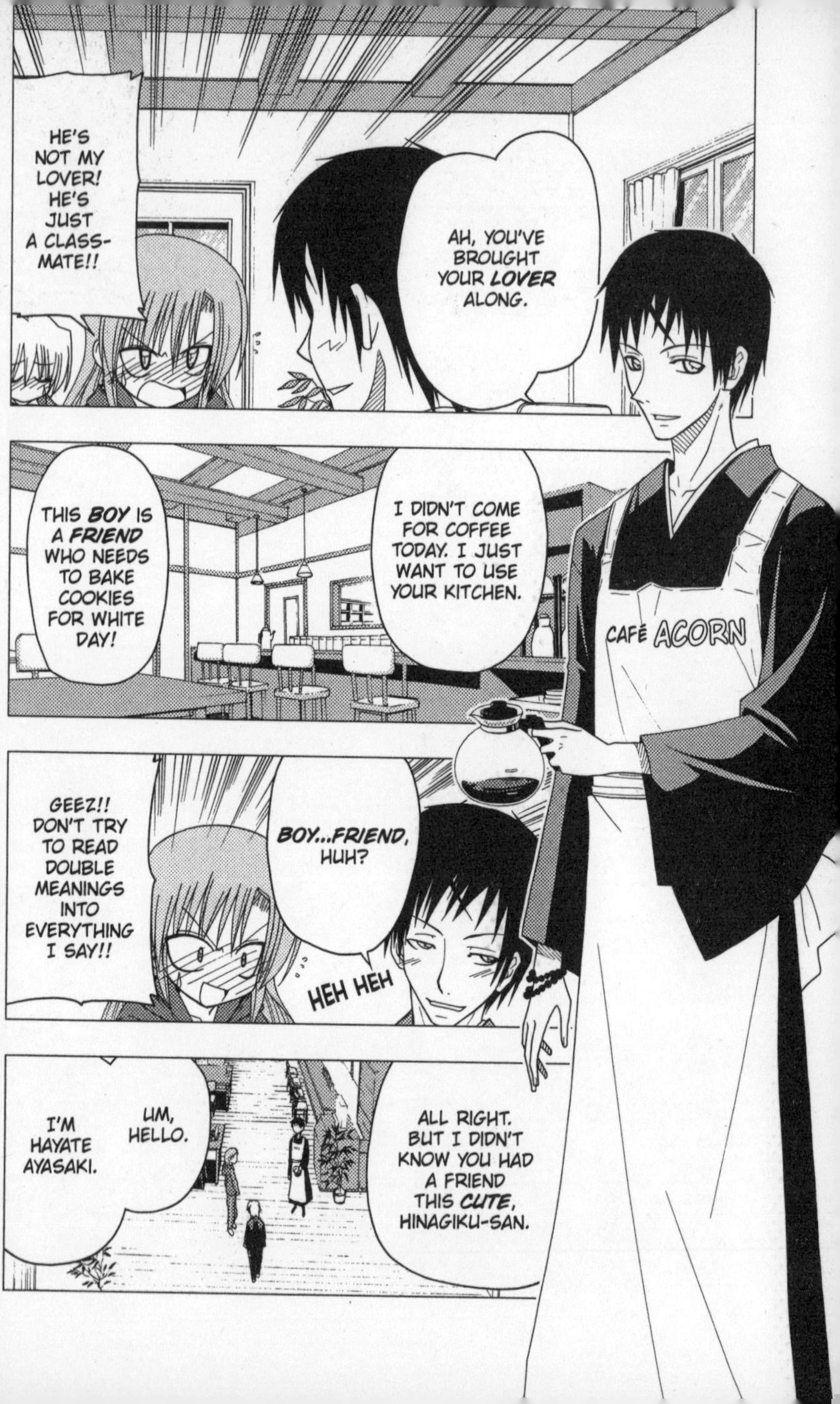
AH, YOU'VE BROUGHT YOUR LOVER ALONG.
HE'S NOT MY LOVER! HE'S JUST A CLASS-MATE!!
CAFÉ ACORN
I DIDN'T COME FOR COFFEE TODAY. I JUST WANT TO USE YOUR KITCHEN.
THIS BOY IS A FRIEND WHO NEEDS TO BAKE COOKIES FOR WHITE DAY!
BOY...FRIEND, HUH?
HEH HEH
GEEZ!! DON'T TRY TO READ DOUBLE MEANINGS INTO EVERYTHING I SAY!!
ALL RIGHT. BUT I DIDN'T KNOW YOU HAD A FRIEND THIS CUTE, HINAGIKU-SAN.
UM, HELLO.
I'M HAYATE AYASAKI.

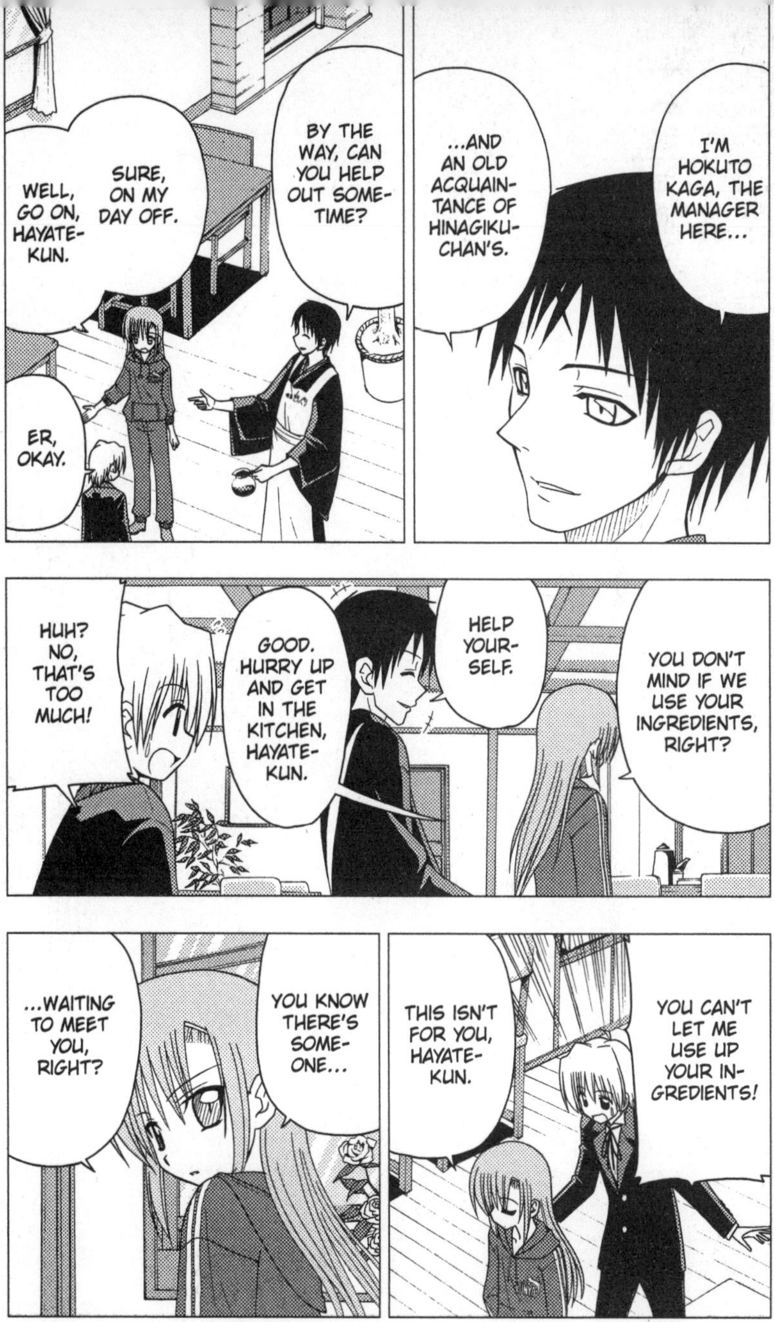
I'M HOKUTO KAGA, THE MANAGER HERE...
...AND AN OLD ACQUAINTANCE OF HINAGIKU-CHAN'S.
BY THE WAY, CAN YOU HELP OUT SOMETIME?
SURE, ON MY DAY OFF.
WELL, GO ON, HAYATE-KUN.
ER, OKAY.
YOU DON'T MIND IF WE USE YOUR INGREDIENTS, RIGHT?
HELP YOURSELF.
GOOD. HURRY UP AND GET IN THE KITCHEN, HAYATE-KUN.
HUH? NO, THAT'S TOO MUCH!
YOU CAN'T LET ME USE UP YOUR INGREDIENTS!
THIS ISN'T FOR YOU, HAYATE-KUN.
YOU KNOW THERE'S SOMEONE...
...WAITING TO MEET YOU, RIGHT?

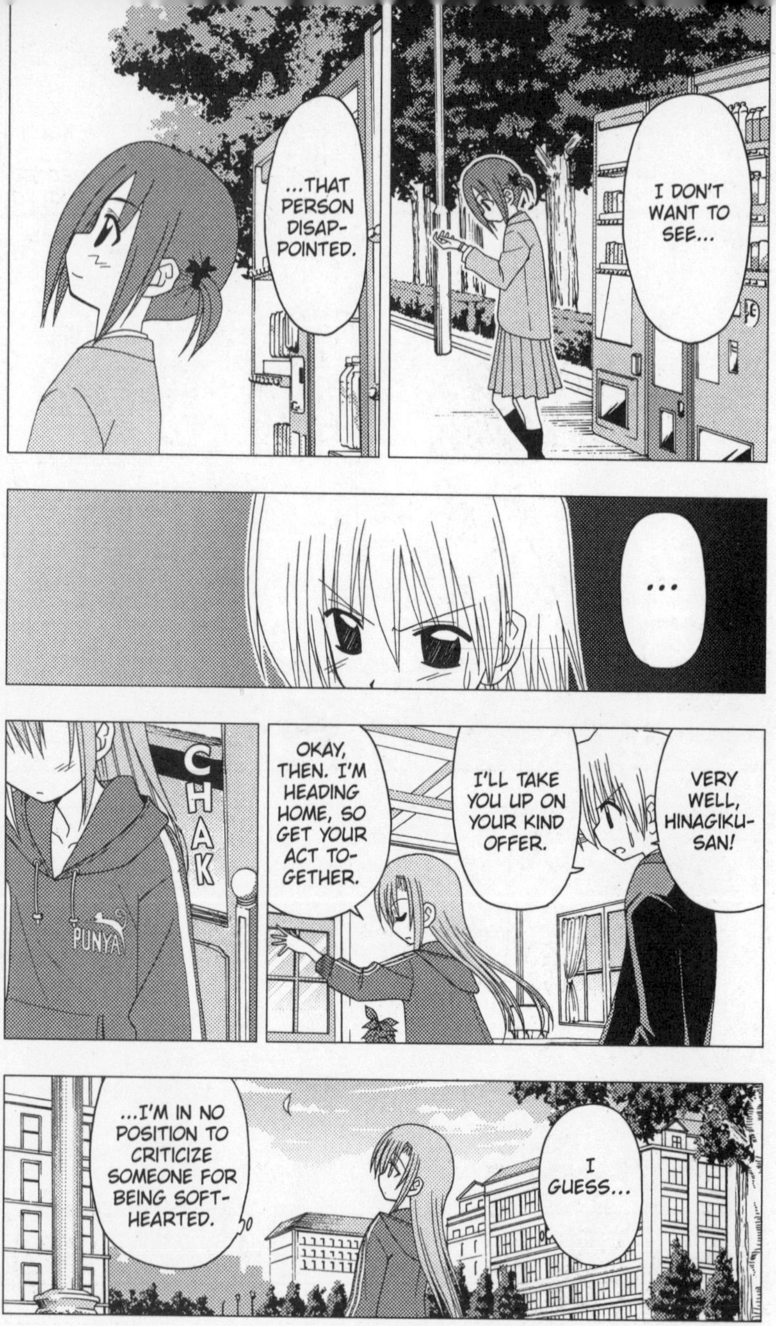
I DON'T WANT TO SEE...
...THAT PERSON DISAPPOINTED.
...
VERY WELL, HINAGIKU-SAN!
I'LL TAKE YOU UP ON YOUR KIND OFFER.
OKAY, THEN. I'M HEADING HOME, SO GET YOUR ACT TOGETHER.
CHAK
PUNYA
I GUESS...
...I'M IN NO POSITION TO CRITICIZE SOMEONE FOR BEING SOFT-HEARTED.

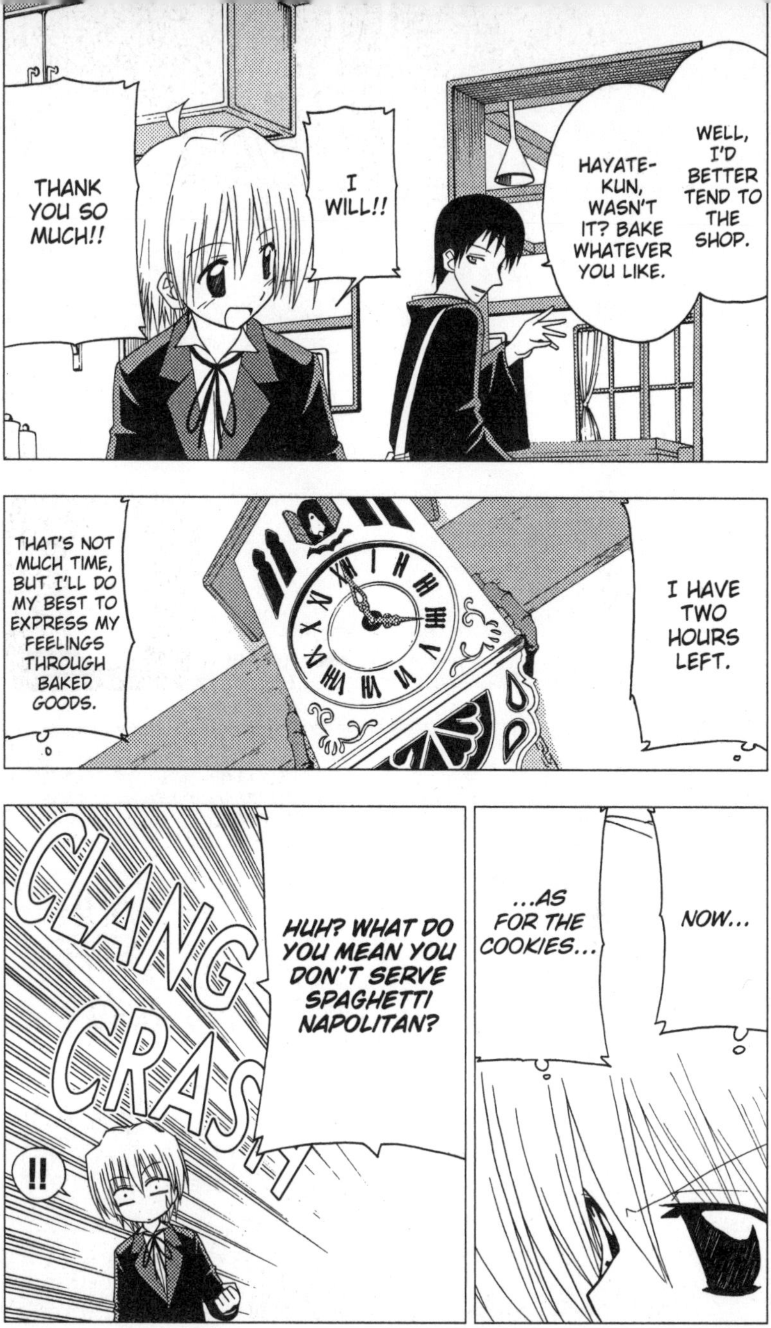
WELL, I'D BETTER TEND TO THE SHOP.
HAYATE-KUN, WASN'T IT? BAKE WHATEVER YOU LIKE.
I WILL!!
THANK YOU SO MUCH!!
I HAVE TWO HOURS LEFT.
THAT'S NOT MUCH TIME, BUT I'LL DO MY BEST TO EXPRESS MY FEELINGS THROUGH BAKED GOODS.
NOW...
...AS FOR THE COOKIES...
HUH? WHAT DO YOU MEAN YOU DON'T SERVE SPAGHETTI NAPOLITAN?
CLANG
CRASH
!!

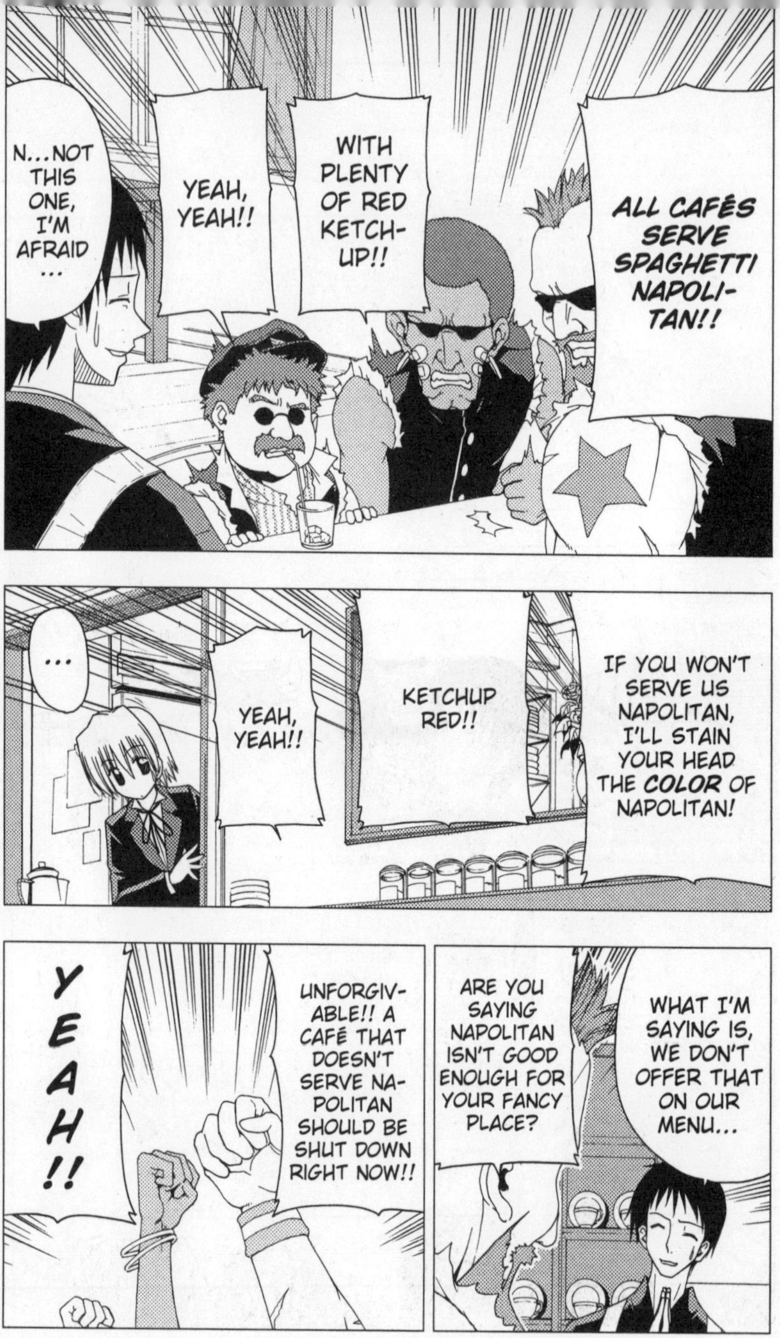
ALL CAFÉS SERVE SPAGHETTI NAPOLITAN!!
WITH PLENTY OF RED KETCH-UP!!
YEAH, YEAH!!
N...NOT THIS ONE, I'M AFRAID...
IF YOU WON'T SERVE US NAPOLITAN, I'LL STAIN YOUR HEAD THE COLOR OF NAPOLITAN!
KETCHUP RED!!
YEAH, YEAH!!
...
WHAT I'M SAYING IS, WE DON'T OFFER THAT ON OUR MENU...
ARE YOU SAYING NAPOLITAN ISN'T GOOD ENOUGH FOR YOUR FANCY PLACE?
UNFORGIVABLE!! A CAFÉ THAT DOESN'T SERVE NA-POLITAN SHOULD BE SHUT DOWN RIGHT NOW!!
YEAH!!

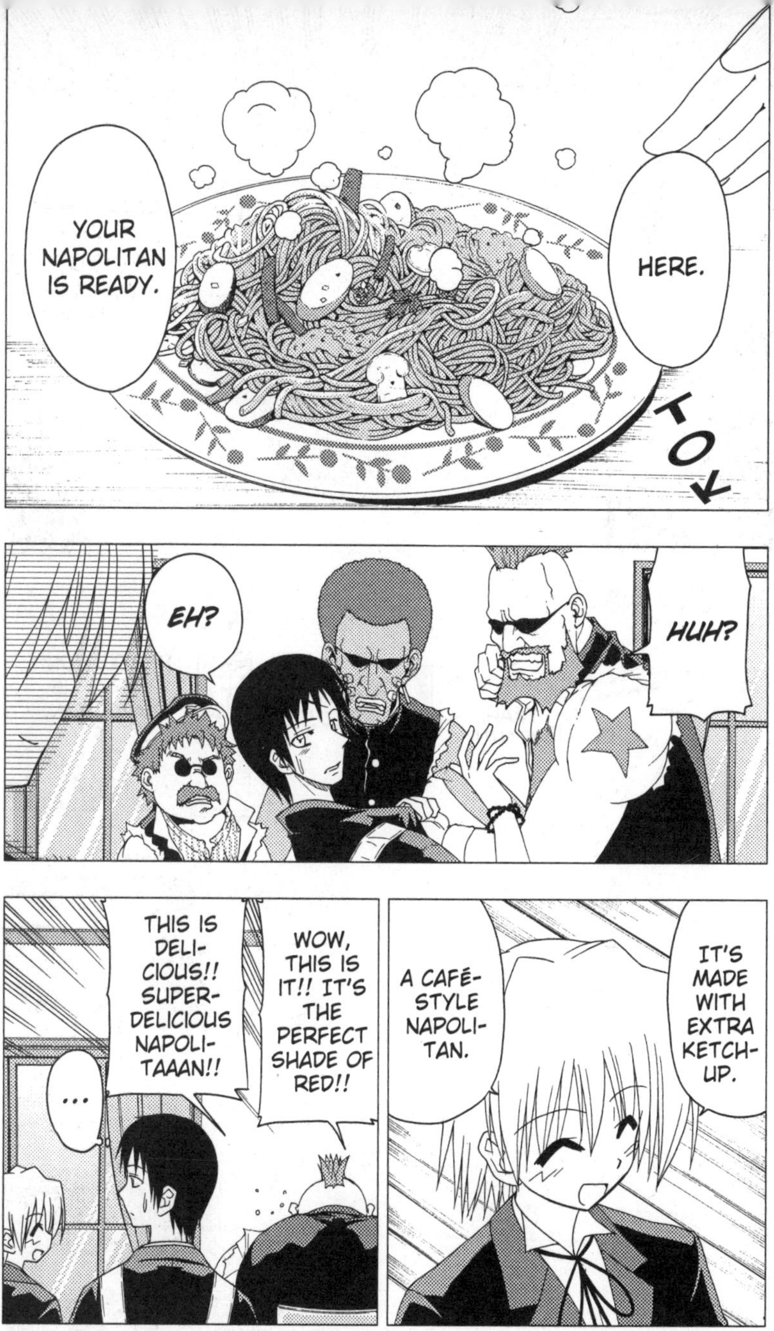
HERE.
YOUR NAPOLITAN IS READY.
TOK
HUH?
EH?
IT'S MADE WITH EXTRA KETCH-UP.
A CAFÉ-STYLE NAPOLI-TAN.
WOW, THIS IS IT!! IT'S THE PERFECT SHADE OF RED!!
THIS IS DELI-CIOUS!! SUPER-DELICIOUS NAPOLI-TAAAN!!
...

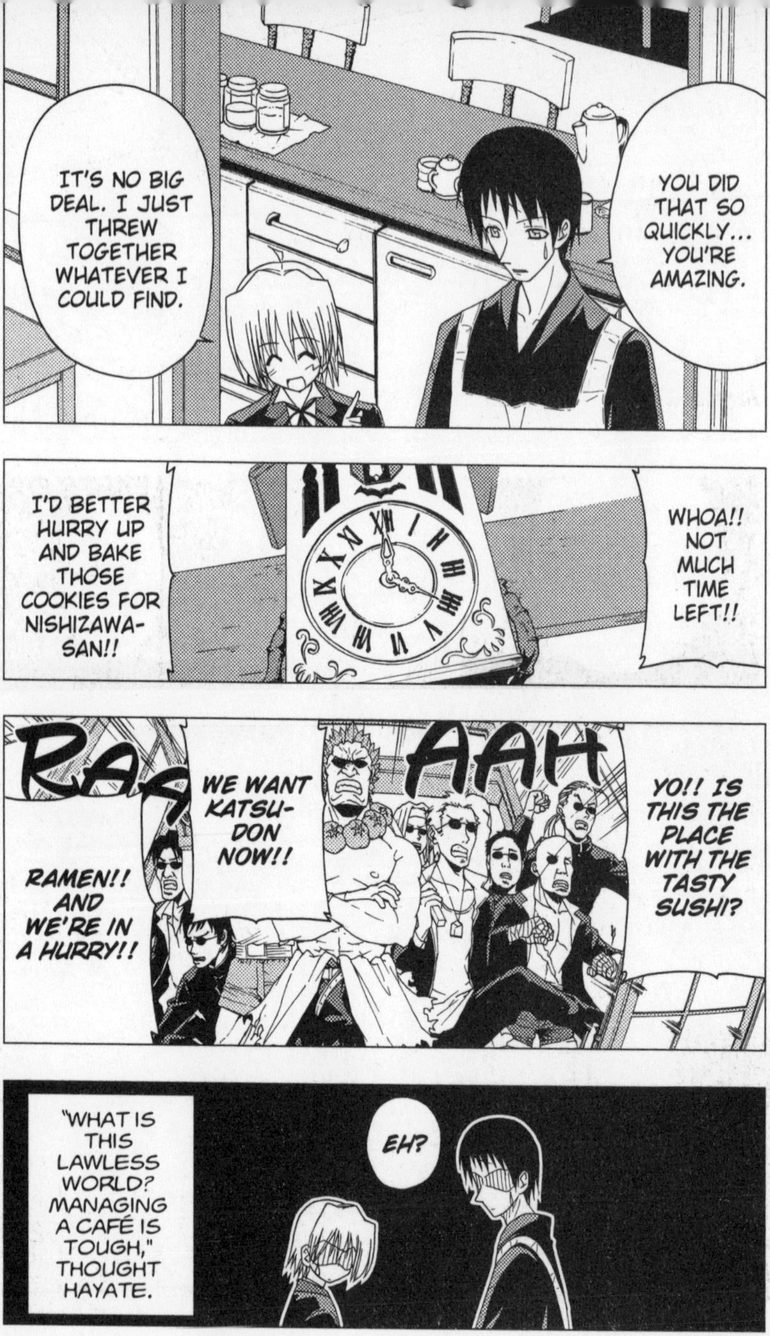
YOU DID THAT SO QUICKLY... YOU'RE AMAZING.
IT'S NO BIG DEAL. I JUST THREW TOGETHER WHATEVER I COULD FIND.
WHOA!! NOT MUCH TIME LEFT!!
I'D BETTER HURRY UP AND BAKE THOSE COOKIES FOR NISHIZAWA-SAN!!
RAAAAH
YO!! IS THIS THE PLACE WITH THE TASTY SUSHI?
WE WANT KATSU-DON NOW!!
RAMEN!! AND WE'RE IN A HURRY!!
EH?
"WHAT IS THIS LAWLESS WORLD? MANAGING A CAFÉ IS TOUGH," THOUGHT HAYATE.

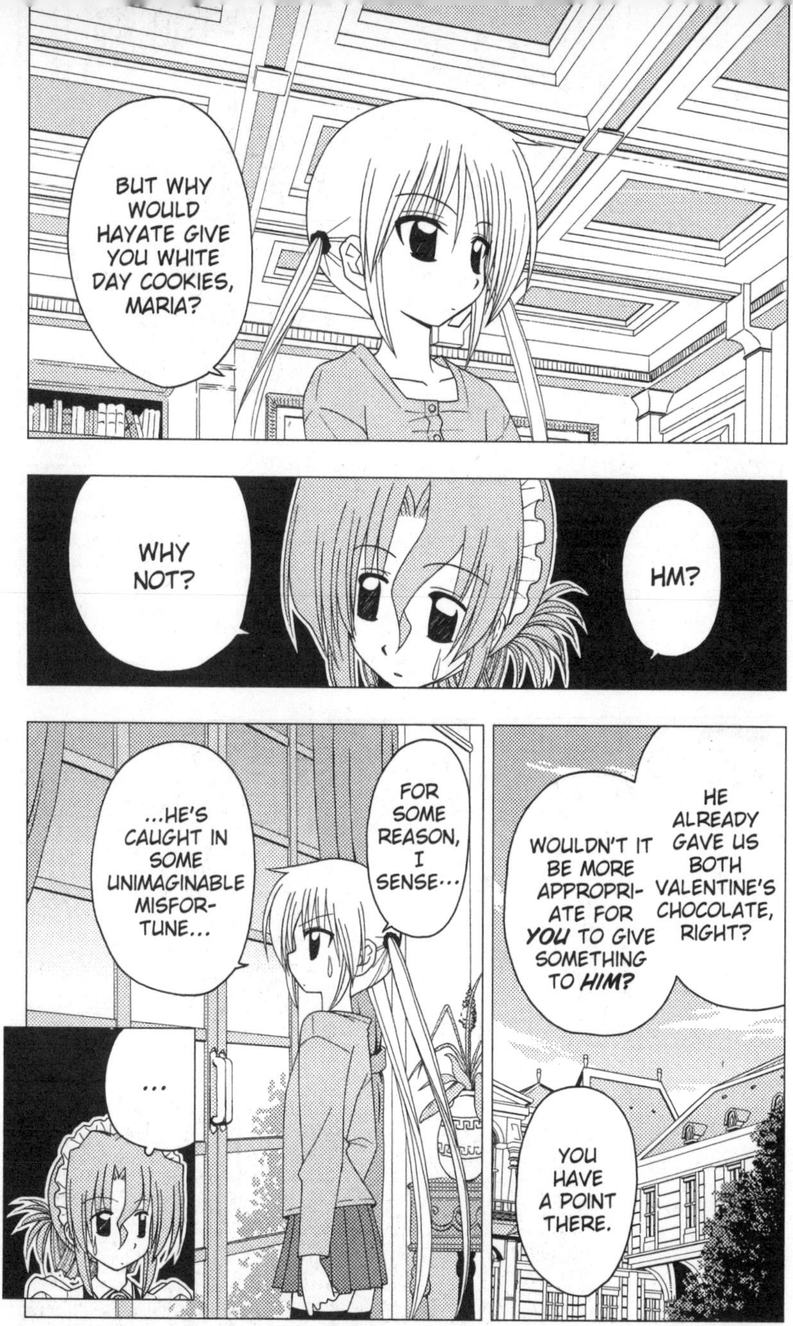
BUT WHY WOULD HAYATE GIVE YOU WHITE DAY COOKIES, MARIA?
HM?
WHY NOT?
HE ALREADY GAVE US BOTH VALENTINE'S CHOCOLATE, RIGHT?
WOULDN'T IT BE MORE APPROPRIATE FOR *YOU* TO GIVE SOMETHING TO *HIM?*
YOU HAVE A POINT THERE.
FOR SOME REASON, I SENSE...
...HE'S CAUGHT IN SOME UNIMAGINABLE MISFORTUNE...
...

Episode 9: "Butter-Fly"

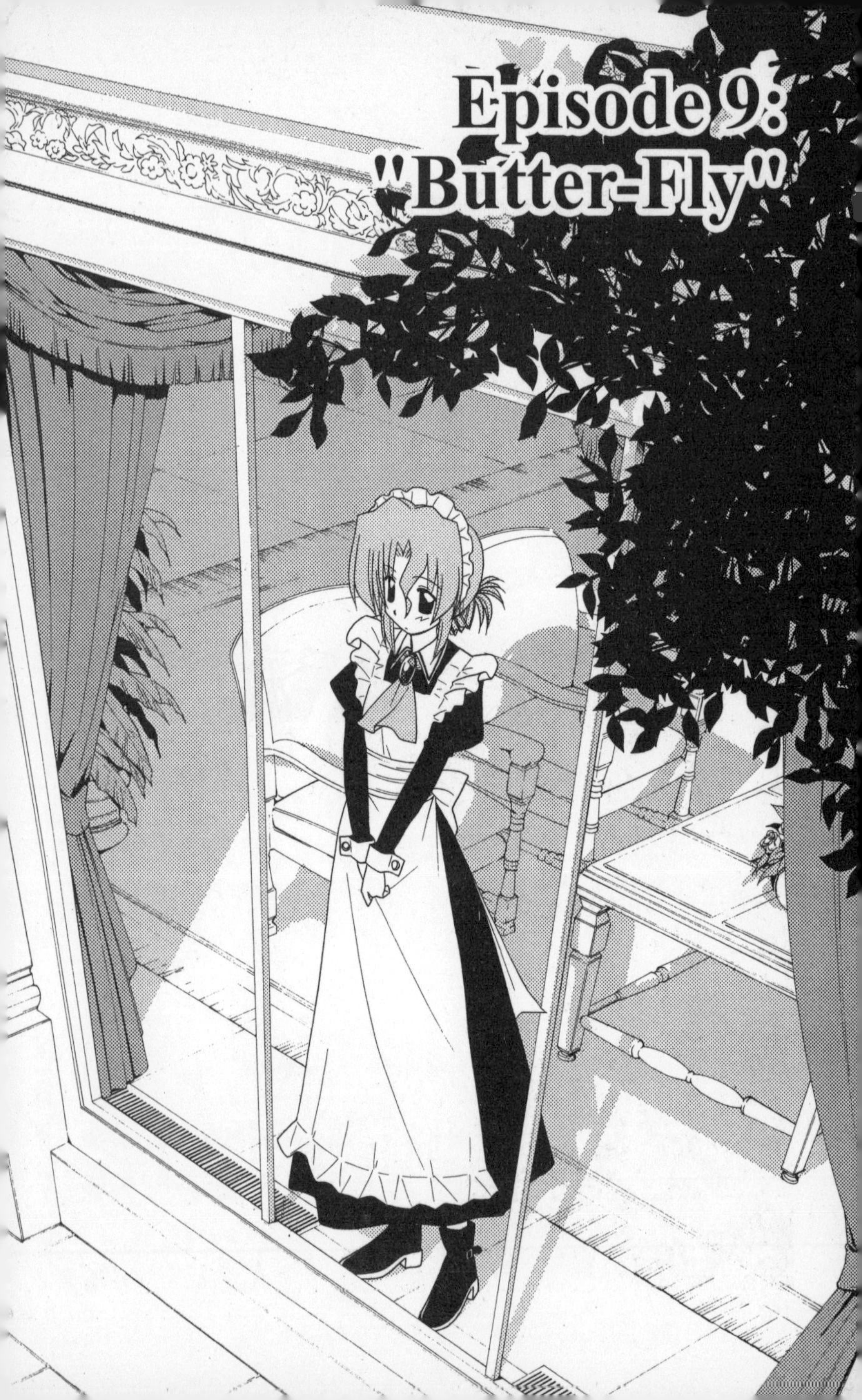
Episode 9:
"Butter-Fly"

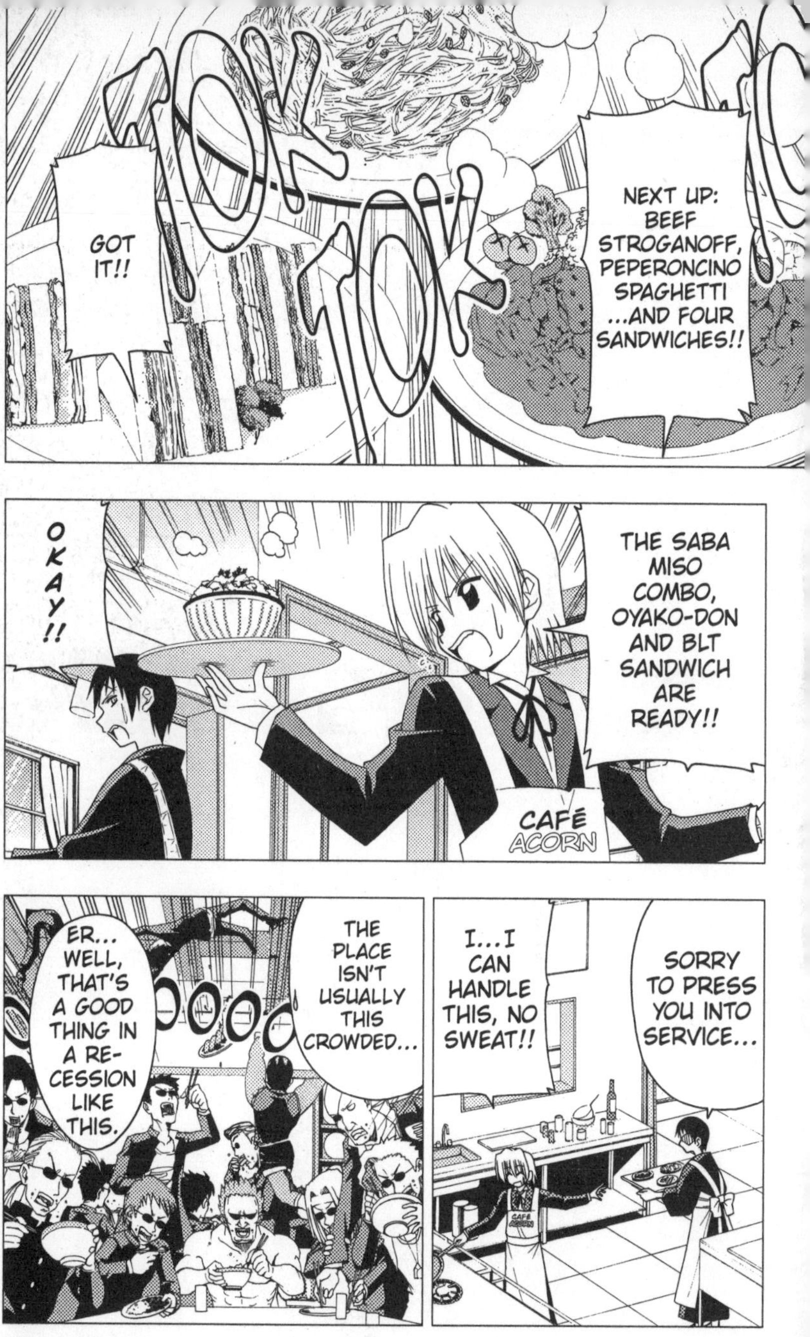
NEXT UP: BEEF STROGANOFF, PEPERONCINO SPAGHETTI ...AND FOUR SANDWICHES!!
TOK
TOK
TOK
GOT IT!!
THE SABA MISO COMBO, OYAKO-DON AND BLT SANDWICH ARE READY!!
OKAY!!
CAFÉ ACORN
SORRY TO PRESS YOU INTO SERVICE...
I...I CAN HANDLE THIS, NO SWEAT!!
THE PLACE ISN'T USUALLY THIS CROWDED...
ER... WELL, THAT'S A GOOD THING IN A RE-CESSION LIKE THIS.

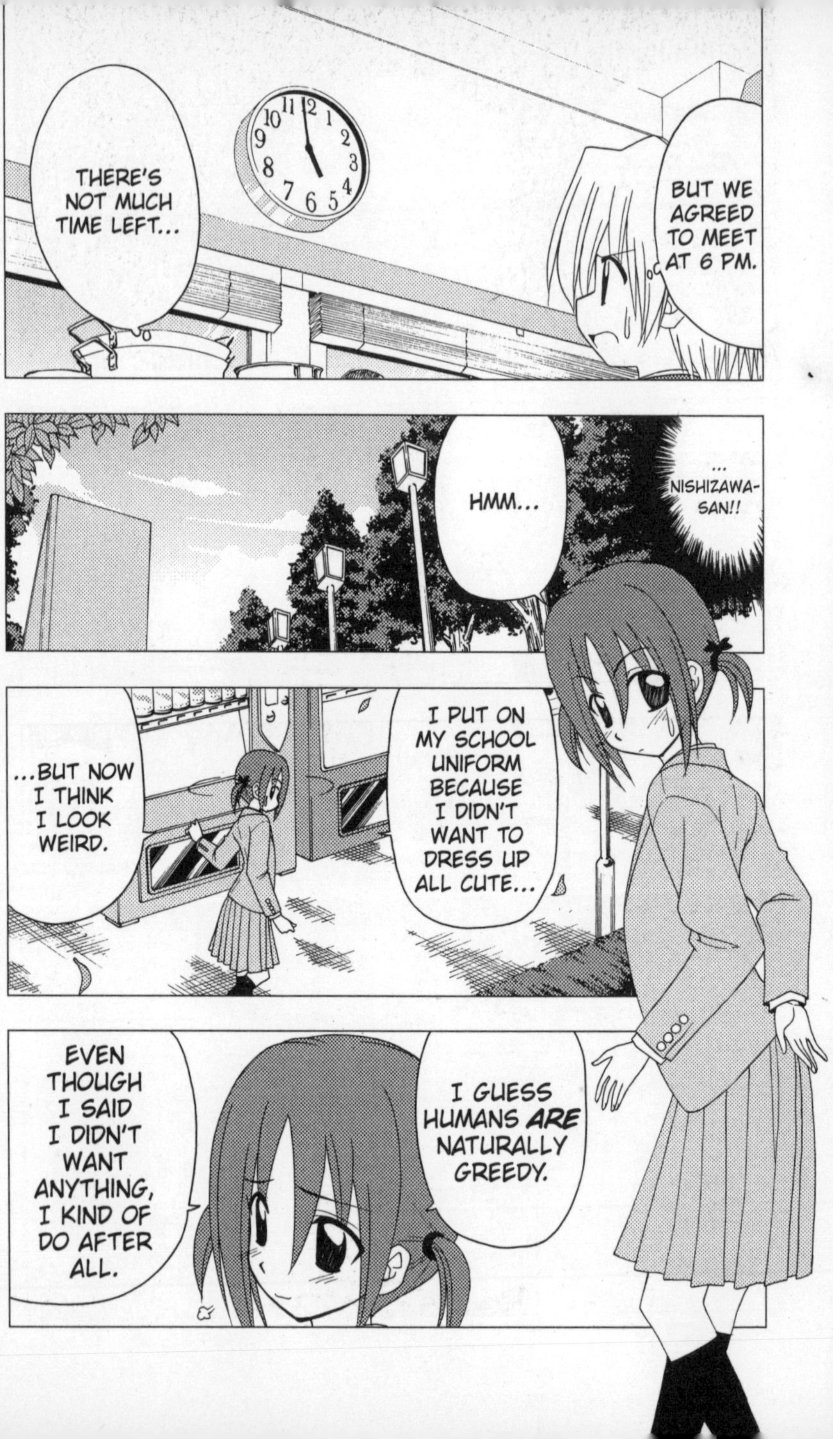
BUT WE AGREED TO MEET AT 6 PM.
THERE'S NOT MUCH TIME LEFT...
... NISHIZAWA-SAN!!
HMM...
I PUT ON MY SCHOOL UNIFORM BECAUSE I DIDN'T WANT TO DRESS UP ALL CUTE...
...BUT NOW I THINK I LOOK WEIRD.
I GUESS HUMANS ARE NATURALLY GREEDY.
EVEN THOUGH I SAID I DIDN'T WANT ANYTHING, I KIND OF DO AFTER ALL.

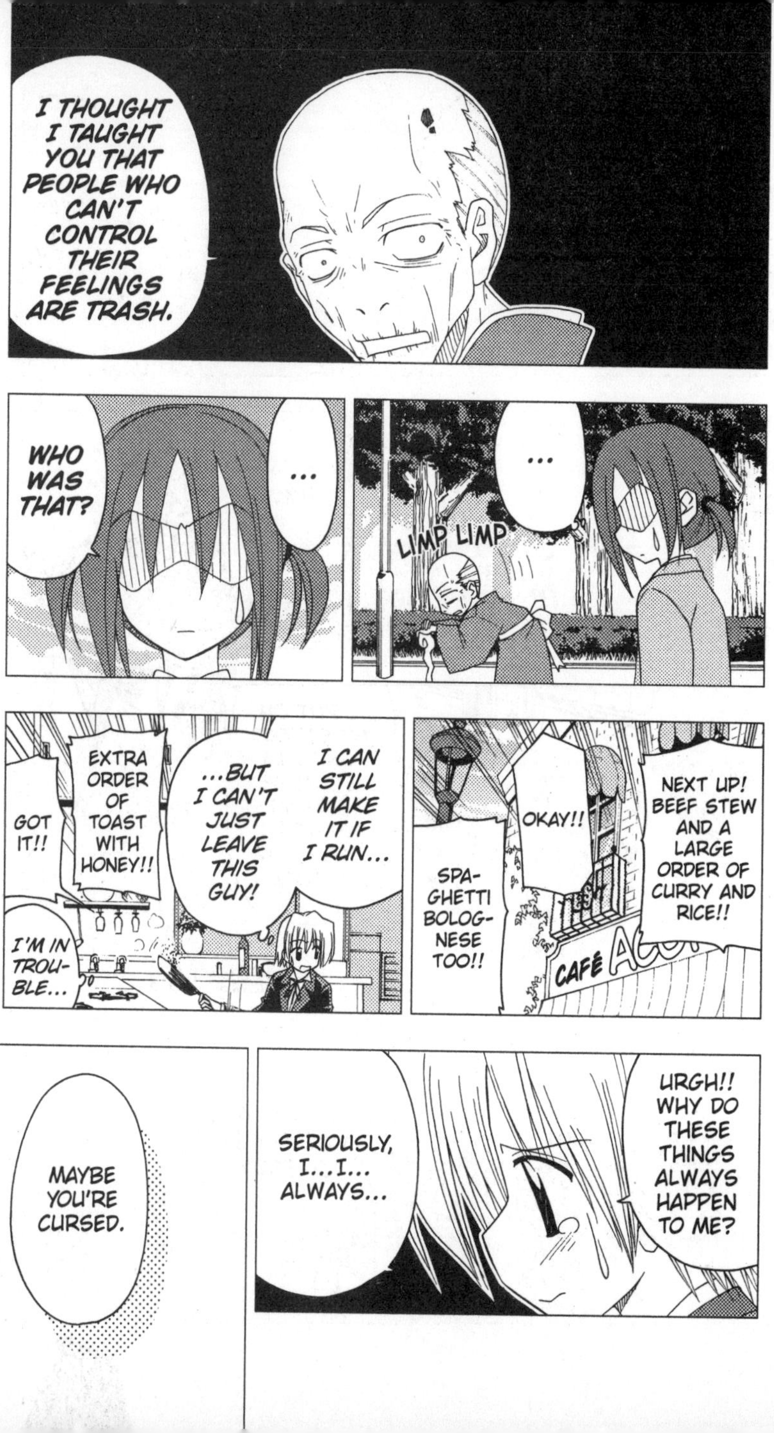
I THOUGHT I TAUGHT YOU THAT PEOPLE WHO CAN'T CONTROL THEIR FEELINGS ARE TRASH.
...
LIMP LIMP
...
WHO WAS THAT?
NEXT UP! BEEF STEW AND A LARGE ORDER OF CURRY AND RICE!!
OKAY!!
SPA-GHETTI BOLOG-NESE TOO!!
CAFÉ
I CAN STILL MAKE IT IF I RUN...
...BUT I CAN'T JUST LEAVE THIS GUY!
EXTRA ORDER OF TOAST WITH HONEY!!
GOT IT!!
I'M IN TROU-BLE...
URGH!! WHY DO THESE THINGS ALWAYS HAPPEN TO ME?
SERIOUSLY, I...I... ALWAYS...
MAYBE YOU'RE CURSED.

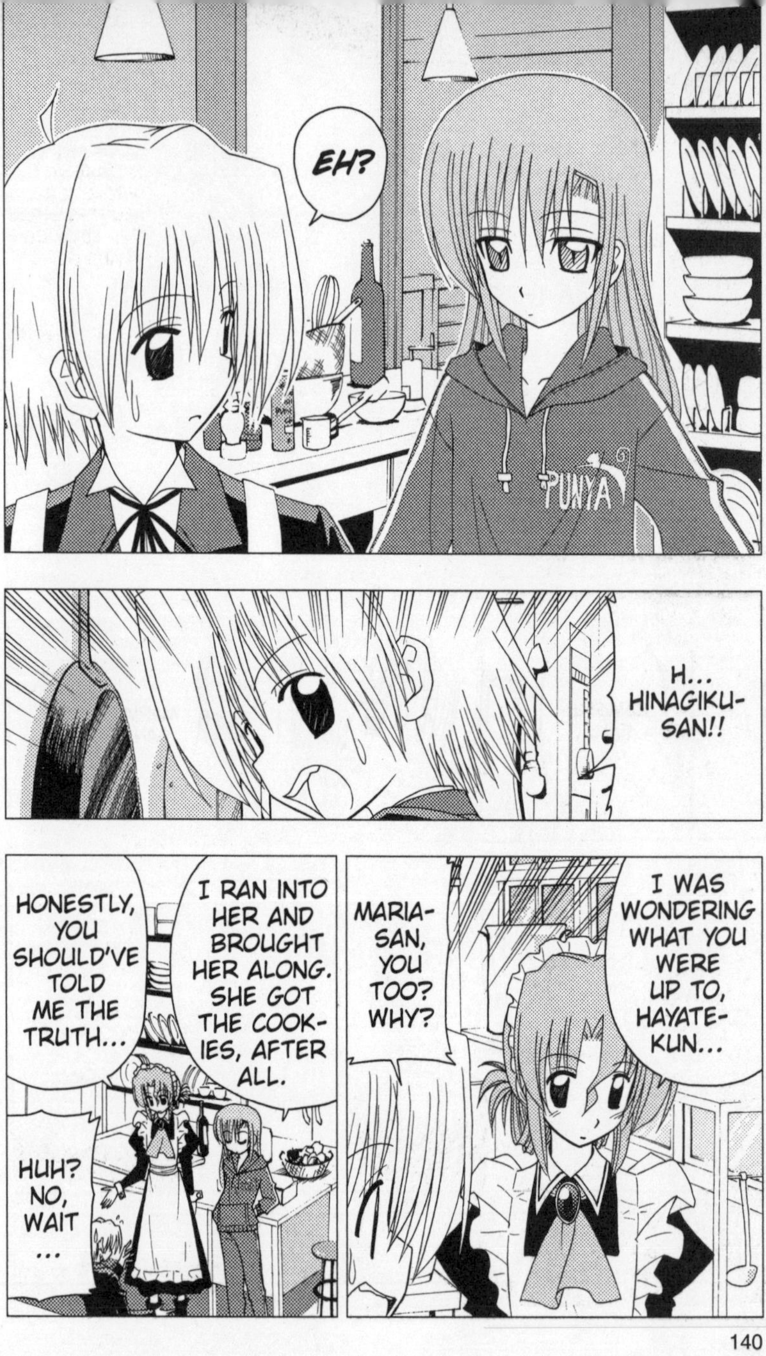
EH?
PUNYA
H... HINAGIKU-SAN!!
I WAS WONDERING WHAT YOU WERE UP TO, HAYATE-KUN...
MARIA-SAN, YOU TOO? WHY?
I RAN INTO HER AND BROUGHT HER ALONG. SHE GOT THE COOKIES, AFTER ALL.
HONESTLY, YOU SHOULD'VE TOLD ME THE TRUTH...
HUH? NO, WAIT ...

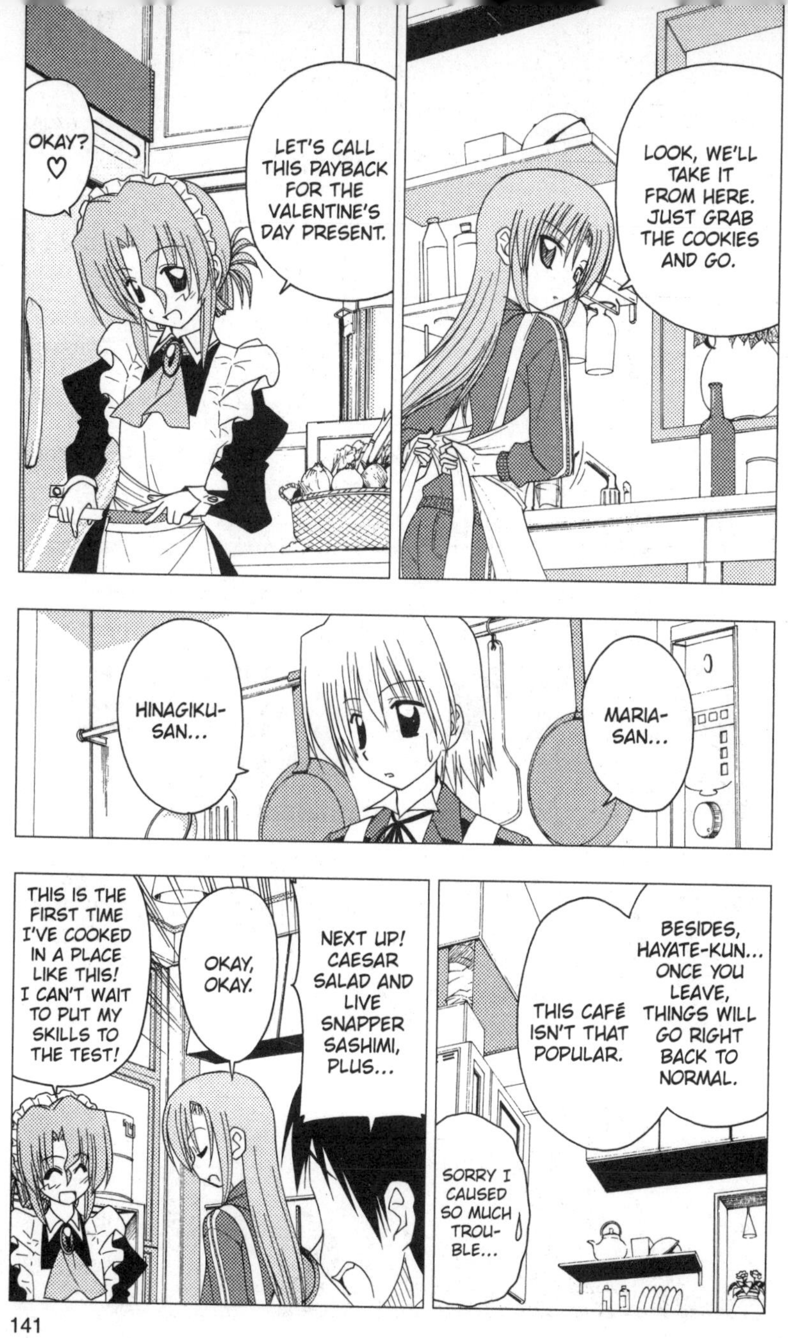
LOOK, WE'LL TAKE IT FROM HERE. JUST GRAB THE COOKIES AND GO.
LET'S CALL THIS PAYBACK FOR THE VALENTINE'S DAY PRESENT.
OKAY? ♡
MARIA-SAN...
HINAGIKU-SAN...
BESIDES, HAYATE-KUN... ONCE YOU LEAVE, THINGS WILL GO RIGHT BACK TO NORMAL.
THIS CAFÉ ISN'T THAT POPULAR.
SORRY I CAUSED SO MUCH TROU-BLE...
NEXT UP! CAESAR SALAD AND LIVE SNAPPER SASHIMI, PLUS...
OKAY, OKAY.
THIS IS THE FIRST TIME I'VE COOKED IN A PLACE LIKE THIS! I CAN'T WAIT TO PUT MY SKILLS TO THE TEST!

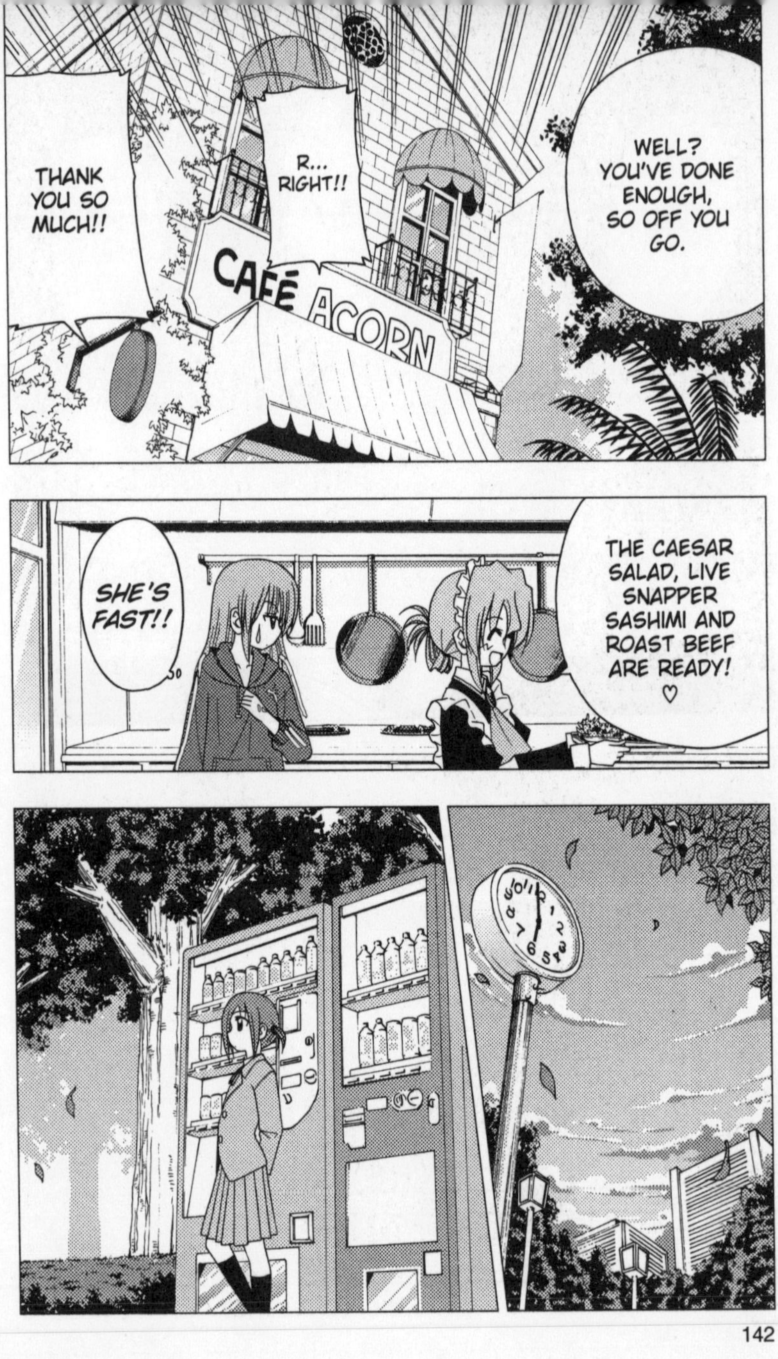
WELL? YOU'VE DONE ENOUGH, SO OFF YOU GO.
R... RIGHT!!
CAFÉ ACORN
THANK YOU SO MUCH!!
THE CAESAR SALAD, LIVE SNAPPER SASHIMI AND ROAST BEEF ARE READY! ♡
SHE'S FAST!!

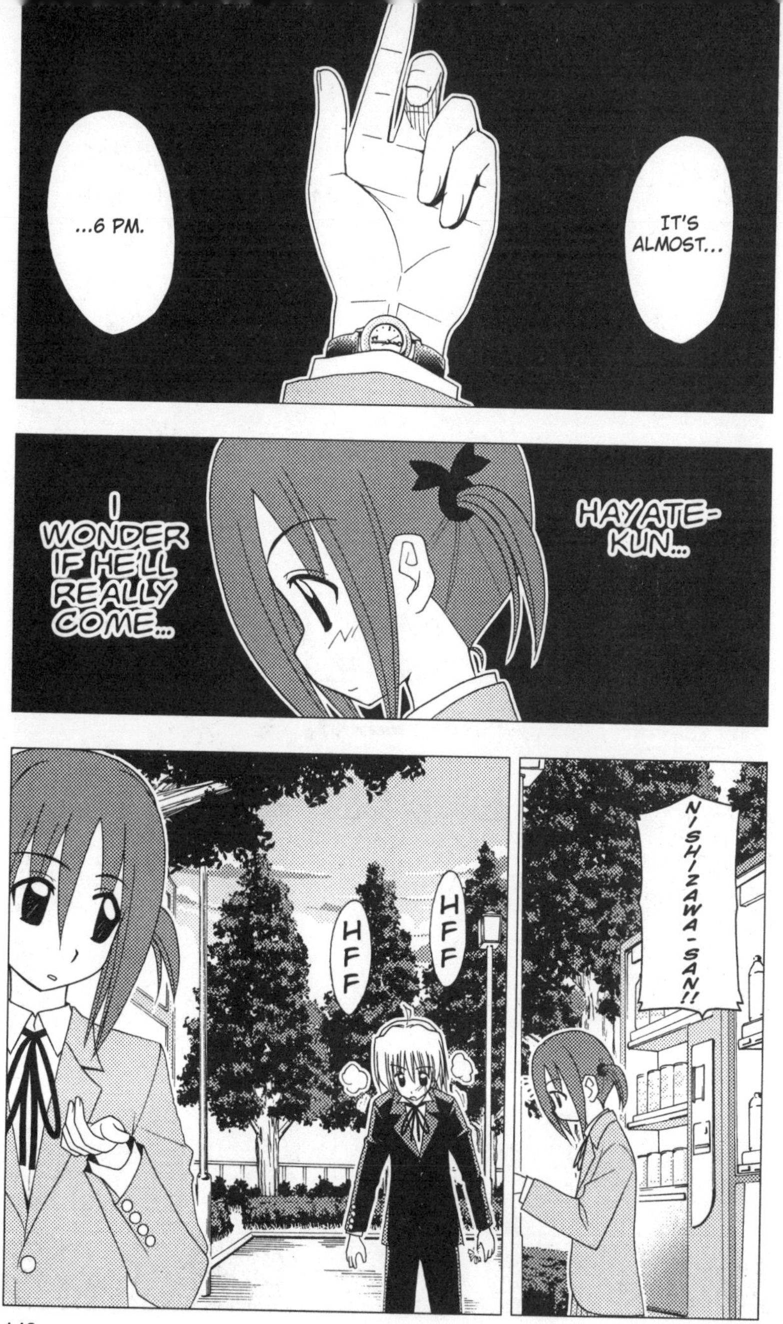
IT'S ALMOST...
...6 PM.
HAYATE-KUN...
I WONDER IF HE'LL REALLY COME...
NISHIZAWA-SAN!!
HFF
HFF

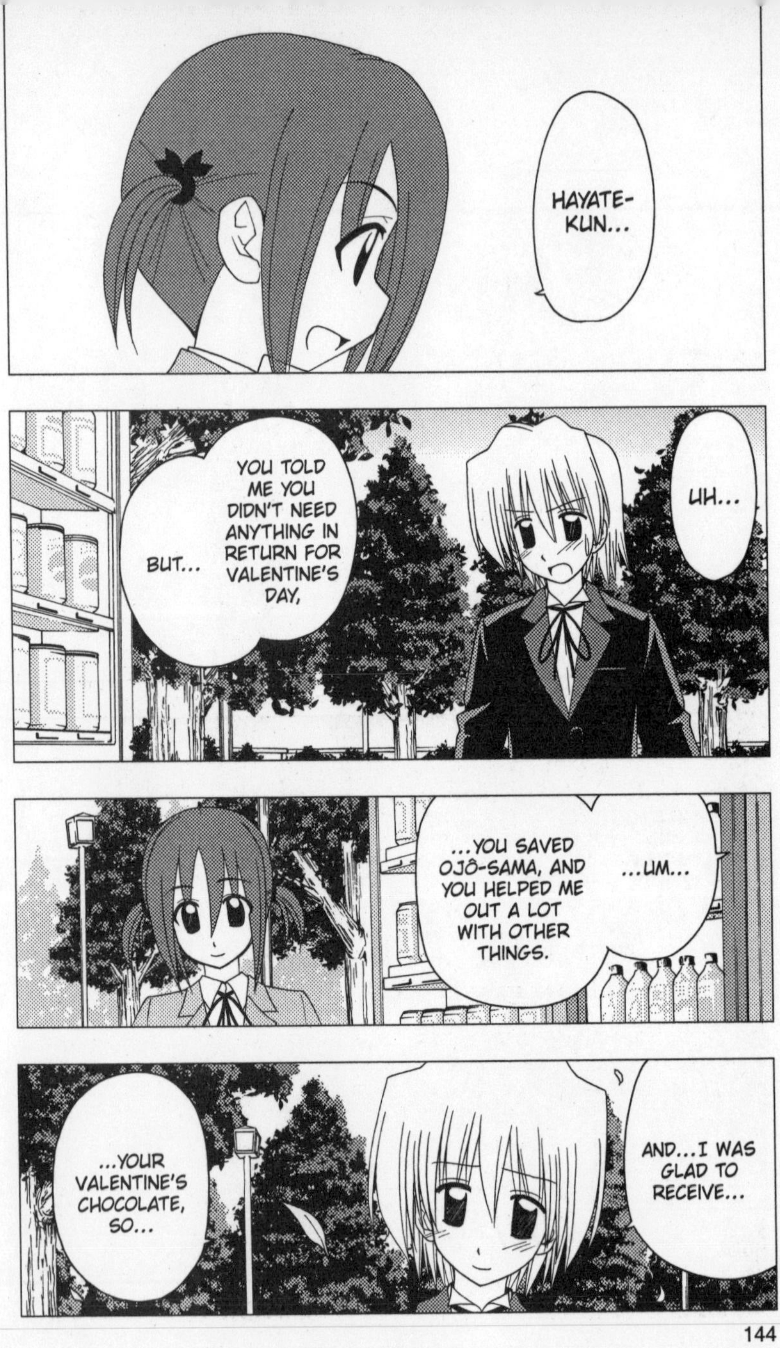
HAYATE-KUN...
UH...
YOU TOLD ME YOU DIDN'T NEED ANYTHING IN RETURN FOR VALENTINE'S DAY,
BUT...
...UM...
...YOU SAVED OJÔ-SAMA, AND YOU HELPED ME OUT A LOT WITH OTHER THINGS.
AND...I WAS GLAD TO RECEIVE...
...YOUR VALENTINE'S CHOCOLATE, SO...

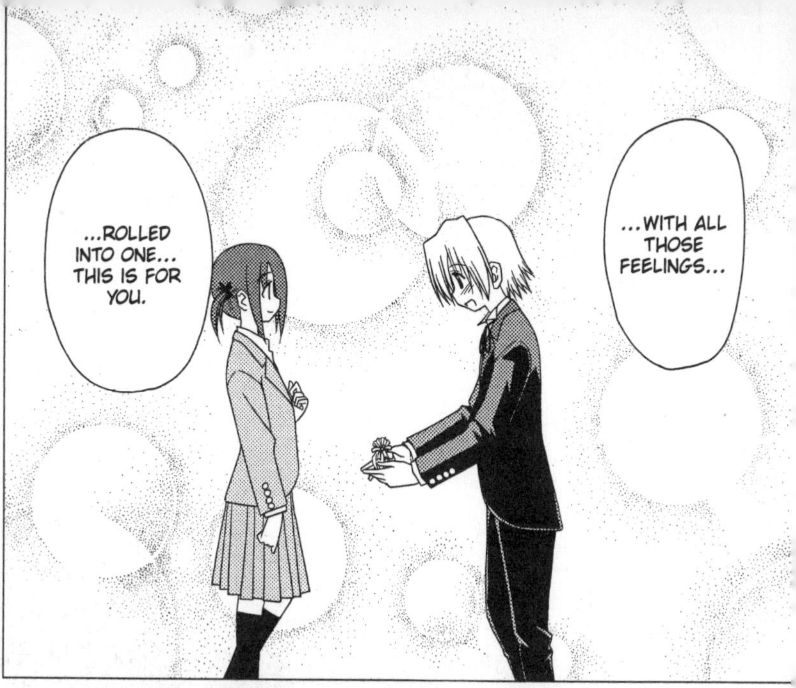
...WITH ALL THOSE FEELINGS...
...ROLLED INTO ONE... THIS IS FOR YOU.

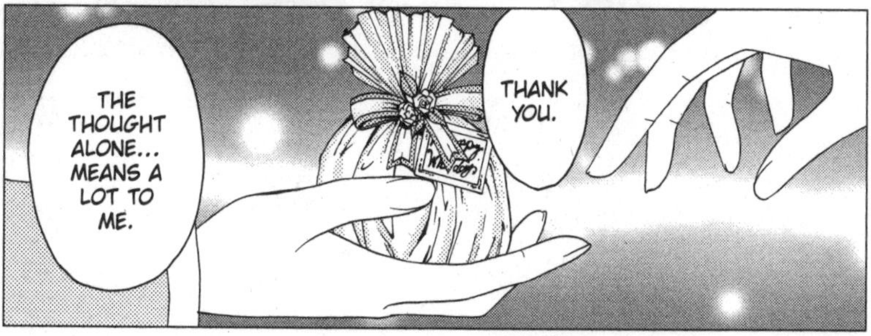
THANK YOU.
THE THOUGHT ALONE... MEANS A LOT TO ME.

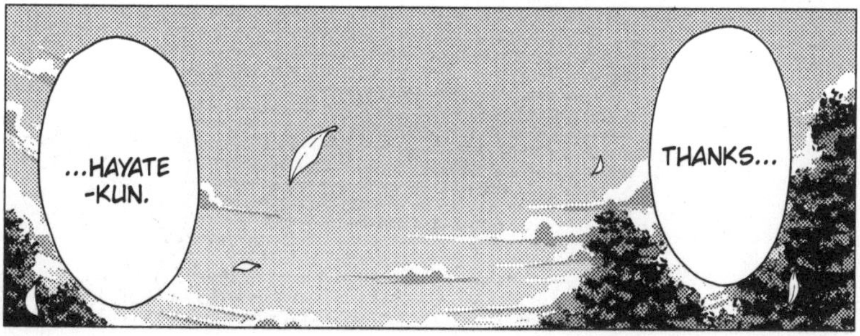
THANKS...
...HAYATE -KUN.

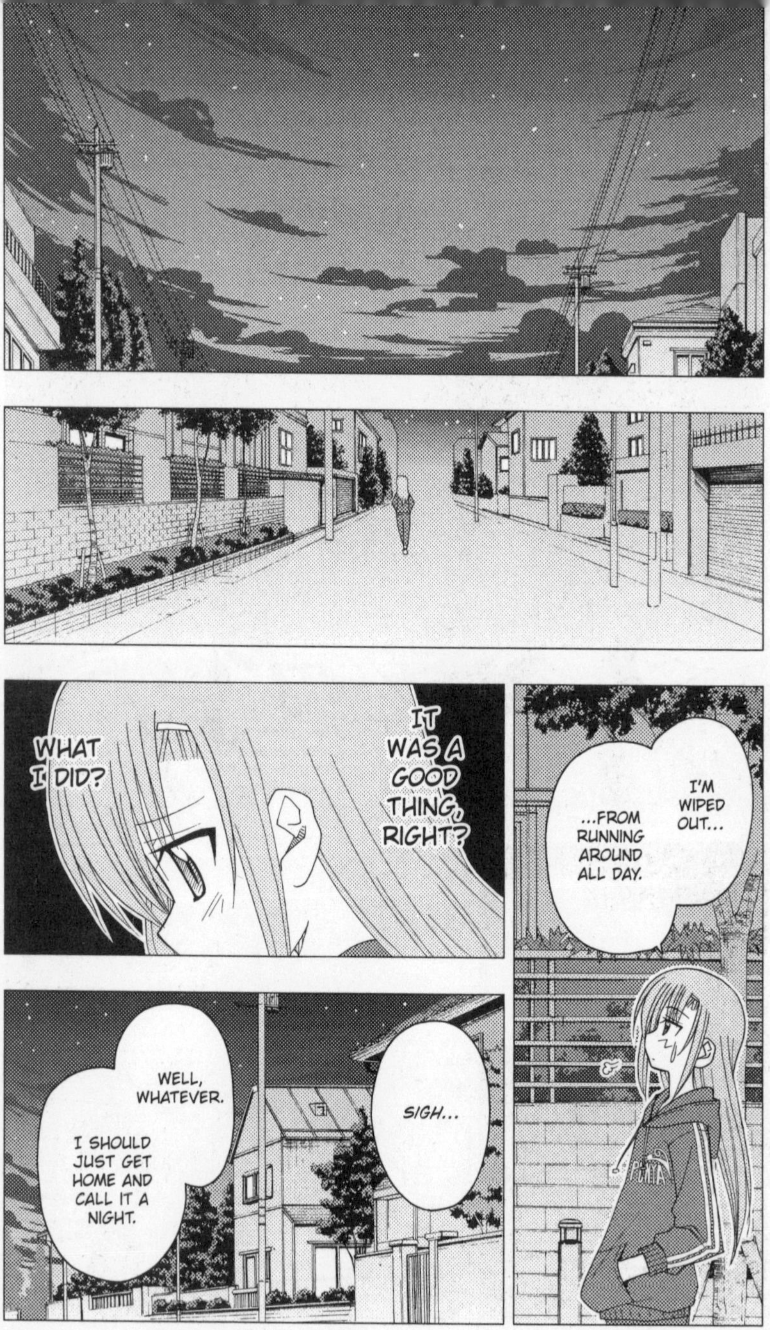
I'M WIPED OUT...
...FROM RUNNING AROUND ALL DAY.
IT WAS A GOOD THING, RIGHT?
WHAT I DID?
SIGH...
WELL, WHATEVER.
I SHOULD JUST GET HOME AND CALL IT A NIGHT.
PUMA

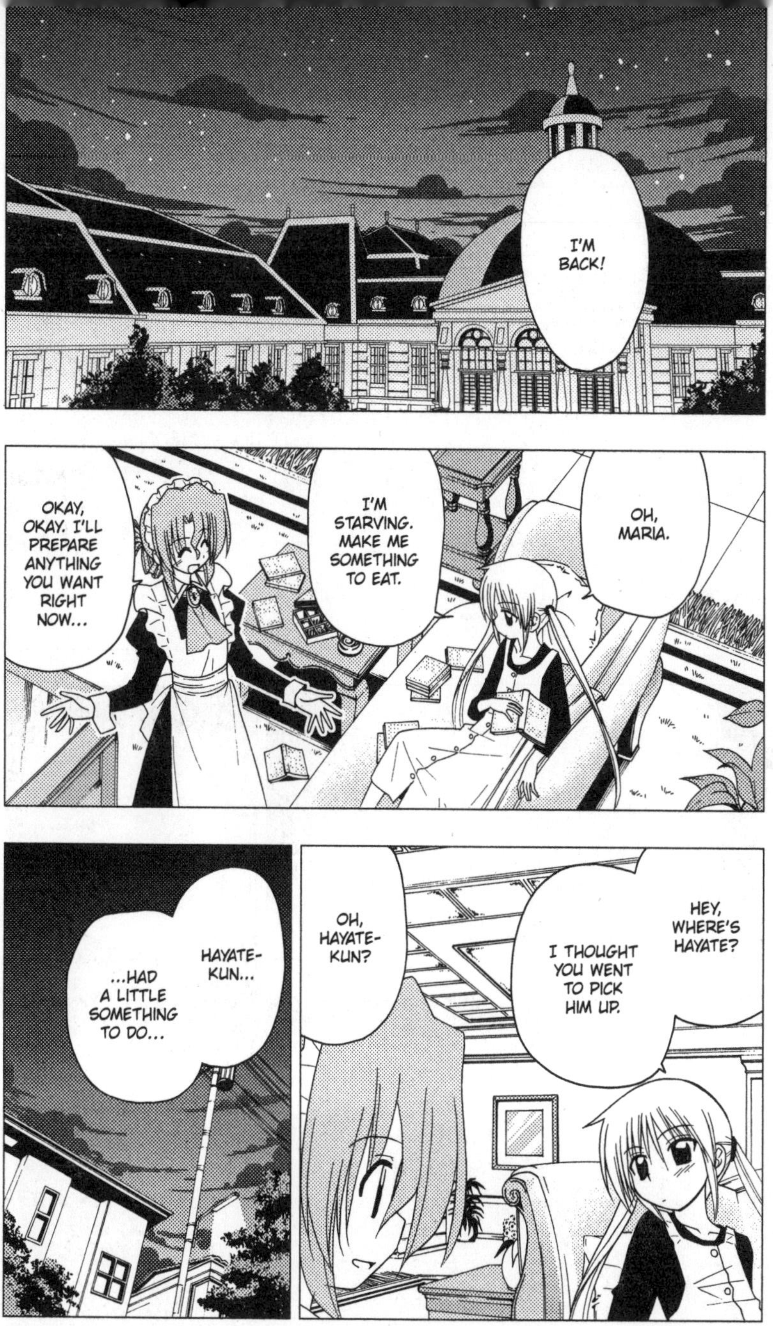
I'M BACK!
OH, MARIA.
I'M STARVING. MAKE ME SOMETHING TO EAT.
OKAY, OKAY. I'LL PREPARE ANYTHING YOU WANT RIGHT NOW...
HEY, WHERE'S HAYATE?
I THOUGHT YOU WENT TO PICK HIM UP.
OH, HAYATE-KUN?
HAYATE-KUN...
...HAD A LITTLE SOMETHING TO DO...

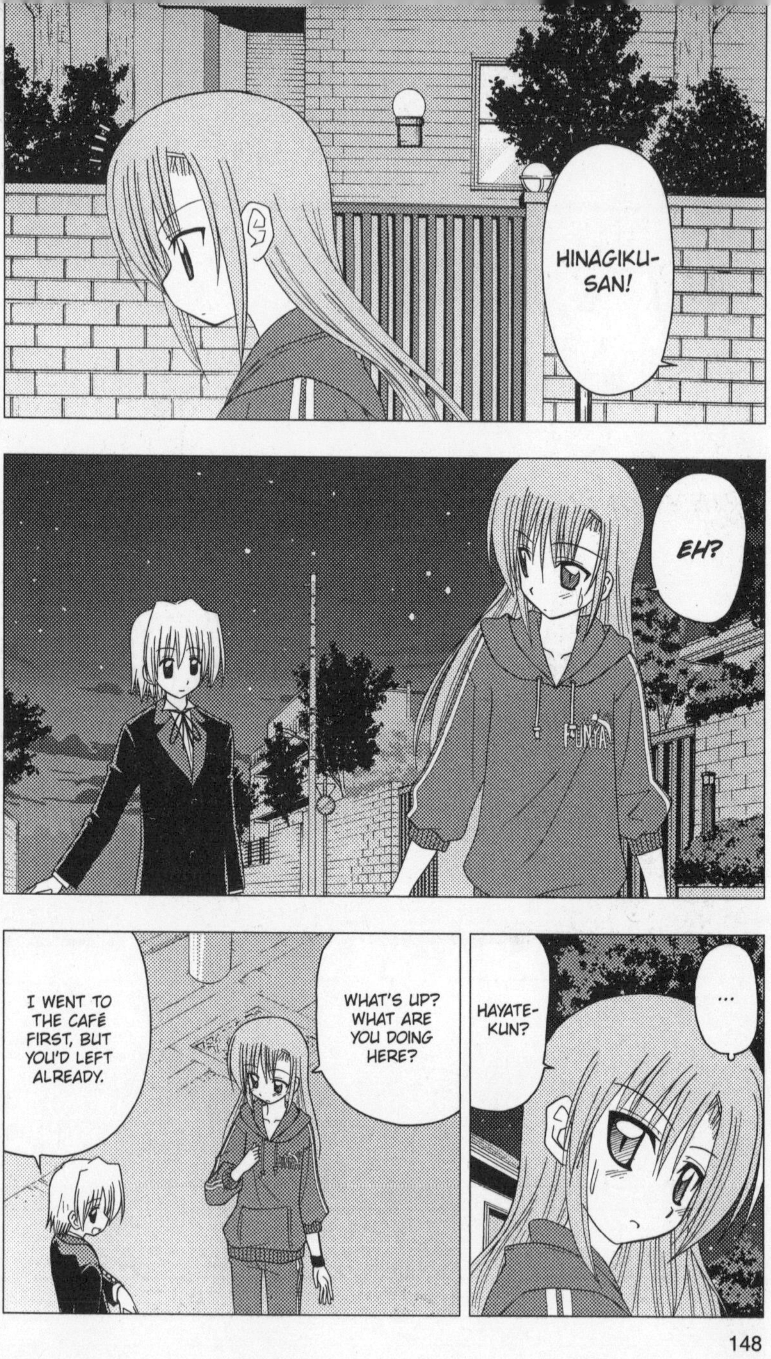
HINAGIKU-SAN!
EH?
...
HAYATE-KUN?
WHAT'S UP? WHAT ARE YOU DOING HERE?
I WENT TO THE CAFÉ FIRST, BUT YOU'D LEFT ALREADY.

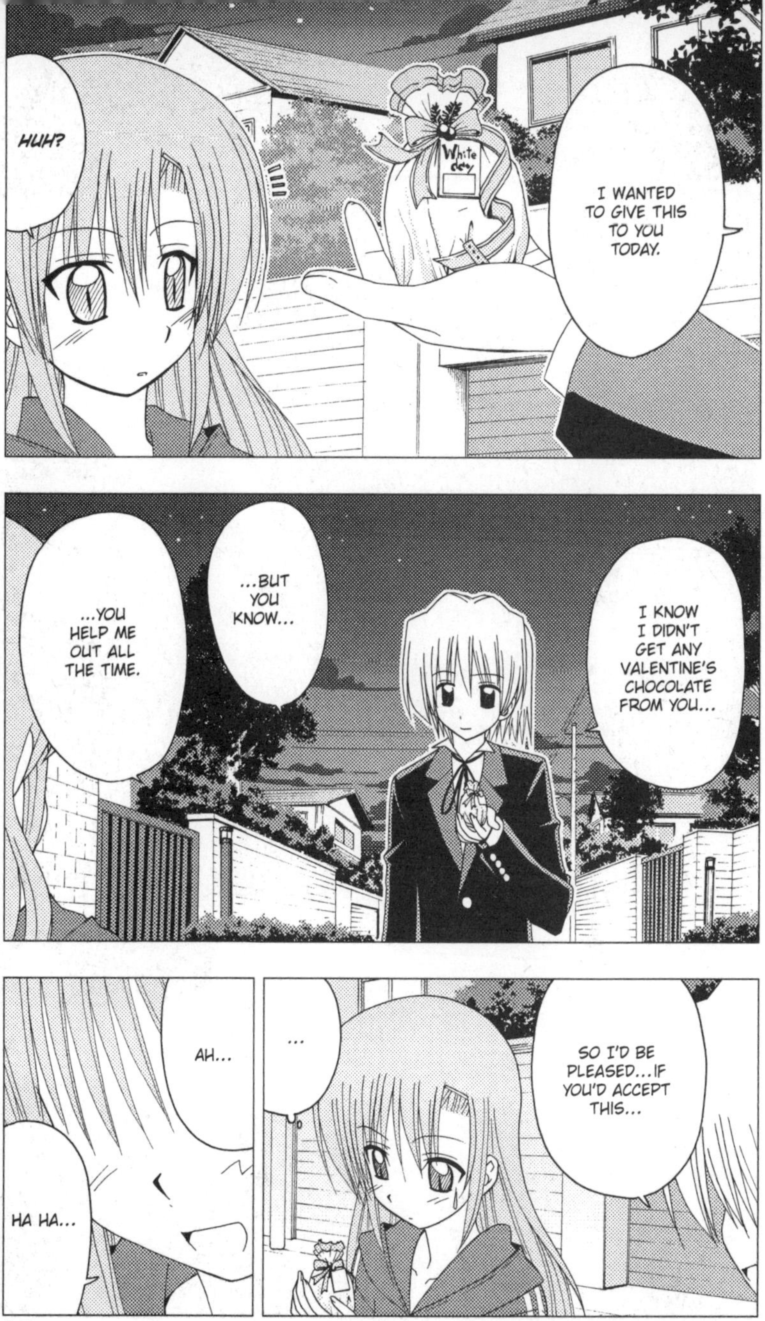
I WANTED TO GIVE THIS TO YOU TODAY.
White day
HUH?
I KNOW I DIDN'T GET ANY VALENTINE'S CHOCOLATE FROM YOU...
...BUT YOU KNOW...
...YOU HELP ME OUT ALL THE TIME.
SO I'D BE PLEASED...IF YOU'D ACCEPT THIS...
...
AH...
HA HA...

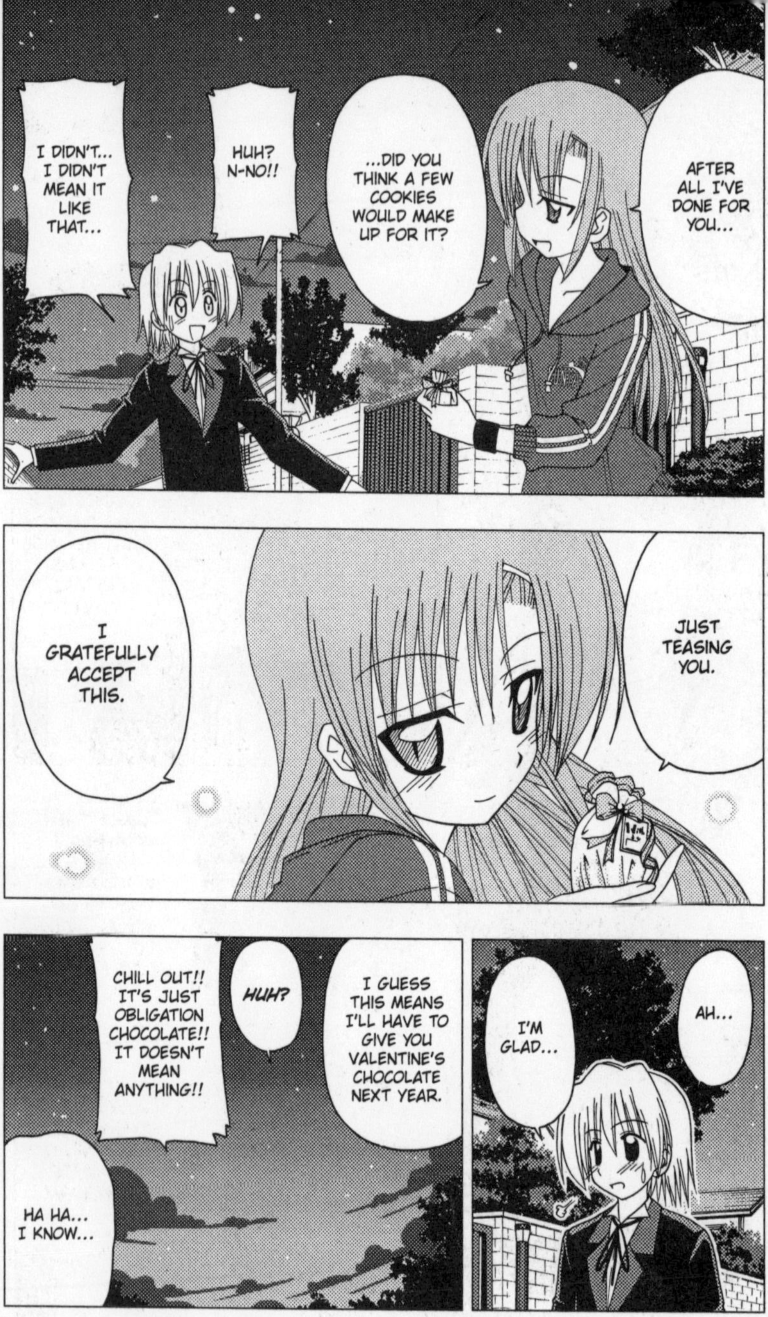
AFTER ALL I'VE DONE FOR YOU...
...DID YOU THINK A FEW COOKIES WOULD MAKE UP FOR IT?
HUH? N-NO!!
I DIDN'T... I DIDN'T MEAN IT LIKE THAT...
JUST TEASING YOU.
I GRATEFULLY ACCEPT THIS.
AH...
I'M GLAD...
I GUESS THIS MEANS I'LL HAVE TO GIVE YOU VALENTINE'S CHOCOLATE NEXT YEAR.
HUH?
CHILL OUT!! IT'S JUST OBLIGATION CHOCOLATE!! IT DOESN'T MEAN ANYTHING!!
HA HA... I KNOW...

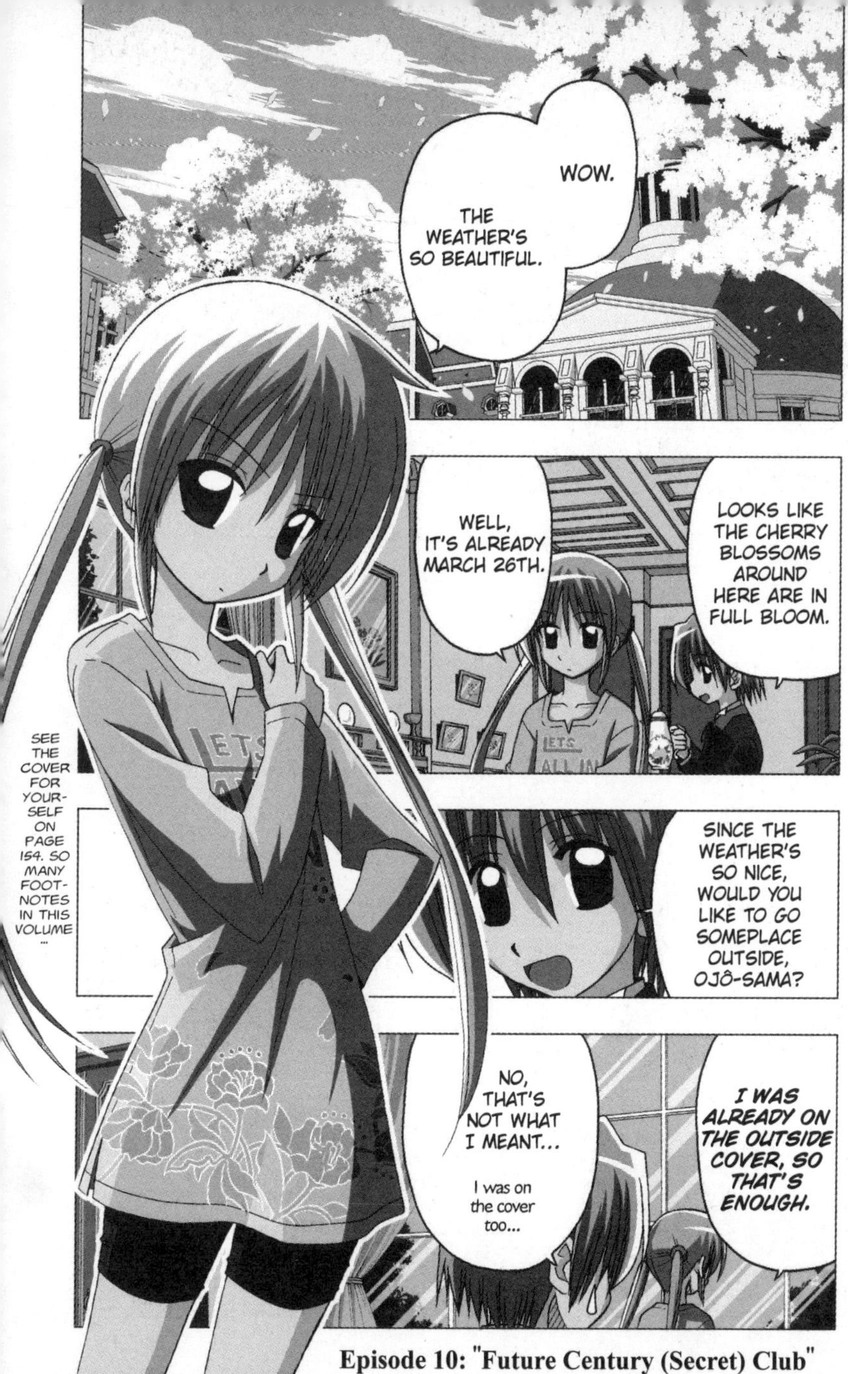
WOW.
THE WEATHER'S SO BEAUTIFUL.
LOOKS LIKE THE CHERRY BLOSSOMS AROUND HERE ARE IN FULL BLOOM.
WELL, IT'S ALREADY MARCH 26TH.
SINCE THE WEATHER'S SO NICE, WOULD YOU LIKE TO GO SOMEPLACE OUTSIDE, OJÔ-SAMA?
I WAS ALREADY ON THE OUTSIDE COVER, SO THAT'S ENOUGH.
NO, THAT'S NOT WHAT I MEANT...
I was on the cover too...
SEE THE COVER FOR YOURSELF ON PAGE 154. SO MANY FOOTNOTES IN THIS VOLUME ...

Episode 10: "Future Century (Secret) Club"

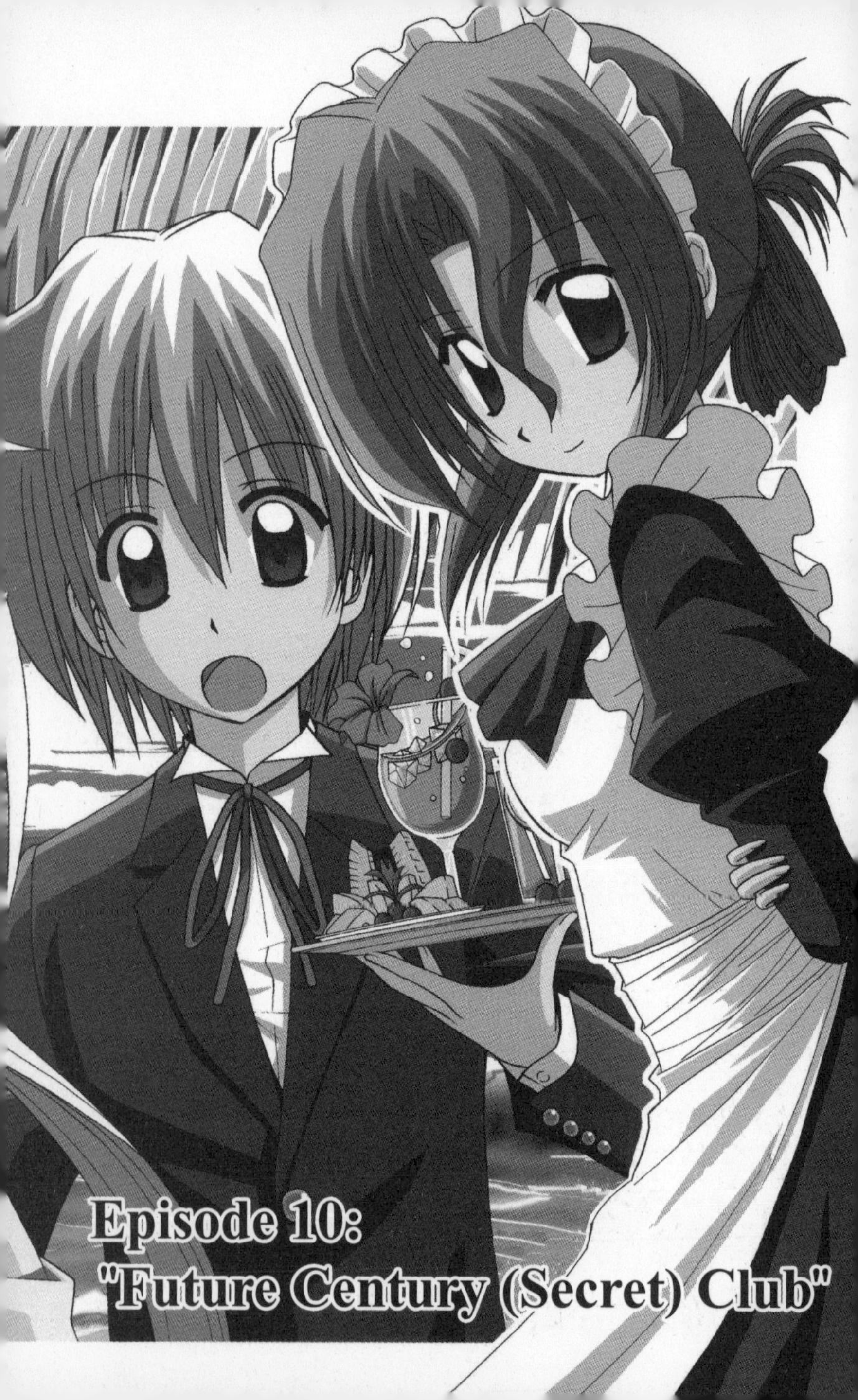
Episode 10:
"Future Century (Secret) Club"

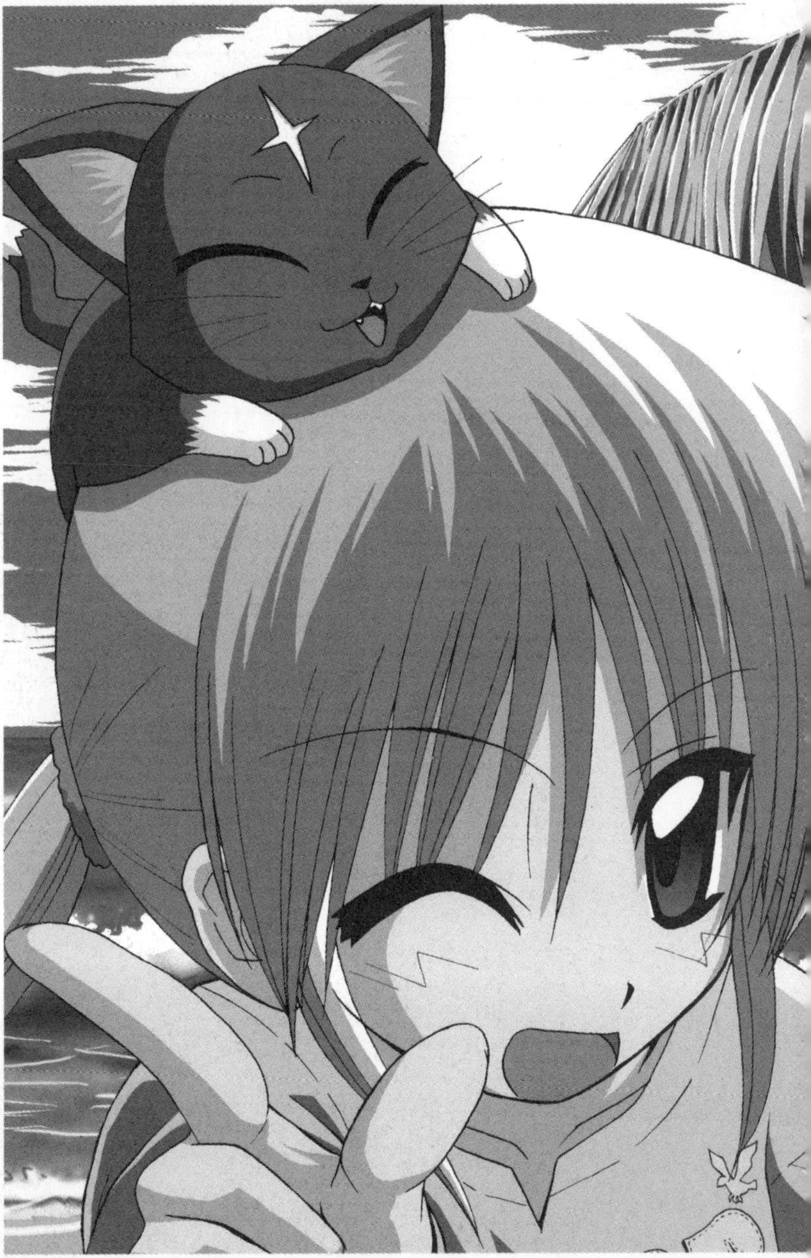

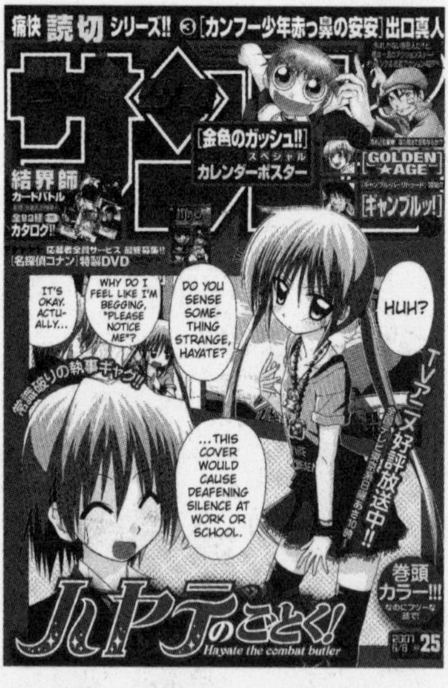
痛快 読切 シリーズ!! ③[カンフー少年赤っ鼻の安安]出口真人
[金色のガッシュ!!] スペシャル カレンダーポスター
[GOLDEN★AGE]
[ギャンブルッ!]
結界師 カードバトル
カタログ!!
[名探偵コナン]特製DVD
HUH?
DO YOU SENSE SOMETHING STRANGE, HAYATE?
WHY DO I FEEL LIKE I'M BEGGING, "PLEASE NOTICE ME"?
IT'S OKAY. ACTUALLY...
テレビアニメ好評放送中!!
常識破りの執事ギャグ!!
...THIS COVER WOULD CAUSE DEAFENING SILENCE AT WORK OR SCHOOL.
巻頭カラー!!!
ハヤテのごとく!
Hayate the combat butler
25

※ SHONEN SUNDAY MAGAZINE #25, 2007.

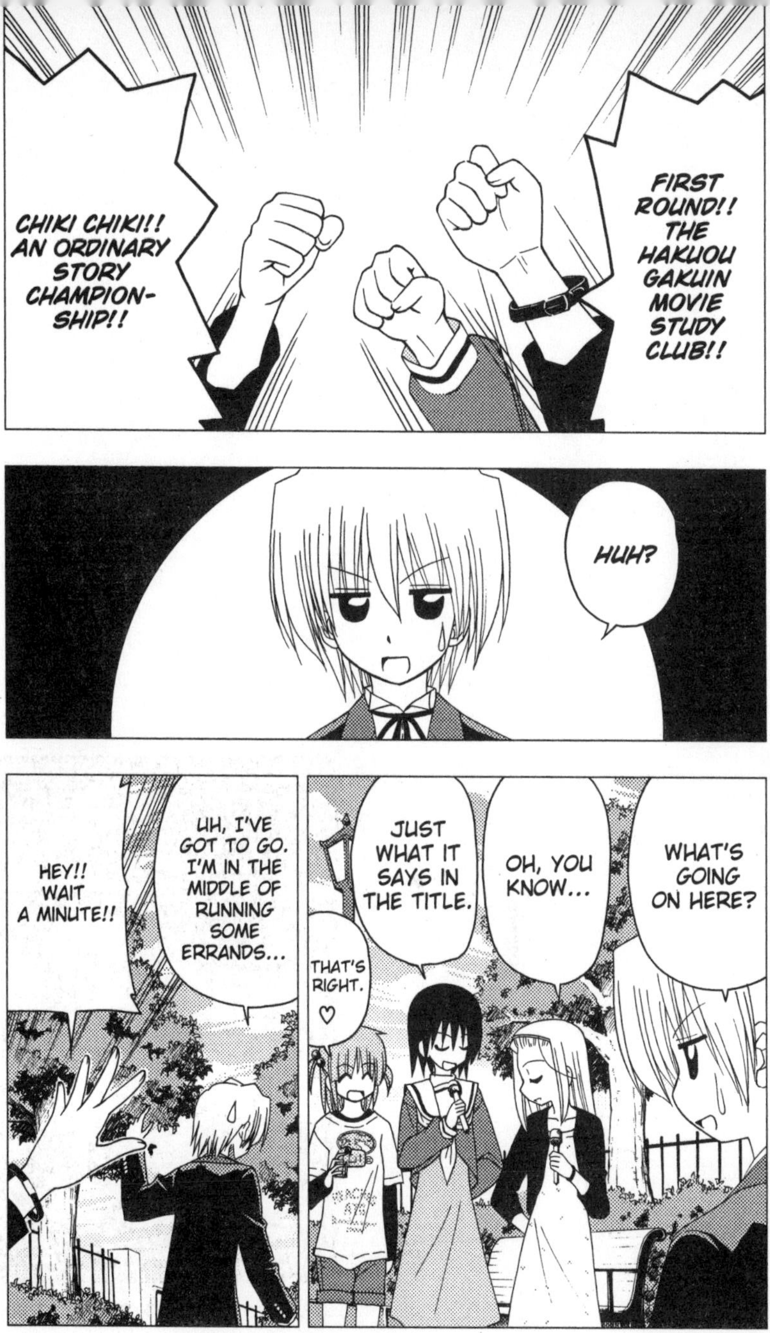
FIRST ROUND!! THE HAKUOU GAKUIN MOVIE STUDY CLUB!!
CHIKI CHIKI!! AN ORDINARY STORY CHAMPIONSHIP!!
HUH?
WHAT'S GOING ON HERE?
OH, YOU KNOW...
JUST WHAT IT SAYS IN THE TITLE.
THAT'S RIGHT. ♡
UH, I'VE GOT TO GO. I'M IN THE MIDDLE OF RUNNING SOME ERRANDS...
HEY!! WAIT A MINUTE!!

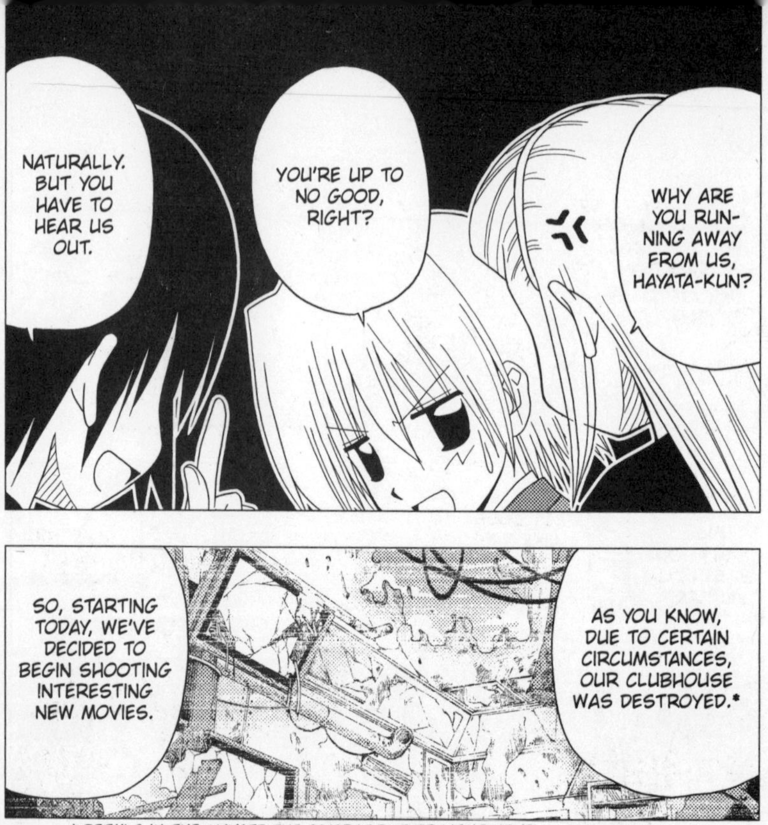
WHY ARE YOU RUNNING AWAY FROM US, HAYATA-KUN?
YOU'RE UP TO NO GOOD, RIGHT?
NATURALLY. BUT YOU HAVE TO HEAR US OUT.
AS YOU KNOW, DUE TO CERTAIN CIRCUMSTANCES, OUR CLUBHOUSE WAS DESTROYED.*
SO, STARTING TODAY, WE'VE DECIDED TO BEGIN SHOOTING INTERESTING NEW MOVIES.

※DETAILS IN THE *HAYATE THE COMBAT BUTLER* LIGHT NOVEL.

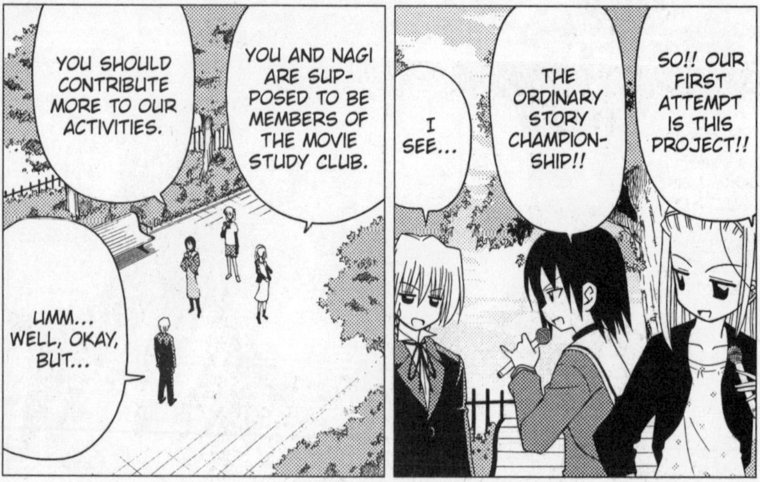
SO!! OUR FIRST ATTEMPT IS THIS PROJECT!!
THE ORDINARY STORY CHAMPIONSHIP!!
I SEE...
YOU AND NAGI ARE SUPPOSED TO BE MEMBERS OF THE MOVIE STUDY CLUB.
YOU SHOULD CONTRIBUTE MORE TO OUR ACTIVITIES.
UMM... WELL, OKAY, BUT...

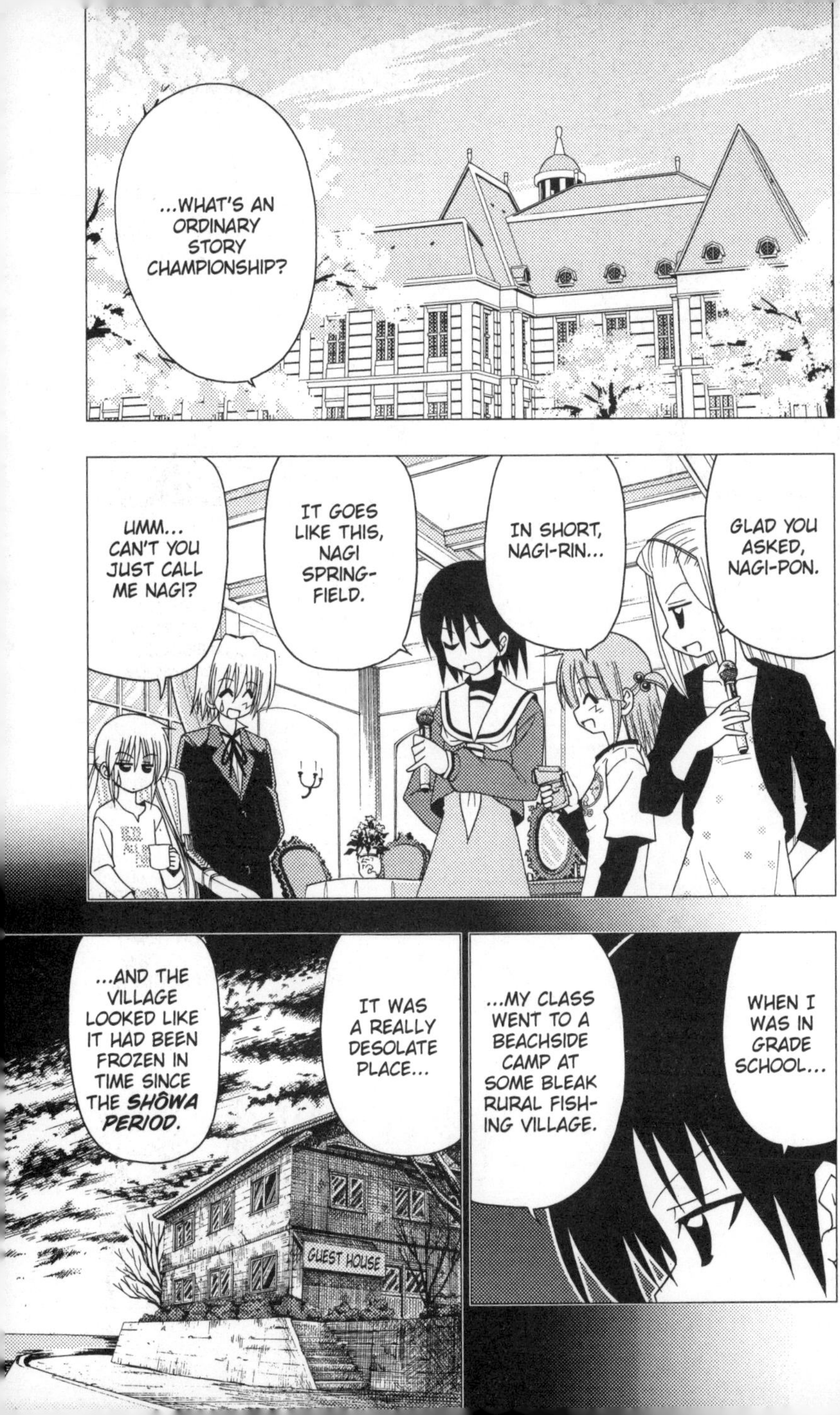
...WHAT'S AN ORDINARY STORY CHAMPIONSHIP?
GLAD YOU ASKED, NAGI-PON.
IN SHORT, NAGI-RIN...
IT GOES LIKE THIS, NAGI SPRING-FIELD.
UMM... CAN'T YOU JUST CALL ME NAGI?
WHEN I WAS IN GRADE SCHOOL...
...MY CLASS WENT TO A BEACHSIDE CAMP AT SOME BLEAK RURAL FISH-ING VILLAGE.
IT WAS A REALLY DESOLATE PLACE...
...AND THE VILLAGE LOOKED LIKE IT HAD BEEN FROZEN IN TIME SINCE THE ***SHŌWA PERIOD***.
GUEST HOUSE

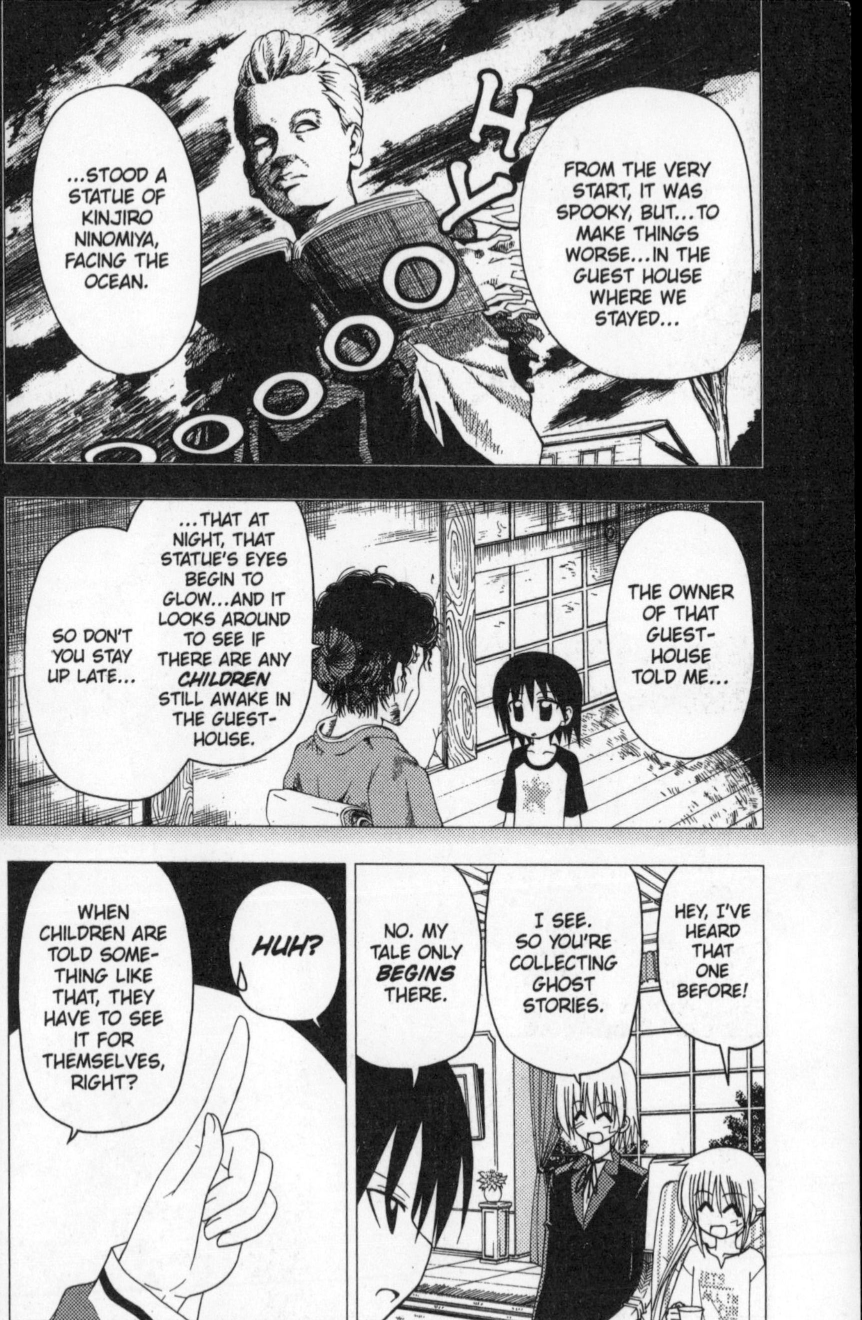
FROM THE VERY START, IT WAS SPOOKY, BUT...TO MAKE THINGS WORSE...IN THE GUEST HOUSE WHERE WE STAYED...
HYOOOOO
...STOOD A STATUE OF KINJIRO NINOMIYA, FACING THE OCEAN.
THE OWNER OF THAT GUEST-HOUSE TOLD ME...
...THAT AT NIGHT, THAT STATUE'S EYES BEGIN TO GLOW...AND IT LOOKS AROUND TO SEE IF THERE ARE ANY CHILDREN STILL AWAKE IN THE GUEST-HOUSE.
SO DON'T YOU STAY UP LATE...
HEY, I'VE HEARD THAT ONE BEFORE!
I SEE. SO YOU'RE COLLECTING GHOST STORIES.
NO. MY TALE ONLY BEGINS THERE.
HUH?
WHEN CHILDREN ARE TOLD SOMETHING LIKE THAT, THEY HAVE TO SEE IT FOR THEMSELVES, RIGHT?

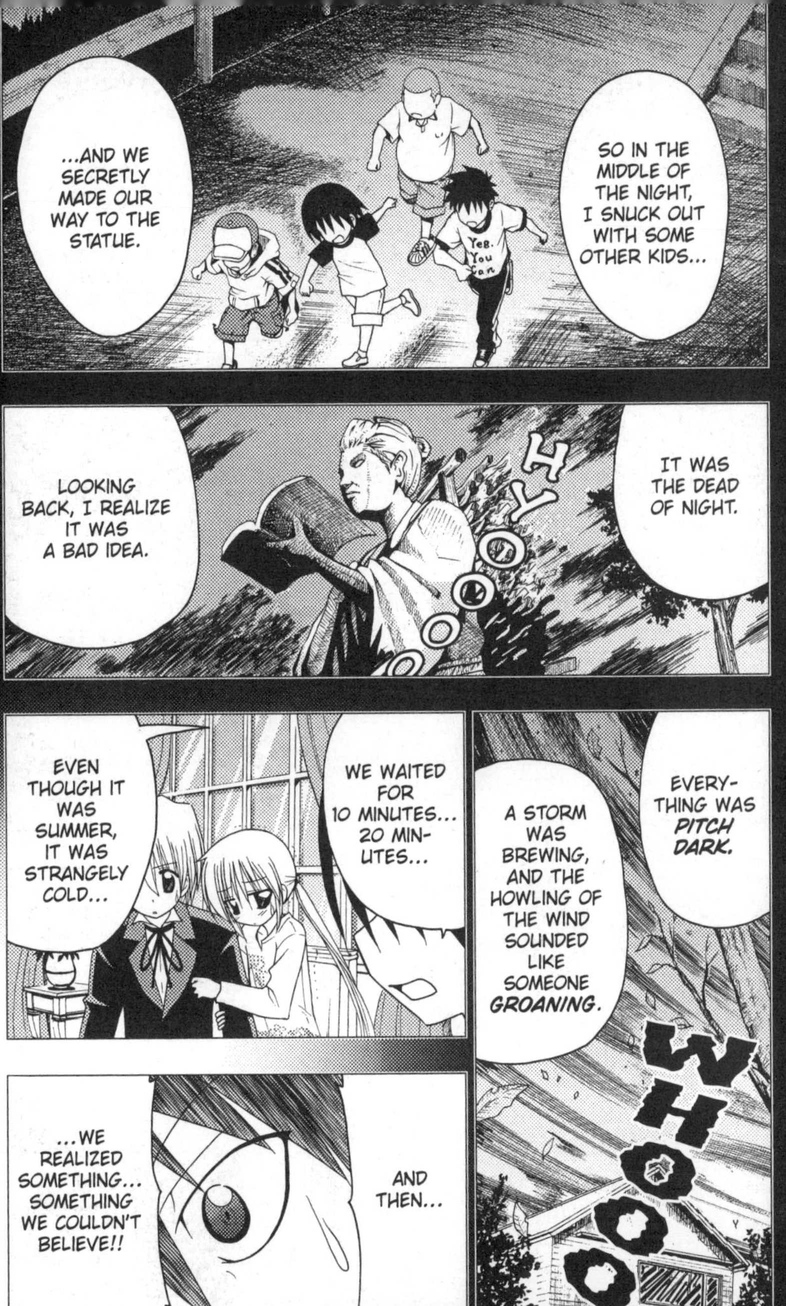
SO IN THE MIDDLE OF THE NIGHT, I SNUCK OUT WITH SOME OTHER KIDS...
...AND WE SECRETLY MADE OUR WAY TO THE STATUE.
Yes. You Can
IT WAS THE DEAD OF NIGHT.
HYOOOOOO
LOOKING BACK, I REALIZE IT WAS A BAD IDEA.
EVERY-THING WAS *PITCH DARK.*
A STORM WAS BREWING, AND THE HOWLING OF THE WIND SOUNDED LIKE SOMEONE ***GROANING***.
WHOOOO
WE WAITED FOR 10 MINUTES... 20 MIN-UTES...
EVEN THOUGH IT WAS SUMMER, IT WAS STRANGELY COLD...
AND THEN...
...WE REALIZED SOMETHING... SOMETHING WE COULDN'T BELIEVE!!

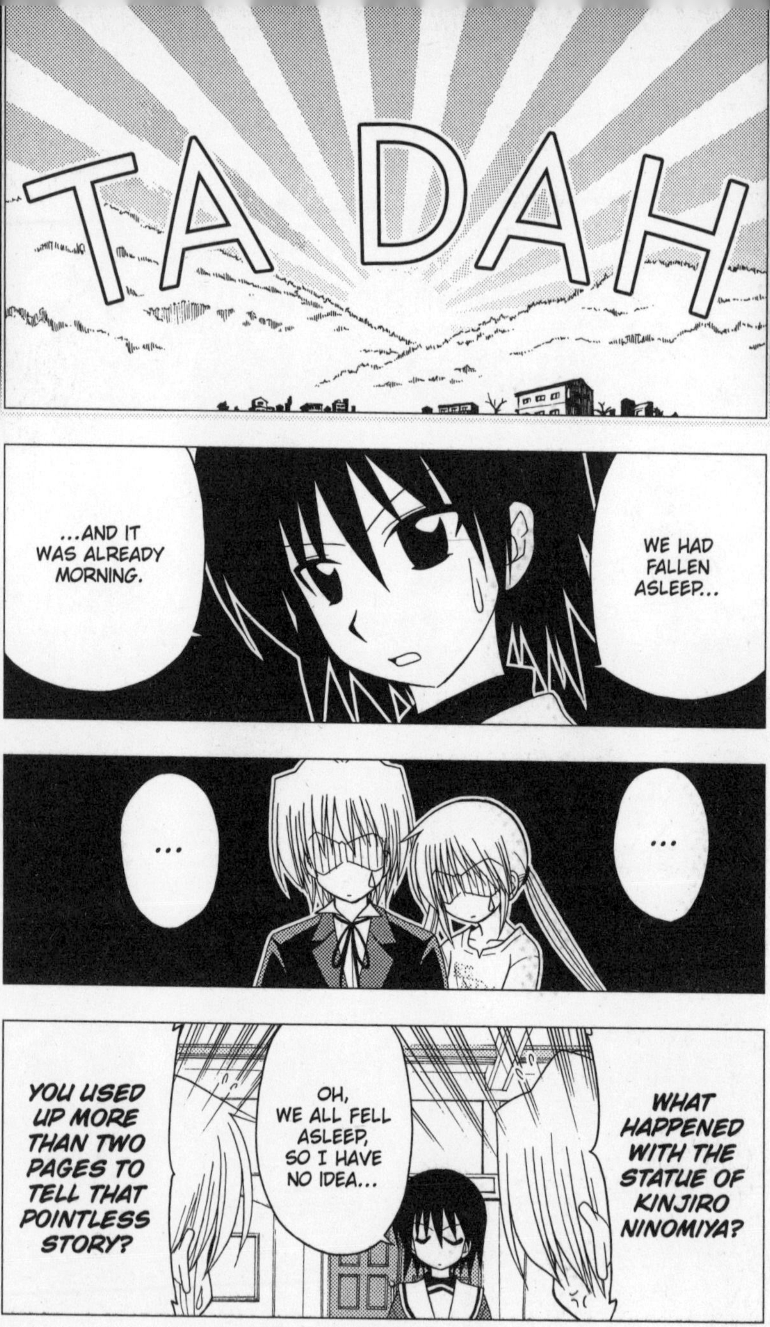
TADAH
WE HAD FALLEN ASLEEP...
...AND IT WAS ALREADY MORNING.
...
...
WHAT HAPPENED WITH THE STATUE OF KINJIRO NINOMIYA?
OH, WE ALL FELL ASLEEP, SO I HAVE NO IDEA...
YOU USED UP MORE THAN TWO PAGES TO TELL THAT POINTLESS STORY?

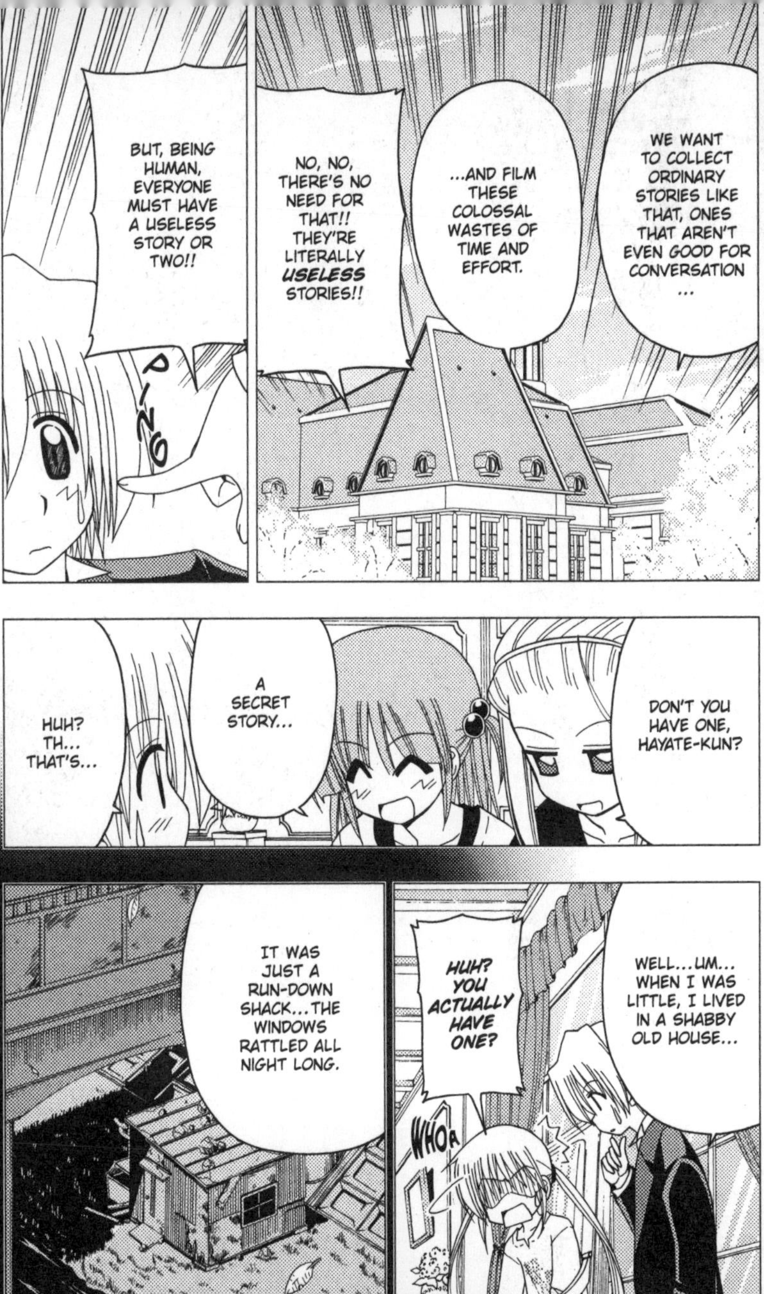
WE WANT TO COLLECT ORDINARY STORIES LIKE THAT, ONES THAT AREN'T EVEN GOOD FOR CONVERSATION ...
...AND FILM THESE COLOSSAL WASTES OF TIME AND EFFORT.
NO, NO, THERE'S NO NEED FOR THAT!! THEY'RE LITERALLY *USELESS* STORIES!!
PING
BUT, BEING HUMAN, EVERYONE MUST HAVE A USELESS STORY OR TWO!!
DON'T YOU HAVE ONE, HAYATE-KUN?
A SECRET STORY...
HUH? TH... THAT'S...
WELL...UM... WHEN I WAS LITTLE, I LIVED IN A SHABBY OLD HOUSE...
HUH? YOU ACTUALLY HAVE ONE?
WHOA!
IT WAS JUST A RUN-DOWN SHACK...THE WINDOWS RATTLED ALL NIGHT LONG.

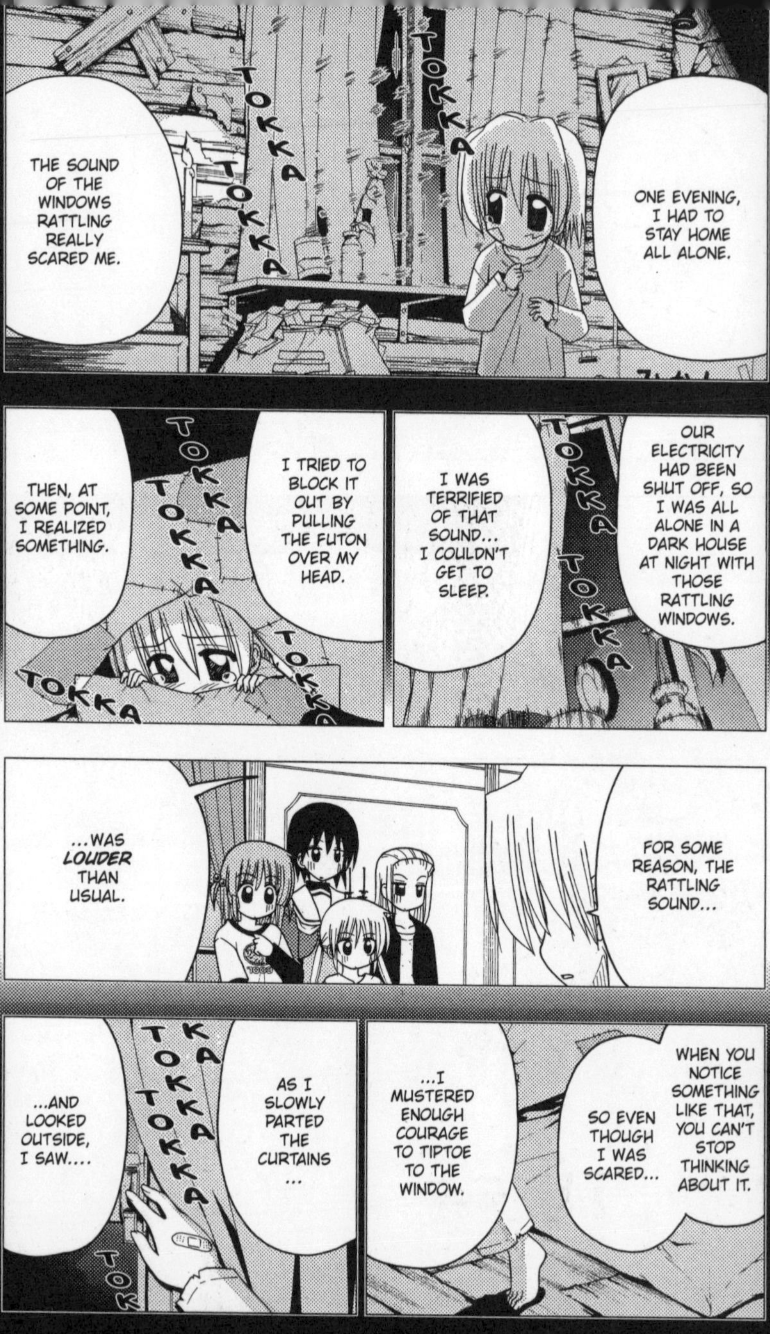
ONE EVENING, I HAD TO STAY HOME ALL ALONE.
TOKKA
TOKKA
TOKKA
THE SOUND OF THE WINDOWS RATTLING REALLY SCARED ME.
OUR ELECTRICITY HAD BEEN SHUT OFF, SO I WAS ALL ALONE IN A DARK HOUSE AT NIGHT WITH THOSE RATTLING WINDOWS.
TOKKA
TOKKA
I WAS TERRIFIED OF THAT SOUND... I COULDN'T GET TO SLEEP.
I TRIED TO BLOCK IT OUT BY PULLING THE FUTON OVER MY HEAD.
TOKKA
TOKKA
TOKKA
TOKKA
THEN, AT SOME POINT, I REALIZED SOMETHING.
FOR SOME REASON, THE RATTLING SOUND...
...WAS *LOUDER* THAN USUAL.
WHEN YOU NOTICE SOMETHING LIKE THAT, YOU CAN'T STOP THINKING ABOUT IT.
SO EVEN THOUGH I WAS SCARED...
...I MUSTERED ENOUGH COURAGE TO TIPTOE TO THE WINDOW.
AS I SLOWLY PARTED THE CURTAINS...
TOKKA
TOKKA
TOK
...AND LOOKED OUTSIDE, I SAW....

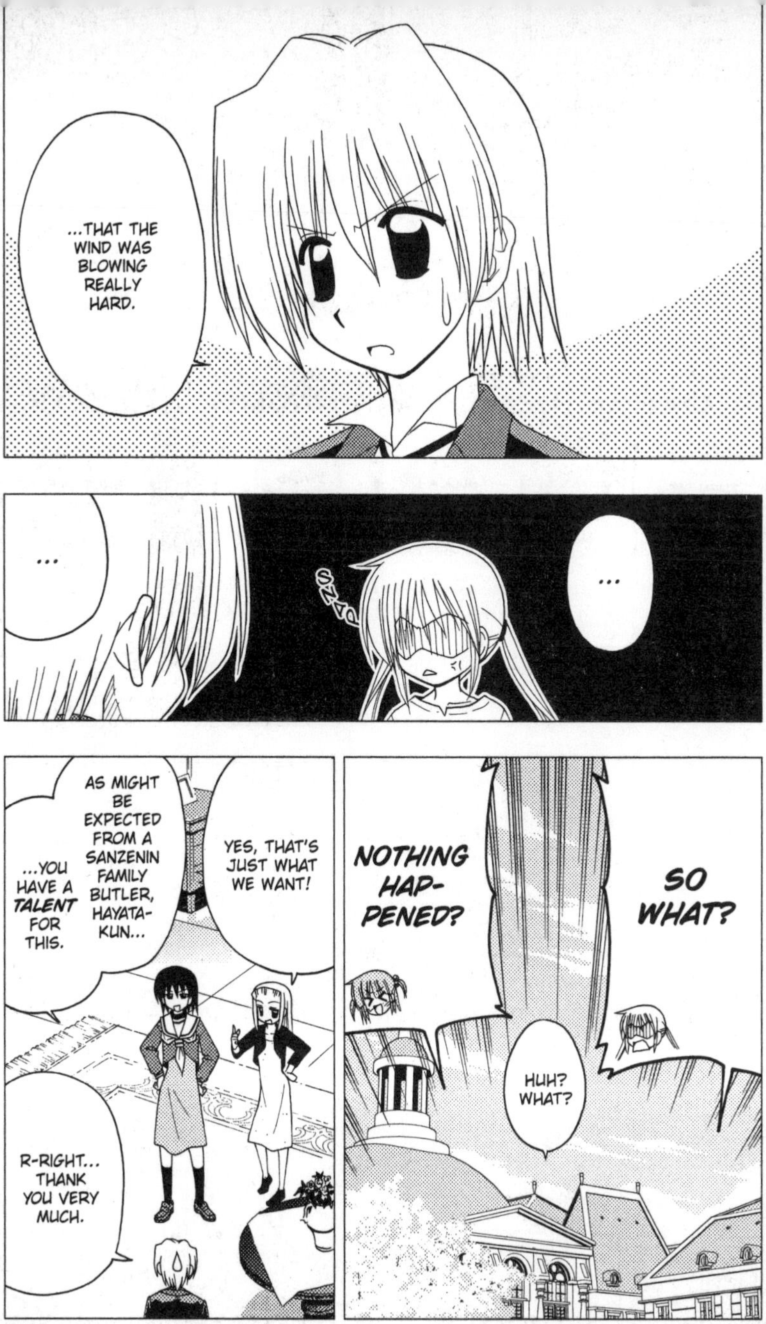
...THAT THE WIND WAS BLOWING REALLY HARD.
...
...
SO WHAT?
NOTHING HAP-PENED?
HUH? WHAT?
YES, THAT'S JUST WHAT WE WANT!
AS MIGHT BE EXPECTED FROM A SANZENIN FAMILY BUTLER, HAYATA-KUN...
...YOU HAVE A *TALENT* FOR THIS.
R-RIGHT... THANK YOU VERY MUCH.

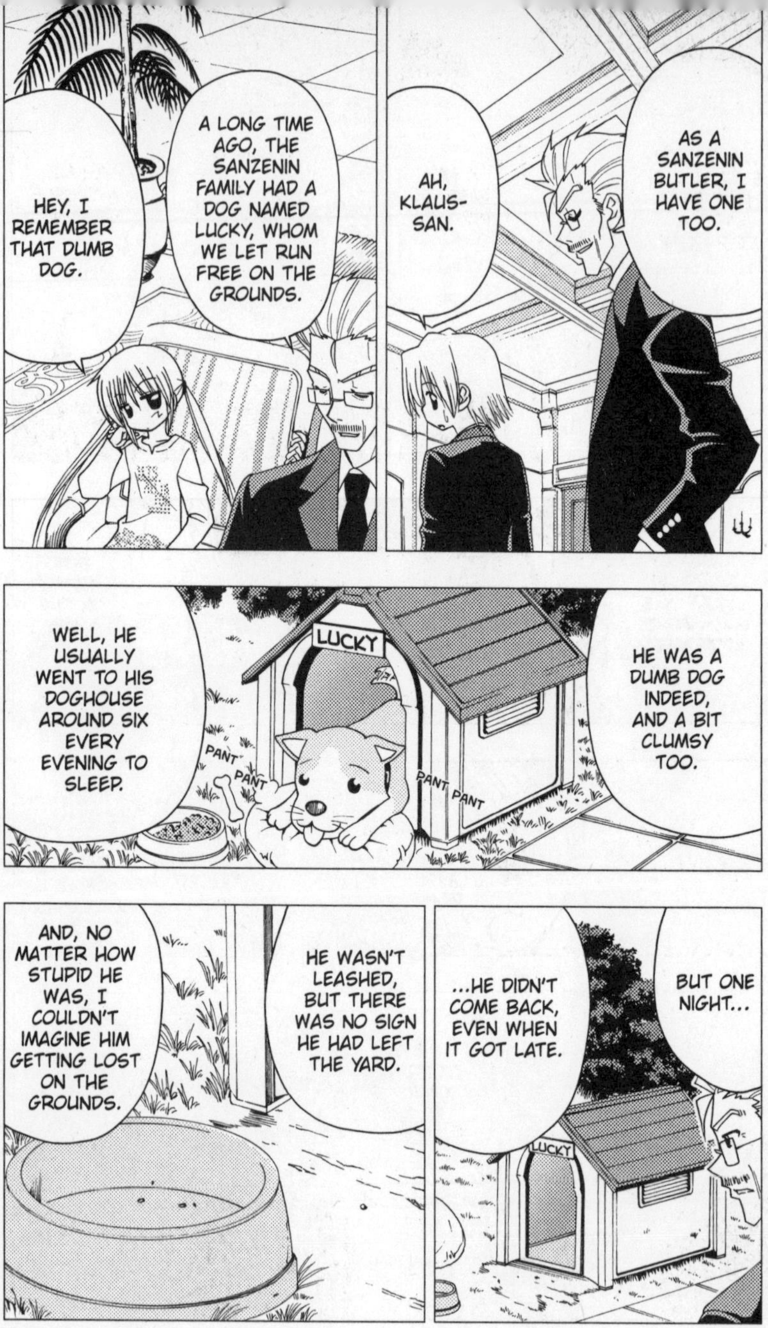
AS A SANZENIN BUTLER, I HAVE ONE TOO.
AH, KLAUS-SAN.
A LONG TIME AGO, THE SANZENIN FAMILY HAD A DOG NAMED LUCKY, WHOM WE LET RUN FREE ON THE GROUNDS.
HEY, I REMEMBER THAT DUMB DOG.
HE WAS A DUMB DOG INDEED, AND A BIT CLUMSY TOO.
LUCKY
PANT PANT
PANT PANT
WELL, HE USUALLY WENT TO HIS DOGHOUSE AROUND SIX EVERY EVENING TO SLEEP.
BUT ONE NIGHT...
...HE DIDN'T COME BACK, EVEN WHEN IT GOT LATE.
LUCKY
HE WASN'T LEASHED, BUT THERE WAS NO SIGN HE HAD LEFT THE YARD.
AND, NO MATTER HOW STUPID HE WAS, I COULDN'T IMAGINE HIM GETTING LOST ON THE GROUNDS.

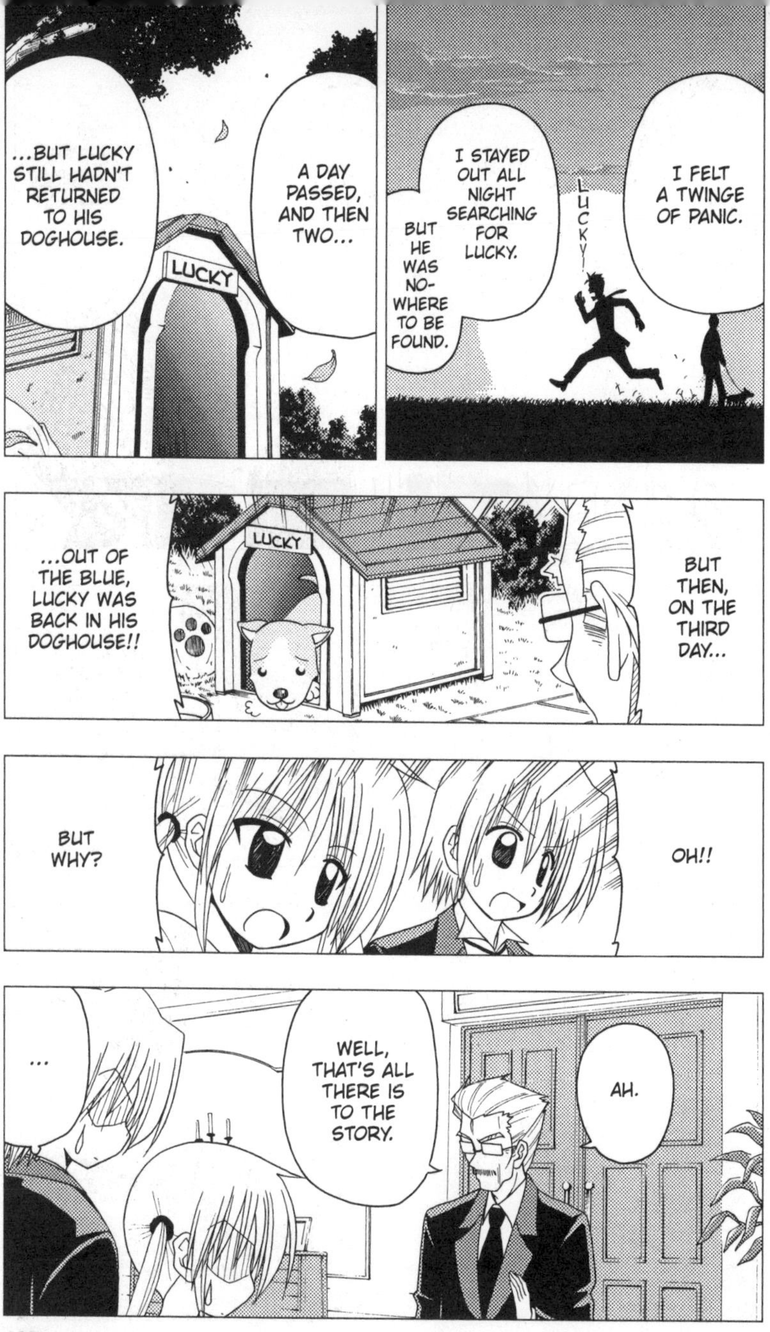
I FELT A TWINGE OF PANIC.
LUCKY!
I STAYED OUT ALL NIGHT SEARCHING FOR LUCKY.
BUT HE WAS NO-WHERE TO BE FOUND.
A DAY PASSED, AND THEN TWO...
...BUT LUCKY STILL HADN'T RETURNED TO HIS DOGHOUSE.
LUCKY
BUT THEN, ON THE THIRD DAY...
LUCKY
...OUT OF THE BLUE, LUCKY WAS BACK IN HIS DOGHOUSE!!
OH!!
BUT WHY?
AH.
WELL, THAT'S ALL THERE IS TO THE STORY.
...

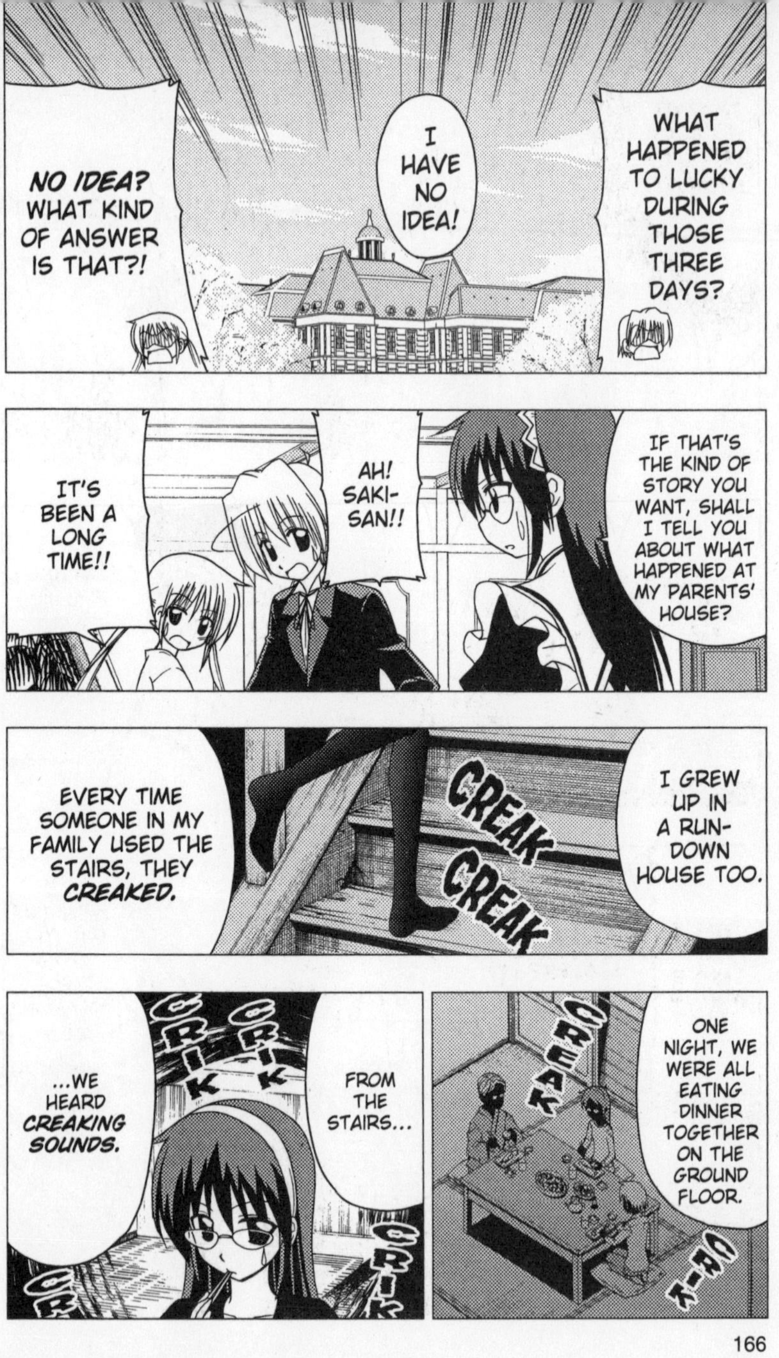
WHAT HAPPENED TO LUCKY DURING THOSE THREE DAYS?
I HAVE NO IDEA!
NO IDEA? WHAT KIND OF ANSWER IS THAT?!
IF THAT'S THE KIND OF STORY YOU WANT, SHALL I TELL YOU ABOUT WHAT HAPPENED AT MY PARENTS' HOUSE?
AH! SAKI-SAN!!
IT'S BEEN A LONG TIME!!
I GREW UP IN A RUN-DOWN HOUSE TOO.
CREAK
CREAK
EVERY TIME SOMEONE IN MY FAMILY USED THE STAIRS, THEY CREAKED.
ONE NIGHT, WE WERE ALL EATING DINNER TOGETHER ON THE GROUND FLOOR.
CREAK
CRIK
FROM THE STAIRS...
CRIK
CRIK
...WE HEARD CREAKING SOUNDS.
CRIK

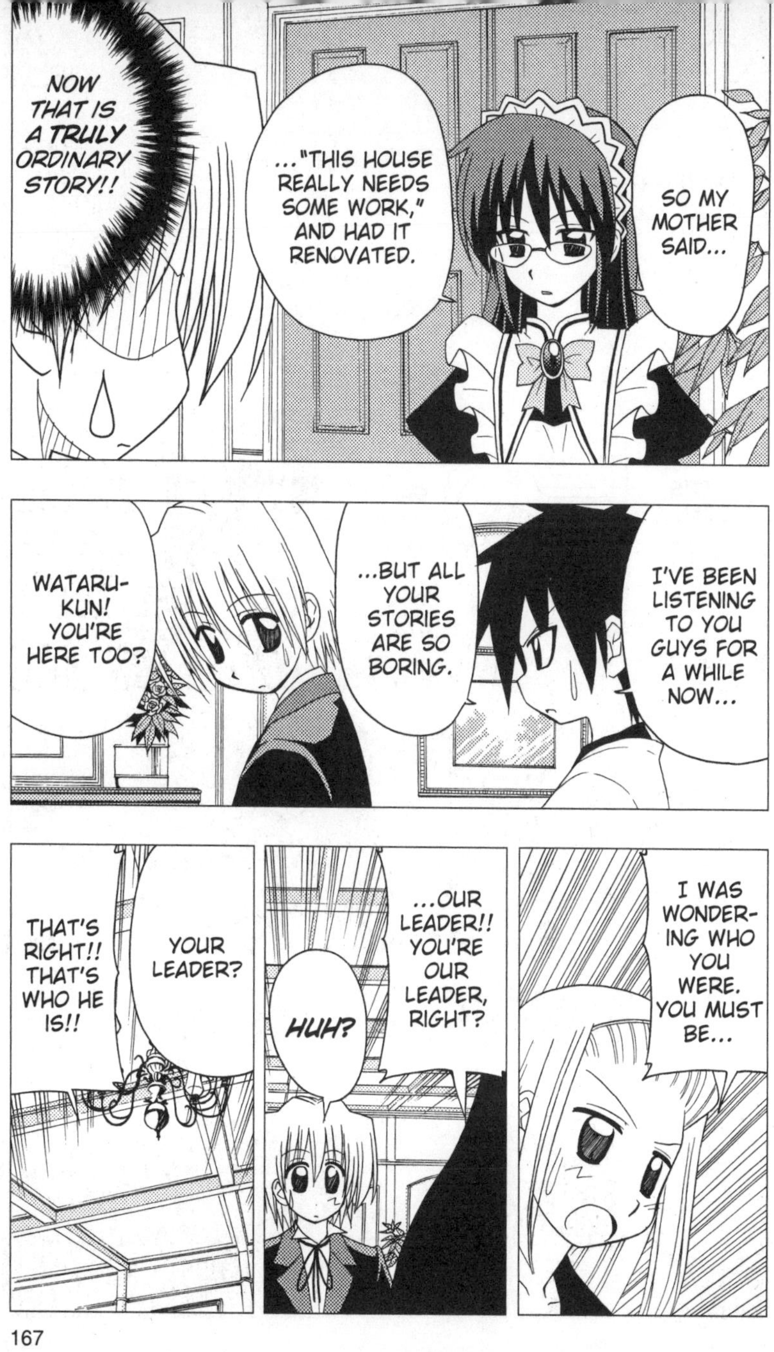
SO MY MOTHER SAID...
..."THIS HOUSE REALLY NEEDS SOME WORK," AND HAD IT RENOVATED.
NOW THAT IS A TRULY ORDINARY STORY!!
I'VE BEEN LISTENING TO YOU GUYS FOR A WHILE NOW...
...BUT ALL YOUR STORIES ARE SO BORING.
WATARU-KUN! YOU'RE HERE TOO?
I WAS WONDERING WHO YOU WERE. YOU MUST BE...
...OUR LEADER!! YOU'RE OUR LEADER, RIGHT?
HUH?
YOUR LEADER?
THAT'S RIGHT!! THAT'S WHO HE IS!!

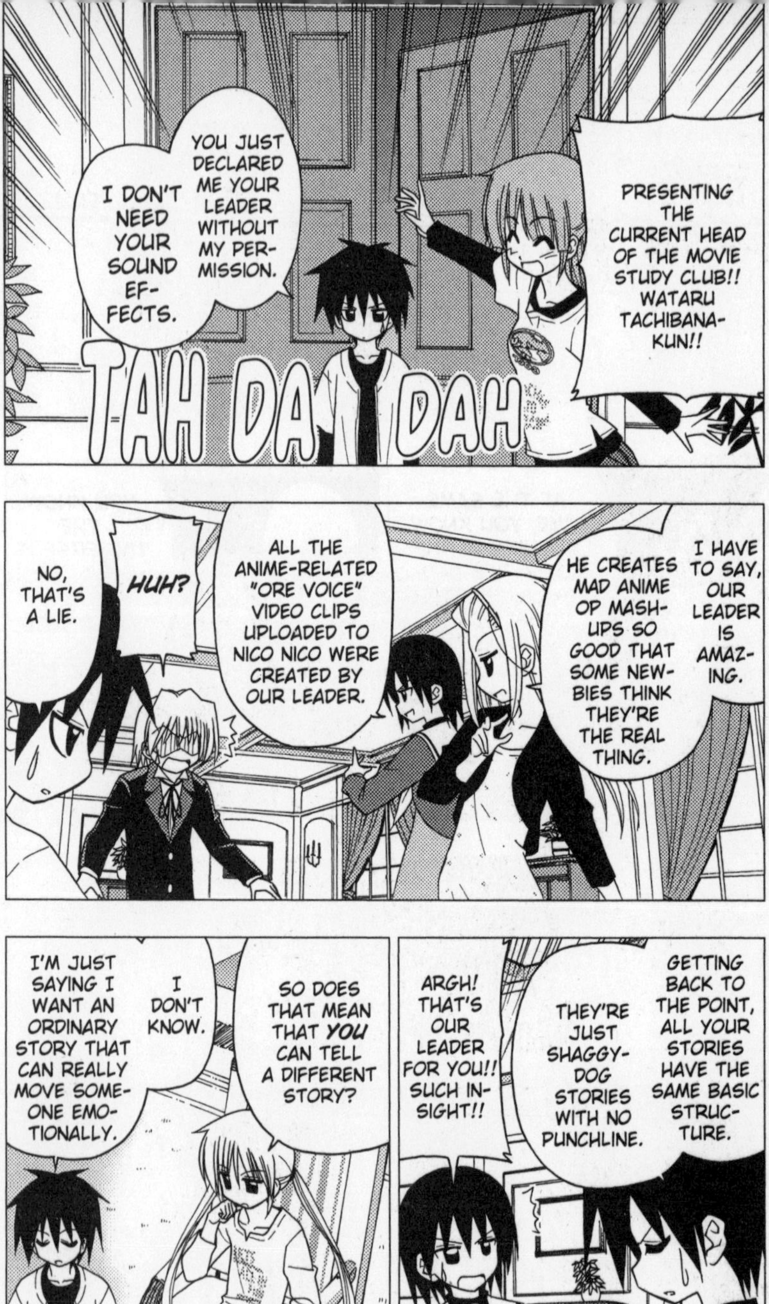
PRESENTING THE CURRENT HEAD OF THE MOVIE STUDY CLUB!! WATARU TACHIBANA-KUN!!
YOU JUST DECLARED ME YOUR LEADER WITHOUT MY PERMISSION.
I DON'T NEED YOUR SOUND EFFECTS.
TAH DA DAH
I HAVE TO SAY, OUR LEADER IS AMAZING.
HE CREATES MAD ANIME OP MASH-UPS SO GOOD THAT SOME NEWBIES THINK THEY'RE THE REAL THING.
ALL THE ANIME-RELATED "ORE VOICE" VIDEO CLIPS UPLOADED TO NICO NICO WERE CREATED BY OUR LEADER.
HUH?
NO, THAT'S A LIE.
GETTING BACK TO THE POINT, ALL YOUR STORIES HAVE THE SAME BASIC STRUCTURE.
THEY'RE JUST SHAGGY-DOG STORIES WITH NO PUNCHLINE.
ARGH! THAT'S OUR LEADER FOR YOU!! SUCH INSIGHT!!
SO DOES THAT MEAN THAT YOU CAN TELL A DIFFERENT STORY?
I DON'T KNOW.
I'M JUST SAYING I WANT AN ORDINARY STORY THAT CAN REALLY MOVE SOMEONE EMOTIONALLY.

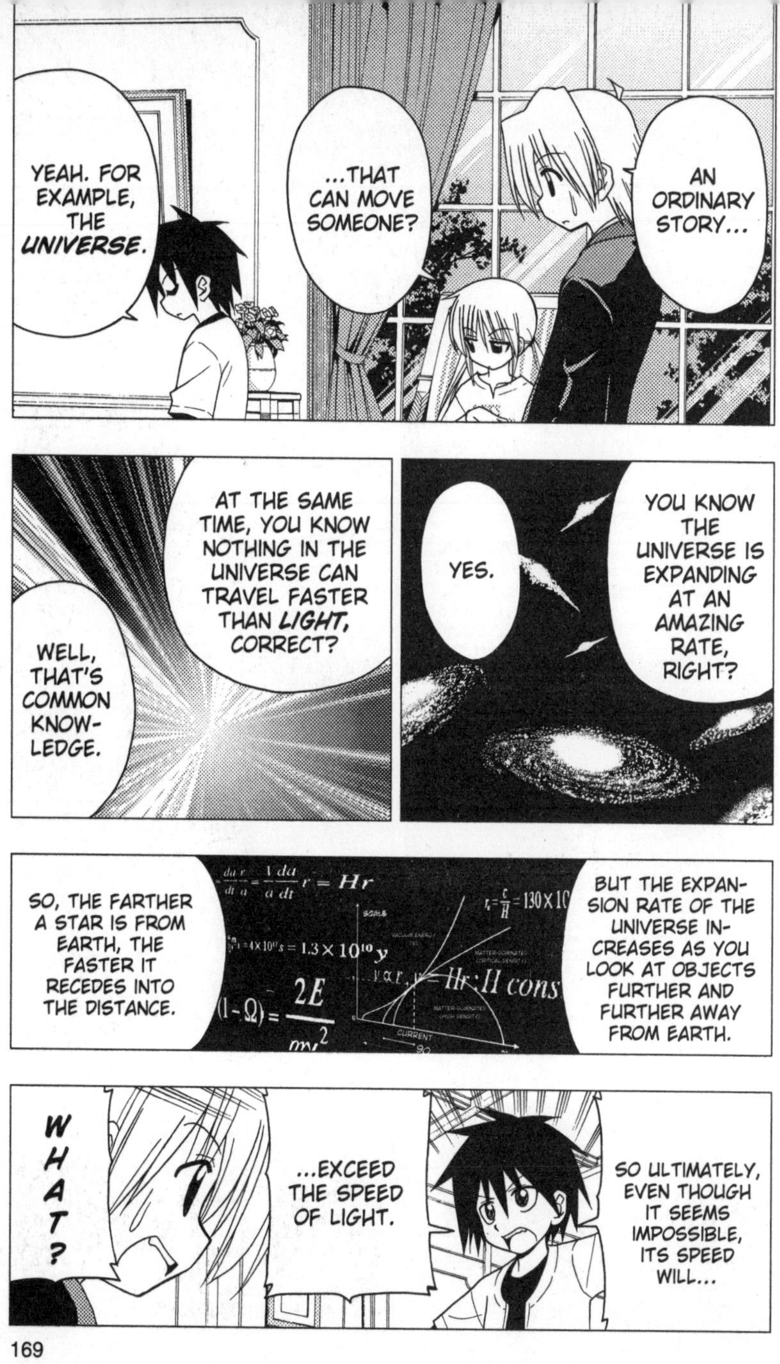
AN ORDINARY STORY...
...THAT CAN MOVE SOMEONE?
YEAH. FOR EXAMPLE, THE UNIVERSE.
YOU KNOW THE UNIVERSE IS EXPANDING AT AN AMAZING RATE, RIGHT?
YES.
AT THE SAME TIME, YOU KNOW NOTHING IN THE UNIVERSE CAN TRAVEL FASTER THAN LIGHT, CORRECT?
WELL, THAT'S COMMON KNOW-LEDGE.
BUT THE EXPAN-SION RATE OF THE UNIVERSE IN-CREASES AS YOU LOOK AT OBJECTS FURTHER AND FURTHER AWAY FROM EARTH.
SO, THE FARTHER A STAR IS FROM EARTH, THE FASTER IT RECEDES INTO THE DISTANCE.
SO ULTIMATELY, EVEN THOUGH IT SEEMS IMPOSSIBLE, ITS SPEED WILL...
...EXCEED THE SPEED OF LIGHT.
WHAT?

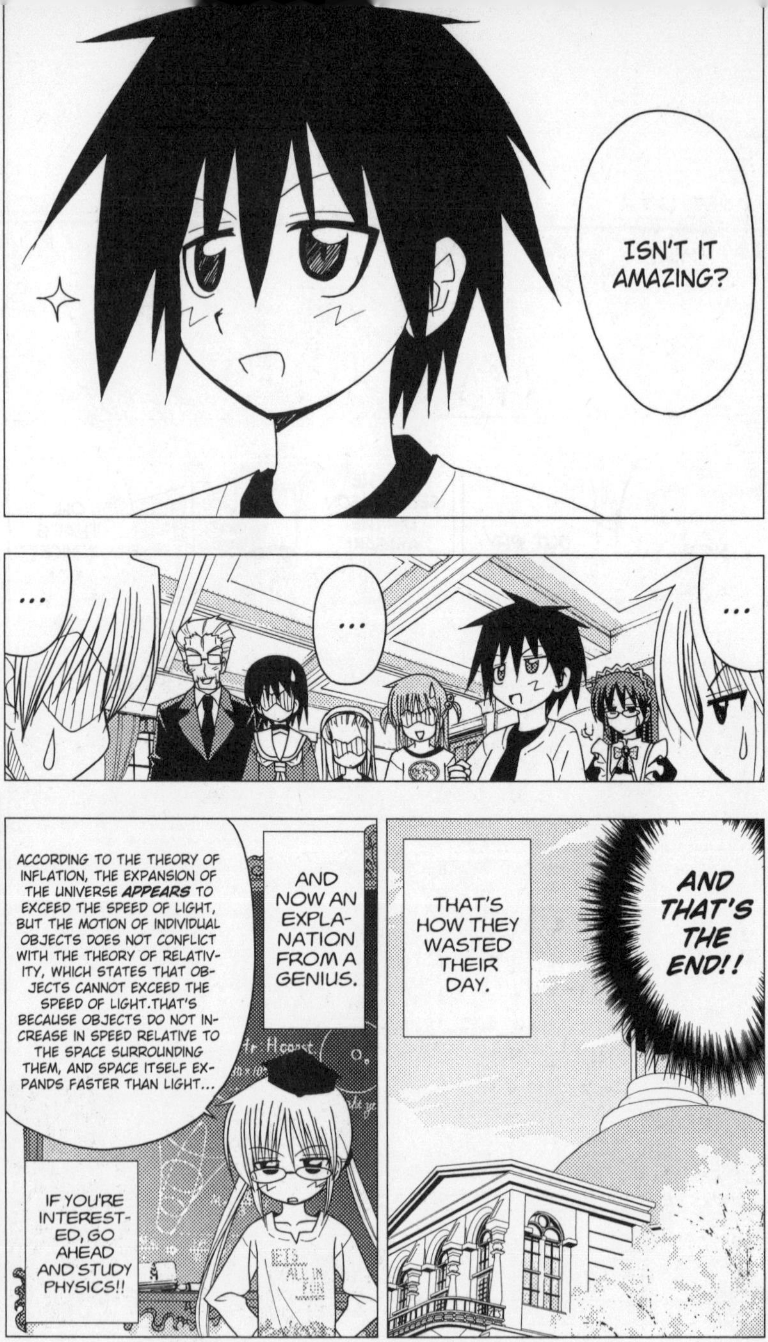
ISN'T IT AMAZING?
...
...
...
AND THAT'S THE END!!
THAT'S HOW THEY WASTED THEIR DAY.
AND NOW AN EXPLANATION FROM A GENIUS.
ACCORDING TO THE THEORY OF INFLATION, THE EXPANSION OF THE UNIVERSE ***APPEARS*** TO EXCEED THE SPEED OF LIGHT, BUT THE MOTION OF INDIVIDUAL OBJECTS DOES NOT CONFLICT WITH THE THEORY OF RELATIVITY, WHICH STATES THAT OBJECTS CANNOT EXCEED THE SPEED OF LIGHT.THAT'S BECAUSE OBJECTS DO NOT INCREASE IN SPEED RELATIVE TO THE SPACE SURROUNDING THEM, AND SPACE ITSELF EXPANDS FASTER THAN LIGHT...
IF YOU'RE INTERESTED, GO AHEAD AND STUDY PHYSICS!!

REFERENCE MATERIAL: *THE CREATION AND EVOLUTION OF THE UNIVERSE*

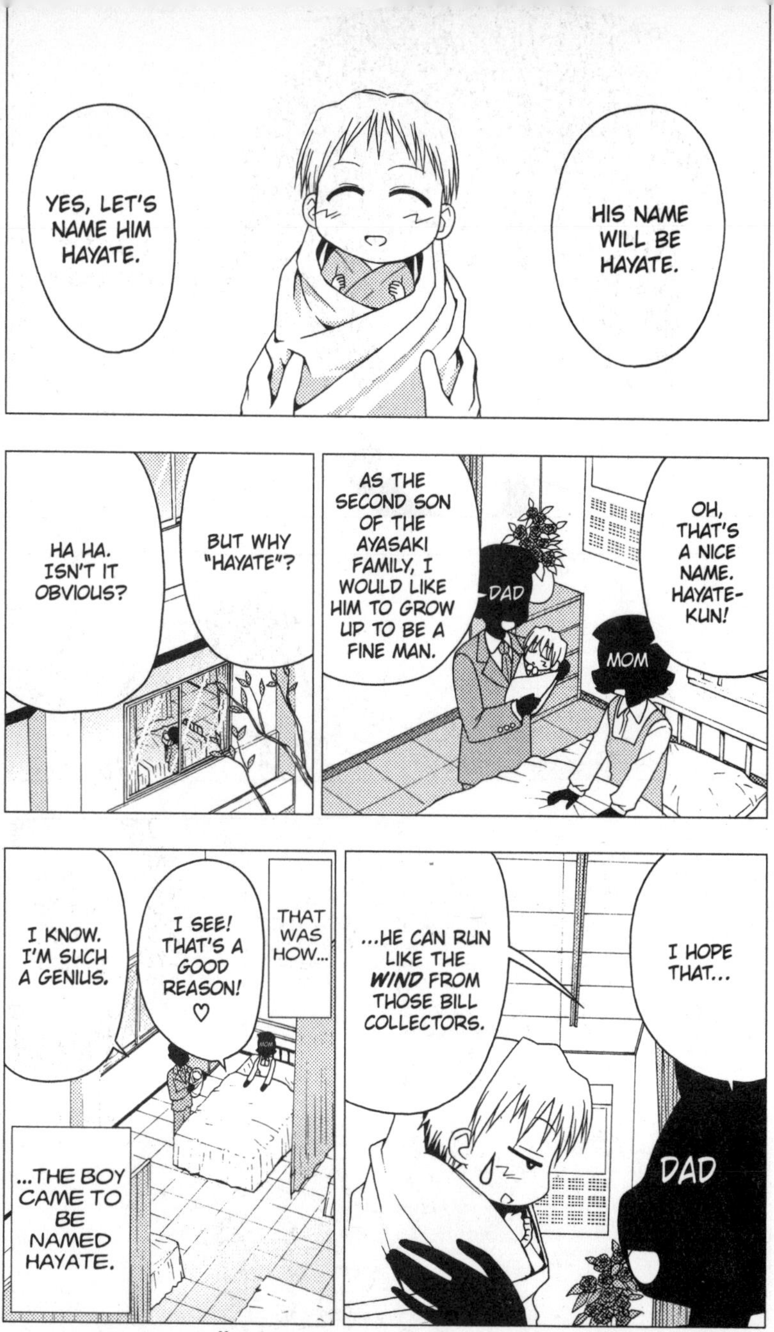

HIS NAME WILL BE HAYATE.
YES, LET'S NAME HIM HAYATE.
OH, THAT'S A NICE NAME. HAYATE-KUN!
MOM
DAD
AS THE SECOND SON OF THE AYASAKI FAMILY, I WOULD LIKE HIM TO GROW UP TO BE A FINE MAN.
BUT WHY "HAYATE"?
HA HA. ISN'T IT OBVIOUS?
I HOPE THAT...
...HE CAN RUN LIKE THE *WIND* FROM THOSE BILL COLLECTORS.
DAD
THAT WAS HOW...
I SEE! THAT'S A GOOD REASON! ♡
I KNOW. I'M SUCH A GENIUS.
...THE BOY CAME TO BE NAMED HAYATE.

Episode 11: "It Was like the Sound of Gill's Flute"

Episode 11:
"It Was like the Sound of Gill's Flute"

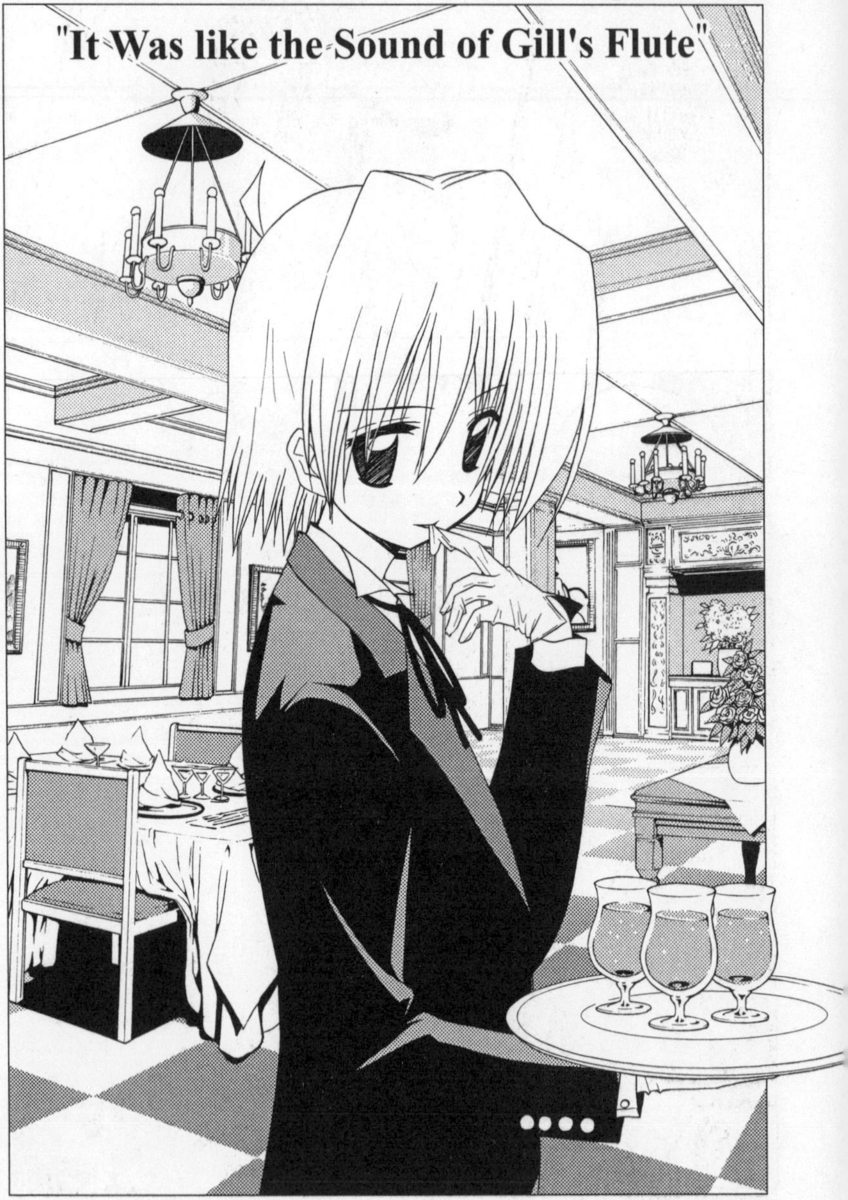

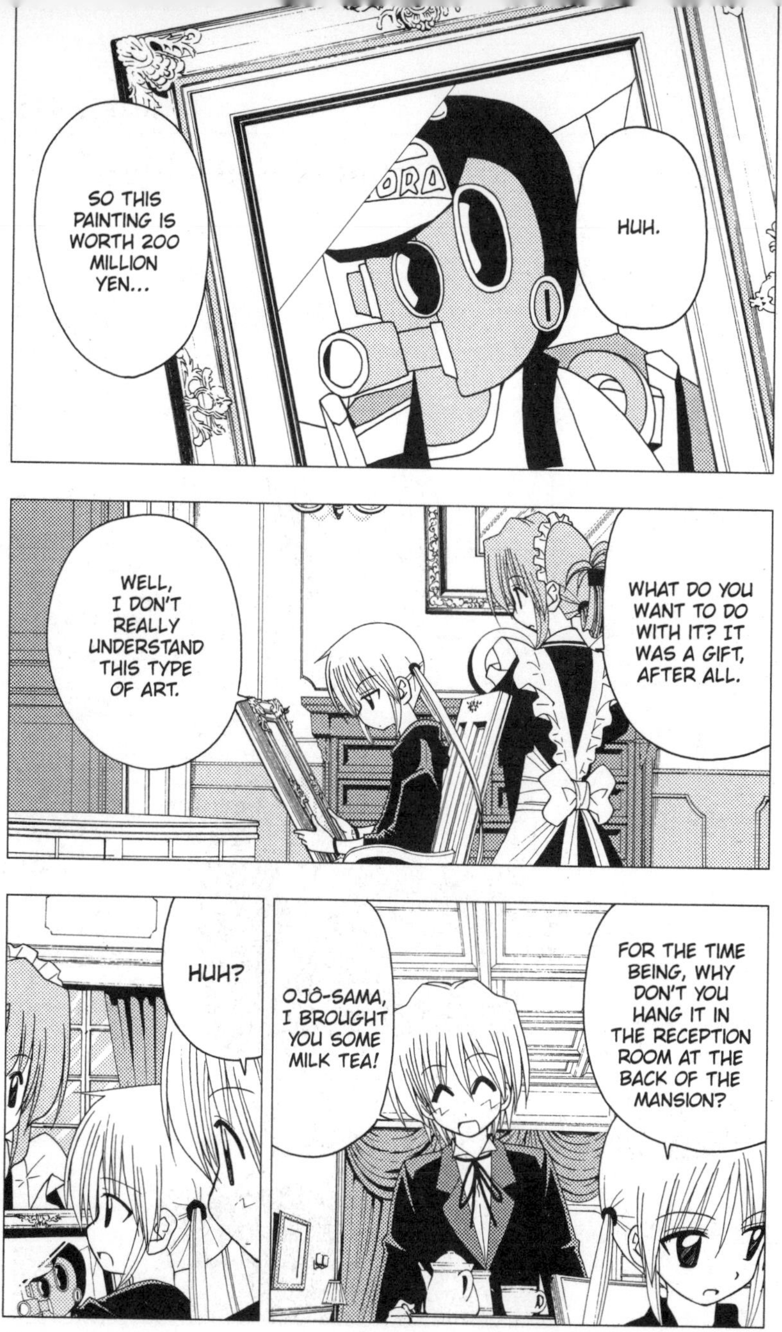

HUH.
SO THIS PAINTING IS WORTH 200 MILLION YEN...
WHAT DO YOU WANT TO DO WITH IT? IT WAS A GIFT, AFTER ALL.
WELL, I DON'T REALLY UNDERSTAND THIS TYPE OF ART.
FOR THE TIME BEING, WHY DON'T YOU HANG IT IN THE RECEPTION ROOM AT THE BACK OF THE MANSION?
OJÔ-SAMA, I BROUGHT YOU SOME MILK TEA!
HUH?

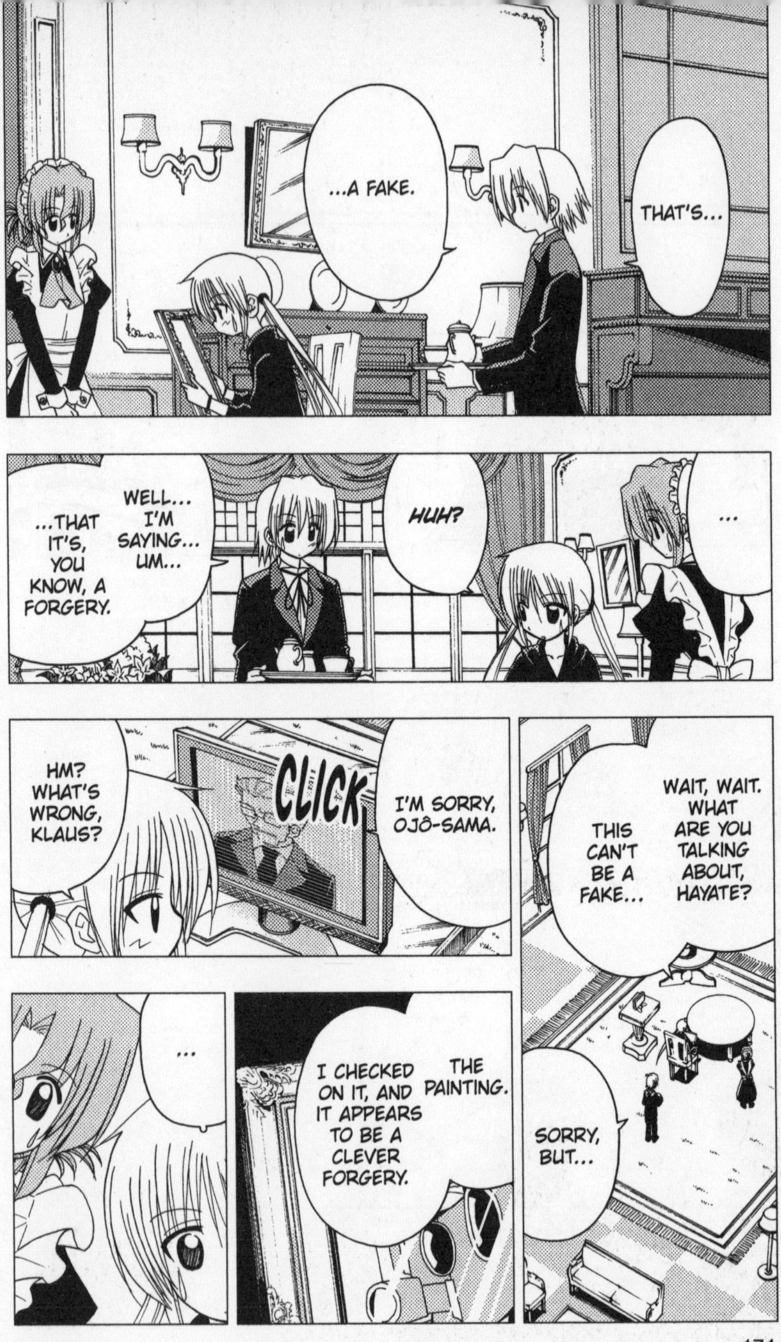
THAT'S...
...A FAKE.
...
HUH?
WELL... I'M SAYING... UM...
...THAT IT'S, YOU KNOW, A FORGERY.
WAIT, WAIT. WHAT ARE YOU TALKING ABOUT, HAYATE?
THIS CAN'T BE A FAKE...
SORRY, BUT...
I'M SORRY, OJÔ-SAMA.
CLICK
HM? WHAT'S WRONG, KLAUS?
THE PAINTING.
I CHECKED ON IT, AND IT APPEARS TO BE A CLEVER FORGERY.
...

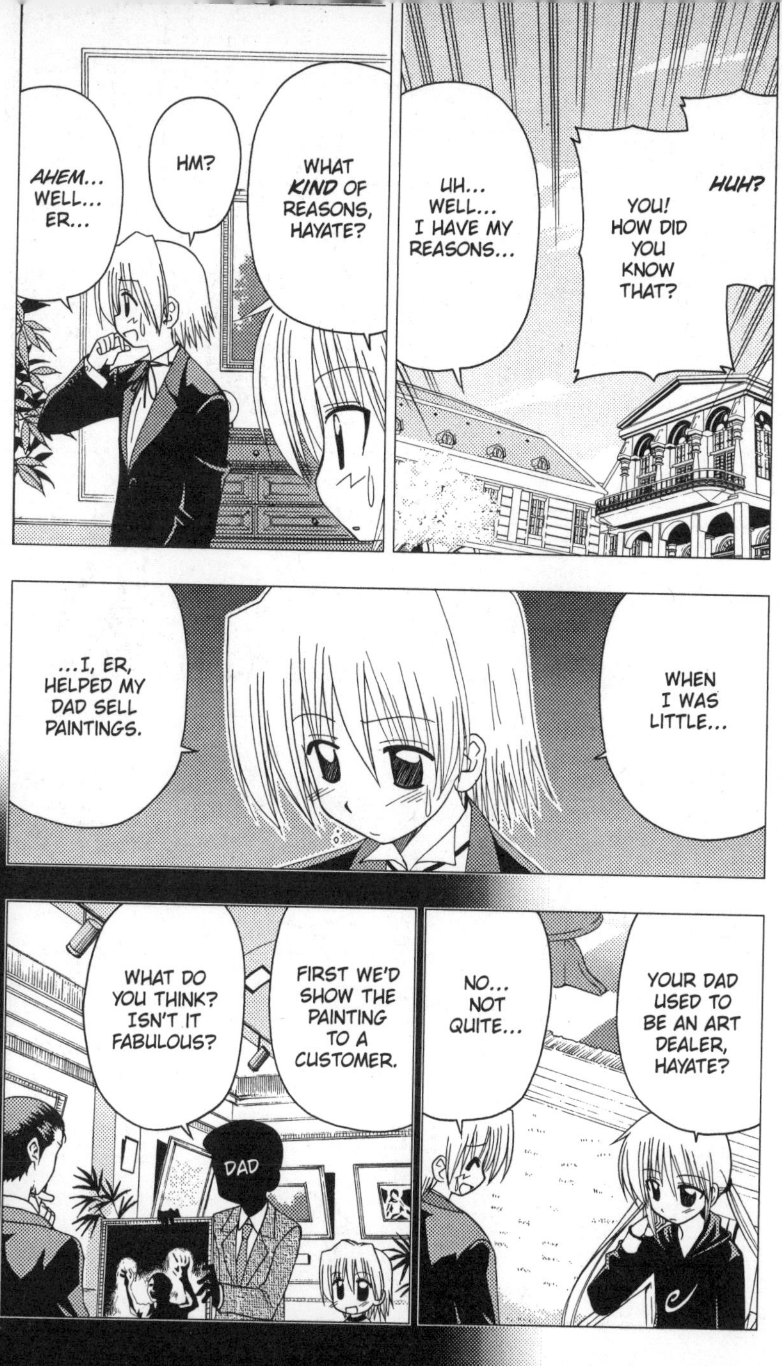
HUH?
YOU! HOW DID YOU KNOW THAT?
UH... WELL... I HAVE MY REASONS...
WHAT KIND OF REASONS, HAYATE?
HM?
AHEM... WELL... ER...
WHEN I WAS LITTLE...
...I, ER, HELPED MY DAD SELL PAINTINGS.
YOUR DAD USED TO BE AN ART DEALER, HAYATE?
NO... NOT QUITE...
FIRST WE'D SHOW THE PAINTING TO A CUSTOMER.
WHAT DO YOU THINK? ISN'T IT FABULOUS?
DAD

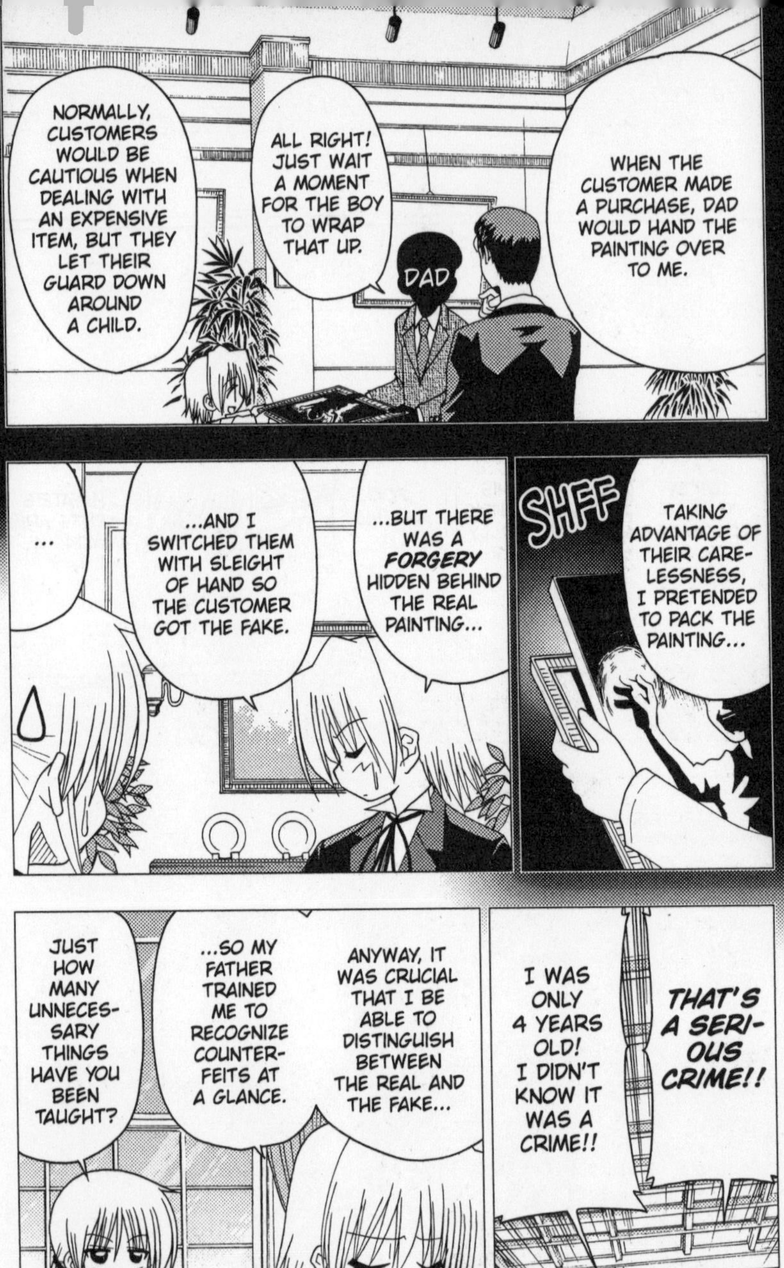

WHEN THE CUSTOMER MADE A PURCHASE, DAD WOULD HAND THE PAINTING OVER TO ME.
ALL RIGHT! JUST WAIT A MOMENT FOR THE BOY TO WRAP THAT UP.
DAD
NORMALLY, CUSTOMERS WOULD BE CAUTIOUS WHEN DEALING WITH AN EXPENSIVE ITEM, BUT THEY LET THEIR GUARD DOWN AROUND A CHILD.
SHFF
TAKING ADVANTAGE OF THEIR CARE-LESSNESS, I PRETENDED TO PACK THE PAINTING...
...BUT THERE WAS A FORGERY HIDDEN BEHIND THE REAL PAINTING...
...AND I SWITCHED THEM WITH SLEIGHT OF HAND SO THE CUSTOMER GOT THE FAKE.
...
THAT'S A SERI-OUS CRIME!!
I WAS ONLY 4 YEARS OLD! I DIDN'T KNOW IT WAS A CRIME!!
ANYWAY, IT WAS CRUCIAL THAT I BE ABLE TO DISTINGUISH BETWEEN THE REAL AND THE FAKE...
...SO MY FATHER TRAINED ME TO RECOGNIZE COUNTER-FEITS AT A GLANCE.
JUST HOW MANY UNNECES-SARY THINGS HAVE YOU BEEN TAUGHT?

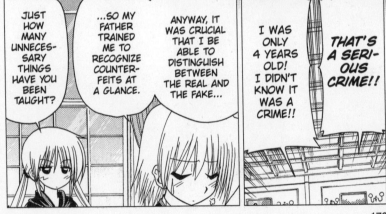

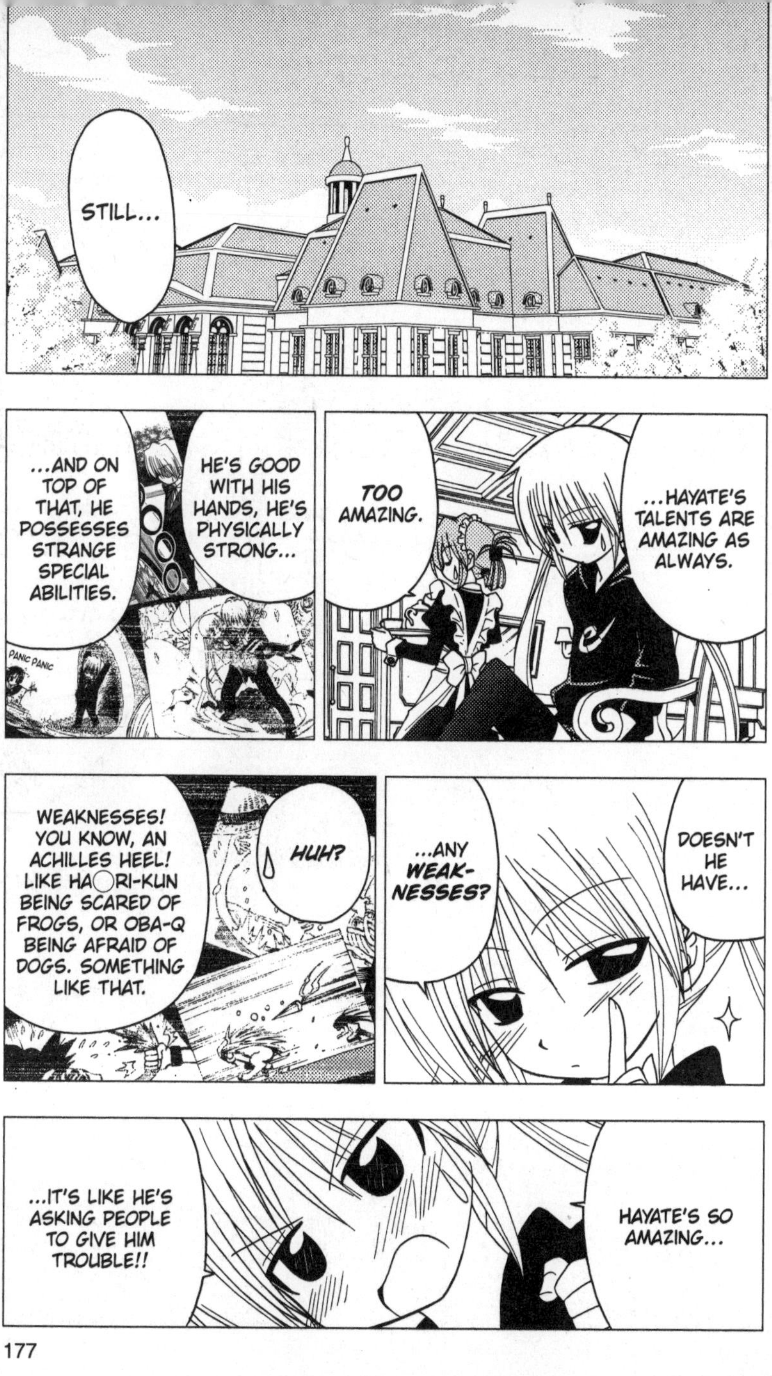
STILL...
...HAYATE'S TALENTS ARE AMAZING AS ALWAYS.
TOO AMAZING.
HE'S GOOD WITH HIS HANDS, HE'S PHYSICALLY STRONG...
...AND ON TOP OF THAT, HE POSSESSES STRANGE SPECIAL ABILITIES.
PANIC PANIC
DOESN'T HE HAVE...
...ANY WEAKNESSES?
HUH?
WEAKNESSES! YOU KNOW, AN ACHILLES HEEL! LIKE HA○RI-KUN BEING SCARED OF FROGS, OR OBA-Q BEING AFRAID OF DOGS. SOMETHING LIKE THAT.
HAYATE'S SO AMAZING...
...IT'S LIKE HE'S ASKING PEOPLE TO GIVE HIM TROUBLE!!

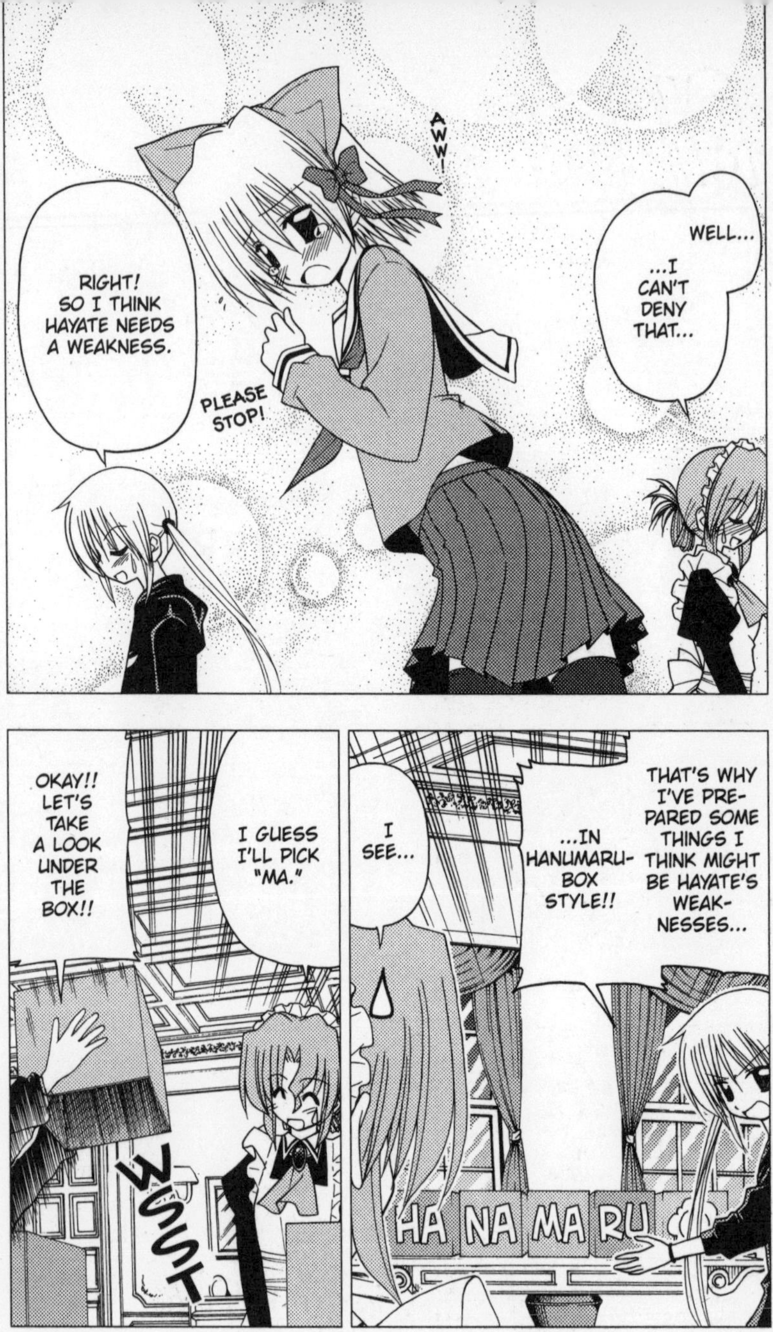
WELL...
...I CAN'T DENY THAT...
AWW!
PLEASE STOP!
RIGHT! SO I THINK HAYATE NEEDS A WEAKNESS.
THAT'S WHY I'VE PREPARED SOME THINGS I THINK MIGHT BE HAYATE'S WEAKNESSES...
...IN HANUMARU-BOX STYLE!!
HA NA MA RU
I SEE...
I GUESS I'LL PICK "MA."
OKAY!! LET'S TAKE A LOOK UNDER THE BOX!!
WSST

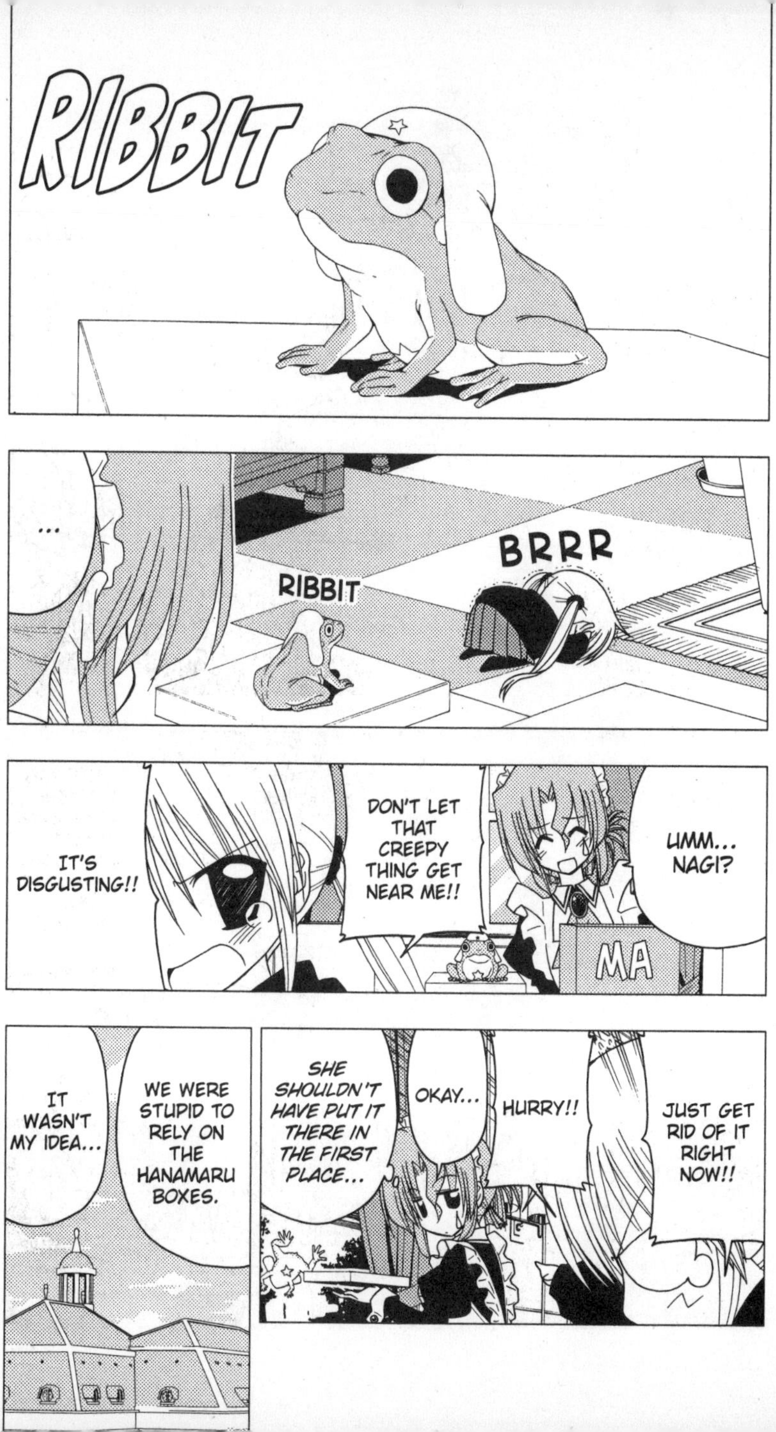
RIBBIT
BRRR
RIBBIT
...
UMM... NAGI?
DON'T LET THAT CREEPY THING GET NEAR ME!!
MA
IT'S DISGUSTING!!
JUST GET RID OF IT RIGHT NOW!!
HURRY!!
OKAY...
SHE SHOULDN'T HAVE PUT IT THERE IN THE FIRST PLACE...
WE WERE STUPID TO RELY ON THE HANAMARU BOXES.
IT WASN'T MY IDEA...

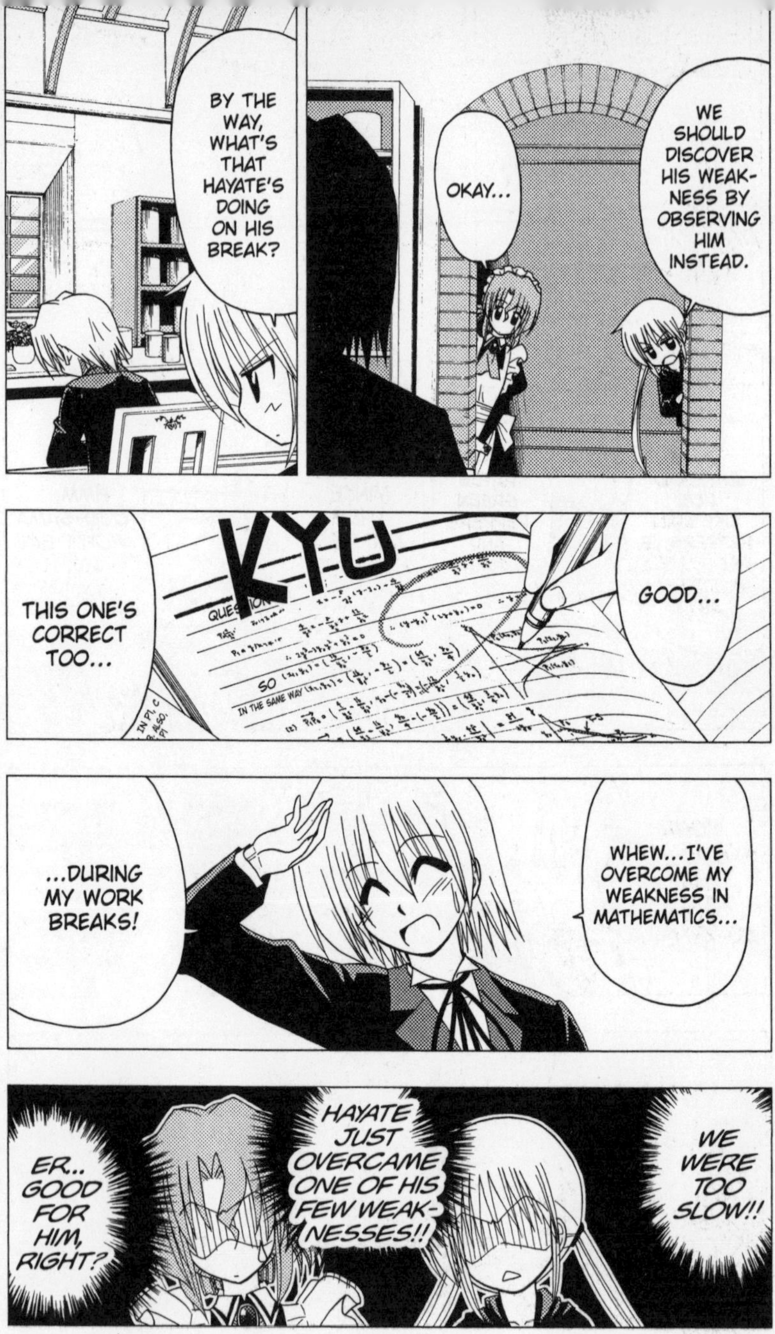
WE SHOULD DISCOVER HIS WEAKNESS BY OBSERVING HIM INSTEAD.
OKAY...
BY THE WAY, WHAT'S THAT HAYATE'S DOING ON HIS BREAK?
GOOD...
KYU
THIS ONE'S CORRECT TOO...
WHEW...I'VE OVERCOME MY WEAKNESS IN MATHEMATICS...
...DURING MY WORK BREAKS!
WE WERE TOO SLOW!!
HAYATE JUST OVERCAME ONE OF HIS FEW WEAKNESSES!!
ER... GOOD FOR HIM, RIGHT?

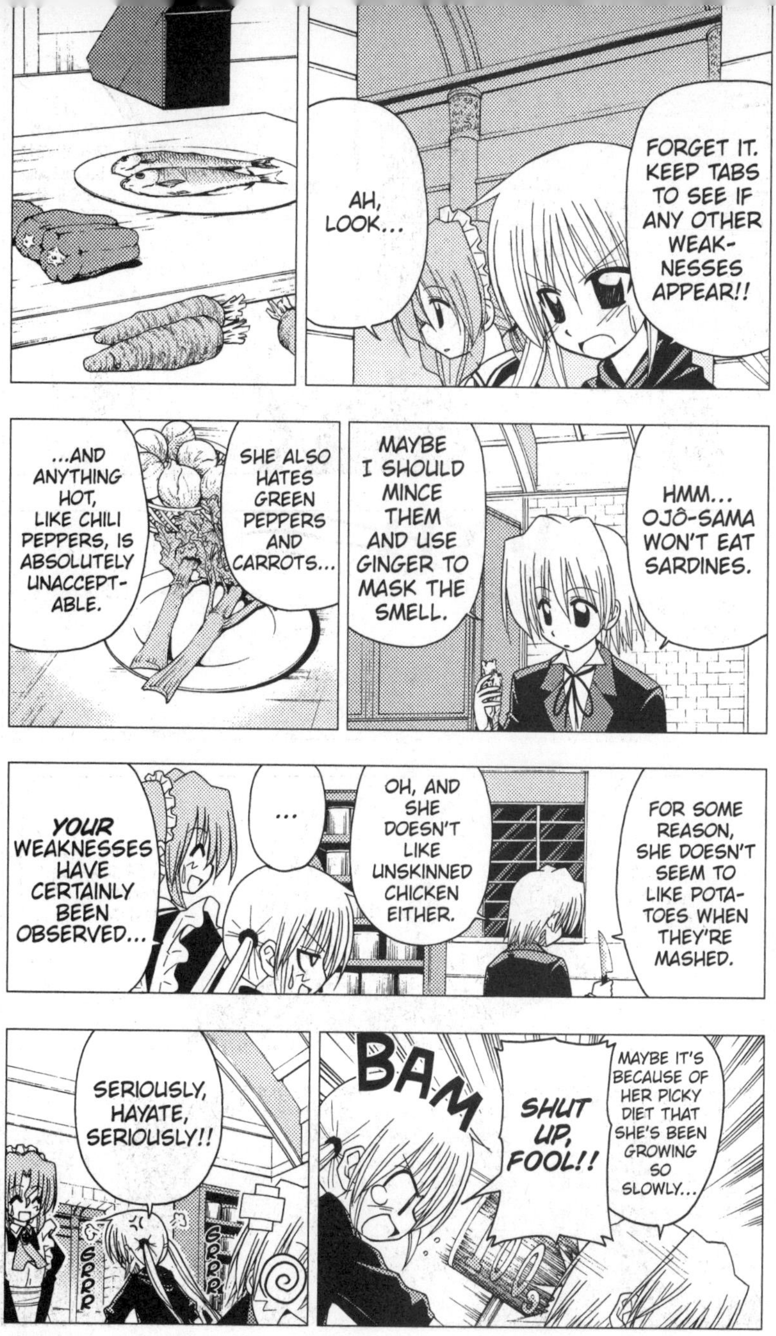
FORGET IT. KEEP TABS TO SEE IF ANY OTHER WEAKNESSES APPEAR!!
AH, LOOK...
HMM... OJÔ-SAMA WON'T EAT SARDINES.
MAYBE I SHOULD MINCE THEM AND USE GINGER TO MASK THE SMELL.
SHE ALSO HATES GREEN PEPPERS AND CARROTS...
...AND ANYTHING HOT, LIKE CHILI PEPPERS, IS ABSOLUTELY UNACCEPTABLE.
FOR SOME REASON, SHE DOESN'T SEEM TO LIKE POTATOES WHEN THEY'RE MASHED.
OH, AND SHE DOESN'T LIKE UNSKINNED CHICKEN EITHER.
...
YOUR WEAKNESSES HAVE CERTAINLY BEEN OBSERVED...
MAYBE IT'S BECAUSE OF HER PICKY DIET THAT SHE'S BEEN GROWING SO SLOWLY...
BAM
SHUT UP, FOOL!!
SERIOUSLY, HAYATE, SERIOUSLY!!
GRRR
GRRR
GRRR

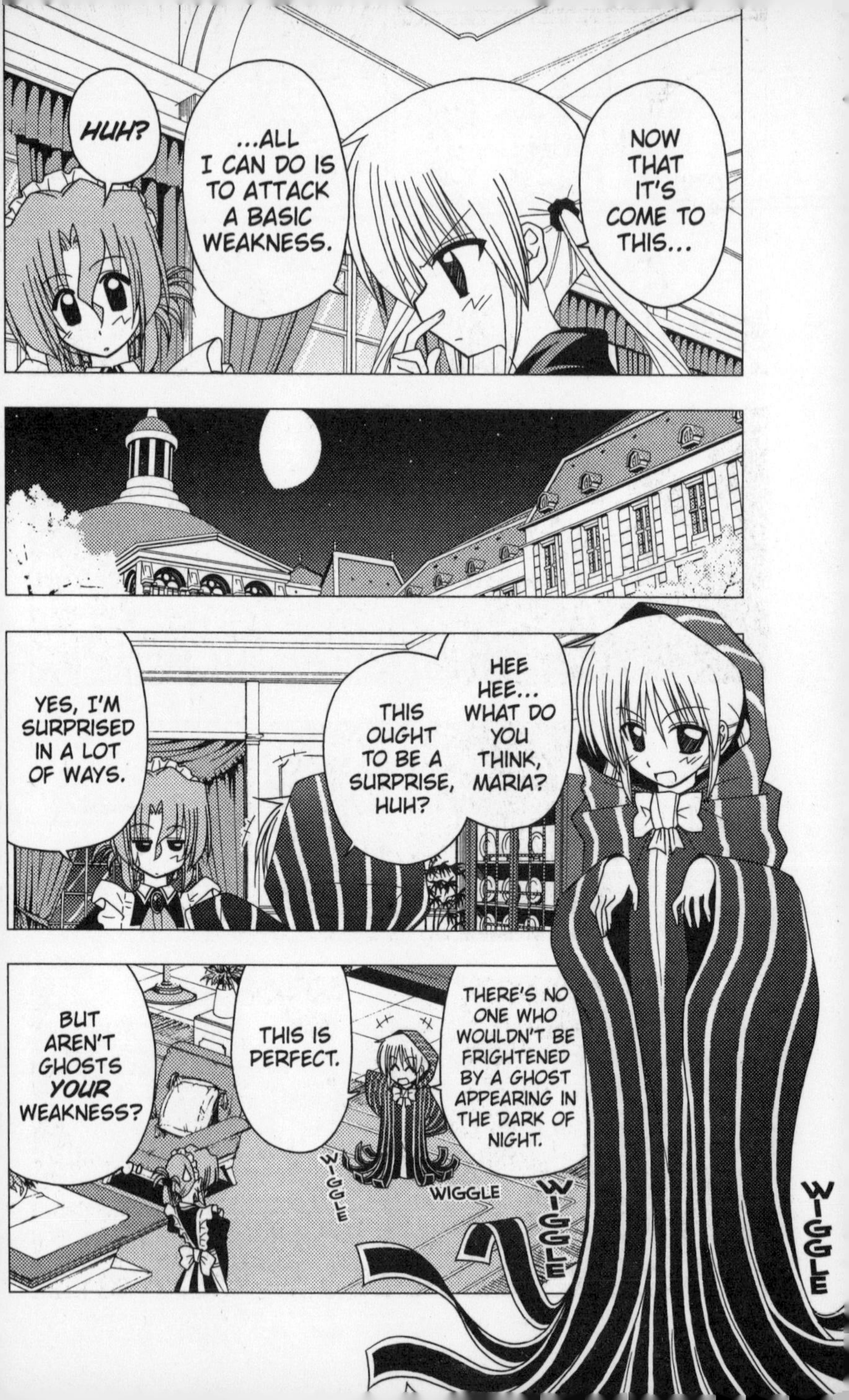
NOW THAT IT'S COME TO THIS...
...ALL I CAN DO IS TO ATTACK A BASIC WEAKNESS.
HUH?
HEE HEE... WHAT DO YOU THINK, MARIA?
THIS OUGHT TO BE A SURPRISE, HUH?
YES, I'M SURPRISED IN A LOT OF WAYS.
WIGGLE
WIGGLE
THERE'S NO ONE WHO WOULDN'T BE FRIGHTENED BY A GHOST APPEARING IN THE DARK OF NIGHT.
WIGGLE
WIGGLE
THIS IS PERFECT.
BUT AREN'T GHOSTS YOUR WEAKNESS?

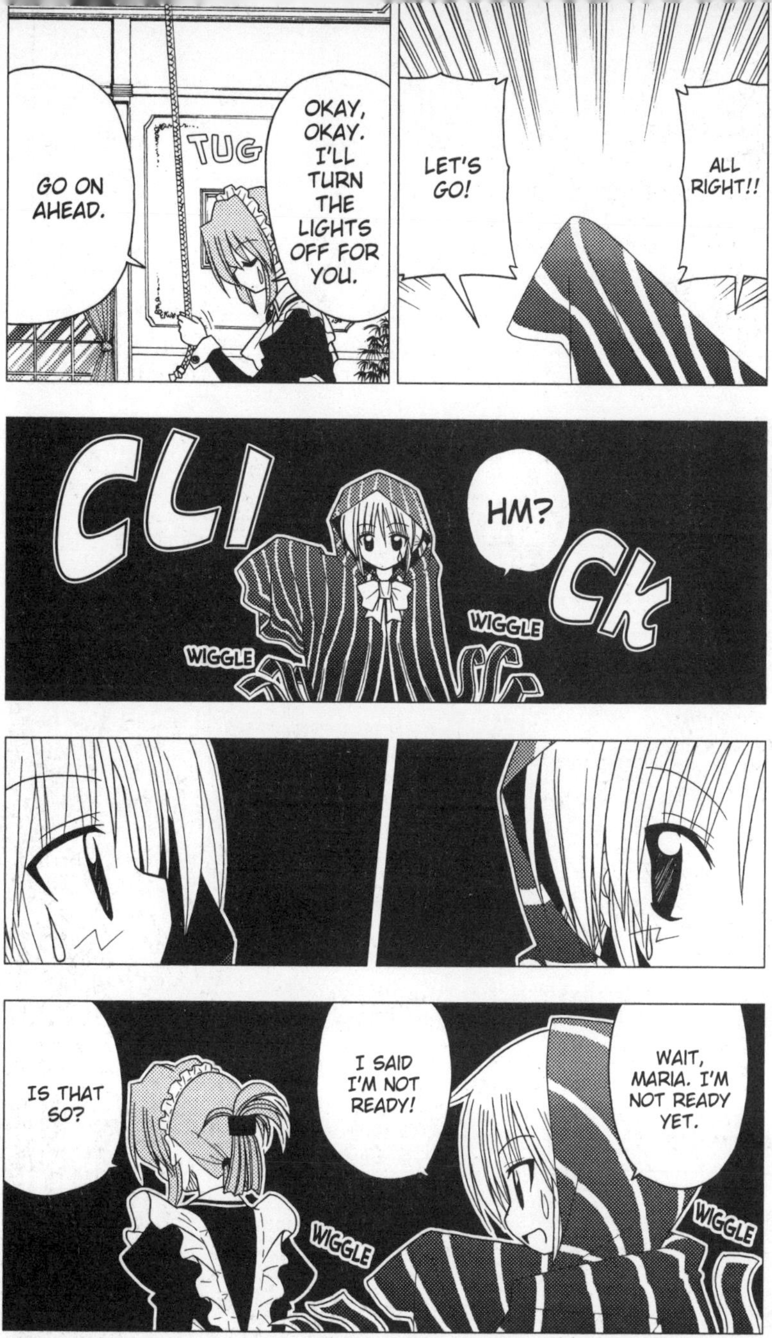
ALL RIGHT!!
LET'S GO!
OKAY, OKAY. I'LL TURN THE LIGHTS OFF FOR YOU.
TUG
GO ON AHEAD.
HM?
CLICK
WIGGLE
WIGGLE
WAIT, MARIA. I'M NOT READY YET.
WIGGLE
I SAID I'M NOT READY!
WIGGLE
IS THAT SO?

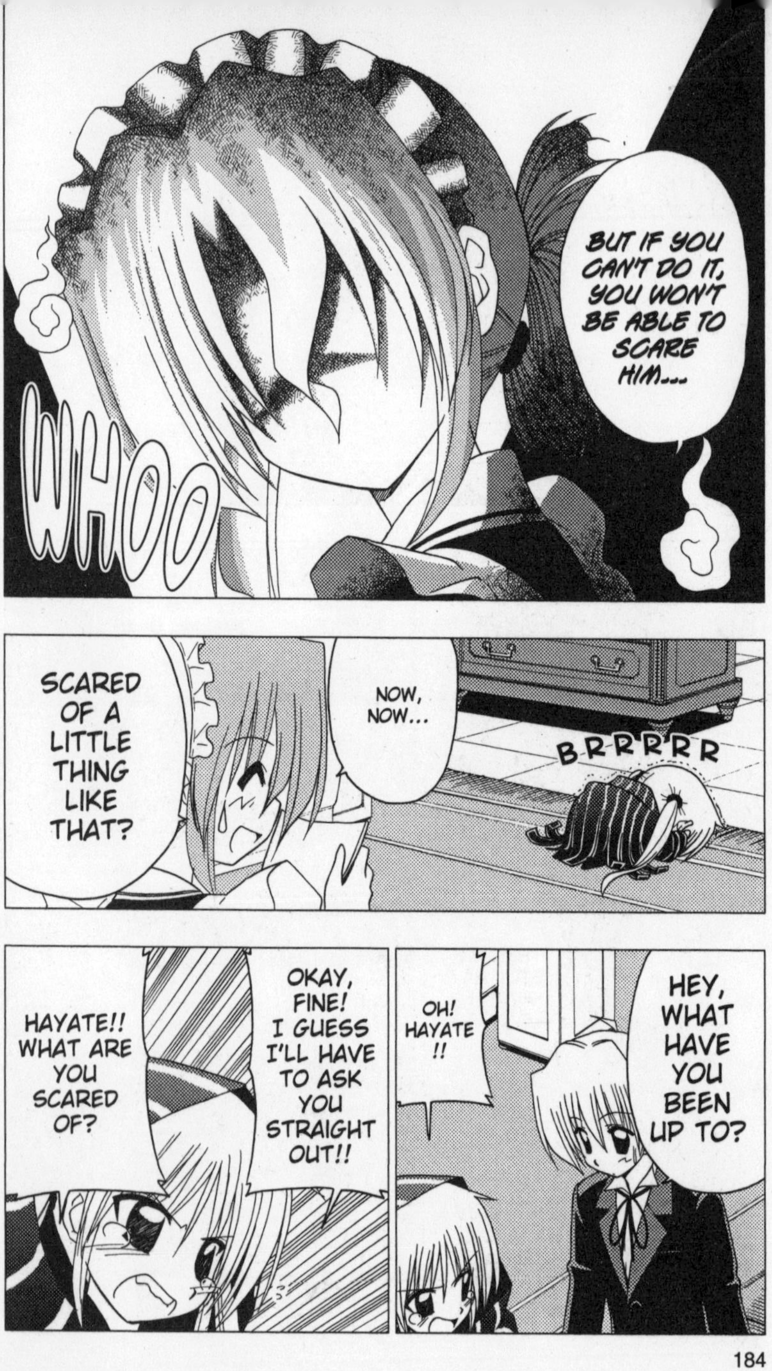
BUT IF YOU CAN'T DO IT, YOU WON'T BE ABLE TO SCARE HIM...
WHOO
BRRRRRR
NOW, NOW...
SCARED OF A LITTLE THING LIKE THAT?
HEY, WHAT HAVE YOU BEEN UP TO?
OH! HAYATE!!
OKAY, FINE! I GUESS I'LL HAVE TO ASK YOU STRAIGHT OUT!!
HAYATE!! WHAT ARE YOU SCARED OF?

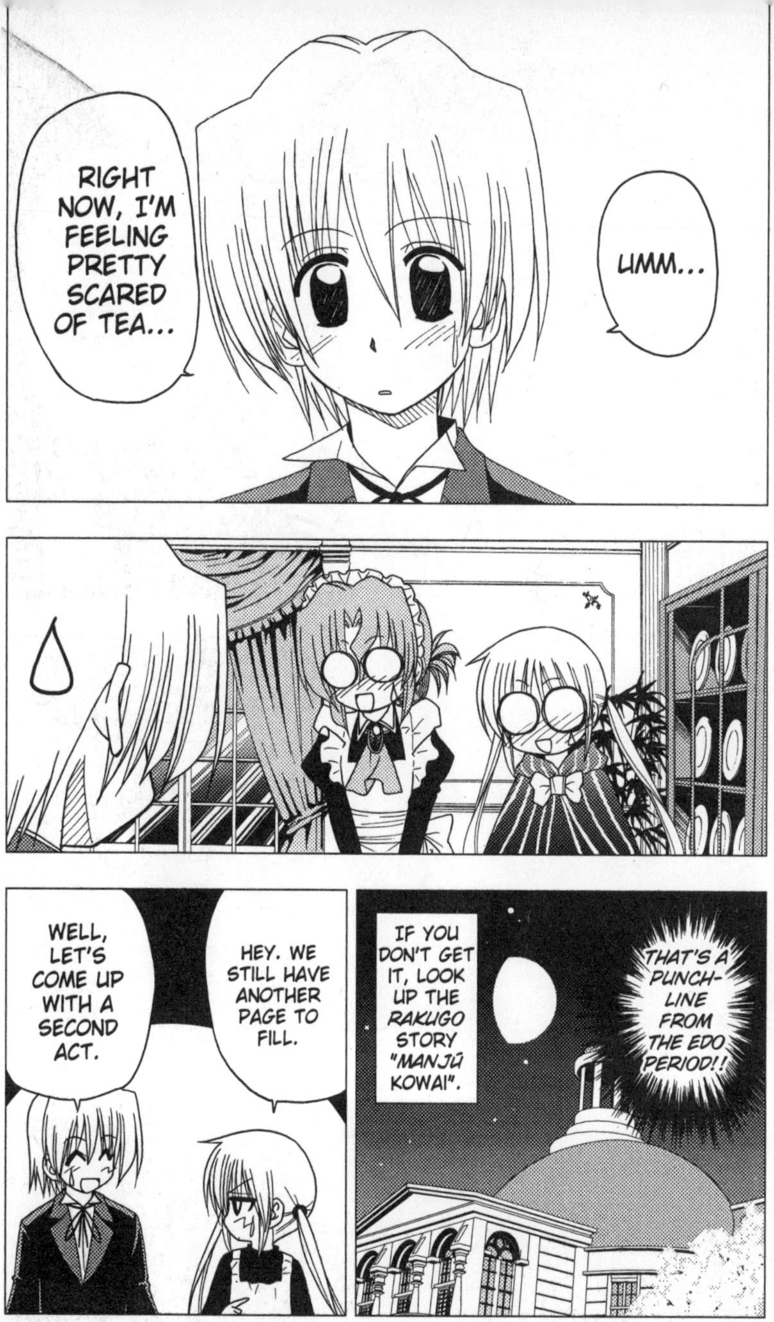
UMM...
RIGHT NOW, I'M FEELING PRETTY SCARED OF TEA...
THAT'S A PUNCHLINE FROM THE EDO PERIOD!!
IF YOU DON'T GET IT, LOOK UP THE *RAKUGO* STORY "MANJŪ KOWAI".
HEY. WE STILL HAVE ANOTHER PAGE TO FILL.
WELL, LET'S COME UP WITH A SECOND ACT.

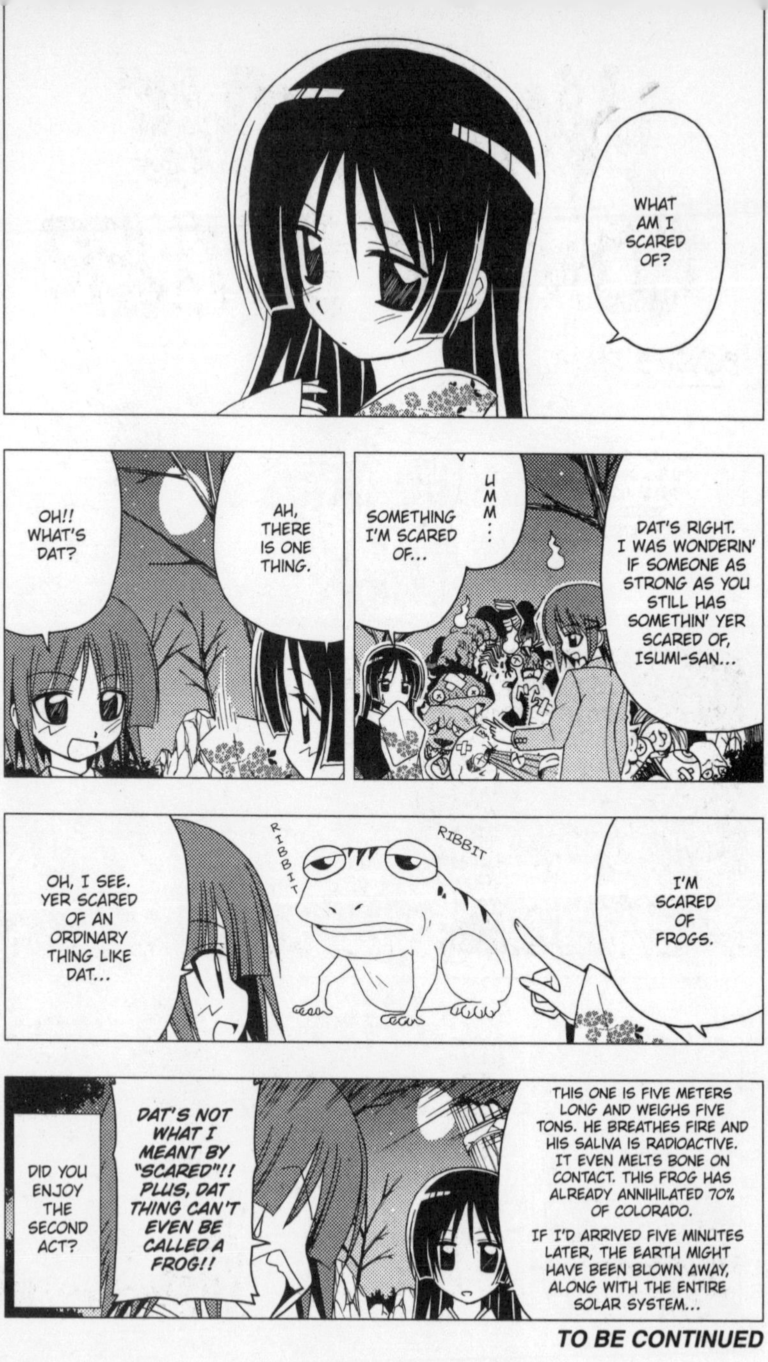
WHAT AM I SCARED OF?
DAT'S RIGHT. I WAS WONDERIN' IF SOMEONE AS STRONG AS YOU STILL HAS SOMETHIN' YER SCARED OF, ISUMI-SAN...
UMM...
SOMETHING I'M SCARED OF...
AH, THERE IS ONE THING.
OH!! WHAT'S DAT?
I'M SCARED OF FROGS.
RIBBIT
RIBBIT
OH, I SEE. YER SCARED OF AN ORDINARY THING LIKE DAT...
THIS ONE IS FIVE METERS LONG AND WEIGHS FIVE TONS. HE BREATHES FIRE AND HIS SALIVA IS RADIOACTIVE. IT EVEN MELTS BONE ON CONTACT. THIS FROG HAS ALREADY ANNIHILATED 70% OF COLORADO.
IF I'D ARRIVED FIVE MINUTES LATER, THE EARTH MIGHT HAVE BEEN BLOWN AWAY, ALONG WITH THE ENTIRE SOLAR SYSTEM...
DAT'S NOT WHAT I MEANT BY "SCARED"!! PLUS, DAT THING CAN'T EVEN BE CALLED A FROG!!
DID YOU ENJOY THE SECOND ACT?

TO BE CONTINUED

HAYATE THE COMBAT BUTLER

BONUS PAGE

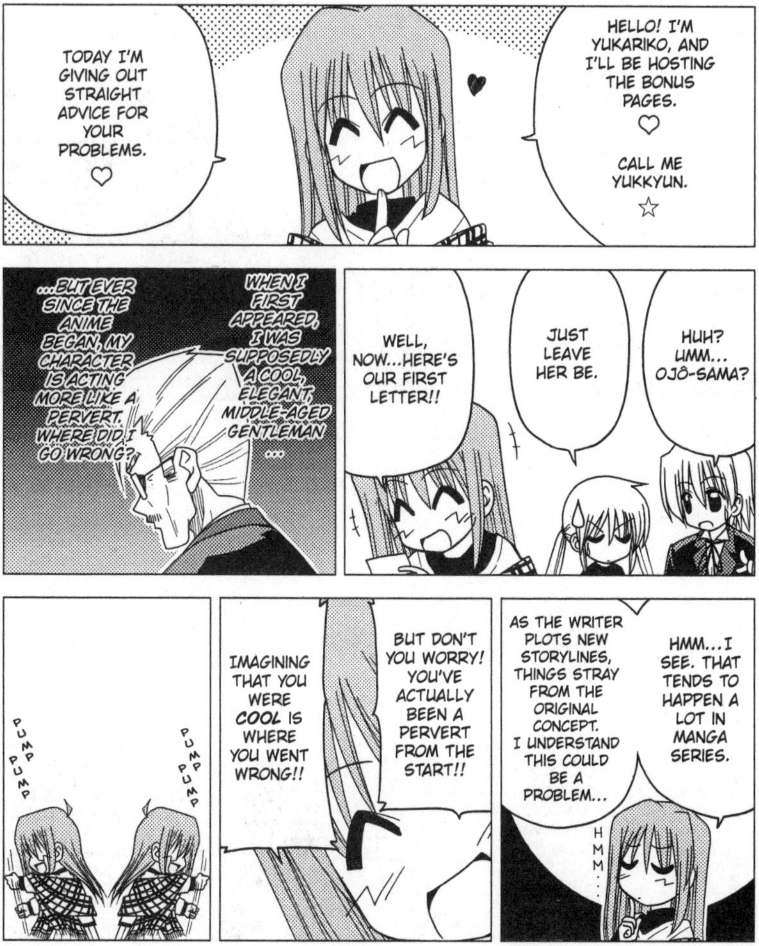

HELLO! I'M YUKARIKO, AND I'LL BE HOSTING THE BONUS PAGES. ♡ CALL ME YUKKYUN. ☆
TODAY I'M GIVING OUT STRAIGHT ADVICE FOR YOUR PROBLEMS. ♡
HUH? UMM... OJÔ-SAMA?
JUST LEAVE HER BE.
WELL, NOW...HERE'S OUR FIRST LETTER!!
WHEN I FIRST APPEARED, I WAS SUPPOSEDLY A COOL, ELEGANT, MIDDLE-AGED GENTLEMAN...
...BUT EVER SINCE THE ANIME BEGAN, MY CHARACTER IS ACTING MORE LIKE A PERVERT. WHERE DID I GO WRONG?
HMM...I SEE. THAT TENDS TO HAPPEN A LOT IN MANGA SERIES.
AS THE WRITER PLOTS NEW STORYLINES, THINGS STRAY FROM THE ORIGINAL CONCEPT. I UNDERSTAND THIS COULD BE A PROBLEM...
HMM...
BUT DON'T YOU WORRY! YOU'VE ACTUALLY BEEN A PERVERT FROM THE START!!
IMAGINING THAT YOU WERE COOL IS WHERE YOU WENT WRONG!!
PUMP PUMP
PUMP PUMP

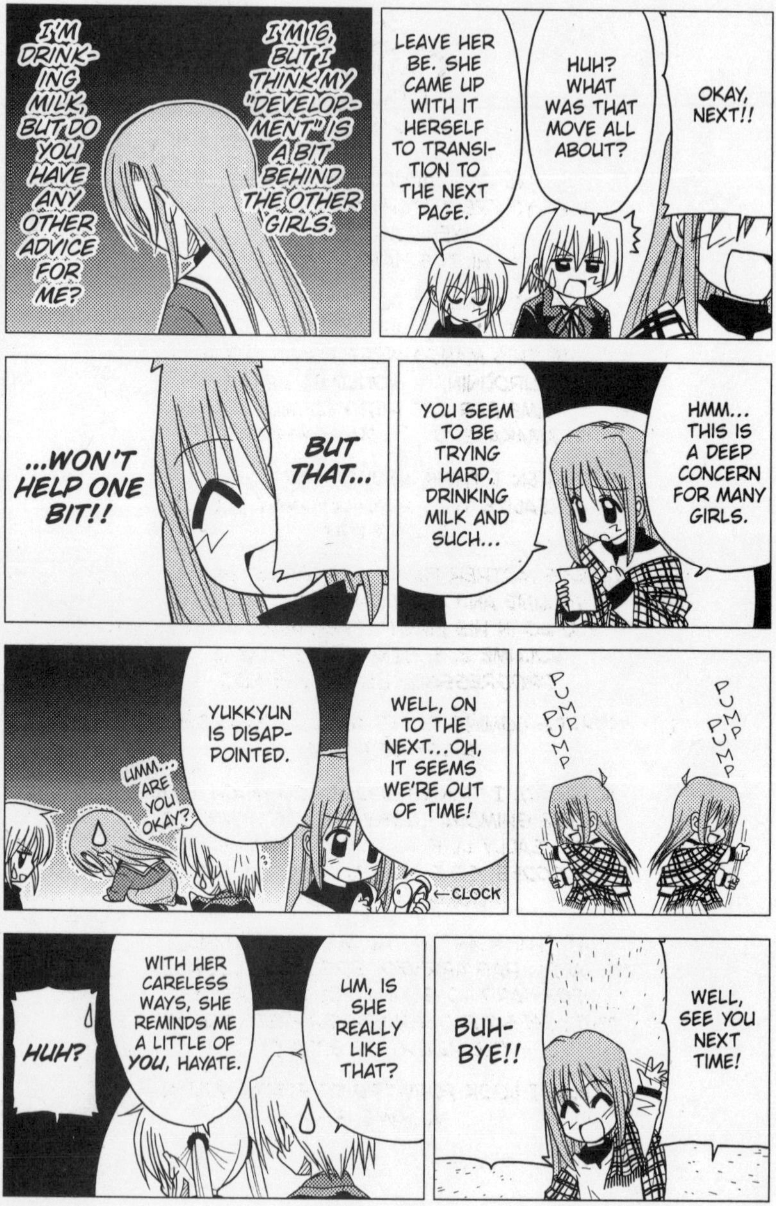
OKAY, NEXT!!
HUH? WHAT WAS THAT MOVE ALL ABOUT?
LEAVE HER BE. SHE CAME UP WITH IT HERSELF TO TRANSITION TO THE NEXT PAGE.
I'M 16, BUT I THINK MY "DEVELOPMENT" IS A BIT BEHIND THE OTHER GIRLS.
I'M DRINKING MILK, BUT DO YOU HAVE ANY OTHER ADVICE FOR ME?
HMM... THIS IS A DEEP CONCERN FOR MANY GIRLS.
YOU SEEM TO BE TRYING HARD, DRINKING MILK AND SUCH...
BUT THAT...
...WON'T HELP ONE BIT!!
PUMP PUMP
PUMP PUMP
WELL, ON TO THE NEXT...OH, IT SEEMS WE'RE OUT OF TIME!
←CLOCK
YUKKYUN IS DISAPPOINTED.
UMM... ARE YOU OKAY?
WELL, SEE YOU NEXT TIME!
BUH-BYE!!
UM, IS SHE REALLY LIKE THAT?
WITH HER CARELESS WAYS, SHE REMINDS ME A LITTLE OF YOU, HAYATE.
HUH?

WE'VE REACHED VOLUME 12!
I HOPE YOU'RE WATCHING THE ANIME EVERY
WEEK AS WELL.
HI, IT'S HATA AGAIN!

TIME'S GONE BY SO QUICKLY. I CAN'T
BELIEVE THIS IS ALREADY VOLUME 12.
IF THIS MANGA WERE ABOUT SOME
RUROUNIN, IT WOULD BE ABOUT
TIME FOR THE HERO TO MASTER
AMAKAKERU ◯◯ OR SOMETHING.

WHEN I THINK ABOUT IT THAT WAY,
I REALIZE THAT I REALLY HAVE COME
A LONG WAY.

NAGI'S MOTHER FINALLY APPEARED IN THIS
VOLUME AND OLD MAN MIKADO MADE A
CAMEO IN HIS FIRST APPEARANCE SINCE
VOLUME 2. I THINK THE STORY IS
PROGRESSING, BUT MAYBE NOT.

WHAT'S COMING NEXT? WELL...YOU KNOW...
A LOT OF STUFF.

ACTUALLY, I THINK I SPENT TOO MUCH TIME
ON THE SHIMODA STORY ARC. AS A WRITER,
I'D REALLY LIKE TO DO MORE ONE-SHOT
EPISODES, SO I PLAN TO FILL THE NEXT
VOLUME WITH THOSE.

AT THIS POINT IN THE MANGA TIMELINE,
APRIL HAS ARRIVED, SO PLEASE LOOK
FORWARD TO SEEING FUTURE *HAYATE
THE COMBAT BUTLER* EPISODES SET DURING
THE HEIGHT OF SPRING!

WELL, I LOOK FORWARD TO SEEING YOU IN
VOLUME 13! ☆

Into a Dream, Into a Dream

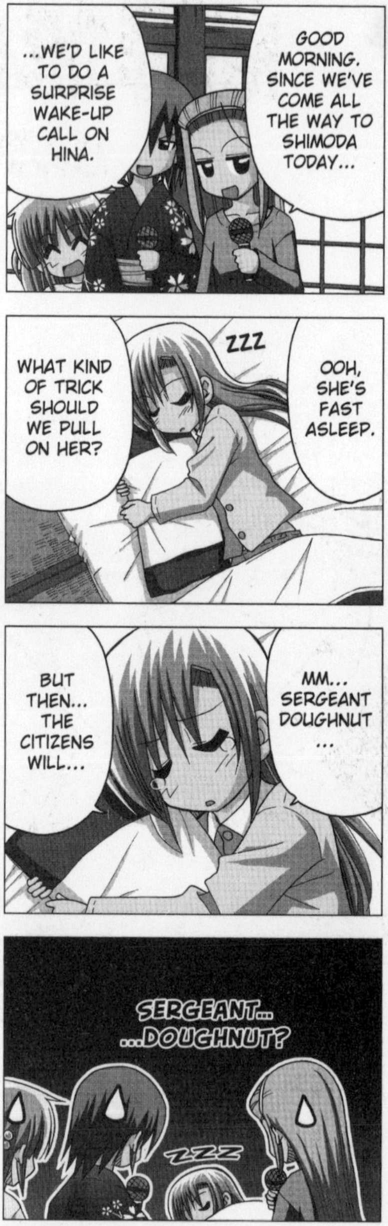

GOOD MORNING. SINCE WE'VE COME ALL THE WAY TO SHIMODA TODAY...
...WE'D LIKE TO DO A SURPRISE WAKE-UP CALL ON HINA.
OOH, SHE'S FAST ASLEEP.
ZZZ
WHAT KIND OF TRICK SHOULD WE PULL ON HER?
MM... SERGEANT DOUGHNUT ...
BUT THEN... THE CITIZENS WILL...
SERGEANT... ...DOUGHNUT?
ZZZ

I Don't Think I Want to Go

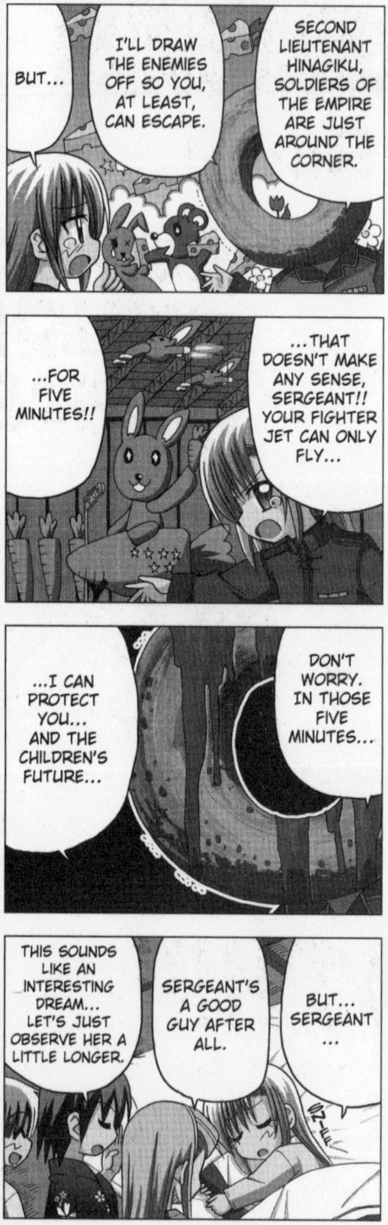

SECOND LIEUTENANT HINAGIKU, SOLDIERS OF THE EMPIRE ARE JUST AROUND THE CORNER.
I'LL DRAW THE ENEMIES OFF SO YOU, AT LEAST, CAN ESCAPE.
BUT...
...THAT DOESN'T MAKE ANY SENSE, SERGEANT!! YOUR FIGHTER JET CAN ONLY FLY...
...FOR FIVE MINUTES!!
DON'T WORRY. IN THOSE FIVE MINUTES...
...I CAN PROTECT YOU... AND THE CHILDREN'S FUTURE...
BUT... SERGEANT ...
SERGEANT'S A GOOD GUY AFTER ALL.
THIS SOUNDS LIKE AN INTERESTING DREAM... LET'S JUST OBSERVE HER A LITTLE LONGER.

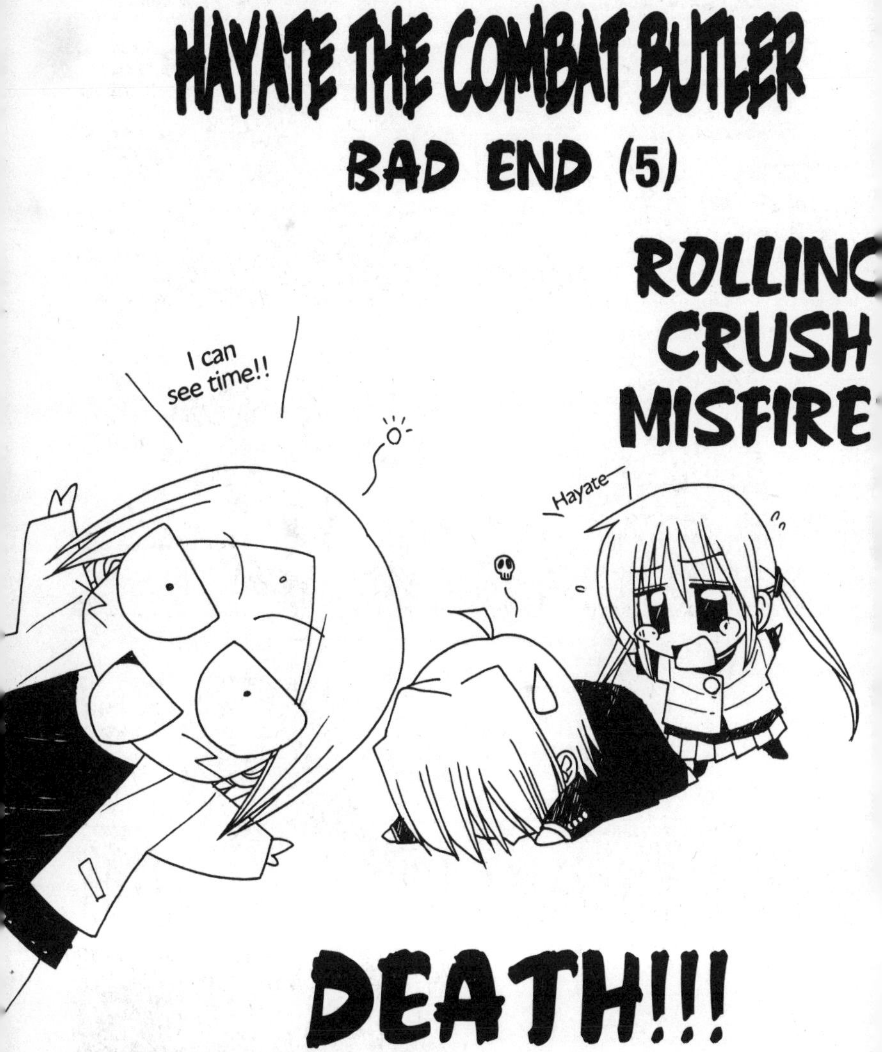
HAYATE THE COMBAT BUTLER
BAD END (5)
ROLLING CRUSH MISFIRE
Hayate—
I can see time!!
DEATH!!!

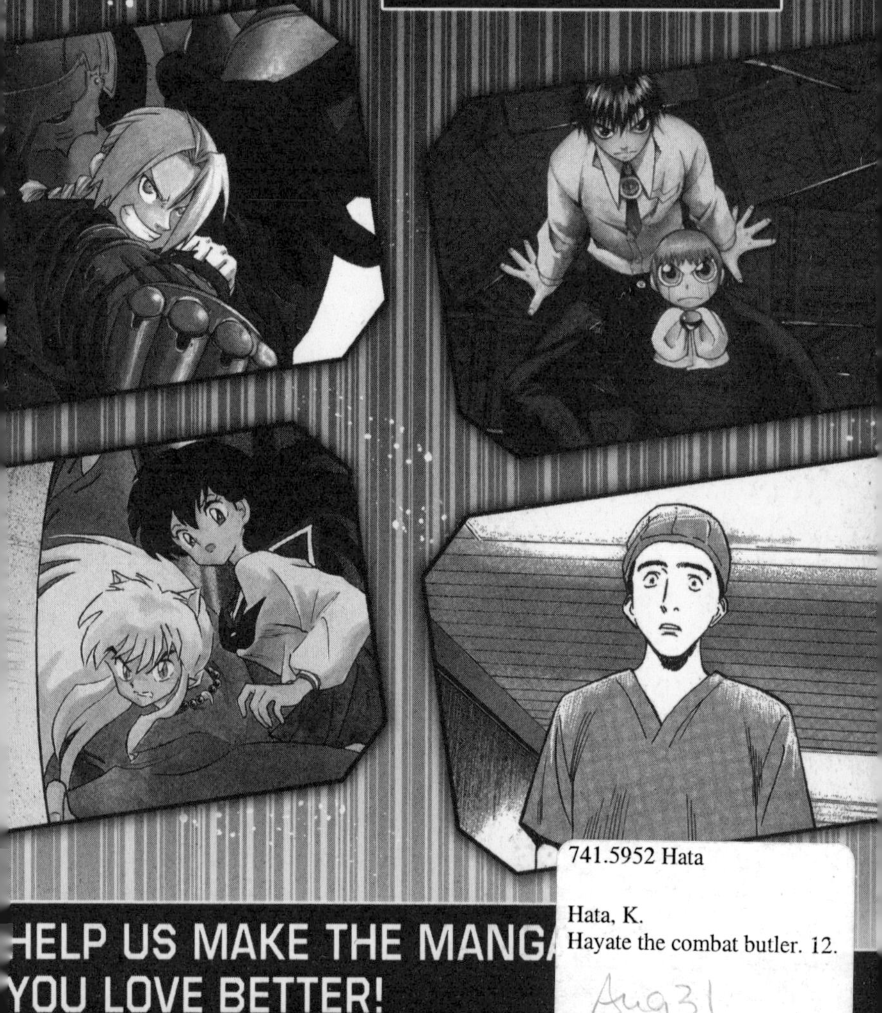